BIG GUN
MONITORS

BIG GUN MONITORS

Design, Construction and Operations
1914–1945

IAN BUXTON

Seaforth PUBLISHING

Copyright © Ian Buxton 1978 & 2008

First published 1978

This second, revised and expanded edition published in Great Britain in 2008 by
Seaforth Publishing
An imprint of Pen & Sword Books Ltd
47 Church Street, Barnsley
S Yorkshire S70 2AS

www.seaforthpublishing.com
Email info@seaforthpublishing.com

British Library Cataloguing in Publication Data
A CIP data record for this book is available from the British Library

ISBN 978-1-84415-719-8

Designed and Typeset by Roger Daniels
Printed in China through Printworks Int.Ltd.

FRONTISPIECE
In this rare view of *Raglan* being towed past Clydebank on 21 June 1915 after having left H & W's Govan yard, she still bears the name *M.3*, although she had already been renamed *Lord Raglan* that very day, before becoming plain *Raglan* on 23 June. The essential simplicity of the early monitors' design is apparent. (JOHN BROWN)

Contents

Abbreviations

Abbreviations marked* are used on illustrations

AA	Anti-aircraft
ADO*	Air defence officer
AEW	Admiralty Experiment Works (Haslar)
AFCT*	Admiralty fire control table
AFD	Admiralty floating dock
ANCXF	Allied Naval Commander, Expeditionary Force
AP	Aft perpendicular
APC	Armour-piercing, capped (projectile)
B	Barbette (mounting)
bhp	brake horsepower (diesels)
BISCO	British Iron and Steel Corporation
BL	Breech-loading (gun)
BLO	Bombardment Liaison Officer
BP, bp	Between perpendiculars (length)
C	Cemented (armour)
cal	calibre (length of gun)
C-in-C	Commander-in-Chief
CG	Centre of gravity
CL*	Cable locker
C & M	Care and maintenance
CNF	Common, nose-fuzed (projectile)
CO	Commanding Officer
COW	Coventry Ordnance Works
CP	Centre-pivot (mounting)
CP	Common, pointed (projectile)
CPC	Common, pointed-capped (projectile)
CPO	Chief Petty Officer
crh	Calibres radius of head (projectile)
CSA*	Chloro-sulphonic smoke apparatus
D and D.1	Designation of Admiralty special high-strength steel
DCB	Distance-controlled boat
DCHQ*	Damage control headquarters
DNC	Director of Naval Construction
DNO	Director of Naval Ordnance
DO*	Diesel Oil
DR*	Dressing room
DS	Detached Squadron
ECM	Electronic countermeasures
efc	equivalent full charge
ehp	effective horsepower
EOC	Elswick Ordnance Company (Armstrong, Whitworth)
FOB	Forward Observer, Bombardment
FOO	Forward Observation Officer
FP	Forward perpendicular
FR*	Frame
FW*	Fresh water
GM	Metacentric height (distance between centre of gravity and metacentre)
H*	Hatch
HA	High angle
HACP	High angle calculating position
HA/LA	High angle/low angle
HE	High-explosive (projectile)
HETF	High-explosive, time fuze (projectile)
HMS	His Majesty's Ship
hp	horsepower
HQ	Headquarters
HT	High-tensile (steel)
H & W	Harland and Wolff
ihp	indicated horsepower (steam reciprocators)
IWM	Imperial War Museum
kts	knots
kW	kilowatt
LA	Low angle
LCG	Landing craft, gun
LCM	Landing craft, mechanised
LCT	Landing craft, tank
LSI	Landing ship, infantry
LST	Landing ship, tank
MAG*	Magazine
MD	Modified (cordite)
Mk	Mark
ML	Motor launch
MP	Member of Parliament
MV	Muzzle velocity
NC	Non-cemented (armour)
NCT	Nitro-cellulose, tubular (propellant)
NMM	National Maritime Museum
OA, oa	Overall, e.g. length
OFT*	Oil fuel tank
P	Pedestal (mounting)
pdr	pounder (gun)
PO	Petty Officer
P & O	Peninsular & Oriental (Steam Navigation Co.)
PRO	Public Record Office (now The National Archives)
P & S*	Port and starboard
QF	Quick-firing (gun)
RAF	Royal Air Force
RFC	Royal Flying Corps
RFW	Reserve feed water
RGF	Royal Gun Factory (Woolwich)
RM	Royal Marines
RN	Royal Navy
RNAS	Royal Naval Air Service
RNVR	Royal Naval Volunteer Reserve
RPC	Remote power control
rpg	rounds per gun
rpm	revolutions per minute
RUL*	Ready use locker
SA*	Small arms
SAP	Semi-armour-piercing (projectile)
SB*	Shell bin
SC	Solventless carbamite (cordite)
SFCP	Shore fire control party
SG*	Steering gear
shp	shaft horsepower (turbines)
SHWR	Swan, Hunter & Wigham Richardson
SL*	Searchlight
SR*	Shell room
ST*	Store
T*	Tank
TNA	The National Archives (formerly the Public Record Office)
TNT	Tri-nitro-toluene (high explosive)
TPD*	Tons per day
TPH*	Tons per hour
TS	Transmitting station
UK	United Kingdom
UP	Unrotated projectile (rocket)
USS	United States Ship
W*	Winch
WB*	Water ballast
WC*	Water closet
WL*	Waterline
WO*	Warrant Officer
W/T	Wireless telegraphy
WTC*	Watertight compartment
WTD*	Watertight door
WW1	World War 1
WW2	World War 2

Fitted in Battle Class Destroyers

Preface

One day in August 1965 I spent many hours aboard Britain's last big gun monitor, *Roberts*, after she had arrived for breaking up at Inverkeithing. When later I tried to find out more about these unusual but relatively little-known warships, I found that very little information was available. There were brief entries in *Jane's Fighting Ships*, a few paragraphs in official histories and a page or two in a handful of other books. The only full-length book on monitors turned out to be a novel, HMS *Saracen* by Douglas Reeman.

The paucity of published material appears to stem largely from the 'hostilities only' character of the monitors, rather from any lack of potential interest. In wartime their construction and operations were shrouded in secrecy, while in peacetime they were soon paid off and either scrapped or relegated to subsidiary duties, away from the public gaze. I therefore determined to fill the gap and publish an account of the origins, design, construction and operations of the forty-two British monitors which served between 1914 and 1965.

The history of the monitors is more than an account of some special ships built for bombardment of enemy-held coastlines. Their requirement for the heaviest guns, up to 18in calibre, had an influence on the battleship building programmes, where availability of heavy ordnance was a determining factor. The monitors' intensive bombardments pushed the science of naval gunnery to its limits in terms of accuracy and sustained fire. Not many such topics have been previously discussed publicly in print, so putting together a comprehensive history required some ten years of research among many original sources of material.

The relaxation of the closed period for official records from 50 to 30 years opened up much new material after 1972, especially on the Second World War. Similarly, many original records, such as drawings and official handbooks, are now available in the National Maritime Museum or the Imperial War Museum. Many who served in the monitors in both World Wars were able to provide invaluable assistance, as noted in the acknowledgements.

I have taken great pains to verify all numerical data; in some cases finding errors in official publications. Where precise figures were not available, estimates have been made as carefully as possible. For example, there is no accurately measured range for the 18in gun as installed in two of the monitors. If the reader finds an above-average measure of discussion on technical and economic aspects of ships and ordnance, this not only reflects my outlook as a professional naval architect, but is a measure of how important these factors are in the design and construction of any novel type of ship.

Nevertheless, my intention has been not only to fill a gap in the naval literature, which was not recognised by the major publishers in the field of naval history, but to make the account one of interest to the general reader as well as a definitive reference for the specialist.

I.L.B.

Preface to Second Edition

The first edition of *Big Gun Monitors* was very well received, and since going out of print some fifteen years ago, it has commanded a high price on the secondhand market. This has been gratifying, as all the regular publishers approached thirty years ago had said that there was no market for such a book. It was pleasing, then, when Chatham (later Seaforth) offered to produce not a reprint but a new edition. It has thus been possible to reinstate some material omitted from the first edition to reduce its length, and generally to flesh out more sections. A modest amount of new material has come to light in the intervening years, on the guns themselves and on the building and disposal of the monitors, including the preservation of *M.33*. A few of the numbers have been slightly modified as a result of later analysis, so where they differ from the first edition, the second should be taken as definitive.

The net effect is an increase in text length of about 15 per cent, mostly on the ships and their guns, rather than on operations, where more detail can be found in National Archive files. A few new drawings have been added, including the cross-section of *Abercrombie*'s 15in turret, and others slightly modified. Most of the original photographs are included, but the longer book has allowed some fifty new views to be added.

The designers at Seaforth have created a more attractive layout than I did in my first amateur attempt in 1978. I trust that all those who have asked over the years for a copy of this long-out-of-print book will be satisfied with the result.

I.L.B.
Tynemouth, 2007

MAIN PHOTOGRAPH
The two warship types mounting the heaviest ordnance, capital ships and monitors, under construction at Clydebank. This view, taken about 15 July 1916, shows *Erebus* having her 15in turret erected under the 150-ton cantilever crane at John Brown's shipyard, with battlecruiser *Repulse*, destroyers *Romola* (alongside forward) and *Peregrine* (aft), and submarine *E.35* in the foreground.
(JOHN BROWN)

CHAPTER 1

The Origins of the British Monitor

'MONITOR — one who admonishes another as to his conduct'

Shorter Oxford English Dictionary

In a letter to Gustavus V. Fox, Assistant Secretary of the United States Navy during the American Civil War, the Swedish engineer John Ericsson claimed of his new design of ironclad ship:[1]

> The impregnable and aggressive character of this structure will admonish the leaders of the Southern Rebellion that the batteries on the banks of their rivers will no longer present barriers to the entrance of the Union forces. The iron-clad intruder will thus prove a severe monitor to those leaders. … On these and many similar grounds, I propose to name the new battery *Monitor*.

The wooden ships of the Federal forces had been unable to overcome the batteries guarding the way to the Confederate strongholds above Hampton Roads, Virginia. Construction of Ericsson's ironclad began in October 1861, and she was completed just in time to counter the destruction that the newly converted Confederate ironclad *Virginia* (ex-*Merrimack*) had been wreaking among the blockading Federal ships. The 987-ton ship was named USS *Monitor*, her principal features being a powerful armament of two 11in smooth-bore muzzle-loading guns in a rotating armoured turret, a well protected low-freeboard hull presenting a very small target, and no rig or sails, as she relied entirely on steam propulsion to provide her modest 6kts speed. The inconclusive action between the *Monitor* and *Virginia* on 9 March 1862 has been recounted many times; neither ship was seriously damaged owing to the protective value of their iron plates. Such a radically new design of fighting ship had a significant influence on warship development, making obsolete at a stroke virtually all the vulnerable wooden sailing vessels whose design had changed little over the centuries; although it must be recognised that the trend towards iron-cladding and the turret was already apparent in contemporary European designs, *Warrior* having been completed in 1861.

The use of special ships to attack well-defended targets has a long history. Both the British and French used bomb vessels at the end of the seventeenth century to bombard forts, as at Tripoli, Algiers and Genoa in 1682-84. From time to time, bomb and mortar vessels continued to be used as required for coast offence purposes. The first serious attempt to ally this type of vessel with the new developments of steam propulsion and iron protection occurred during the Crimean War. In July 1854 French Emperor Napoleon III ordered ten ironclad floating batteries to be constructed which could be used against the Russian Crimean and Baltic forts. Five vessels were built in Britain and five in France, each of about 1,600 tons, mounting sixteen 68pdr or 50pdr muzzle-loading guns. Four-inch wrought iron plating covered the sides of their hulls, and they could steam at about 4kts.

During the 1860s the unprotected broadside-armed sailing vessels and wooden screw battleships of the major navies were rapidly superseded by a wide variety of steam-propelled ironclad designs. The principles of Ericsson's *Monitor* found favour among the smaller powers for coast defence vessels, but low freeboard made the type unsuitable for overseas operations. Even the mighty Royal Navy embarked on building vessels suitable only for coast defence, starting with the *Prince Albert* in 1862. Over the next decade a motley fleet of some dozen such vessels was built. Apart from the three designed for colonial defence,

these ships were almost valueless. It was strategically unsound for a major power to build coast-defence vessels. The best defence against attack or invasion was the destruction of the enemy fleet, in effect making the enemy's own shores the defence perimeter of the British Isles. Subsequent development of armoured ships for the RN therefore concentrated on well armed, well protected vessels with a reasonable speed and capable of keeping the seas in all weathers. Such ships were necessarily large and could not be afforded in great numbers. When coast-offence vessels were needed, as at the Bombardment of Alexandria in 1882, the regular ships of the line were employed. Thus for some forty years the RN built neither coast-offence nor coast-defence vessels, although the latter remained popular with most of the smaller navies. The United States continued to build monitors up to 1903, when the last of a line of seventy-one vessels ordered was commissioned, the 3,225-ton USS *Florida*. Several navies also built river monitors, in effect shallow-draft armoured gunboats, but they were intended only for service on rivers like the Danube or Amur, not on the open sea.

With the outbreak of World War 1 in August 1914 the RN was committed to its first full-scale war for a century. The Grand Fleet's role was that of neutralising the German High Seas Fleet, so enabling Britain to keep command of the seas and her overseas communications while blockading Germany. Germany's rapid thrust on land through Belgium towards Paris had been brought to a halt by October, when the war was already showing signs of dragging on for a year or more. In addition to the main belligerents of Britain, France and Russia on the one hand, and Germany and Austria-Hungary on the other, attempts were made to persuade other nations to join either the Allied Powers or the Central Powers. At the end of October it was plain that Turkey would join the latter bloc, but Italy could not yet be persuaded to join the former.

When Lord Fisher replaced Prince Louis of Battenberg as First Sea Lord on 30 October 1914, it was clear that some form of naval initiative would be desirable to break the impending stalemate on land and attempt to strike Germany decisively in a vulnerable spot. Winston Churchill, First Lord of the Admiralty, and Fisher had been mulling over various possibilities. Fisher had long been a proponent of a Baltic strategy, where an offensive against the Pomeranian coast could enable a landing to be made with Russian support only 90 miles from Berlin. To be successful such a scheme required the prior disablement or neutralisation of the High Seas Fleet, which otherwise could emerge from Wilhelmshaven or the Kiel Canal and wreak havoc among the invasion fleet. The shallow waters of the Baltic were easily mined, which would hamper and endanger the deep-draft big-gun ships of the RN. It would therefore be necessary to undertake the hazardous operation of seizing some form of advanced base across the North Sea in the Friesian Islands or off the Danish coast, either to force the High Seas Fleet out of its well protected base at Wilhelmshaven and enable the Grand Fleet to destroy it by battle, or to permit surface forces and submarines to blockade movements from the German bases.

The stabilisation of the Western Front on the Belgian Coast also offered opportunities for landing forces under the cover of heavy guns to turn the enemy's flank and prevent ports such as Zeebrugge from being used as submarine bases by the Germans. Any hostilities against Turkey would probably entail an attempt to force the Dardanelles to open the direct supply route to Russia. Ships of the Grand Fleet could not be risked from their vital strategic role for such operations, while most of the older British ships had insufficiently powerful guns or were of too deep draft for working close inshore near strong shore defences. The makeshift fleet which had bombarded the Belgian Coast at the end of October (see p.95) had demonstrated the potential of coast-offence vessels, as it had been instrumental in stemming the German advance towards the French Channel ports.

All of these possibilities for coastal bombardment, some more practical than others, were at the backs of the minds of Churchill and Fisher when an important visitor called at the Admiralty on Tuesday 3 November 1914. The visitor was Charles M. Schwab, President of the Bethlehem Steel Corporation, who had left New York a fortnight earlier in the White Star liner *Olympic* to try to sell arms and munitions to Britain. In addition to steel and armour plate, Bethlehem manufactured ordnance as well as owning several shipyards. After some delay because the passengers on the *Olympic* had witnessed the sinking of the British battleship *Audacious,* mined off the north coast of Ulster on 27 October, Admiral Sir John Jellicoe, C-in-C of the Grand Fleet, permitted Schwab to travel to London, when he learned that Schwab had arranged to see Lord Kitchener at the War Office and that Bethlehem had submarine-building capacity available. At the Admiralty the new construction programme was discussed and agreement was reached with Schwab to build twenty submarines for Britain in the USA. That evening Schwab was asked by Churchill and Fisher if he had any other naval material which might be of use to Britain. He then disclosed that he had four twin 14in turrets nearing completion, which had been ordered for the Greek battlecruiser *Salamis,* then building in Germany. As the British blockade would obstruct their delivery, he was quite willing to sell them to Britain

instead, together with their outfit of ammunition.

At this moment the British monitor was conceived. A supply of modern heavy ordnance was the main prerequisite for building coast-offence vessels. While hulls and machinery could be constructed quite quickly, heavy gun mountings took well over a year to build. The only source of supply in Britain would have been the requisition of mountings ordered for some of the battleships of the 1912 and 1913 new construction programmes. Any such diversion would have a serious effect on the completions that were needed to ensure an adequate margin of capital ship numbers over the High Seas Fleet. Schwab's offer opened up the prospect of rapidly obtaining a significant coast-offence capability, so Churchill and Fisher eagerly accepted.

After the meeting the Third Sea Lord, Rear-Admiral F.C.T. Tudor, who was responsible for naval construction, immediately minuted to the Director of Naval Construction (DNC), Eustace Tennyson d'Eyncourt:[2]

To design immediately 2 Armoured Monitors, to be built in 4 months — each to carry 2-14in guns or equivalent. Draft 10 feet. Speed 10 knots. To have crinoline. An armoured conning tower. Armoured deck. Who could build them?

A design to satisfy these requirements was worked up very quickly, as detailed in the next chapter. It was a revolutionary design in that it owed nothing to previous ship designs, unlike the normal evolutionary process of naval architecture. By the standards of Ericsson's original design, the British concept was not strictly a 'monitor', but over the intervening half-century the term could reasonably be considered as having evolved somewhat to embrace a new type which still owed something of its characteristics to the first monitor. Within the RN the description 'monitor' would be distinctive and unambiguous, while not giving away too much as to their expected operational role.

Over the next four months thirty-three vessels were authorised; thus, with the two vessels ordered later, the RN had by 1916 a fleet of thirty-five monitors, sixteen large and nineteen small, mounting guns from 6in to 15in calibre. Including three ex-Brazilian river gunboats and two ex-Norwegian converted coast-defence ships, a total of forty vessels saw service during World War 1. Further vessels were built exclusively for river work, the so-called China gunboats of the *Insect* and *Fly* classes but, as they were not intended primarily for bombardment operations, they are only mentioned in passing in this history of British big-gun monitors.

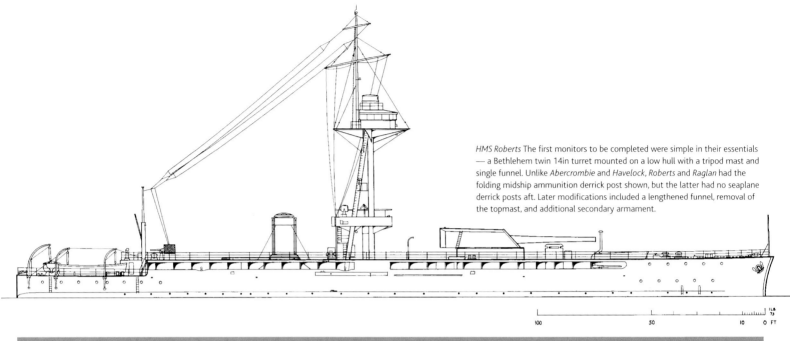

HMS Roberts The first monitors to be completed were simple in their essentials — a Bethlehem twin 14in turret mounted on a low hull with a tripod mast and single funnel. Unlike *Abercrombie* and *Havelock*, *Roberts* and *Raglan* had the folding midship ammunition derrick post shown, but the latter had no seaplane derrick posts aft. Later modifications included a lengthened funnel, removal of the topmast, and additional secondary armament.

CHAPTER 2

The 14in-gun Monitors

2.1 Design of the First British Monitor

Churchill and Fisher were in their element in November 1914, planning a vast new fleet of ships. The projected cruisers, destroyers and submarines were all relatively well established types, but the monitors were a totally new concept. While some of the latter's characteristics might be similar to those of coast-defence vessels or river gun-boats, neither of these types formed a suitable basis for designing seagoing vessels. The main requirements could be summarised:

    (i) Twin 14in turret to be carried on a good gun platform

    (ii) 10ft shallow draft, to get close inshore

    (iii) Maximum protection against mines and torpedoes, with reasonable protection against gunfire

    (iv) Hull and machinery as simple as possible for rapid construction

    (v) Modest speed of 10kts

    (vi) Reasonable seagoing capability.

By the time Schwab returned to the Admiralty on 6 November to discuss further details of the proposed

contracts, a Constructor, A.M. Worthington, had sketched out a preliminary specification of a monitor of about 6,000 tons displacement.[1] After the weekend, formal instructions were given on the 9th to a young Assistant Constructor, Charles S. Lillicrap. It was a challenging task even for a talented man who was later to become DNC himself; a totally new type of ship to be designed and built with the greatest urgency, with the formidable Fisher continually appearing in the office to hasten progress.

Unfortunately no Ship's Cover (the file kept by DNC Department recording the design of each new class of ship) was prepared for the early monitors, probably owing to Fisher's impatience and to the secrecy surrounding them. However, it is possible to glean something of the considerations applied in the monitor design from the calculations recorded in Lillicrap's calculation workbooks. The turret was the heaviest single item, about 620 tons revolving weight, plus about 350 tons for ammunition and barbette armour. Such a concentrated weight would have to be placed nearly amidships to avoid problems of trim. The width of the hull would need to be about 60ft to contain the turret comfortably and its magazines. Protection spaces were to be fitted outboard, as a monitor was the ideal vessel on which to demonstrate d'Eyncourt's newly developed design of an anti-torpedo bulge. The bulges, sometimes called blisters, were added outside the hull proper, being 15ft wide on each side, as described on p.14, The breadth of the ship would thus be about 90ft; anything wider would severely restrict the number of drydocks that could be used (and would be too wide for the Chatham Dockyard entrance lock). The hull needed only to be long enough to provide the necessary internal space for the turret, machinery, accommodation and stores. The depth of the ship (height of deck above keel) was established from the length of the turret trunk containing ammunition hoists and working machinery, the height of the engines and boilers, and the need for adequate freeboard forward.

The dimensions which resulted from a consideration of all these factors were: length between perpendiculars (BP) 320ft, moulded breadth over bulges 90ft, depth to upper deck 18½ft (i.e. the uppermost continuous deck), on top of which was added a forecastle deck 7ft high, draft 10ft forward and aft. The hull form amidships was composed of a rectangle for the main hull, with the bulges added below water at each side, as illustrated on pages 21 and 45. The form was parallel-sided for over half the length, before tapering in towards the very bluff ends considered acceptable owing to the low speed. The resulting effective block coefficient[2] was the highest of any British warship type, at 0.84, compared with a normal 0.55 to 0.65. By Archimedes' principle, the buoyancy of this hull in seawater was about 7,000 tons, but as the bulges contained compartments open to the sea, the net figure was reduced to about 6,150 tons.

Part of the naval architect's skill lies in achieving balance between a ship's weight and its buoyancy at the designed draft. Once the underwater hull form has been established,

the buoyancy at any given draft is fixed. If the completed ship is to float at the correct waterline, the weight of all materials built into the ship together with fuel, ammunition, stores, etc. must exactly equal the buoyancy. The weight of a warship (and thus its displacement of water) can be regarded as being made up of:

   (i) Armament and ammunition
   (ii) Hull structure and fittings
   (iii) Machinery and fuel
   (iv) Armour and protection
   (v) Crew, stores, equipment etc.

For the monitors, (i) had already been specified, (ii) largely depended upon the proposed hull dimensions, (iii) was determined mainly by the power of the machinery and the endurance requirements, both low for monitors. As (v) was relatively small, the protection that could be afforded tended to be the balancing item, using up all the remaining buoyancy after deduction of the other items. Lillicrap finalised the hull form by 17 November, so with d'Eyncourt's approval he was able to give an outline of its shape to the Admiralty Experiment Works (AEW) at Haslar, near Portsmouth. Here the Superintendent, R.E. Froude, son of the pioneer of scientific ship-model testing, would arrange for a scale model to be made and towed along the test tank to measure its resistance at various speeds and hence deduce the horsepower required for the actual ship. As it would take a few weeks to make full tests, a preliminary estimate had to be made from data for existing ships. Unfortunately there had never been any other British naval vessel of remotely similar form, so it was difficult to estimate not only the resistance of such an unusual design, but also its propulsive efficiency. The best estimate that could be made from existing data suggested that about 2,000hp would be required for a speed of 10kts, which would easily be obtained from steam reciprocating machinery. The shallow draft and very full form aft limited propeller diameter, so it was

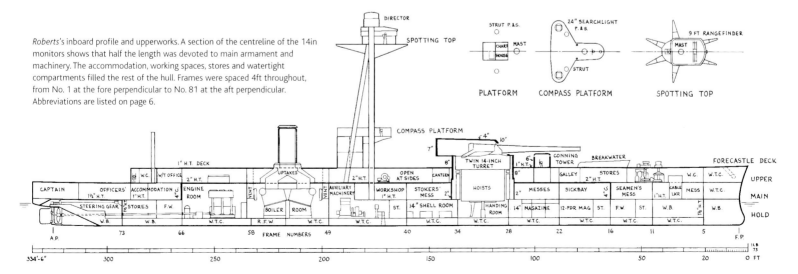

Roberts's inboard profile and upperworks. A section of the centreline of the 14in monitors shows that half the length was devoted to main armament and machinery. The accommodation, working spaces, stores and watertight compartments filled the rest of the hull. Frames were spaced 4ft throughout, from No. 1 at the fore perpendicular to No. 81 at the aft perpendicular. Abbreviations are listed on page 6.

necessary to have twin screws no larger than about 7½ft in diameter.

Having established the arrangement of the turret, magazine and propulsion machinery, the remainder of the ship features could then be worked in. On the lower decks: coal bunkers around the boiler room, auxiliary machinery between the magazine and boiler room, stores and accommodation for the crew of about 200 — officers aft, men forward. The upper deck was open at the sides, containing galleys and washplaces together with the barbette structure surrounding the ammunition trunks to the turret. The forecastle deck, which ran over three-quarters of the length of the ship, was comparatively bare: a huge tripod mast amidships carrying the gunnery

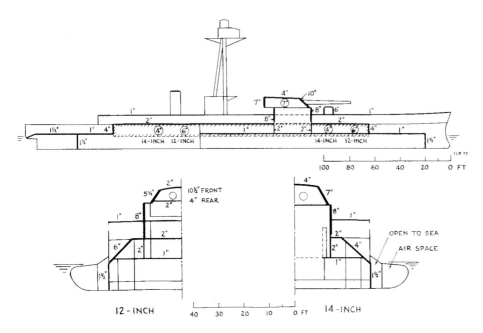

12 - INCH   14 - INCH

The principal hull protection for the 14in monitors was provided by a 4in sloping belt, a 2in upper deck and a 1½in longitudinal bulkhead, covering magazines and machinery. The 1in forecastle deck provided splinter protection. The main anti-torpedo and mine protection was provided by the bulge with its air and water spaces, the latter open to the sea at top and bottom through holes in the shell plating. Turret protection was the same as in the original battleship design. The protection for the 12in monitors was identical except for the turret and the 6in sloping belt.

spotting top and director, the heavy turret forward of the mast, with a small armoured conning tower nestling beneath its guns, and a stumpy funnel abaft the mast. The great expanse of deck abaft the funnel provided sufficient space to arrange stowage for two observation seaplanes, making the monitors the first ships designed from the outset to carry aircraft.

The protection of these first monitors was arranged primarily against torpedo and mine attack, secondarily against gunfire, thirdly against air attack. The threat of torpedoes came both from destroyers and U-boats, although the danger from the latter would be reduced by operating principally in shallow coastal waters, while the modest draft offered a chance that torpedoes would pass harmlessly underneath the hull without exploding. The main protection, however, came from the underwater bulges which, contrary to popular belief, were not fitted to improve stability, as they were below the waterline. The bulges were divided into two compartments by a vertical

longitudinal bulkhead, the outer being 10ft wide and watertight, the inner 5ft wide and open to the sea via holes in the top and bottom. The principle was that a torpedo would detonate against the outer chamber some distance away from the main hull, while the inner flooded chamber absorbed the splinters and distributed the energy of the explosion over a larger area of the main hull. The structure of the latter at this point consisted of a strong protective bulkhead formed of two thicknesses each of ¾in high-tensile (HT) steel. Behind this was another watertight compartment to contain any leakage resulting from deformation of the protective bulkhead. The effectiveness of such an arrangement had recently been proved in full-scale tests on the old pre-dreadnought *Hood*. Although the bulge was intended mainly as a defence against torpedoes, it also afforded some protection against mines. To prevent moored mines being carried under the less well protected bottom before exploding, tripper mine-catcher wires were fitted along the outer edge of the bulge. The 14in monitors were the first new-construction ships to have these underwater protection features.

The main protection against gunfire was provided by a sloping belt of 4in cemented armour[3] 12ft wide fitted inside the main hull, stretching from the ship's side at the waterline up to the upper deck, closed at the ends by 4in transverse bulkheads, proof against 6in gunfire. An armoured citadel was thus provided which would preserve flotation if the ends of the ship were damaged. One-inch HT steel extended over the full area of the forecastle deck to detonate any shells or light bombs, while the 2in HT steel upper deck would take care of any resulting splinters. The armour and protective plating amounted to a considerable weight, about 1,850 tons, or about 30 per cent of the displacement, as shown in the Technical Data at the end of this chapter (p.43).

As soon as Froude received the drawings of the monitor hull he was aghast at its shape. The very full form with steep buttock lines along which the water flowed from underneath the hull upwards towards the propellers would have an appalling hydrodynamic performance compared with the usual fine-lined warship. He wrote immediately to d'Eyncourt, pointing out that the resistance would be very high, the propulsive efficiency very low and the steering unsatisfactory. Work on making the 1/36th-scale wax model was nevertheless put in hand, although it proved difficult to make because of the bulges. All other work was suspended owing to the urgency; the first runs in the tank were made on 27 November. Over the next few days tests continued at different drafts and speeds up to 15kts. Results at low speeds were erratic, probably owing to the presence of some laminar flow and separation of the flow at the bluff forward and after ends. All

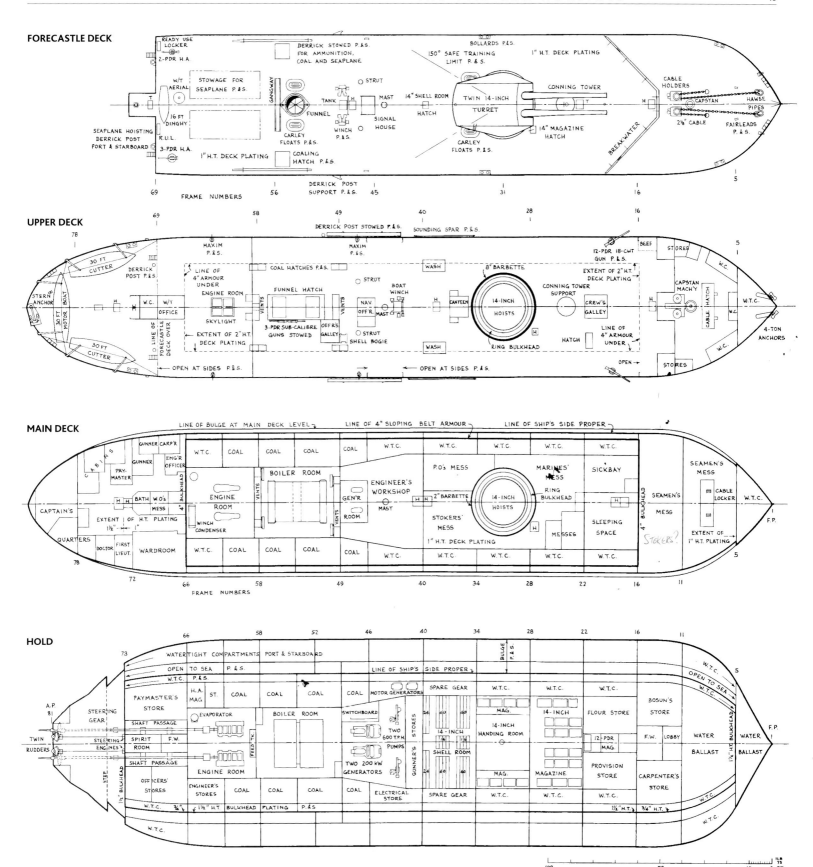

FORECASTLE DECK

UPPER DECK

MAIN DECK

HOLD

Roberts's decks. The forecastle deck was uncluttered, leaving plenty of space for the planned stowage of two seaplanes. The upper deck was open at the sides above bulwark height for most of its length, but a number of small compartments also served to support the forecastle deck. Both decks were painted steel except for the planked quarterdeck. The hold plan clearly shows the beamy below-water hull, the bluff angle of entrance and the extensive watertight subdivision. Accommodation spaces were floored with linoleum; other areas were painted steel.

of Froude's fears were confirmed; the resistance was even higher than expected, while the steering resembled that of the circular *Popoffka*s, which steamed sideways almost as readily as forwards. The measurements showed that to overcome the towing resistance alone, about 2,000 effective horsepower (ehp) would be needed at 10kts. The power required to be supplied by the engines would have to be considerably greater, due to the inherent losses of propellers in converting engine torque into propulsive thrust.[4] Froude estimated that the propulsive efficiency would be well under the 50-60 per cent typical of warships of this period, so that appreciably more than 4,000hp would be needed for 10kts, which was double the power being proposed by DNC. Froude had telegraphed the preliminary results to d'Eyncourt on 27 November, following up with full results and comments a week later, pointing out the reasons for the poor performance and proposing modifications to the afterbody lines. But it was too late to change the design of the hull; the first ship was about to be laid down. However much the constructors would have liked to improve the lines or increase the power of the engines, Fisher would permit no delays in construction. The design was committed; the monitors' speed would have to be accepted, whatever it was.

2.2 Armament

The Greek Government had ordered the 19,500-ton battlecruiser *Salamis* from Germany in July 1912, with her four twin 14in turrets to be supplied by Bethlehem Steel to a design generally similar to the US Navy 14in Mk I. The battlecruiser was launched at Vulcan Werke in Hamburg on 11 November 1914, having been renamed *Vassilefs Giorgios*.[5] Meanwhile, the first gun had been proof-fired in March 1914, and construction of the mountings was progressing well. By the outbreak of war *Salamis*'s armament had nearly been completed, but then, as described earlier, Schwab offered it to Britain, as it would not be permitted through the British blockade. A new contract was therefore quickly signed with the Admiralty on 10 November for the eight 14in guns, four twin mountings, their turret shield armour and two sets of 8in barbette armour, plus 500 rounds of ammunition per gun.

The RN designated the 45cal guns as 14in BL Mk II.[6] Their range was 19,900yd at their maximum elevation of 15 degrees. The design of both gun and mounting differed appreciably from current British practice. For example, the propellant was nitro-cellulose, compared with the RN's cordite. Being electrically instead of hydraulically worked, two 200 kW generators were required — double the capacity of a cruiser. Magazine arrangements were

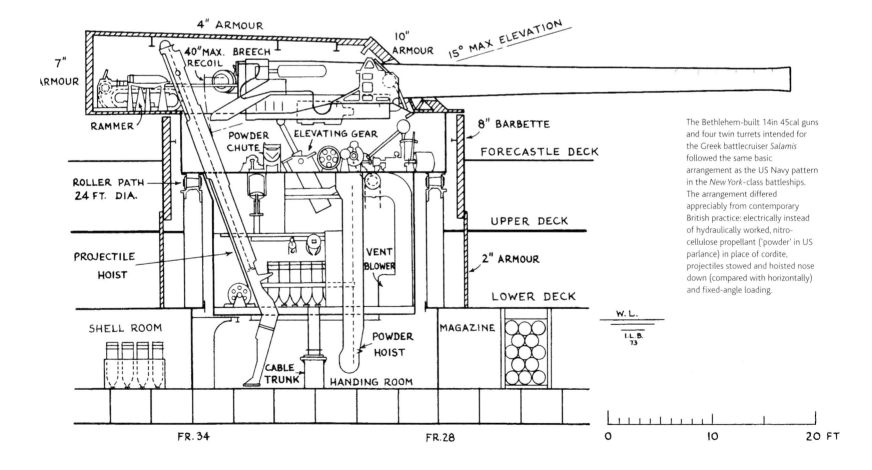

The Bethlehem-built 14in 45cal guns and four twin turrets intended for the Greek battlecruiser *Salamis* followed the same basic arrangement as the US Navy pattern in the *New York*-class battleships. The arrangement differed appreciably from contemporary British practice: electrically instead of hydraulically worked, nitro-cellulose propellant ('powder' in US parlance) in place of cordite, projectiles stowed and hoisted nose down (compared with horizontally) and fixed-angle loading.

also different, stowage for the 120 projectiles per gun being arranged vertically, nose down. The magazine and shell room were arranged on one level to keep them below the waterline as far as possible. Further details of the 14in guns are given in Chapter 10.4 on p.229.

A light secondary armament of 3in or 4in guns was proposed, sited on the upper deck to repel torpedo craft. Four (later reduced to two) 12pdr 18cwt QF guns[7] of 3in calibre were therefore selected; a weapon normally mounted in the older battleships. Later, high-angle (HA) guns were added at the after end of the forecastle deck. Although their main target was expected to be airships rather than aeroplanes, the designers were far-seeing in appreciating the conditions under which the monitors were likely to operate close to hostile shores, exposed to air attack. The British monitor stands out as being one of the first warships to take aircraft into account at the design stage, with their two seaplanes, two HA guns and protected forecastle deck. The anti-aircraft (AA) weapon chosen was the new 3in 45cal gun but, owing to shortage of supply, alternative weapons were actually fitted as detailed in 2.4. Four 0.303in Maxim machine guns were also supplied, normally mounted on the upper deck, but also capable of being carried in the larger ships' boats.

Although only local control was fitted for the secondary armament, the main guns had director control. The gunnery director was placed on the roof of the spotting top, which also contained the rangefinder. The director housed the gunlayer's and trainer's sights, whose movements were passed electrically to the layer and trainer in the turret. The system was similar to that being fitted in British capital ships but, as it had been designed primarily for direct fire at other ships, it was not entirely suitable for shore bombardment, where the target was usually invisible from the ship; nor was a transmitting station fitted. Consequently, new fire control techniques had to be developed as described in Chapter 10.7.

2.3 Construction

While full details of the monitors' design were being worked out, arrangements were being made to find suitable shipbuilders to undertake construction. Very wide building berths would be necessary for the beamy hulls but, because most ships of that period had breadths under 65ft, only a few shipyards would be capable of building them. There were only a dozen British shipbuilders who regularly built broad ships: capital ships and large passenger liners.

Fisher called a meeting of all the important shipbuilders at the Admiralty on 11 November 1914 to allocate orders for his massive new construction programme, mostly destroyers and submarines, but also

including the first monitors. None of the regular builders of large warships had a slipway free for the monitors, as they all had capital ships in hand already. One other major builder, Harland and Wolff (H & W) of Belfast, could offer quick delivery since, although it had full orderbooks, its contracts for large vessels were all for passenger liners. Since the outbreak of war the passenger and emigrant trade had slumped disastrously with the threat of enemy sinkings of merchant ships, so shipowners were not pressing for delivery of their new tonnage. Thus H & W would be able to switch its resources to building monitors, even though it had not built a warship at Belfast since completing two gunboats in 1887. However, in 1912 the company had taken over the London & Glasgow Company's shipyard at Govan, Glasgow, which had recently built a number of cruisers and destroyers. H & W had a massive orderbook totalling 400,000 gross tons, mostly for passenger-cargo liners, spread between their Belfast and Clyde yards. Two of the orders were for the Belgian Red Star Line, a subsidiary of J.P. Morgan's giant shipping combine International Mercantile Marine, which also owned White Star Line. As Belgium had just been overrun by the Germans, including Red Star's home port of Antwerp, the company had little use for its 27,000-ton liner *Belgenland*, nearly ready for launching, and even less for its as yet unnamed 35,000-tonner which had been laid down earlier in the year. However, not very much steel had been erected for this second vessel, H & W's No. 469, so it would be possible to clear the 860ft x 99ft No. 2 slipway fairly quickly. Lord Pirrie, H & W's chairman, could therefore offer to build two monitors. Fisher eagerly accepted. Thus were placed the orders for the first two monitor hulls, H & W's Hull Nos 472 and 473.

Arrangements for the other two vessels took a few days longer. Nine shipbuilders were circulated with invitations to tender for the construction of either one or two monitors. They were advised that the Admiralty would make arrangements to supply machinery, armament, armour, searchlights, boats and steering gear. As a result orders were placed on 21 November: one ship with Swan, Hunter & Wigham Richardson at Wallsend-on-Tyne, which also had had merchant ship orders suspended (including the Italian liner *Giulio Cesare)*, the other with H & W's Govan yard, to be numbered 476G.[8] Swan Hunter's large covered berth next to that on which the *Mauretania* had been built would be freed after the forthcoming launch of the cruiser *Comus,* so capacity was available to start work almost immediately on a monitor.

Arrangements to supply their machinery recognised that many engineering works were capable of supplying steam reciprocating machinery of modest power. Tenders

Admiral Farragut, later *Abercrombie,* on 15 March 1915, a month before her launch at Belfast. The crane is lowering a 4in slab of the sloping side armour into place. In the left foreground the stern of *General Grant* can be seen; in the background the pre-dreadnoughts *Mars* (left) and *Magnificent* (right) are about to have their turrets removed for the 12in monitors.
(HARLAND & WOLFF)

were invited for the supply of engines, boilers, auxiliaries, shafting, propellers and their installation. The machinery contracts were then allocated: H & W was to build the machinery for its first two monitors at Belfast, while McKie & Baxter was to engine H & W's third ship, its works at that time being near the Govan yard. Swan Hunter received the machinery contract for its monitor, which was allocated to their Neptune Engine Works as No. 984. The engines were a repeat of those the company fitted in the Canadian lighthouse tender *Simcoe.* The hull was to be built at its Wallsend yard as No. 991, the latter works using the odd numbers in the SHWR yard number series. H & W arranged to build its engines with quadruple expansion, each set developing 1,000 indicated horsepower (ihp.).[9] The other two engine builders chose triple-expansion engines of slightly less power, 800ihp each for McKie & Baxter, 900ihp for Swan Hunter, as the Admiralty had not specified any precise power to be installed, while Froude's model tests had not yet been run. The two coal-fired boilers would be of Babcock & Wilcox design, watertube, which gave a quicker response to changes of speed than mercantile firetube or Scotch boilers.

The ships were described as 'monitors' from the very beginning, so it was necessary to change the name of the destroyer *Monitor* then building at Thornycroft to *Munster.* In the period before names were selected the four monitors were identified by numbers only, *M.1* to *M.4.* Churchill, Fisher and Schwab used the codeword 'Styx' to describe the vessels in correspondence.

The urgency of construction was paramount. The builders were instructed by Fisher that there were to be 'no fall-lalls or comforts of any kind', as it was not expected that the ships would survive long in their intended role of bombarding heavily defended coastlines. The first keel, *M.3* at Govan, was laid on 1 December and that of the last, *M.4* at Wallsend, on 17 December, the day after *Comus* was launched. The two Belfast ships, *M.1* and *M.2,* were laid down simultaneously on the same slipway, that on which the White Star liners *Olympic* and *Britannic* had been built. As virtually all work had ceased on merchant ship construction, it was possible for H & W to devote a large proportion of its resources to the monitors. Work went on round the clock seven days a week but, as these were still early days in a war which was not expected to last long, it was sometimes difficult to persuade the night-shift workers that the customary procedure of taking naps on the job was no longer appropriate. With the long hours of overtime, riveters were able to make £13 a week, compared with about £2 to £3 in normal times. Many put in over 70 hours a week.

To reduce construction delays, the usual process

LEFT

General Grant on 28 April 1915, the day before her launch. Her name was changed before completion to *M.2*, finally becoming *Havelock* in mid-June. The full lines aft of the early monitors produced both a high resistance and a low propulsive efficiency. The mine-catcher wires can be seen underneath the bulge. (HARLAND & WOLFF)

ABOVE

The first British big-gun monitor *Admiral Farragut* takes to the water, on 15 April 1915, at Harland & Wolff's Belfast yard, from the same slipway on which *Olympic* was launched. There even seems to be steam up on the boilers. (HARLAND & WOLFF)

whereby the builder submitted drawings of the structure or proposals for equipment to the Admiralty for approval was omitted. Instead such matters were decided on the spot by the overseers who stood by the building of naval vessels. Merchant ship quality fittings were used wherever possible to speed the orders for such items as pumping and ventilating equipment, although the Admiralty were to supply major fittings such as steering gear, fire control instruments and boats. Lloyds Register of Shipping's surveyors were employed to approve progress on the machinery. Most of the hull was of simple construction, with much of the plating a standard ½in in thickness. Only the quarterdeck was planked, all other exposed decks being bare or painted steel.

The monitors were allocated names in February 1915. In recognition of the USA being the source of their main armament and the original *Monitor*, they were named after American Civil War leaders, *M.1* to *M.4* becoming respectively: *Admiral Farragut* (originally just *Farragut*), *General Grant*, *Robert E. Lee* and *Stonewall Jackson*. The compliment was ill received. The US Government was anxious to maintain its neutral status and to confine any shipments of war material to relatively minor items. A roundabout way of delivering Schwab's submarines had to be found, and these arrangements rather diverted attention from his other deal. The 14in guns were safely shipped across the Atlantic in Cunard's passenger-cargo vessels *Ausonia* and *Transylvania* in February 1915. When the monitors were given names so unusual for British warships, and which drew attention to the origin of their armament, the Americans were not pleased. After representations from the American Ambassador in London, the names were changed in May, as detailed later.

While construction of the hulls and machinery was progressing, arrangements were being made to erect the turrets in the monitors. Because of its proximity on the Tyne, Armstrong Whitworth's Elswick Ordnance Company (EOC) was to erect *M.4*'s turret, while Coventry Ordnance Works (COW)[10] handled the three H & W ships, all under the supervision of Bethlehem staff. H & W and Swan Hunter tied for the launch of the first monitor; both *Admiral Farragut* and *Stonewall Jackson* were sent down the ways on 15 April 1915, just four months after their keels were laid, the other pair following a fortnight later. Such rapid construction constituted a remarkable achievement for the builders, especially as the monitors were launched in a relatively complete state. Most of the machinery, armour and superstructure was aboard, leaving only the shipping of the armament and the final outfitting to be done afloat.

With delivery of the ships so urgent, formalities were kept to a minimum. No detailed cost records exist in Admiralty files, apart from Churchill's estimate to the Cabinet in December 1914 of £2,207,000 for the four vessels, i.e. £551,750 each. From a few surviving records at Swan Hunter, plus comparative cost rates for other ships of this period, it is possible to estimate the likely breakdown of total costs as shown in the table. As Bethlehem have no record of the value of Schwab's deal, it is also necessary to estimate likely costs based on

General Grant's launch on 29 April 1915 provides an excellent view of the monitors' bulged hull form. As the monitor was built at the head of the same slipway as *Admiral Farragut*, the drag chains were placed well aft as seen in the photograph opposite, connected by wires running under the hull to the hawsepipes. The launch was the only occasion on which any of the early monitors achieved their designed speed of 10kts!
(HARLAND & WOLFF)

comparable ordnance. The cost of naval construction in the USA was about 25 per cent higher than in Britain at this period, when the pound was worth about $4.87 and had a purchasing power about 70 to 80 times greater than in the mid-2000s. Schwab would certainly have demanded a substantial premium for his immediately available guns, possibly about 10-20 per cent, so that total contract value per ship would have been about 40 per cent above the equivalent British costs based on the comparable 13.5in gun, say about £335,000. Ammunition alone comprised nearly half the total, as not only was it necessary to buy about four outfits but nitro-cellulose was an expensive propellant. Bethlehem benefited by about $6.5 million. The final probable cost of each 14in monitor to the British taxpayer of about £550,000 was thus close to Churchill's estimate.

Estimated cost of a 14in-gun monitor

1. Actual cost records for Swan Hunter's No. 991 (*Roberts*)			
Item	Tons	£/ton	£
High-tensile steel plates	1,182	10.02	11,852
Mild steel plates and sections	1,979	7.01	13,880
Miscellaneous steel and rivets	227	15.50	3,515
Total purchased steel	3,388		29,247
Labour on steel hull			31,567
Labour on outfitting			20,119
Outfit materials and subcontractors			21,131
Overhead charges			8,101
Total cost of hull to shipbuilder			110,165
Engines, boilers and installation			23,625
Shipbuilder's profit on hull and machinery			23,987
Shipbuilder's price to Admiralty			157,777
2. Estimated costs for other items			
Armour plating, belt, bulkheads etc.			43,000
Items of Admiralty supply, boats, small guns, etc.			7,223
Admiralty overheads and incidentals			7,000
Total cost of ship excluding main armament			215,000
3. Estimated cost of main armament if built in UK			
Twin 14in mounting			85,000
Two 14in guns			26,000
Barbette armour			17,000
500 rounds of ammunition per gun			110,000
Total cost if in UK			238,000
4. Estimated price of armament charged by Schwab			
(40 per cent extra)			335,000
5. Estimated total cost of monitor to the Admiralty			**550,000**

2.4 As Completed

Four weeks after launch, *Admiral Farragut* was the first big monitor to be commissioned, Capt H. M. Doughty assuming command on 12 May 1915. There were twelve officers in all: Captain, First Lieutenant *cum* Gunnery Officer ('First and G'), Navigating Officer, two Lieutenants, Surgeon, Paymaster, Mate, Artificer Engineer, two Gunners and Shipwright. The last five were Warrant Officers, men of long experience promoted from the lower deck, most of whom had been standing by the ship for several weeks and preparing to receive the ship's full complement. The 186 ratings, largely reservists, were from Chatham, 89 in the Seaman branch, 45 Engine Room, 15 Artisans, 14 Stewards and Miscellaneous, together with 23 Royal Marines to man the secondary armament. The total complement of 198 for a ship carrying two big guns was in proportion to that of a battleship with about 900 to 1,000 men for eight to ten big guns.

The crew quickly settled in to their somewhat spartan quarters. Conditions were similar to those aboard most RN ships; large communal mess-decks used for sleeping, eating and recreation. Each man had a place to sling his hammock, a space on a bench at the wooden tables and a small kit locker. Heating was by means of a small coal stove, ventilation was by a mechanical supply fan with natural exhaust through hatches, skylights and sidelights. The officers were much better off for space; each had his own cabin, complete with portable bath, the captain having a separate day cabin, sleeping cabin and bathroom. The warrant officers had a mess separate from the wardroom, as it was considered that their pay was too low for them to afford the additional expenses of wardroom messing.

Three days after commissioning she was ready for her steam trials. The intention was to steam the ship at full power for 4hr continuously and during this time, make a number of runs up and down the measured mile in Belfast Lough. The trials were not a success. After 3½hr the ship could only make about 6kts rather than the designed 10, although developing 1,864ihp, not far short of the designed power. Such a poor result came as no surprise to Froude at AEW, who had predicted from the beginning that the performance would be bad. D'Eyncourt thought that the low speed might have been due to the bulge being so close to the surface, or to the trim of the ship in the trial condition. Froude was not impressed with these explanations, and re-emphasised that the low speed was due to the steep buttock lines aft producing not only a high resistance but also a low propulsive efficiency, owing to the poor flow of water past the propellers, resulting in very high propeller slip.

While a 6kts speed might just be sufficient to get along in fine weather, in bad weather, or with a heavily fouled hull, or against wind, tide or current, the ship would make little headway at all. The hull form could not now be altered, but two small changes could be made which might increase the speed a little. New propellers could be

ABOVE
Roberts, launched as *Stonewall Jackson*, alongside Swan Hunter & Wigham Richardson's Wallsend yard in June 1915, with steam up and temporary coal bunkers being fitted on the upper deck.
(SWAN HUNTER)

LEFT
Abercrombie getting her final touches on 27 April, berthed in the Musgrave Channel at Belfast (H & W's building dock from 1970) with the gantries over her launch slipway in the background.
(HARLAND & WOLFF)

tried and the mine-catcher wires with their high drag removed. New propellers were therefore ordered, with four blades of increased area compared with three, diameter reduced by 3in to 7ft 3in and pitch reduced by 12in to 7ft 6in, thus permitting the engines to run closer to their designed rpm and reducing the propeller loading. After the wires were removed a further trial on 22 May showed a slight increase of speed to about 6½kts. Other trials of the ship were also carried out: anchoring, turning, stopping, running astern, compasses. The all-important gun trials took place that same day, four rounds being fired from each 14in gun, with only a few minor defects appearing. After a further week of ammunitioning, storing

and fitting temporary additional coal bunkers on the upper deck, HMS *Admiral Farragut* was handed over by her builders and left Belfast on 29 May.

The other ships all commissioned within a fortnight of each other; *Stonewall Jackson* on 21 May under Capt P.N. Garnett, *General Grant* on 26 May under Cdr G. Hamilton, and *Robert E. Lee* on 3 June under Capt C.D.S. Raikes. The last ship was actually commissioned as HMS *M.3*, as on 31 May a directive had come from the Admiralty that the names were to be changed as a result of American pressure. All four ships thus reverted to their original numbers, *M.1* to *M.4*. This change did not last long: it was appreciated that it was inappropriate for such large ships to be identified by numbers only. With King George V's approval new names were selected on 19 June, this time of former British military leaders. *M.1*, late *Admiral Farragut*, became *Abercrombie*, named after Maj-Gen Sir Ralph Abercromby of the Napoleonic era. This was the second use of the name for a British warship, perpetuating the misspelling first adopted on a third-rate of 1809. *M.2*, late *General Grant*, became *Havelock*, named after Maj-Gen Sir Henry Havelock, a hero of the Indian Mutiny fighting. *M.3*, late *Robert E. Lee*, became first *Lord Raglan*, then, on 23 June, simply *Raglan*, named after Field-Marshal Lord Raglan, who had fought with Wellington and in the Crimea. *M.4*, late *Stonewall Jackson*, became *Earl Roberts*, shortened on 22 June to *Roberts*, named after Field-Marshal Earl Roberts, who had fought in nearly every campaign in the latter half of the nineteenth century, and who had died only the previous year. During their lives the ships were sometimes referred to erroneously as *Lord Raglan*, *Earl Roberts* or *Lord Roberts*, while the title *General* was likewise occasionally added to *Abercrombie* and *Havelock*. The rapid succession of names caused confusion not only in administrative circles but also on board the ships.

The trial performance of the three later ships was also disappointing. *Havelock* managed 6.32kts on 29 May, but *Raglan*, which had now been fitted with higher-powered engines by H & W (see p.47), produced the best perform-ance of the class, with 7.64kts. *Roberts*, handicapped by the lowest installed power and over-pitched propellers, had only been able to achieve 5.70kts.

Little official data has survived on the characteristics of the monitors as completed. Displacement, dimensions, armament, speed, stability and most technical features usually differ slightly from the designed figures, owing to changes during construction and to the difficulty of making fully detailed calculations from the limited information available at the design stage. The Technical Data show the details of the ships, distinguishing where possible between the 'designed' and 'completed' conditions. No record of the actual displacement as completed can be found in either Admiralty or builders' records, but it can be estimated from the drafts recorded in service that the deep displacement (i.e. fully loaded) was almost exactly as designed: about 6,150 tons, compared with 6,157 tons with a full load of coal.

Although all the ships were intended to be identical, there were the usual minor differences between each vessel as completed. All except *Raglan* were fitted with two derricks at the after end of the forecastle deck for hoisting the seaplanes in and out. The aircraft were not aboard when the ships were completed and, to preserve secrecy, they were referred to on the ships' plans as 'boxes', with overall dimensions corresponding to their size with folded wings, 31ft long × 12ft wide × 13ft high; probably a Sopwith Admiralty Type 807. All ships were initially fitted with the very tall topmasts needed to support the aerials of the long-range battleship-type wireless transmitter. The actual HA armament fitted was a single 3pdr semi-automatic and one of the new 2pdr pom-poms, each on specially designed HA mountings.

2.5 The Deployment of the First Monitors

The first large monitors had been conceived and ordered in great haste, without any detailed plans being made for their employment. Fisher's original intention had been to use them for his Baltic plan, but Churchill regarded the North Sea area or the Dardanelles as more promising. By January 1915 it was clear that there were very serious risks in the Baltic scheme, not least from mines, while nothing could be done until the High Seas Fleet had been neutralised. A memorandum prepared by Churchill on 27 January 1915 included the following paragraph:[11]

Between the beginning of April and the end of July we shall also receive 14 heavily armoured, shallow draft Monitors; 2 armed with two 15in guns, 4 armed with two 14in guns, and 8 armed with two 12in guns. These last 8 will be armed by taking the turrets out of 4 of the *Majestic*s. It is this force which it is proposed to use for special services and for bombarding as may be necessary from time to time in furtherance of objects of great strategic and political importance, among which the following may be specifically mentioned:
    1. The operations at the Dardanelles;
    2. The support of the left flank of the Army;
    3. The bombardment of Zeebrugge; and later on
    4. The seizure of Borkum.

The priorities listed reflected the current military and political situation. It was already evident to Churchill that the stalemate on the Western Front in France was likely to continue indefinitely. A strongly defended line was held from neutral Switzerland to the Belgian Coast. With the high losses resulting from frontal attacks, it was vital to turn one of the enemy's flanks. Long before the entry of Turkey into the war in early November 1914, Churchill had appreciated that the Dardanelles, the gateway to Constantinople (now Istanbul), would be a key objective. The rewards for the seizure of this strategic waterway would be many, including the opening of a direct supply route to the ally Russia, the relief of Turkish pressure on the Suez Canal and a favourable influence on the Balkan states.

Compared with the prize of the Dardanelles, the support of the Army's left flank was of secondary importance. Useful work had been done by the makeshift bombarding fleet of October-December 1914, and this work could be continued, provided that the German shore defences did not become too strong. The bombardment of Zeebrugge and Ostende was desirable to discourage their use as advanced bases for German destroyers and U-boats, although there was little possibility of backing up the operations by landings at that time. The seizure of Borkum could be considered when the necessary naval and military forces had become available, although an attempt to capture and retain the island as a forward base against strong German opposition would be a most hazardous undertaking.

The Dardanelles scheme was officially approved in January, and the campaign began on 19 February with a naval bombardment of the Turkish forts by British and French ships, which included the newly completed battleship *Queen Elizabeth*. A major naval offensive was launched on 18 March to try to force a passage; some progress was made for the loss of three pre-dreadnoughts from mines, *Ocean*, *Irresistible* and French *Bouvet*. As with so many WW1 operations, the opportunities were not followed up. No Army landing was made nor any sustained naval attack continued while the Turkish defences were still weak. It was not until 25 April that troops were landed on the Gallipoli peninsula, with gunfire support from the warships. The Army was able to make little progress ashore in the very difficult conditions; it became clear that additional forces were required. Churchill telegraphed Vice-Admiral John M. de Robeck, the Allied Fleet commander, on 12 May:[12]

Two more infantry divisions with other reinforcements leave about 17th and 30th. Meanwhile arrival of German submarines in Turkish waters makes it undesirable to expose *Queen Elizabeth*. We are therefore sending you at once instead *Exmouth* and *Venerable*, and also, before the end of the month, the first two new monitors, *Admiral Farragut* and *Stonewall Jackson*, with 2 14in guns apiece, an effective range of 20,000 yards, firing a 1,400-pd high-explosive shell, 10ft draught, and special bulges against mine and torpedo. You will be able to use the two monitors much more freely for all purposes, as they have been specially built for this work.

Kitchener and the Army were disturbed at the prospect of losing the support of the *Queen Elizabeth*, but Fisher was adamant that she should be brought home, especially after the news was received that the pre-dreadnought *Goliath* had been torpedoed in the Dardanelles on the 13th. The monitors were expected to be able to play a valuable role, not least because they were considered relatively expendable, both in support of Army operations and in forcing a passage of the Dardanelles. Loss of a monitor would have less psychological effect than loss of a battleship, even though it was an obsolete pre-dreadnought.

The anticipated departure date was optimistic; the monitors were not ready until well into June. Churchill was determined that they should be used to the fullest extent. On 14 May, he minuted:[13]

The following nine heavy monitors should go in succession to the Dardanelles, as soon as they are ready:- *Admiral Farragut*, *General Grant*, *Stonewall Jackson*, *Robert E. Lee*, *Lord Clive*, *Prince Rupert*, *Sir John Moore*, *General Craufurd*, and *Marshal Ney*. The first six of the 9.2in monitors should also go, unless the Admiral [de Robeck] chooses to have two of their guns for work on shore, in which case the first four only will go.

The first four named carried two 14in guns, the next four two 12in and *Ney* two 15in, while the 9.2in were small monitors with a single gun. In addition, the four old *Edgar* class cruisers were to go: *Edgar*, *Endymion*, *Grafton* and *Theseus*, each now carrying twelve 6in and fitted with bulges. Against this fleet of well protected vessels the U-boats would be less of a menace.

During the preceding weeks Fisher had become increasingly opposed to any extension of the Dardanelles operation, including anything involving the vessels intended for his specially created Baltic fleet. Sending nine large monitors was more than Fisher had agreed, so Churchill wrote to him: 'I shall not press my wish about reinforcements beyond the point to which you were willing to go – namely the six earliest monitors'. Disagreements between Churchill and Fisher had been building up for some time, and matters came to a head on 15 May, when Fisher resigned. Churchill and others tried to dissuade him, but the old man was determined. A train of political changes was set off; Churchill was forced out as First Lord and was succeeded by Arthur J. Balfour on 25 May. There followed a dangerous hiatus between Fisher's resignation and the settling-in of the new government in June, when the whole question of reinforcing the Dardanelles had to be reconsidered. On 7 June it was agreed to send a monitor fleet: the four 14in vessels, together with eleven small monitors and a number of other vessels. As with all matters concerning the monitor fleet at that time, all these plans were shrouded in secrecy. Even the monitor officers were not told of their final destination, although they could make an intelligent guess.

2.6 At the Dardanelles

Now that the despatch of the monitors had been finally agreed, additional preparations had to be made for the 3,000-mile voyage. *Abercrombie* had to be drydocked at Avonmouth, which had one of the few graving docks sufficiently wide to take her, to have her new propellers fitted. She then undertook a full power trial in Milford Haven on 6 June, making 7.04kts, a gain in speed of about one knot, while vibration was reduced. Further work at Pembroke included the replacement of her underpowered steering gear and the loading of 170 tons of extra coal into temporary bunkers, making a total of 550 tons. She sailed on 24 June for the Dardanelles, with *Theseus* giving her a tow to speed her up. *Theseus* had been newly fitted with bulges and her 9.2in guns had been transferred to small monitors. Even with both ships' engines at full power, the unwieldy pair were only able to make 9kts, although this was enough to leave their escort of four trawlers astern. After *Havelock* had also got modified propellers at Avonmouth, giving her an extra knot, she departed from Pembroke on 30 June, assisted by a tow from the old cruiser *Juno*. After a call at Plymouth, *Roberts* was taken in tow by *Endymion* on 28 June, while *Raglan* also left that same day from Pembroke, later towed by the old cruiser *Diana*. After brief stops at Gibraltar and Malta

Abercrombie arrived on 12 July at the main British naval base in the fine natural harbour of Mudros on the Greek island of Lemnos, some 50 miles west of the Dardanelles (see map on p.127), and the others within the next ten days.

The monitors' arrival was particularly welcome to the troops at Gallipoli. For several weeks U-boats had made it dangerous to expose heavy ships to give close-support bombardment to supplement the Army's limited artillery, but now it became possible to deploy extremely powerful guns without the same risk of loss. *Abercrombie* was inspected by de Robeck shortly after her arrival at the anchorage at Kephalo on the south-east corner of the island of Imbros. Although barely ten miles from Cape Helles (see map on p.35), the south-western point of the Gallipoli peninsula, Kephalo was just out of range of the Turkish batteries on the mainland. The same day she hoisted Rear-Admiral Nicholson's flag, the commander of the supporting forces, and fired her first twelve rounds at the enemy. Her targets were Turkish ammunition dumps at Eren Keui on the Asiatic shore of the Dardanelles, but no hits were reported after the 50min bombardment. The Turks were not slow to reply; a 150mm (5.9in) shell hit *Abercrombie*'s quarterdeck, penetrating the captain's cabin, fortunately without exploding.

Roberts arrived on 15 July and was allocated to bombard the batteries on the Asiatic side of the Dardanelles which were severely harassing the British and French troops on the European side. As the slowest monitor she was anchored on the 23rd south of Rabbit Island (Mavro

Roberts arriving at Malta on 10 July 1915, on her way to the Dardanelles. The planked-in parts of the upper deck housed temporary coal bunkers.
(IWM SP637)

Roberts firing on the Turkish coast from her Rabbit Island berth in 1915, with her 14in guns at their maximum elevation.
(IWM SP3202)

LEFT
Roberts fires at the Turkish batteries on the Asiatic shore of the Dardanelles from her berth at Rabbit Island. She is heeled to starboard to increase gun elevation and maximum range. The left gun is just recoiling after firing, while the right gun appears to have already been reloaded.
(IWM SP150)

Island), four miles from the Turkish coastline. Hidden behind the island's cliffs, she and one of the small monitors engaged the enemy at leisure, protected by anti-submarine nets, with aiming marks erected on the island and connected by telephone to the Naval Observation Station on shore at Cape Helles. She continued in this stationary role for five months, suffering the occasional minor shell hit and bombing attack by enemy aircraft. However, de Robeck had warned Gen Sir Ian Hamilton, commanding the Allied Armies, not to expect too much:[14]

> The presence of naval monitors at Rabbit Island will no doubt assist a little to neutralise the Asiatic batteries, but owing to the distance involved (18,000 yards) large guns with a consequent small supply of ammunition will be required, and it is not to be expected that direct hits will be obtained; moreover it will not be possible to reach the batteries beyond In Tepe.

Meanwhile both *Havelock* and *Raglan* arrived on 22 July and were quickly in action. The Army reinforcement programme culminated in the Suvla Bay landings on 6–7 August, which were supported by the monitors, large and small, and the bulged cruisers. During the simultaneous offensive from Anzac just to the south, *Havelock* was assigned to deal with any enemy ships that might fire

from the Narrows, while *Abercrombie* and *Raglan* were further south, firing at Krithia village and the heights of Achi Baba, where large numbers of Turkish troops and guns were ranged against the British Helles position. The guns were mobile and difficult targets among the smoke and dust of the bombardments, as only a direct hit would silence them completely. *Abercrombie* did manage to hit one Turkish redoubt, which according to an eyewitness sent 'whole Turks whirling in the air'. Most of the fire in direct support of the Allied troops came from the cruisers *Bacchante*, *Endymion*, *Grafton* and *Theseus*, backed up by the small monitors. On one unfortunate occasion one of *Raglan*'s guns went off prematurely while still at a low elevation and the shell landed among British troops, killing one man and wounding three. Such episodes had occurred before the monitors arrived, and discouraged the Army from calling on the full weight of naval bombardment support available.

Havelock moved into Suvla Bay on 8 August to give closer support, firing occasionally and with a clear view of the fighting ashore. On the 12th she was hit four times by Turkish shells, three men being injured. During the Suvla landings the large monitors had fired 138 rounds of 14in HE (high-explosive) in two days. Such a rate of expenditure was considered excessive for the available targets and the limited stocks of ammunition. Thereafter the monitors' big guns were ordered to be used only with the Senior Officer's permission against specific targets out of range of other guns and when spotting conditions were favourable. Later they were rationed to ten rounds per week. Generally, Army forward observation posts on shore were used for spotting, but aircraft and balloon spotting were also being experimented with. An officer from the firing ship would often be carried in the aircraft, although it was some time before effective wireless communications and spotting code procedures were developed. Although the monitors were designed to carry two spotting seaplanes, they rarely ever carried even one, as the shore-based Royal Naval Air Service (RNAS) aircraft were found to be more suitable. During September *Roberts* embarked a Short Admiralty Type 166 seaplane, which was quite effective, although there were problems as the aeroplane had to be hoisted off whenever the guns were fired, to avoid blast damage. On one occasion *Abercrombie* experimented with a Sopwith Schneider. *Raglan* also embarked a Short Type 166 for several days for her bombardment, in company with small monitors, of enemy lines of communication and flour mills near Gallipoli town on 12 October. The weather proved too poor for successful spotting, and it proved difficult to handle the seaplane on board and in the water.

The monitors usually anchored close offshore for their bombardments, using aiming marks on the rocky coastline. In these exposed positions they were vulnerable to return fire from the Turkish batteries between Suvla and Helles. Fortunately the Turks were not very good shots and their shells were prone to be duds. By keeping nearly all the monitors' crews under cover, the shell hits caused little injury. On 8 September *Abercrombie* was hit several times by 75mm (2.95in) shells, which damaged a winch and severed rigging. *Roberts* was hit on two occasions in October, the first time on the forecastle, the second on the port bulge. Fragments of one of the shells showed that it was a 4.7in made by Bethlehem Steel in 1910, indicating that Schwab's munitions were now being used by both sides. The Suvla landings were not followed up with vigour ashore, and failed to break the stalemate, although a link was made with the Anzac position to the south. The Allied troops were thus confined to two small areas, unable to break past the dominating ridges to the Narrows to open the way for the ships. With the decline in demand for heavy gun support following the landings, the opportunity was taken during September to check over the monitors. *Roberts* conducted special trials to determine the reason for the occasional erratic firing of the 14in guns. One of the causes was found to be copper deposited in the gun bores from the driving bands of the projectiles, which had to be scraped away.

De Robeck reported to the Admiralty:[15]

Each class of monitor has her own particular trouble; 14in, the steering engines are too weak; 9.2in, the exhaust fumes in the funnel; 6in, weakness of decks under the guns; but they are mostly being successfully dealt with by *Reliance*, where Engineer-Captain Humphreys is worth his weight in gold and never makes a difficulty. We must not expect too much from these monitors, especially the 14in, which could not navigate the Dardanelles without tugs, so the question of forcing the Narrows with monitors is, I am afraid, for the present not a workable proposition.

A Special Squadron for bombardment was organised, the First Division comprising the four 14in monitors, the Second the ten small 9.2in monitors *M.15* to *M.23* and *M.28*; the Third the five 6in monitors *M.29* to *M.33* (see Chapter 7) plus the ex-Brazilian river monitor *Humber*, and the Fourth the four bulged cruisers. Over the remaining months of 1915 *Abercrombie* continued to support the left flank of the Helles position, generally firing against the Turkish redoubts on the northern slopes of Achi Baba, which were hidden from shore artillery fire. Captain A.U. Moore took over from Doughty, who took command of the battleship *Agincourt* now that *Abercrombie* was fully worked up. *Roberts* remained off Rabbit Island, while *Havelock* made an occasional bombardment of the Narrows, firing right over the peninsula. Her bombardment of the iron foundries at Chanak (now Cannakale) from 17,000yd on 3 October was quite successful: 15 rounds in 45min, 11 reported hits, two missed short and two duds. In reply, 33 rounds were fired at her, which included four hits by 12pdr shells. With practice, all the ships greatly improved their bombardment performance, the large monitors eventually proving themselves good platforms for firing accurately close to Allied troops. During all these operations none of the monitors was attacked by U-boat, an immunity partly due to the extensive use of anti-submarine nets at their anchorages.

Separate suggestions by Churchill and by Cdre Roger Keyes, de Robeck's Chief of Staff, to use a fleet of old battleships and monitors to force the Dardanelles were turned down by the Admiralty. Not only were the losses of 18 March too well remembered, but the monitors' slow speed and poor manoeuvrability would give them little chance of getting past the Turkish forts. No further attempts were made to use the monitors in other than a purely harassing role at Gallipoli, a modest enough contribution compared with Churchill's original ambitious plans for devastating the Turkish defences and breaking into the Sea of Marmara.

Meanwhile, in an effort to assist Serbia, British and French troops had landed at Salonika (now Thessaloniki) in October, Bulgaria already having thrown in her lot with the Central Powers. *Raglan* spent a month with the British squadron at Salonika from 14 November, but there was little for her to do there. At the same time *Havelock* and *M.18* were at Milo in the southern Aegean from 22 November, where a number of ships was being held ready to put pressure on Greece not to interfere with Allied operations, if the political situation so demanded. By this time the monitors' firing had improved to the point where VIII Army Corps at Helles could signal on 16 November:[16]

The Corps Commander [Lt Gen Sir F. Davies] wishes me to express to you his appreciation of the excellent shooting of the cruiser and monitors yesterday [*Edgar, Abercrombie* and *Havelock*], which undoubtedly contributed very largely to the ease with which our troops seized two very important positions in the enemy's line and added enormously to the moral effect and material damage done to the enemy. All who saw it agree as to the accuracy and value of the monitors' fire, but the chief point is that

it has been established that co-operation in an attack has now become a practical reality, and that a system has been established which with further development will prove a powerful factor both in attack and defence.

Abercrombie's firing was also commended unofficially by one of the naval observers ashore: 'You have, I think, got the best shooting monitor out here (between ourselves that is)'. On *Raglan*, another officer's comment was less complimentary: '*Raglan* in his usual inconsequential fashion dropped half a dozen shell anywhere on the same continent as Krithia'. *Raglan's* then Gunnery Officer was Lt A.J. Power, destined to become Admiral C-in-C of the East Indies Fleet in 1944.

All four 14in monitors, the two 12in which had just arrived *(Sir Thomas Picton* and *Earl of Peterborough,* see p.68), plus most of the small monitors, were concentrated off the Dardanelles in December after it had been decided to evacuate the Gallipoli peninsula, starting with the northern positions at Suvla and Anzac. *Havelock* took over *Roberts'* Rabbit Island berth on 16 December while the latter retired to Mudros, having fired about 150 rounds since July, some of them at a range of 22,000yd, requiring the ship to be heeled about 5 degrees by flooding the bulges on one side to increase the guns' elevation. The other four large monitors supported the diversionary attacks being made on the Turkish lines at Helles; their powerful guns wrought a heavy execution on the Turkish counterattacks. The monitors did not escape unscathed; *Raglan* was hit six times on 17 December but was only slightly damaged. The evacuation of Suvla and Anzac went off without the loss of a single man, being completed on the night of 19/20 December.

At the end of the month it was decided to evacuate the remaining position at Helles early in the New Year, so all six large monitors again foregathered. The orders to *Roberts* to join the East Indies Command in Egyptian waters were cancelled. *Roberts*, *Peterborough*, *Picton*, *M.18* and *M.31* were stationed at Rabbit Island in early January to neutralise the Turkish Asiatic batteries. *Raglan* and *Havelock* were with the reserve squadron at Imbros, ready to move up in close support off Helles as necessary, while *Abercrombie* was in her usual position off the left flank. An unexpectedly heavy Turkish attack was launched on the British lines on 7 January, supported by fire from across the Dardanelles. *Abercrombie*, *Havelock*, *Raglan* and *Peterborough*, together with three bulged cruisers and several destroyers, moved in to pour a heavy fire on to the Turkish lines and the Asiatic batteries. The ships amply compensated for the previous withdrawal of a high proportion of the Army's artillery, the attack being beaten off with many Turkish casualties. The evacuation was completed on the night of 8/9 January 1916 with the loss of only one man, although a considerable amount of stores had to be abandoned.

Thus ended the only major Allied attempt to make a decisive thrust away from the stalemate of the Western Front. Despite Churchill's high hopes for the monitors, plans for forcing the Dardanelles by sea were not really practicable by the time the ships were ready. There was very little more that they could have done beyond their purely supporting role from July 1915 onwards, and even this was limited until bombarding technical efficiency had been built up.

2.7 The Rest of the War

With the withdrawal from Gallipoli there was no need to keep six large monitors in the Mediterranean. Accordingly, after final bombardments of the Turkish and Bulgarian coastlines, *Roberts* (the slowest monitor) and *Havelock* (the most junior CO) were sent back to Britain. Both ships departed Mudros on 14 February, under tow by a collier or tug most of the way, and arrived at Portsmouth during April for overhaul. *Havelock* had been

delayed at Gibraltar for five weeks waiting for a tug. As she entered the English Channel at a leisurely 5kts on 24 April a message was received that the German High Seas Fleet had sortied. If the Fleet forced a passage of the Straits of Dover, *Havelock* feared that she might face this armada alone. In the event they were only covering the raid on Lowestoft by German battlecruisers. This attack on 24 April aroused public indignation over the vulnerability of British East Coast towns, but it was very difficult for the RN to defend the lengthy coastline against such 'hit-and-run' operations, with the major Fleet bases far away to the north. However, Balfour was able to write to the Mayors of Lowestoft and Yarmouth in a letter also published in *The Times* of 10 May 1916, assuring them that steps were being taken to discourage such raids by redistributing naval forces. In addition to moving some pre-dreadnoughts and cruisers further south, 'submarines and monitors, which form no portion of the Grand Fleet, are now available in growing numbers for coast defence'. In consequence, *Havelock* and *Roberts* were ordered to Lowestoft and Yarmouth respectively as guardships at these patrol craft bases. The only alternative deployment for them would have been off the Belgian Coast, but their 14in guns would have been even further outranged than were the 12in monitors' guns by this time. *Havelock* arrived on 14 May, securing in the Hamilton Dock just north of the harbour entrance. Here she remained until the end of the war, apart from a short drydocking in the big 32,000-ton Admiralty floating dock in the Tyne in July 1917. Although her AA guns were occasionally in action, there was little for her to do except for endless drills, the occasional target practice firing and a few false alarms.

Roberts' subsequent career was hardly more exciting. She arrived at Gorleston at the entrance to Yarmouth harbour on 27 May 1916. Her new CO was Commander K.G.B. Dewar, a clear-thinking but outspoken gunnery specialist who was none too pleased with his new static command. She was camouflaged at her moorings so that from a distance she merged with the background. Searchlight and observation posts were set up on shore so that good bearings and range could be obtained on any attacking ships. The posts were linked by telephone to the ship, which was always at short notice for fire. There was great excitement one day in October 1916 when five two-funnelled battlecruisers were reported by aircraft a few miles offshore. *Roberts* went to 'Action Stations', ready to fire her 14in guns, when out of the mist steamed, not battlecruisers, but five British two-funnelled minesweepers about to enter harbour, blissfully unaware of the alarm they had caused. On 28 November the German Navy Zeppelin *L.21* passed close overhead, so that

Roberts' new 6in HA was able to get off two or three rounds. Shortly afterwards *L.21* came down in flames, but the credit belonged to the pursuing fighters. During June 1917 *Roberts* was drydocked in the Tyne and then moved to the Thames Estuary. She joined the monitor squadron which was preparing for the Great Landing, as a reserve vessel (see p.62). She returned to Yarmouth in October, remaining there until the end of the war, apart from a refit at Portsmouth in July 1918, where she finally got her new propellers. Although she came to 'Action Stations' she had no opportunity to open fire during the minor German raid on the East Coast on 14 January 1918.

The two monitors remaining in the Mediterranean had a more varied life. In early 1916 the Admiralty orders for the Aegean Squadron were 'to watch the Dardanelles, and safeguard Greek islands in our occupation, to maintain the blockade and submarine patrols in the Aegean, and to support the Army at Salonica'.[17] In the weeks following the evacuation of Gallipoli *Abercrombie* continued to be based on Imbros, now an almost deserted island, whence she could harrass Turkish troops picking over the abandoned stores on the peninsula. She made occasional bombardments of Turkish shipping lying in the Narrows and generally kept the Turkish batteries alert, but there were few worthwhile targets. The monitors were often attacked by aircraft as large, relatively static targets. On one occasion *Abercrombie* was machine-gunned and bombed, being narrowly missed by two bombs. Her HA guns did their best to drive off the aeroplane, although her 3pdr had acquired a number of peculiarities as a result of years of previous service as a drill gun at Devonport Gunnery School. In an endeavour to force the gun to run out again to its firing position after recoil, a round was accidentally fired into a stack of petrol and paraffin cans stored nearby. The resulting blaze was accompanied by so much smoke that the Turks claimed a direct hit, and even nearby British ships thought she had been seriously damaged. In fact the only damage was to some food stocks; in attempting to flood the 3pdr magazine as a precaution it had been forgotten that this compartment now served as the canteen store.

In an effort to reassure public opinion after the Lowestoft Raid in April 1916, journalists are shown round *Havelock*, moored as a floating battery in the Hamilton Dock at Lowestoft. One 14in gun is at the maximum 15 degrees elevation. The unsuitability of the conning tower for navigation is evident; the searchlight platform has been built up to serve as a bridge, with splinter protection visible. (IWM SP3209)

Abercrombie also formed part of the squadron at Kephalo detailed to prevent a break-out by the German battlecruiser *Goeben*, which initially included pre-dreadnoughts such as *Russell*. She was anchored out of sight behind cliffs, her guns trained over the land towards the Dardanelles entrance. Fire control depended on shore spotting stations and she had to remain ready to open fire at short notice, even though her HE projectiles would be of limited value against an armoured ship. In May 1916 she sailed to Malta for a well earned rest, refit and drydocking, then returned to Imbros and a quiet life through the hot summer months. She sailed north on 5 October to bombard the railway line connecting Constantinople to the Salonika front, which had already been the target for the small monitors twelve months earlier (see p.123) and for *Raglan* and *Havelock* in January. She anchored with *M.32* off the small Bulgarian port of Dedeagatch (now Greek Alexandroupolis), taking her time to select aiming marks and organise the spotting aircraft. The resulting fire was very accurate from a range of about 18,000yd. The fifth round was a direct hit on the rail switch at Bodoma Junction a few miles inland, the mean error of the seventeen rounds fired being only about 20yd. This was one of the last large shoots that *Abercrombie* carried out; she had already fired over 500 rounds of 14in in about 15 months.

The remainder of her time was spent in a variety of places in the Aegean with the various Detached Squadrons (see p.126), generally for a few weeks at a time. For the closing months of 1916 she was at Port Iero in the island of Mitylene (now Lesbos) with ships blockading Smyrna (now Izmir) and the Turkish coast. The Squadron also tried to keep the Turks at a high pitch of readiness in expectation of another landing, as well as discouraging the use of the ports as submarine bases. She returned to Kephalo early in 1917 to the *Goeben* watch. In April she went north to Stavros, 40 miles east of Salonika at the north-west corner of the Gulf of Strimon, on the right flank of the Allied Balkan front. As Lt-Cdr L.A.W. Spooner, her 'First and G', later wrote: 'This was a most peaceful war zone, and it seemed a great pity to disturb it by bombardment'. So *Abercrombie* fired only a few rounds before departing for refit at Malta in May 1917. She returned to Stavros, staying until September, and then pottered around the islands off the Turkish coast — Samos, Imbros, Mitylene, Khios — until January 1918. After the loss of *Raglan* (see 2.8), she became the only large monitor available to support the Salonika front, so she spent virtually the whole of 1918 at Stavros, making brief visits to Mudros for bunkers and rest. At the end of August she was near-missed by the U-boat which torpedoed *Endymion*, although the cruiser's bulges saved her from sinking. She returned to Mudros after the Bulgarian Armistice on 29 September, until Turkey also surrendered. On Armistice Day, 11 November 1918, she joined the Allied Fleet steaming up the Dardanelles and she anchored off Chanak, unmolested by the batteries she had been bombarding over the preceding years. *Abercrombie*'s war was over; she had been the hardest worked of all the 14in monitors. Although it had not been

Abercrombie, probably at Mudros in 1916, sporting her new lengthened funnel, with her men painting her side.
(IWM SP253)

possible to put into effect the ambitious plans of her creators, she had performed much useful service in her shore bombardment role and, in her patrol work, had relieved vessels which could be better employed elsewhere.

Raglan's last two years were rather more exciting than *Abercrombie*'s. In February and March 1916 she enlivened the Mitylene patrols with bombardments of Smyrna and the Turkish west coast, supporting the small monitors off Long Island (see p.125). She transferred to the Salonika front in April and occasionally fired a few rounds at targets on the Bulgarian coastline, sometimes setting fire to crops. Kitchener's nephew, Cdr Viscount Broome, took command on 22 May, only two weeks before his uncle was drowned when the cruiser *Hampshire* was mined. After a six-week refit at Malta she returned to Imbros in October, taking over the *Goeben* watch from *Abercrombie*. In December she relieved *Peterborough* at Stavros and continued to support the Allied Armies ashore, occasionally being fired on or attacked by aircraft, but without result. From this time on there were only two large monitors out of the original six in the Aegean, so they concentrated on the Imbros and Stavros patrols, backed up by small monitors.

Raglan remained on watch off the Dardanelles for

OPPOSITE

This view shows a number of the ships of the Aegean Squadron used to blockade the Turkish coast anchored at Port Iero on Mitylene. In the nearest row are *Triad*, the C-in-C's HQ ship, left, and *M.22* (probably) right. In the next row are *Roberts*, left, and *Canopus*, right. Behind *Canopus* is *Raglan*, while the two small vessels furthest off are probably *M.16* and *M.30*. Although the original photograph is undated, study of the logs of the ships present puts it at between 26 and 29 January 1916.
(IWM Q13751)

BELOW

This map of the Dardanelles shows the area of operations of the large and small monitors during the First World War, together with the track of the sortie by *Goeben* and *Breslau* in January 1918. The whole of the Aegean area is shown on the map on p.127.

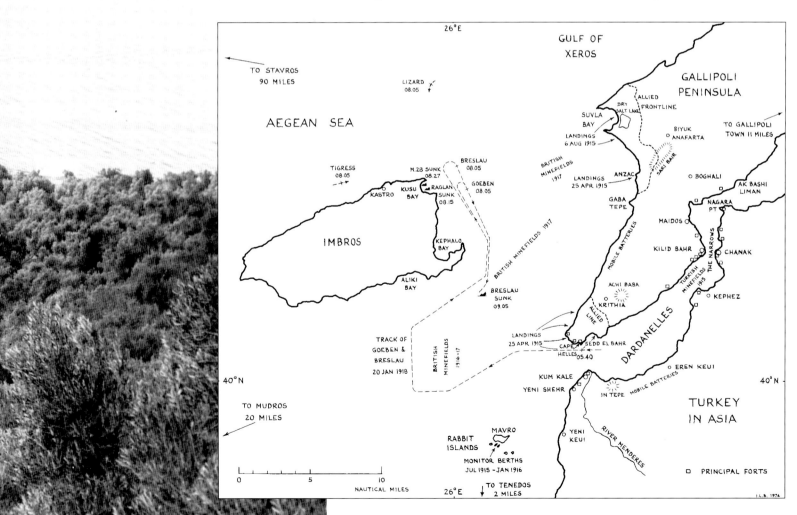

several months in mid-1917, interspersed with bombardments of the Turkish coastal batteries around Smyrna. She moved to Port Said in September, where she prepared to assist Gen Edmund Allenby's forthcoming offensive from Egypt against the Turks in southern Palestine. A Short Admiralty Type 184 spotter from the seaplane carrier *City of Oxford* was embarked on top of her 14in turret when she joined the other ships at the anchorage of Deir el Belah, 9 miles south-west of Gaza. A naval feint attack was to be made north of Gaza, while the main Army thrust was to be inland at Beersheba. On 30 October *Raglan* began to bombard the railway station and bridge four miles inland at Deir Seneid, while four of the small monitors tackled other targets as described on p.132. The bombardment continued on and off for a week, as the land attack pushed forward. An ammunition dump was exploded, bridges hit and the supply railway damaged. As the Turkish line broke and fell back northwards, *Raglan* moved up to Askalon in support but, as the Army penetrated inland, possible targets were soon out of range of her guns. She spent the next few weeks at Port Said before returning to her old base at Imbros. According to the direction of the prevailing weather and the harassing gunfire from the Turkish batteries, she moved between the netted anchorages at Kephalo, Aliki on the south coast and Kusu on the north-east coast of Imbros.

2.8 The Loss of *Raglan* and *M.28*

The German battlecruiser *Goeben* and the light cruiser *Breslau* had been bottled up above the Dardanelles since taking refuge in Constantinople in August 1914. Although the ships were given Turkish names — *Yavuz Sultan Selim* and *Midilli* respectively — the German crew members remained on board, and several sorties were made into the Black Sea. The British had taken precautions against a sortie into the Mediterranean by these two vessels, which included the laying of extensive minefields off the Dardanelles from April 1916 onwards. Towards the end of 1917 there were indications that such a sortie might be made, although it was thought that it would be preceded by minesweeping, thus giving sufficient warning to permit concentration of superior British forces. The ships available included the 12in pre-dreadnoughts *Lord Nelson* and *Agamemnon* based at Mudros, together with three cruisers, destroyers and supporting forces, usually including *Abercrombie* or *Raglan* as well as small monitors.

Following her bombardments off Palestine, *Raglan* had returned to Imbros on 26 December 1917, anchoring frequently in Kusu Bay, 15 miles from the entrance to the Dardanelles and out of range of the batteries on Cape Helles. Together with the small 9.2in monitor *M.28*, four

destroyers and other vessels, she formed the Second Detached Squadron of the Aegean Squadron. Submarine *E.12*, normally stationed at Kephalo, was out of action with a broken propeller shaft.

In January 1918 highly secret preparations were being made for *Goeben* and *Breslau* to attack British ships in their Aegean bases and to destroy any vessels on patrol. In the half-light of the early morning of 20 January the two ships slipped out of the Dardanelles. The lookouts on Mavro Island (see map) failed to spot the enemy ships in the poor visibility before sunrise on that misty winter Sunday morning. Half an hour later, when they were 10 miles to the westward, *Goeben* struck a mine. Despite having captured a rough chart of the British minefields, the Germans had misjudged their full extent. However, her damage was not serious, so, after seeing that the Aliki anchorage was empty, the two ships turned north up the east coast of Imbros, bombarding the wireless station at Kephalo on the way. The destroyer *Lizard*, patrolling north-east of Imbros, was the first to sight them at 07.20, *Breslau* steaming ahead of *Goeben*. Owing to enemy wireless jamming, it was several minutes before she could get in visual contact with *Raglan* and flash 'GOBLO', the signal that *Goeben* was out. Almost simultaneously *Raglan* sighted the ships herself, as did the net drifters and shore lookouts. At 07.35 *Raglan* managed to get off a wireless message to *Agamemnon* at Mudros, passed on to Rear-Admiral, Aegean, A. Hayes-Sadler at Salonika, where he had unwisely taken his flagship *Lord Nelson* four days earlier.

Meanwhile, *Raglan* came to 'Action Stations' and started raising steam on her second boiler. Her twin 14in turret and single 6in trained round to port but withheld their fire temporarily, as it was thought that she might not have been spotted by *Breslau* against the background of cliffs. It was a forlorn hope; after some well-directed shots to prevent *Lizard* from launching torpedoes, *Breslau*'s first salvo of 150mm (5.9in)[18] from 10,000yd crashed into the sea 1,000yd short of *Raglan*. The latter's 6in then opened fire in local control, the first round missing. *Breslau*'s second salvo was 500yd short, but by this time *Raglan*'s 14in had opened fire, the single round falling astern of the German. *Breslau*'s third salvo landed 400yd over, but with a very small spread of shot. In *Raglan* a correction was applied before firing the second round, but it too missed. *M.28* also opened fire with her 9.2in at a range of 11,500yd. Meanwhile the drifters had been attempting to cover the monitors by smokescreens, but the enemy gunfire was too heavy for them to get into position.

Breslau's fourth salvo included a lucky shot that hit *Raglan*'s spotting top, killing the Gunnery Officer, wounding Broome and wrecking the control gear. Now that *Breslau* had the range, she began firing rapid salvoes,

knocking out the 6in ammunition supply party. The engine room was hit twice, putting all telephones and lights out and damaging the port engine. Before running out of ready-use ammunition the 6in got off seven rounds, one of which was reported by the drifters to have hit *Breslau* and another *Goeben*, but German accounts mention no damage. The latter ship had just appeared round the southern headland of Kusu Bay to add her 280mm and 150mm fire.[19] On board *Raglan* attempts were being made to get the 14in turret into local control. Just as the guns were reloaded a 280mm shell from *Goeben* penetrated the barbette armour on the port side below *Raglan*'s turret and ignited the charges in the hand-ups. Although the flash did not reach the magazine, several of the turret's crew were killed, the impression being that one of the guns had burst. The survivors escaped out of the back of the turret, including the First Lieutenant. The latter, on seeing the ship's hopeless position and presuming the CO killed, gave the order to abandon ship. Those who had been taking cover below the protected main deck jumped overboard and swam for the shore.

After nine salvoes at *Raglan*, *Breslau* turned her attention to *M.28*, hitting her amidships with her second salvo, which ignited her cordite and her oil fuel tanks in one fierce flash. The two British monitors were now helpless, caught at anchor close to the shore, their armament out of action and their hulls on fire; *Lizard* had been driven off. The German fire was rapid and accurate

at a range which had now shortened to only about 4,000yd. *Raglan* received more hits forward, the resulting fire reaching the 12pdr magazine, which then blew up. She sank quickly by the head at about 08.15, the incoming water preventing the fire from reaching the 14in magazine. She settled on an even keel in about 40ft of water with her mast, funnel and part of the bridge projecting above the water. A drifter was able to come alongside the spotting top to take off Broome and the other survivors. When *M.28*'s CO, Lt-Cdr D.P. Macgregor, saw that *Raglan* was sinking, he ordered his whaler over to pick up survivors.

Meanwhile, *M.28*'s 9.2in had got off its second round, but no further charge could be loaded, owing to the flames in the magazine welling up through the hatch in the deck. A shell from *Breslau* then hit *M.28*'s gun, killing most of its crew and the CO, who was standing close by, and blowing others into the water. The whaler then returned to assist and had just moored alongside aft when the fire reached the shell room and *M.28* blew up at 08.27 with a huge explosion, scattering debris and bodies over *Lizard*, which was approaching to help.

Goeben and *Breslau* then made off to the south, intending to bombard Mudros Harbour, although by now the alarm had been raised in British ships all over the Aegean. Both vessels were again caught in the minefield and *Breslau* soon struck a mine, followed shortly by *Goeben* hitting another. *Breslau* found herself right in the middle

Raglan at Mudros, probably late 1916 or early 1917. She is sporting a camouflage scheme on her upperworks, including her newly installed 6in gun visible abaft the funnel. One of her 12pdr can be seen on its new HA mounting abreast the turret. (P.A. VICARY)

of the minefield and under attack from British aircraft, and she hit four more mines before finally sinking at 09.05. Meanwhile, *Lizard* and *Tigress* were trying to press home a torpedo attack on *Goeben* but were driven off. All German plans to continue the sortie had to be abandoned, *Goeben* turning back to the Dardanelles. Despite striking a third mine and suffering more serious damage, she reached the safety of the Narrows, but ran aground off Nagara Point.

Continuous attempts were then made to bomb her from the air, but, despite many attacks, no serious damage was inflicted. On 23 January Hayes-Sadler sent a telegram to the Admiralty:[19] 'Suggest there is a fair prospect of completely disabling *Goeben* by gunfire if a 15in monitor could be sent'. This was a curious request. Firstly, he had a perfectly adequate 14in monitor available. *Abercrombie* had left Samos on the 20th and arrived at Mudros on the 22nd, departing the next day for Stavros. Although muzzle velocity had been falling off, her guns were still quite capable of reaching *Goeben* if she went fairly close in to the peninsula, but she was never called upon to try. Her steeply plunging HE projectiles would have been able to inflict serious damage if they hit *Goeben*. Secondly, Hayes-Sadler should have been well aware that the RN had only three 15in monitors, that they were all based at Dover and that, given their slow speed, it would take at least three weeks for one to reach the Dardanelles. Not surprisingly, the Admiralty turned down his request but did offer him the 12in monitors from the Adriatic.

However, one of the more immediately available small monitors was used instead. *M.18* was immobilised at Mudros by engine repairs, so *M.17* was called up from Stavros. She arrived at Kusu on the night of 23/24 January and moved up to the peninsula the following evening. She anchored bow and stern in 240ft of water and opened fire on *Goeben* shortly before 22.00. The haze made air spotting of her indirect fire difficult and she was harassed by shore batteries. Only ten rounds were got off, without any visible result. No further attempts were made to bombard the battlecruiser from the sea before she was finally towed off on 26 January, returning safely to Constantinople.

Back on Imbros the wounded from *Raglan* and *M.28* were being treated and a start was made on salvaging equipment from the ships. In all, 127 of *Raglan*'s crew had been killed, leaving 93 survivors, while *M.28* lost eight killed out of 66 on board at the time. The then customary Court Martial following the loss of an HM ship in questionable circumstances took place on 31 January. Evidence was given by Broome and the other survivors on board *Lord Nelson*. There was no disputing the surprise of the attack and the overwhelming odds of

MAIN PHOTOGRAPH
Overwhelmed by the gunfire of *Goeben* and *Breslau* on 20 January 1918, *Raglan* lies on the bottom of Kusu Bay on Imbros. The bulged cruiser *Edgar* is assisting salvage operations.
(IWM SP767)

INSET
Raglan on an even keel in 40ft of water in Kusu Bay. The wreck is being inspected by naval divers to salvage as much equipment as possible.
(IWM SP768A)

ten 280mm and eighteen 150mm guns against two 14in, one 9.2in and one 6in. An incorrect claim was made that *Raglan*'s guns had been condemned for excessive wear. Although they had fired nearly 300 equivalent full charges, which was the normal life of large British guns using cordite, they were less than half worn on US NCT propellant. *M.28* had been under orders to wait until *Raglan* opened fire, so she had little chance to do much damage with her slow-firing 9.2in.

Although unprepared, the monitors' crews had put up a reasonable fight against superior forces, so they were all acquitted. The report to the Admiralty stated:[21] '… loss [of *Raglan* and *M.28*] was due to overwhelming gunfire causing fire and explosions, and that the conduct of the survivors was in accordance with the traditions of the Service, and that blame is not attributable to any of them.'

They were thus able to participate in the £6,000 Prize Bounty awarded for *Breslau*'s sinking. The C-in-C Mediterranean, Vice-Admiral Sir S.A. Gough-Calthorpe, expressed himself: 'not satisfied that the watch kept at some of the lookout stations was as alert as it should have been, especially in the case of Mavro'. Hayes-Sadler also incurred the C-in-C's displeasure concerning the divided disposition of his main forces, and was relieved of his command only a few months after having taken up his post.

Without sufficient warning allowing superior forces time to concentrate, the two monitors were doomed against *Goeben* and *Breslau.* With longer warning the monitors would certainly have been better prepared, but their loss would still have been almost inevitable. Without *Breslau*'s lucky hit on *Raglan*'s spotting top, the latter could have kept up her fire longer, inflicted greater damage on the enemy and possibly given the other ships a chance to arrive. Although the pre-dreadnoughts were too slow to catch an undamaged *Goeben* and the cruisers were not powerful enough to sink her, it might have been possible to cause sufficient damage to restrict seriously any further operations. As it was, *Goeben* had re-entered the Dardanelles almost before *Lord Nelson* had cleared the fog present at Salonika, *Agamemnon* having left Mudros to rendezvous with her.

Nonetheless, the outcome was, on balance, favourable to the British, although this was not fully appreciated at the time. The two German ships had long been a potential menace to British forces, especially the vessels supplying the Salonika Army. Now one was sunk, the other damaged, for the loss of two relatively expendable British vessels. The British surface patrols could be reduced and even greater reliance placed on air reconnaissance, especially as the minefields were to be reinforced. A number of the ships so relieved could make a greater contribution strengthening the convoy system then being

introduced into the Mediterranean. It was also decided that in future no monitors or bulged vessels would be kept at unprotected netted anchorages such as Kusu.

2.9 Performance in Service

The speed of the 14in monitors on their first trials had been very low, and they continued to be handicapped in service by their poor performance. Fresh from drydock with newly painted bottoms and replacement propellers, they were capable (except *Roberts*) of a shade over 6kts without forcing in good weather. With several month's fouling on their broad underwater areas, the average speed dropped to about 5½kts. Even the modest 700 miles from Mudros to Malta used to take *Abercrombie* and *Raglan* five days if conditions were good, but over a week if they were bad.

AEW had followed up their preliminary reports on the proposed monitor hull form in December 1914 with a full analysis of subsequent model tests in March 1915, which confirmed all their earlier predictions. Subsequent experience bore out their pessimism. Although nothing was done to modify the 12in and first 15in monitors which immediately followed the 14in, the lessons learnt were used to improve all subsequent designs of large monitor.

Despite the monitors' modest speed, their fuel consumption was considerable. Steam reciprocating engines supplied with saturated steam did not have a high thermal efficiency (only about 8 per cent), while there was additional extensive steam consumption by the auxiliary machinery, which included the two high-powered 600 tons-per-hour ballast pumps. Each of the two 200kW generators was driven by a steam engine of about 300hp, in total nearly one-third of the main engines' power. On trials the specific fuel consumption was about 2.25lb of coal per ihp per hour (equivalent to about 1.6lb of oil), corresponding to about 48 tons of coal per day in *Abercrombie* and *Havelock*. In service the ships generally consumed about 40 tons of coal a day at sea, and in harbour about 6-8 tons; fresh water consumption was about 5-9 tons per day. Coal capacity limited endurance to only about eight days without emergency bunkers; consequently any voyage had to be undertaken in stages of a few hundred miles. *Abercrombie* required five intermediate bunkering stops on her way home from the Dardanelles in 1919. Bunkering was usually done from colliers sent out from Britain to supply the ships of the Fleet. As the monitor lay at anchor in Mudros or Kephalo harbour the collier would come alongside. About 150 to 200 tons of best Welsh steam coal would be slung aboard from derricks in 2cwt (224lb) sacks at the rate of about 50 to 70 tons per hour.

While the speed in fine weather was just about

sufficient for the monitors to carry out their bombarding duties, there was no margin at all for bad weather. The very full form was quite unsuitable for pushing through heavy seas as, in addition to increased hull resistance, the wind resistance was appreciable too. The shallow draft allowed little immersion for the propellers, which were liable to emerge from the water when pitching in the short Mediterranean seas. In beam winds considerable leeway was made, so that progress was distinctly crabwise. Against moderate wind and sea, speed dropped rapidly to two to four knots, at which point it was not unknown for small Greek sailing craft to overhaul them. In anything over Force 7, speed dropped further to one to two knots and, even when a tow was available, no appreciable headway could be made until the weather moderated. Returning home early in 1916, *Roberts* tried rigging fore and mizzen staysails, thus using three means of propulsion simultaneously: engines, sails and towline from a tug. In the heavy weather of the Bay of Biscay this combination of propulsive power yielded a speed of just 3½ knots!

Although the loss of speed was inconvenient, the ships were safe enough in a seaway. With their broad flat bottoms most rolling and pitching were damped out, which made them good gun platforms. The hulls would slap the sea, however, causing much spray over the forecastle and on to the upper deck through the side-screens. The top of the bulge was just about submerged at deep load, so causing a broken wave profile and a considerable wake. In harbour, the top of the bulge was usually dry enough for men to work alongside the hull for painting, repairing boats 'docked' by heeling the ship under them, or even for bathing.

As was to be expected, the steering characteristics remained unsatisfactory. A hull with a length:breadth ratio of 3.7 is not well endowed with directional stability, especially when the rudders operate in an irregular wake. The ships were hard to manoeuvre, difficult to control and required great skill in helmsmanship, especially when entering or leaving harbour, when minor collisions could occur. To add to the monitors' troubles, the steering gear was underpowered. Their performance does not bear thinking about had only a single rudder been fitted.

Ammunition and stores were received from store-ships or lighters which came alongside in Mudros. Here, also, maintenance and minor damage repairs could be undertaken by the repair ship *Reliance*. The food was adequate but limited by the lack of refrigerated stores and bakery. Bully beef and biscuit was a frequent menu, with some vegetables available from Egypt. Rice sometimes replaced potatoes. Although fresh water could be distilled on board for feed water and drinking, the crews preferred the tanks to be filled from a shore supply. The ships' boats were

used continually as the monitors spent much time at anchor. Three 30ft boats were slung in davits aft, one being a motor boat, the other two pulling cutters. There was also a 16ft dinghy stowed on the deck abaft the funnel. The motor boat was hard-worked and its engine none too reliable, so two motor boats and one pulling boat would have been a more useful outfit.

Despite their not being regarded as real Navy ships, the monitors were popular with their crews. Most of the officers were young and were holding positions of responsibility much earlier than they would have expected normally. For the men, the less formal routine and moderate numbers made for reasonable conditions. Living quarters were spacious by warship standards, although they could become hot in the Mediterranean, even when the steel decks were cooled by fire hoses. Under these conditions, sleeping on the upper deck with its open sides was preferred.

Taken overall, the performance of the first monitors was barely adequate for their role in service. As the first of a totally new type built in great haste, any shortcomings were understandable, and did lead to modifications to existing vessels and to improved design of the later monitors.

2.10 Modifications

The 14in monitors underwent fewer changes than most of the later vessels, which were largely deployed in the more demanding conditions off the Belgian Coast. The most obvious change was the lengthening of the funnel by about 12ft. As the conning tower was badly sited for normal navigation, the exposed searchlight platform halfway up the mast was preferred. Unfortunately it was just level with the top of the funnel so, as the ships were so slow, it only required the lightest of breezes from abaft the beam to cover the watchkeepers in smoke. At the first refit, therefore, an extension was added to the funnel of the same diameter as the inner casing, resulting a somewhat stovepipe appearance. *Havelock*, however, had a superior version with a double casing, which was not as tall as the other three. At the same time the navigating position was provided with some modest shelter.

Apart from general overhauling on their annual refits, modifications were also made on these occasions to the secondary armament. To relieve the 14in guns of routine harassment fire, a 6in BL XII[22] was added to the two Mediterranean monitors, similar to the guns in *M.29* and *M.33*. It was fitted on the forecastle deck abaft the funnel, in the space originally allocated for seaplane stowage. The seaplane derricks were removed to improve the arcs of fire. *Raglan*'s gun was fitted in 1916 and was one of the pair salvaged from *M.30* (see p.125); *Abercrombie*'s was fitted a year later. *Roberts* had a 6in QF I on an improvised

Havelock alongside Ward's Preston shipbreaking yard in 1927. Her gun barrels have already been removed. Her funnel has just been cut off, and is lying on the deck. Weeds on her hull aft are indicative of a long lay-up. (JOHN CLARKSON)

After WW1 *Roberts* was used for experimental purposes, including tests of new designs of underwater protective structure. This view shows her later at Portsmouth in July 1928 in a poor state, with part of the bulge removed amidships. (WRIGHT & LOGAN)

first ever made of that design; calling it a 'pom-pom' was a distinctly optimistic description, as its usual mode of operation was merely to 'pom', much coaxing being needed to persuade it to fire more than one round at a time. The armament changes are summarised below, showing the ships' armaments as finally fitted towards the end of the war:

Abercrombie	2 x 14in, 1 x 6in, 2 x 12pdr HA, 1 x 3in HA, 1 x 3pdr, 1 x 2pdr
Havelock	2 x 14in, 2 x 12pdr HA, 2 x 3in HA
Raglan	2 x 14in, 1 x 6in, 2 x 12pdr HA, 1 x 3pdr, 1 x 2pdr
Roberts	2 x 14in, 1 x 6in HA, 2 x 12pdr HA, 1 x 3in HA, 1 x 3pdr, 2 x 2pdr

Consideration was given in March 1917 to replacing the twin 14in turret in some of the class by one of the single 18in turrets designed for the large light cruiser *Furious*. No action was taken because reconstruction would have been too extensive, although a modified 18in mounting was fitted in two of the 12in monitors in 1918, as described in 3.6.

The elaborate camouflage paint schemes common to some ships in home waters were not used. In *Raglan*, only the bridge, funnel, turret and spotting top had a modest disruptive pattern; *Abercrombie* simply had very light coloured upperworks, with a slightly darker grey hull beneath. While all four ships were in the Mediterranean together, each carried identification bands on the funnel, three for *Roberts*, two for *Raglan*, one for *Havelock*, none for *Abercrombie*. The false bow wave painted on the

HA mounting fitted on the starboard side aft, the mounting being fixed to the upper deck, but the trunnions and the gun itself projecting through the forecastle deck, from which it was loaded. The gun was found to be too heavy, slow and unwieldy to make a successful AA weapon, yet it remained in *Roberts* for the rest of her life. This piece, together with its near-sisters fitted in *General Wolfe* and some of the China gunboats, holds the RN record for the largest-calibre gun fitted primarily for HA firing.

Other more useful changes were made to improve the monitors' AA armament. The 12pdrs were moved from their restricted position on the upper deck and remounted on the forecastle deck on mountings modified for HA firing. *Abercrombie*'s 2pdr automatic had been one of the

monitors when new to give an impression of speed to mislead U-boats was soon removed.

Minor internal changes were made in all ships, including the provision of secondary armament magazines and rearrangement of the stores and accommodation spaces, the crew number having been increased slightly to 208 to man the additional guns.

2.11 Post-war Careers

Following the Armistice in November 1918 there was no further need for monitors as guardships, nor was there a role in the post-war fleet for most of those engaged on patrol and bombardment work. Accordingly, *Abercrombie* set off from Chanak on 19 February 1919 on the long voyage home, arriving at Devonport on 19 April. After de-ammunitioning she was sent round to Immingham with a Care and Maintenance (C & M) party. There she joined eight other monitors already on the Disposal List, as there was insufficient berthing accommodation at the dockyards. She finally paid off on 9 May. *Havelock* arrived at Immingham from Lowestoft shortly afterwards, paying off on 14 May, while *Roberts* arrived from Yarmouth, paying off on 26 May.

By the summer of 1920 there was capacity at the dockyards to take the monitors in hand for de-equipping. *Abercrombie* and *Havelock* were towed to Portsmouth in June to have their 14in gun barrels and secondary armament removed. *Roberts* followed in October, but retained her guns. All three vessels were put on the Sale List and formed part of the massive purchase of warships for scrap by T.W. Ward Ltd of Sheffield. On 9 May 1921 the Admiralty sold the company 113 obsolete naval vessels at the flat rate of £2.50 per ton, later reduced to £2.20. The purchase included five battleships, 12 cruisers and 88 destroyers and torpedo boats, as well as three 12in monitors (*General Wolfe*, *General Craufurd* and *Prince Eugene*) and two of the ex-Brazilian river monitors (*Severn* and *Mersey*), totalling about 300,000 tons in all. The effective price for one of the large monitors was thus about £11,000. Most of the ships were towed away to the breaker's yards over the next two years. The Admiralty had reserved the right to withdraw any of the vessels if required and to substitute others, and the three 14in monitors were in fact retained. They remained laid up in Spithead or in Portsmouth Harbour until 1927, when *Abercrombie* and *Havelock* were resold to Ward at the previously agreed price and scrapped that same year.

Roberts was retained for experimental purposes for a number of years. Consideration had been given about 1925 to converting her for use as a mobile mooring mast and fuelling station for airships. In the early 1930s she was involved in trials for new designs of underwater

protection. To correlate model experiments with large-scale results, a structure representing a proposed double bottom and bulge was built on to *Roberts*. With her 10ft draft the structure was one-third the full scale for a battleship. Various charges representing different sizes of bomb were exploded against her; the results provided information for the design of the aircraft carrier *Ark Royal* and battleship *King George V*.

By 1936 she was of no further use, so she was handed over to Ward with 33 other warships in part exchange for the Cunard-White Star liner *Majestic*. Ward had recently purchased the latter for scrap, but now the Admiralty wanted her to provide accommodation for young artificers under training at Rosyth. The total exchange value was about £143,000, of which *Roberts* constituted about £11,000. *Roberts* was allocated to Ward's Preston yard, leaving Portsmouth on 10 September in tow of the tug *Seaman*. Some weeks after arrival she broke adrift during a December gale and was blown down the River Ribble to strand off Lytham, later being towed back. She had outlived all of her sisters and her near-sisters the 12in monitors, and it was to be only three years before a new *Roberts* was to be designed, who would herself become the last to survive of all the large monitors (see Chapter 9).

The 14in Monitors – TECHNICAL DATA

Displacement: 6,150 tons Navy List, 6,150 tons deep as completed on 10ft 0in draft, 5,300 tons light on 8ft 6in.

Dimensions: Length 334ft 6in overall, 320ft 0in bp, breadth 90ft 2in oa, 60ft 0in main hull, depth to forecastle deck 25ft 6in.

Weight distribution as designed (tons): Armament 650, ammunition 195, armour plating 682, protective plating 1,170, hull structure 2,091, hull fittings 393, general equipment 220, machinery and reserve feed water 376, coal (nominal) 200. Total 5,977 tons.

Complement: 12 officers, 186 men.

Armament: (As completed) 2 x 14in (twin) (120 HE + 15 practice rounds per gun), 2 x 12pdr 18cwt (200rpg) 1 x 3pdr Vickers HA (500rpg), 1 x 2pdr HA (1,000rpg), 4 x 0.303in Maxim machine guns (5,000rpg).

Protection: Forecastle deck 1in HT; upper deck amidships 2in HT; main deck, forward and aft 1in HT; sloping internal belt 4in C; bulkheads at end of belt 4in C; torpedo protective bulkhead 1½in HT (1in at ends); steering gear 1½in HT; barbette 8in C; gunhouse 10in front, 7in sides and rear, 4in roof; conning tower 6in sides, 2½in roof, cast steel; spotting top 1in HT sides and floor.

Machinery: Twin screw steam reciprocating engines. Two Babcock & Wilcox watertube boilers, 200lb/in². *Abercrombie* and *Havelock*: two quadruple-expansion by Harland & Wolff, Belfast, 13½in, 19½in, 28in, 40in bore x 28in stroke 2,000ihp at 175rpm. *Raglan*: two 4-cylinder triple-expansion by H & W Belfast 15in, 25in, 30in, 30in x 24in 2,310ihp at 200rpm. *Roberts*: two 3-cylinder triple-expansion by Swan Hunter & Wigham Richardson 13½in, 22in, 36in x 27in 1,800ihp at 180rpm. Coal 380 tons maximum.

Speed: 10kts designed, 6½ in service. Trials: *Abercrombie* 7.04, *Havelock* 7.35, *Raglan* 7.64, *Roberts* 5.70 kts.

Endurance: 1,340 miles at 6kts on 1.7 tons coal per hour (*Abercrombie* and *Havelock*)

Construction: Harland & Wolff, Belfast: *Abercrombie* (No.472) laid down 12.12.14/launched 15.4.15/completed 29.5.15; *Havelock* (No.473) 12.12.14/29.4.15/18.6.15. *Raglan* H & W, Govan (No.476G/B) 1.12.14/29.4.15/24.6.15. *Roberts* Swan Hunter & Wigham Richardson, Wallsend (No.991) 17.12.14/15.4.15/14.6.15.

Disposal: *Abercrombie* scrapped by T.W. Ward, sold 25.6.27, arrived Inverkeithing 29.7.27; *Havelock* scrapped by T.W. Ward, sold 25.6.27, arr Preston 20.7.27; *Raglan* sunk 20.1.18; *Roberts* scrapped by T.W. Ward, sold 4.9.36, arr Preston 19.9.36.

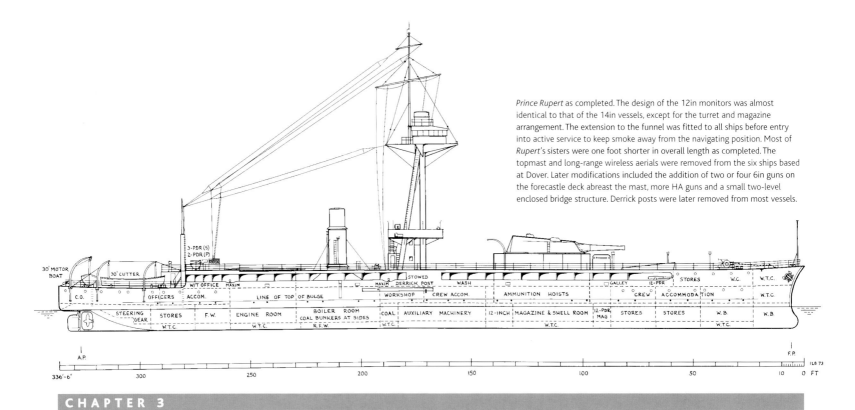

Prince Rupert as completed. The design of the 12in monitors was almost identical to that of the 14in vessels, except for the turret and magazine arrangement. The extension to the funnel was fitted to all ships before entry into active service to keep smoke away from the navigating position. Most of *Rupert*'s sisters were one foot shorter in overall length as completed. The topmast and long-range wireless aerials were removed from the six ships based at Dover. Later modifications included the addition of two or four 6in guns on the forecastle deck abreast the mast, more HA guns and a small two-level enclosed bridge structure. Derrick posts were later removed from most vessels.

CHAPTER 3

The 12in-gun Monitors

3.1 Design

The rapidity with which construction of the 14in monitors got under way, plus the extent of the coastal bombardment opportunities beginning to present themselves with Turkey's entry into the war, encouraged Churchill to plan further big gun monitors. On 11 December 1914 he minuted to Fisher and the Secretary to the Admiralty:[1]

We ought without delay to order more 'Styx' class for heavy in-shore work. There are, for instance, the four reserve 13.5in guns of the *Audacious*, which should certainly be mounted in new monitors. It should also be possible to draw from the reserve of 15in guns, and to make in a short time 15in or 18in howitzers. We require now to make ships which can be built in 6 or 7 months at the outside, and which can certainly go close in shore and attack the German Fleet in its harbours. These are special vessels built for a definite war operation, and we must look to them in default of a general action for giving us the power of forcing a naval decision at latest in the autumn of 1915.

Our thought is proceeding independently on the same lines. I propose, as a basis of discussion, that in addition to the 4 Schwab monitors, we prepare 8 more at a cost of not more than £700,000 apiece. These vessels should be armed either with 13.5in or 15in guns, two or four in each as convenient. Or, alternatively, they should be armed with four 18in howitzers in separate cupolas sunk low on their heavily-armoured turtle backs. They should draw 8ft at most, and be propelled entirely by internal combustion at a speed not exceeding 10kts; no funnels; three or four alternative telescopic masts for fire observation; strong crinolines 20ft away all round to make them immune from mine and torpedo, etc. A third alternative variant would be two heavy guns in turrets in the centre and two mortars in 'cupolad' pits on each side of the deck.

Fisher was also in favour, so the idea was passed to the Third Sea Lord for examination by DNC and the Director of Naval Ordnance (DNO), Rear-Admiral Morgan Singer. The loss of *Audacious* had indeed released spare 13.5in guns, and there was also one spare mounting kept for each ship. But in the context of heavy non-transferable ordnance, 'mounting'[2] meant only the elevating parts, i.e. one gun cradle, slide and fittings, not the complete turret and equipment. Thus there was no installation suitable for use and it would take at least a year to build one. Similarly with 15in guns; it was not enough to possess spare guns, cradles and slides, which were useless without the complete mounting for loading, training and elevating. 15in howitzers were a possibility as COW was building twelve for use in France, but it was considered that their range would be insufficient when matched against shore defences.

Although none of Churchill's suggestions for armament was found to be practicable, there remained one further possibility: taking mountings from existing ships. There were still a fair number of pre-dreadnoughts in service carrying 12in guns, which were now of limited value. The oldest class comprised the nine *Majestic*s, designed in 1893, which were now being used largely for coast defence purposes. Each ship carried two twin 12in mountings of an Elswick pattern which marked a big step forward in naval ordnance at the time, as described in 10.2. It was therefore proposed that eight new monitors could be armed by disarming four of the battleships. Admiral Sir Percy Scott, who had done so much to improve the RN's gunnery before the war and who had now returned to the Admiralty from retirement, appreciated that the range of the *Majestic*s' 35cal 12in Mk VIII at its maximum elevation of 13½ degrees was only 13,700yd. While this was adequate for the 1890s, it was well below the range of modern coast defence guns, so he pointed out that, if 30 degree elevation could be obtained, over 21,000yd was possible. Scott telephoned Elswick, receiving next morning a sketch confirming that 30 degrees was feasible without major modifications to the turret, so Fisher immediately approved Scott's

suggestion, who directed Elswick to carry out the modifications.

Meanwhile, design of the hull had been going ahead, but leaving sufficient space for whatever armament was likely to be fitted. The design was virtually a repeat of the 14in monitors, as it was not found possible to adopt Churchill's other suggestions. A draft of only 8ft was insufficient to provide the required buoyancy, so 10ft was substituted, while 20ft crinolines became 15ft bulges. Diesel engines were still in their infancy for marine propulsion, so it was quite impossible to provide eight sets of 2,000hp machinery in as little as six months. Steam reciprocators were the only practicable propulsion units, although machinery of slightly greater than 2,000hp was sought.

The proposed armament and its ammunition was about 367 tons lighter than the 14in, so the hulls of the 12in monitors could be made slightly narrower. A reduction from 90 to 87ft would also simplify the problem of finding sufficiently wide building berths. Weight was available to increase the thickness of the sloping armour belt from 4in to 6in (see diagram on p.14). The resulting designed displacement was 5,599 tons, compared with 5,977 in the earlier class, the difference being mostly due to the lighter armament. Such a reduction could have permitted finer lines as recommended by Froude, but d'Eyncourt would not allow any significant changes. There was no time to make a detailed cost estimate, but in seeking Cabinet approval it was anticipated that the combined cost of all eight monitors would be about £3½ million, i.e. about £437,500 each. This figure is almost certainly too high, as it would have been based on the estimate for the 14in monitors with their expensively purchased armament. As the 12in monitors' armament already existed, the major components of their cost would be hull and machinery, and it is unlikely that actual expenditure exceeded about £260,000 each.

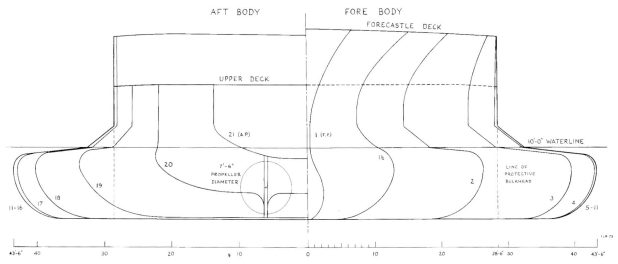

The body plan of the 12in monitors shows the cross-sections of the hull at the 21 constructional stations, each one-twentieth of the 320ft length BP apart (16ft). Station No. 1 was at the fore perpendicular and No. 21 at the aft perpendicular. The hull was parallel-sided from Station No. 5 to No. 16, or 176ft, over half the ship's length. The rectangular cross-section of the main hull and the large area of flat bottom simplified construction, as did the angled transition between bulge and main hull.

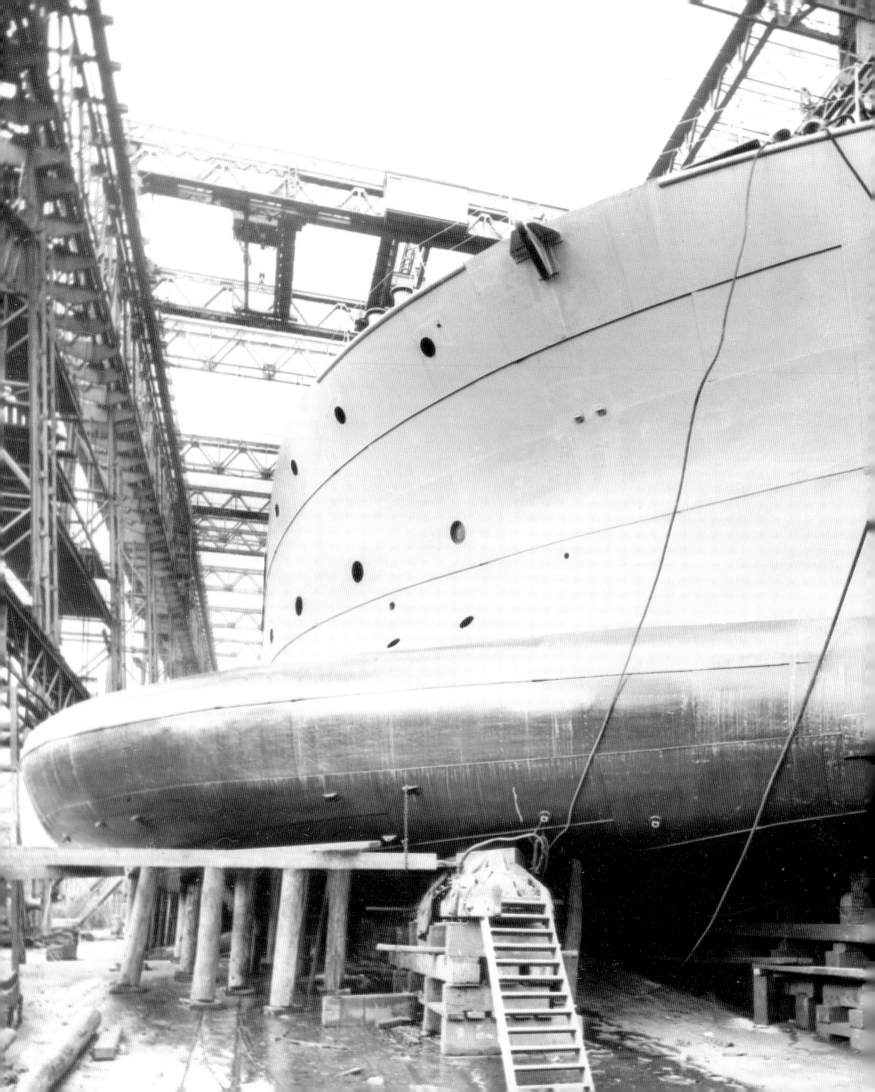

3.2 Construction

It was not easy to find the shipbuilding capacity to tackle a further eight beamy ships, at a time when most shipyards with wide berths were already fully occupied. However, with more shipowners deferring their passenger liner contracts, Pirrie could offer to build five more monitors as Nos. 477 to 481. Two would go on Berth 1 at Belfast following the launch of Red Star's *Belgenland* on 31 December (the berth originally allocated to Union-Castle's *Amroth Castle*, which was not completed until 1921 as *Arundel Castle*), two on Berth 3 after the modest amount of steel erected for White Star's 33,000-ton *Homeric* had been dismantled (never to be recommenced), and one more at Govan. The three other berths were provided by Clyde yards after tenders were received: Scotts' of Greenock, Hamilton of Port Glasgow and Fairfield of Govan.

With the postponement of so many big ships, H & W's engine works also had considerable spare capacity. The company offered to produce a special design of twin-screw triple-expansion machinery for the monitors, developing a total of 2,310ihp Each engine actually had four cylinders with two low-pressure cylinders, an arrangement which gave better balancing characteristics than three cylinders. Although H & W needed only five sets for its 12in ships, it could easily manage a sixth and fit it in *M.3* (*Raglan*) at its Govan yard. So McKie & Baxter's existing contract for *M.3*'s 1,600ihp machinery was transferred to the Hamilton monitor, as the latter company had no engine

OPPOSITE

General Craufurd, second of H & W's 12in monitors, on the day before her launch from the same berth on which *Titanic* was built. The steps lead up to the hydraulic rams at the head of each sliding way. The platers' skills in shaping the sharply curved steel plates is evident.
(HARLAND & WOLFF)

BELOW

This portion of Harland & Wolff's berth chart shows how merchant ship construction rapidly gave way to monitor construction after the outbreak of war. The monitors are shown as heavy lines from keel laying to launching, with their hull numbers. Not shown are the small 6in monitors *M.32* and *M.33* (488-9WC) subcontracted to Workman, Clark. Berths 2 and 3 were the pair under the large gantry in the Queen's yard, seen in the photograph on p.20. There were also merchant ships on the other four berths at Belfast and the other seven at Govan, on which work was suspended throughout 1915. No. 469 was never recommenced, No. 470 was re-ordered post-war as the smaller *Laurentic* built on another berth, while *Narkunda*'s keel was transferred to Berth 8 in the Abercorn yard in 1917. The berths in the Queen's, Abercorn and Govan yards of H & W were dismantled in the 1960s.

BERTH AND YARD		1914	1915	1916
BELFAST	1 QUEEN'S	BELGENLAND (391)	EARL OF PETERBOROUGH (480) / SIR THOMAS PICTON (481)	ARUNDEL CASTLE (455)
	2 QUEEN'S	BRITANNIC (433) / RED STAR (469)	ABERCROMBIE (472) GLORIOUS (482) / HAVELOCK (473)	VINDICTIVE (500)
	3 QUEEN'S	STATENDAM (436) / HOMERIC (470)	LORD CLIVE (478) TERROR (493) / GENERAL CRAUFURD (479)	
	5 ABERCORN	ALMANZORA (441)	M.29 (485) NARKUNDA (471) / M.30 (486) / M.31 (487)	
GOVAN	E	APAPA (443)	RAGLAN (476)	EREBUS (492) TENACIOUS (498) / TETRARCH (499)
	F	GLENGYLE (466)	PRINCE EUGENE (477)	SALMON (494) / SYLPH (495)

works, unlike Scotts', who was to engine their hull. The switch was a sensible one, as the more powerful machinery would be more usefully deployed in a monitor armed with modern 14in guns rather than one with old 12in guns. McKie & Baxter also received the order for the machinery of the Fairfield ship, but the power was increased to 2,500ihp. Orders to build went out about 23 December 1914. Following the transfer of the battlecruiser *Repulse* from Palmer to John Brown at Clydebank and acceleration of *Renown* at Fairfield, the latter yard's monitor order and its machinery was transferred to Palmer on 6 January, although to its shipyard at Hebburn-on-Tyne, rather than the main yard at Jarrow, a mile downstream.

The eight ships had been given provisional *M* numbers, the Scott's ship being *M.5*, Palmer's *M.9* and Hamilton's *M.10*, while the H & W ships filled the gaps up to *M.12*. Names of British generals were chosen early in 1915 and, after some reconsideration as to the exact titles[3], those

ABOVE
McKie and Baxter received an order for a pair of 800ihp triple-expansion engines (Nos. 807-8) in November 1914. Originally intended for *Raglan*, they were re-allocated to *Prince Rupert* in December. This view shows the engines (looking aft) in the company's Glasgow works, nearly ready for shipping, at a weight of 18 tons each.
(McKIE & BAXTER)

RIGHT
Earl of Peterborough on 16 August, ten days before launch, her quarterdeck planking being laid. Her machinery has evidently already been shipped, as there are no openings in the deck and the funnel has been erected. The timber kept the tide off the lower end of the slipway. Barely visible ahead of her on the same slipway are the frames of *Sir Thomas Picton*.
(HARLAND & WOLFF)

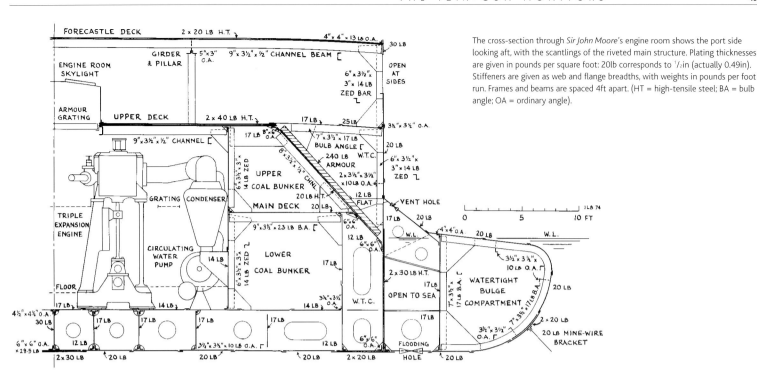

The cross-section through *Sir John Moore*'s engine room shows the port side looking aft, with the scantlings of the riveted main structure. Plating thicknesses are given in pounds per square foot: 20lb corresponds to ¹⁄₂in (actually 0.49in). Stiffeners are given as web and flange breadths, with weights in pounds per foot run. Frames and beams are spaced 4ft apart. (HT = high-tensile steel; BA = bulb angle; OA = ordinary angle).

finally selected in March were:

M.5:   Sir John Moore, of Peninsular War fame.

M.6:   Lord Clive, the soldier-statesman who established British domination in India

M.7:   General Craufurd, of the Peninsular War (whose name was frequently misspelt)

M.8:   Earl of Peterborough, of the War of the Spanish Succession

M.9:   General Wolfe, the victor of Quebec

M.10: Prince Rupert, the English Civil War Royalist leader

M.11: Prince Eugene, the Savoy prince who fought with Marlborough

M.12: Sir Thomas Picton, of the Peninsular War and Waterloo.

The decision as to which four pre-dreadnoughts were to surrender their armament had been made on 1 January 1915. Early in February *Mars* and *Magnificent* arrived at Belfast, *Hannibal* at Dalmuir on the Clyde and *Victorious* at Elswick. The work of conversion was done aboard ship and the mountings then lifted out and placed on the dockside to await re-erection, although the barbette armour was not transferred, new flat plates being provided. Belfast Harbour Commissioners' 100-ton derrick crane had recently collapsed, so H & W's 150-ton floating crane had to be used instead. Conversion was divided amongst the big three ordnance companies as follows:

Ship	Conversion by	From
Prince Rupert	EOC	Victorious
General Wolfe	EOC	Victorious
Lord Clive	COW	Magnificent
General Craufurd	COW	Magnificent
Prince Eugene	COW	Hannibal
Sir John Moore	Vickers	Hannibal
Earl of Peterborough	Vickers	Mars
Sir Thomas Picton	Vickers	Mars

Prince Rupert had the shortest time on the berth, being laid down on 12 January, launched on 20 May and immediately towed up to Clydebank, where her turret was shipped using John Brown's 150-ton derrick crane. Back at Greenock, J & G Kincaid finished installing her machinery and she was ready for trials on 1 July, twenty-four weeks after construction started. McKie & Baxter had delivered her engines as early as February, as not only did their ex-*M.3* contract precede that of the hull by one month, but the design was a repeat of the machinery supplied to the steamer *Lampo*, so that drawings and wooden patterns for castings already existed. *Rupert*[4] was the first to go out on gun trials, but several faults showed up. The additional elevation had greatly increased firing stresses, which caused the gunmetal run-in and run-out ram to distort. This was cured by fitting a steel ram, but then other faults appeared, particularly in the hydraulic piping. Considerable pressures were developed, especially at maximum elevation, which soon produced leaks from inadequately brazed joints.[5] The problem was partly due to a shortage of skilled labour for refitting the mountings, but those converted by Vickers suffered more than others; perhaps its men did not relish working on mountings built by arch-rival Elswick.

After the fiasco of the 14in monitors' speed trials, care

Prince Rupert at Clydebank to have her 12in turret erected by John Brown's 150-ton derrick crane in May 1915. The original short funnel is fitted, which was lengthened soon after entry into service. The 6in guns in the foreground belong to *Barham*. (JOHN BROWN)

had been taken to redesign the propellers and leave the mine-wires off the later ships, but even so there was no chance of their making the originally specified 10kts. As anticipated with her particularly low-powered machinery, *Rupert* turned out to be slowest ship, just making 7kts. *Wolfe* and *Clive* both made 8kts, while 8.2kts was claimed for *Eugene*, but this was probably an overestimate of about 0.6kts as the speed had been assessed from a towed log, not on a measured mile, and did not match the measured power and rpm. So *Clive* must be reckoned the fastest of the class on trials, with her 8.02kts. All ships except *Clive* and *Rupert* ran their trials with the increased funnel height found necessary on the 14in monitors.

As with the 14in monitors, little check seems to have been made on stability and displacement as completed, although *Prince Rupert* with her lighter low-powered machinery was recorded at 5,683 tons deep. However, from the drafts recorded in the ships' logs, the deep displacement for the others was about 5,850 tons, which compared well with the estimated weights after allowing for the full stowage of coal. Design calculations of the stability characteristics had been less accurate, the measured vertical CG being 2ft above the estimate at 13.6ft above the keel; a serious error in a normal ship, but nothing to worry about in a monitor with its broad beam and ample stability. The corresponding metacentric height, GM,[6] was 13.4ft, much the same as the 14in monitors. As with the 14in monitors, insufficient 3in guns

Earl of Peterborough at Harland & Wolff's Belfast yard on 29 March 1915, ten weeks after keel laying. Most of the double bottom and inner hull (two thicknesses of ¾in higher-tensile steel) has been erected on No. 1 slipway. In the background *Mars* and *Magnificent* are about to have their 12in mountings lifted out by the floating crane.
(HARLAND & WOLFF)

had been completed for them to ship their designed HA armament of two 3in, so they were generally equipped with one 3pdr and one 2pdr. There were a few minor differences between ships of the class as completed, such as in details of rig and in bow profile and thus overall length.

As mentioned on p.25, *Prince Rupert*, *Sir John Moore*, *Lord Clive* and *General Craufurd* were initially intended to go out to the Dardanelles. These orders were cancelled by the new Board of Admiralty and the ships were allocated to the Dover Squadron, where the German-occupied coast of Belgium offered tempting targets for bombardment. *Clive* was the first to leave her builder's, on 10 July, having been commissioned on the 4th by Cdr N.H. Carter. *Rupert* followed two days later under Cdr H.O. Reinold, having commissioned on 22 June. Both vessels put into Devonport for three weeks, where the dockyard ordnance department sorted out all the minor problems that had shown up on trials. Commander S.R. Miller had commissioned *Moore* on 1 July and was anxious to press on to Dover, so, although she did not leave Greenock until 22 July, she was the first ship to join

the Monitor Squadron when she arrived at Dover on the 27th. The other five commissioned at their builder's yards, with COs and dates as shown:

General Craufurd	Cdr. E. Altham	19 August
Prince Eugene	Capt E. Wigram	21 August
Earl of Peterborough	Capt H.G.C. Somerville	21 September
General Wolfe	Cdr N.W. Diggle	27 October
Sir Thomas Picton	Capt W.R. Napier	31 October

There had been some competition to get command of a monitor, as it was expected that they would see plenty of action. Although some of the COs selected were relatively young, others were older men passed over for further promotion, who were glad to get such a command. With *General Wolfe* completing on 9 November, the whole newbuilding programme of 33 monitors was completed twelve months to the day from Lillicrap being ordered to start their design.

3.3 Wartime Service in Home Waters, 1915-1916

Churchill had identified the Belgian Coast and the area

Prince Rupert was towed to John Brown's Clydebank shipyard immediately after her launch at Port Glasgow on 20 May 1915 to have her twin 12in turret installed by Elswick Ordnance Co. This fine view, typical of the work of Clydebank's resident photographer, shows the roof plates being fitted, before she returned on 25 May. The vent holes in the bulge water space are clearly seen; more closely spaced than in most of the monitors. In the background the battleship *Barham* is seen completing. The gap in her main deck shows where one of the 6in guns which was used to arm the small monitors was to have been fitted.
(JOHN BROWN)

General Craufurd on her way to trials in Belfast Lough on 21 August 1915. (HARLAND & WOLFF)

covered by the Dover Squadron as second only in importance to the Dardanelles for the monitors, as it would permit support of the Allied armies' left flank, the bombardment of U-boat bases such as Zeebrugge and the possibility of seizing Borkum as a forward base. Following the 'Race to the Sea' in October 1914 and the naval gunfire support which helped stabilise the Allied line (see p.94), occasional bombardments had been made during the early months of 1915 by the pre-dreadnought *Venerable* and the gunboats *Excellent* and *Bustard*, although their guns were of limited range. The Germans now held 27 miles[7] of the Belgian Coast from Nieuport, 8 miles east of the French border, right up to neutral Dutch territory at the mouth of the Scheldt. Two important ports were held: Ostende and Bruges, the latter being 8 miles inland and connected by canal to the North Sea at Zeebrugge. From these bases, only 60 miles from the Kent coast, U-boats and destroyers menaced British control of the narrow seas by torpedo, mine and gun. The all-important transports crossing the Straits of Dover to supply the armies in France were particularly vulnerable, necessitating keeping strong forces of British ships in the Dover area. To protect their bases and their Army's flank, the Germans strongly fortified the Belgian Coast.

The RN faced conditions quite different from those in the Dardanelles. A short length of heavily defended coastline was flanked by shallow waters abounding in tricky tidal currents. The shore was low-lying and offered few visible points of aim for bombardment. Many of the most important targets were in areas still occupied by Belgian civilians. Weather conditions were notoriously unpredictable; poor visibility and gales could severely limit operations. All the time there hovered in the background the threat of a sortie by the High Seas Fleet, considerably nearer at Wilhelmshaven than the Grand Fleet at Scapa Flow.

Vice-Admiral Reginald H. Bacon took over the Dover Command from Rear-Admiral H.L.A. Hood on 13 April 1915. A tireless man who often slept in the office, he brought a fresh and ingenious mind full of technical innovations, but their implementation was not helped by his autocratic tendencies and a refusal to delegate. As he had been a previous DNO (1907-09) and more recently the not-very-successful managing director of COW (1909-14), it was natural that he should devote much of his attention to bombardment operations. As COW's managing director he had gone to France to take charge of his company's 15in howitzers, so was familiar with the Army's needs. At Churchill's request he now resumed naval duties. While waiting for the monitors to arrive, Bacon had been busy making plans for their use. The problem was that of obtaining hits at long range against small targets invisible from the sea. This required an accurate knowledge of the position of both ship and target, as well as the development of reliable spotting methods. Experiments had been carried out in April by Altham before his posting to *General Craufurd*, using seaplanes to observe firings from the pre-dreadnought

Revenge[8] in the Thames Estuary. Portable tripod observation islands were also prepared, to be carried by ship and dropped in shallow water at suitable points off the coast. The danger of mines was to be reduced by sweeping operations before a bombardment, while the U-boat menace was to be countered by surrounding the firing area with drifter-laid nets. Bacon's book *The Dover Patrol 1915-1917*[9] is one of the few published works which give monitors any more than the briefest of passing references. He gives considerable detail of his plans and operations, especially the initial bombardments from which so much was expected.

After *Lord Clive* and *Prince Rupert* had joined *Sir John Moore* off Sheerness on 9 August 1915, bombardment practice could start in earnest in the broad waters of the Thames Estuary. For a fortnight the three ships put their newly converted 12in mountings through their paces. These trials proved a great disappointment to the keen young Gunnery Officers. There were continual breakdowns, makeshift repairs and endless re-tests of the 20-year-old equipment, with Bacon lending an experienced hand to get the guns right. A replica of some of the principal features of the Belgian Coast near Zeebrugge had been laid out in the Thames, enabling the monitors to practise their manoeuvring and spotting arrangements. For the latter, Bacon had two observation tripods, which were to be positioned in the sea about 6 miles offshore before bombardment. The signals from the two groups of observers, coupled with the monitors' own spotting, would give three bearings from which to fix the fall of shot. Bacon considered that spotting from seaplanes alone was not yet sufficiently reliable for such operations. By 21 August all was deemed ready for the first bombardment of German-held territory by big gun monitors, one month after the 14in monitors had opened fire on the Turks. A considerable fleet of supporting vessels was required: ten escorting destroyers, nine minesweepers, the seaplane carrier *Riviera*, four observation tripod handling ships and no fewer than fifty drifters to manoeuvre the explosive anti-submarine nets around the monitors. Bad weather delayed departure on the 21st, and operations had to be postponed for twenty-four hours. During the night of 22/23 August the ships took up their stations about ten miles off Zeebrugge (see map opposite). Marker buoys were laid, tripods were lowered into position and nets were laid around the monitors on all sides except to landward, where it was considered that shoals would prevent any U-boat approach. These activities were not accomplished without difficulty; some of the positions laid were inaccurate, while the enemy had observed the drifters' operations and proceeded to drop some shells among them, fortunately none being hit.

Moore with Bacon aboard, *Clive* and *Rupert* then anchored by the stern within the zareba of nets and opened fire at 05.36 on the 23rd. Their primary target was the locks of the Zeebrugge Canal leading to the naval base at Bruges, but a secondary target was nearby industrial works. From 18,000yd *Clive*'s guns quickly found the range, so she kept up a steady fire for 1½hr, dropping thirty-one rounds in the vicinity of the locks. She then switched to the works, firing a further eleven rounds at maximum range on the gunsights. *Moore* was less fortunate; after nine rounds, which included some misfires, the leather in one of the walking pipes blew. As these pipes carried the hydraulic fluid from the fixed to the revolving part of the mounting, the turret was effectively put out of action for the rest of the operation. *Rupert* was scarcely more fortunate; the electrical connections from the director to the turret broke down and training had to be undertaken by verbal message. She was thus only able to get off nineteen rounds before the cease-fire was ordered. Although none of the German batteries could reach the monitors, Bacon judged two hours a sufficient exposure to risk off Zeebrugge. It had been hoped to go on to bombard Ostende, but with the turret troubles this was not possible and the fleet returned safely to Dover. Preliminary reports indicated considerable damage from the bombardment, including two submarines and two dredgers sunk, one lock damaged and part of the works destroyed.

German accounts, however, show that these reports were much exaggerated, damage being limited to two barges sunk, some buildings and works damaged, two Belgian civilians killed and some German workmen wounded. Although the locks were not hit, Admiral A.D. Jacobsen, commanding the marine artillery in Flanders, later wrote commending the good British shooting in which shells had landed close all around the target. With short-range batteries of old-fashioned guns transferred from Germany and no U-boats ready for action, the enemy were powerless to retaliate. Jacobsen wrote:[10] 'We stood there with clenched fists, gritting our teeth, and had to let the onslaught roll over us. After we had expended so much effort on building our coastal batteries, the enemy simply remained outside their range and could do just as he liked.'
From the British viewpoint the operation could be regarded as reasonably successful for a first attempt and, if the technical difficulties could be overcome, promised well for the future.

Plans were then made for a second bombardment, this time of Ostende, where the dockyard was being used as a forward base for German torpedo-boats and U-boats. Westende, seven miles west, was also included; it was

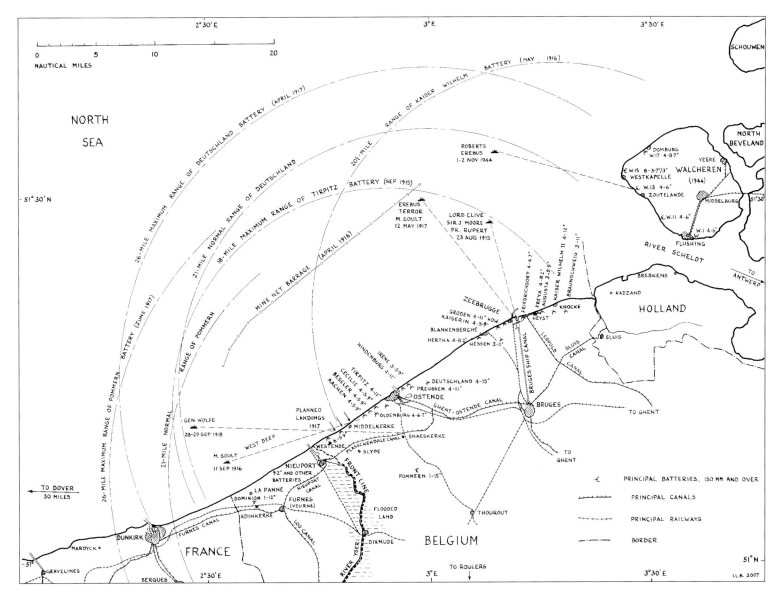

nearer the front line and contained numerous small batteries and observation posts. Following the weak retaliation at Zeebrugge, no great enemy response was anticipated, although several 150mm (5.9in) batteries had been located, together with the Hindenburg battery, which mounted four old 280mm (11in) guns of only 13,500yd range east of Ostende. Meanwhile, *Moore* and *Rupert* had retired to Chatham to have their turrets and steering gear overhauled, *Clive* remaining at Dover. *General Craufurd* had just arrived from Belfast on 30 August, so that by early September there were four large and one small monitor (*M.25* carrying one 9.2in gun) ready to bombard Ostende. Arrangements remained basically similar to those for the Zeebrugge operation, except that the ships would fire whilst under way. The force was divided into two divisions, the first with the monitors going to Ostende, the second with *Redoubtable*, *Excellent* and *Bustard* to Westende.

Two false starts were made; bad weather both on 2 September and on the 5th forced the eighty-seven-ship fleet to return to Dover. The weather cleared on the 6th, so by early morning on the 7th the fleet was in position off Ostende, the mines swept and the nets laid. Unfortunately the weather was clear everywhere except over the target, where a haze prevented observation. Rather than risk exposure to the enemy shore batteries, Bacon ordered the fleet to retire until visibility improved. Attacks were made by German U-boats and aircraft, but the monitors sustained no damage. By mid-afternoon the weather had cleared and the monitors again took up their positions. However, it was found that the observation tripods could not be used effectively after their temporary withdrawal in the morning, so they were unable to provide any worthwhile spotting information. Fortunately the shore spotting posts near Nieuport had not yet been located by the Germans, and these could also be supplemented by three Short seaplanes put up by *Riviera*.

At 15.30 *Lord Clive* opened fire with a ranging shot at

This map of the Belgian Coast shows the area of operation of the large and small Dover monitors during WW1, as well as the 1944 Walcheren assault. Apart from a small loss of Allied territory at the mouth of the Yser, the front line remained static from 1914 to 1918. The German defences were continually being strengthened; the map shows them as in 1918, although more coast defences were still under construction. The maximum range of the German 15in could only be attained with special ammunition.

Ostende lighthouse from 17,500yd but, as the other monitors started to shoot, a hitherto unsuspected shore battery began to drop heavy shells close to *General Craufurd.* The enemy fire soon switched to the flagship *Clive,* and there ensued a very lively half-hour. The Germans had the range accurately as they were using an observation kite balloon, and proceeded to surround *Clive* with an alarming number of near-misses. In an endeavour to open the range she turned to steam out to sea, but, as her speed was so slow, the shells continued to follow and fall all around her. At about 1550 she received four hits in quick succession; one on the port bulge aft, one on the starboard 2pdr (fortunately this shell did not explode, although it knocked the gun down on to the quarterdeck), one hit alongside the bulge forward and another on the bows, which severely shook the turret. It was obvious to Bacon that it would not be long before one of the steeply plunging shells would hit *Clive* fair and square and penetrate right through her decks to explode near her keel. Furthermore, falling rigging had severely injured Carter, so he gave the order to retire.

Meanwhile, the other monitors had got off a few rounds, but *Moore*'s hydraulic pump had broken down after only two rounds. In all, only fourteen rounds had been fired between the four ships, one setting fire to part of the dockyard. The enemy fire slackened as the monitors waddled out of range, but the ships were unable to reply as their turrets would not train far enough aft. During this time the seaplane crews had had a grandstand view from 7,000ft. Not only could they see the gun flashes, but

they could even watch the individual shells passing through the air on their way towards their targets and landing with a splash that almost obscured the monitors.

The strength of the enemy defences in this sector had come as a nasty surprise. It was afterwards discovered that the damage had been wrought by twenty-eight rounds from the newly installed Tirpitz battery, two miles south-west of Ostende, mounting four 280mm coast-defence guns in single mountings which had originally been ordered by Belgium from Krupp. The guns could normally range about 31,000yd, although this was later increased to about 38,000yd using special ammunition. Fortunately the Germans ceased firing at only 25,000yd, as the guns had only just been installed and the fire control equipment had not been completed. Although *Clive*'s damage was little more than scratches, it was evident that Bacon's system of nets and tripods would not work within range of such powerful shore batteries. Once again it was demonstrated that ships were at a severe handicap in a duel with shore guns.

Prince Eugene had arrived at Dover on this same day, followed shortly after by *Marshal Ney.* With the latter's longer-range 15in guns it was considered possible to bombard Ostende docks and the Tirpitz battery from the West Deep, an offshore channel between Dunkirk and Nieuport, which was thought to be outside the training sector of the Tirpitz guns, and which would be too shallow for U-boats. *Lord Clive* and *Sir John Moore* would again tackle Ostende targets, while *Prince Eugene* and *Marshal Ney* attempted to suppress the batteries' fire. After

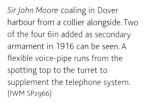

Sir John Moore coaling in Dover harbour from a collier alongside. Two of the four 6in added as secondary armament in 1916 can be seen. A flexible voice-pipe runs from the spotting top to the turret to supplement the telephone system. (IWM SP2966)

another postponed start, the ships set off on 19 September, but *Eugene* had to drop out as she had depleted her bunkers while waiting. *Ney*'s activities are related on p.83, but *Clive* had little more success than on the last occasion. The enemy guns were found to be quite capable of all-round training, and quickly drove her out of range, although later in the afternoon she managed a few retaliatory rounds.

The Allies' autumn offensive was due to start on 25 September, and Sir John French wished the Germans to keep as many of their troops as possible tied up at the coast, away from Champagne and Artois, where the main blow was to fall. Bacon therefore planned a feint landing and arranged for the monitors to bombard near Nieuport to cover an imaginary advance, and near the Dutch border as if covering a landing. So on the 25th *Craufurd* and *Eugene* shelled the coast near Zeebrugge while *Clive*, *Moore and Ney* bombarded Westende. In all, 194 rounds were fired that day, but such a rate of fire could not long be maintained as ammunition stocks were limited; so also was the supply of spare gun barrels. An intermittent fire was kept up till the end of the month, then bad weather interfered with operations. A final bombardment to support the Army was made at night on 3 October by *Moore*, *Eugene* and *Rupert*.

The monitors had come under attack from shore batteries, from the air and from U-boats, but by keeping on the move they avoided damage; *UB.17* had fired a torpedo which had passed right under a monitor off Middelkerke. The effect of these bombardments was not known at the time, but in fact the Germans did reinforce their troops in the coastal sector as they feared a British landing. They also put in hand the construction of additional coastal batteries. During October the batteries near Westende were fired at on several occasions but, although the shells fell close and one battery was temporarily evacuated, no gun positions were actually destroyed. Under the strain of these repeated firings some of the 12in guns were beginning to give trouble, necessitating their replacement as described on p.224. Both *Clive* and *Moore* arrived at Portsmouth on 23 October, the former for a new left gun, the latter for a right gun. Captain B.St G. Collard, later of *Royal Oak*'s bandmaster controversy in 1928, took over command of *Clive*.

General Wolfe, the last 12in monitor to be completed, arrived at Dover on 12 November, bringing the squadron up to six 12in- and two 15in-gun ships, plus four small monitors. For operations off the Belgian Coast the monitors normally used Dunkirk as a forward base. At night one of them would usually anchor off Nieuport to deter enemy torpedo boats from raiding Dunkirk or the Army's left flank or laying mines, but in fact the Germans

considered such operations too risky. With winter setting in, the daylight hours fading and the gales increasing in frequency, it was time to take stock of operations to date. Two major difficulties had arisen: the lack of satisfactory observation methods, and the outranging of the monitors' guns by the shore batteries. As a result of earlier experience with the *Revenge* trials, Altham was sent to the Thames Estuary with *Craufurd* and *Riviera* on 15 November. A series of trials were undertaken to develop the use of wireless in seaplanes and to practise methods of spotting the simultaneous fire of several ships. The observers were required to learn the positions of all the topographical features surrounding each target, so that corrections could be more accurately translated into 'yards, left or right, over or short'. With the keen co-operation of the RNAS the trials were successfully completed, but bad weather prevented the adoption of the new methods in service until January 1916.

The problem of the shore batteries remained, as they were sited to protect the most important targets. Smoke-screens showed promise for shielding the monitors, so experiments were made with different types of smoke producer. To date the Germans were not very impressed by the monitors' performance. A report on 5 December by the Commander of the Flanders Naval Corps, Admiral von Schröder, stated:[11]

They always took good care to keep out of range of our coastal guns, for if they had not done so, the danger of being hit was far greater for them than the prospect of hitting anything themselves; as soon as they were under fire they steamed off again. At the long ranges thus made necessary, spotting and sufficient hitting power were not possible. In fact hitting was merely accidental. Long-range coast artillery practically nullifies the navigational advantage possessed by these ships in their light draft; the completion of the new battery at Knocke will therefore be of great importance to Zeebrugge section. Again the immunity of the monitors from mines and submarine attacks is only relative. At all events the English obtained better results with the old cruisers and battleships in which they first appeared off our coast than they now get with the new type of ship.

During December and January all the Dover monitors except *Wolfe* were ordered to the Thames Estuary to try to intercept German rigid airships coming in from over the North Sea to raid London. The intention was for the small monitors to fix the airships in their searchlights while the large monitors fired 12in shrapnel at maximum elevation, so that lead balls might fall on to the airship. However, given the lack any form of high-angle fire control, even getting close to such a moving target was difficult. In the event, the few airships sighted were far out of range.

During these quieter spells Bacon's thoughts were turning towards other means of restricting German use of the bases at Ostende, Bruges and Zeebrugge. Three plans were considered, all fully described in *The Dover Patrol*:

(i) Landing on the mole (breakwater) at Zeebrugge and blowing up the lock gates of the Bruges Canal

(ii) Closing the entrance to Ostende harbour with blockships

(iii) Landing a force of 10,000 men at Ostende to capture the Tirpitz battery and link up with Allied forces advancing from Nieuport.

In all of these operations it was planned to use the large and small monitors both as bombardment ships and as landing vessels. Upon detailed examination the first scheme had to be abandoned until an effective type of smokescreen had been developed. The second planned to use an old cruiser to manoeuvre two blockships across the narrow harbour entrance. The scheme was well advanced when the Army vetoed it; it was considered unwise to block a harbour the Allies might need after a subsequent advance into Belgium. In addition it was realised that no blocking could be permanent; it would not take the Germans long to salvage the blockships. The third scheme replaced the second; it was intended that all six 12in monitors would force their way right into Ostende

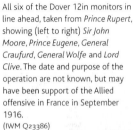

All six of the Dover 12in monitors in line ahead, taken from *Prince Rupert*, showing (left to right) *Sir John Moore*, *Prince Eugene*, *General Craufurd*, *General Wolfe* and *Lord Clive*. The date and purpose of the operation are not known, but may have been support of the Allied offensive in France in September 1916.
(IWM Q23386)

harbour, together with three of the small monitors and 90 troop-carrying trawlers. Planning and co-operation with the Army was going well when, early in 1916, news came of the installation of a new German battery at Knocke near Zeebrugge, named after Kaiser Wilhelm II. Following the first bombardment of Zeebrugge the Germans had pressed on with the construction of a battery there which could outrange the monitors. Its four 305mm (12in) guns with a range of 41,000yd, capable of reaching Ostende, made the position of any British ships forcing a way into the harbour completely untenable. Reluctantly, the plan had to be abandoned.

The monitors continued to meet short-term calls on their services. During January 1916 Marshal Foch requested a demonstration to support Army operations. Here was the chance to put into effect the newly developed air-spotting procedures. Bacon set off in *General Wolfe* on the 25th, accompanied by *Lord Clive*, *General Craufurd*, *Prince Eugene*, *Marshal Ney*, *M.25* and *M.27*. *Wolfe* was now commanded by Capt J.A. Moreton, who had previously served under Bacon as a pioneer submariner. The monitors anchored in the mid-afternoon of the 26th and, from an extreme range of 21,000yd, proceeded to bombard the batteries around Westende. The ships fired in rotation so that shells landed at roughly 20sec intervals, thus permitting corrections to be signalled to individual ships. The spotting proved reasonably effective but, as might be expected, *Craufurd* was the most efficient at making use of the corrections. Each large monitor fired about eleven rounds, meeting with little response from the enemy during the half-hour operation.

This proved to be the last bombardment for seven months, until the faster 15in monitors *Erebus* and *Terror* joined the squadron. In the interim the 12in monitors

remained based at Dover, undertaking a multitude of activities. The opportunity was taken to refit each ship at Chatham or Portsmouth, where 6in guns were added on the forecastle deck to strengthen their anti-destroyer defences and supplement short-range bombardment capability. Early in April *Craufurd* started ferrying spare naval guns from Chatham to Dunkirk to be used as heavy shore artillery in France. Initially one 12in Mk X weighing 58 tons, the model that was fitted in *Dreadnought,* was brought over, followed in July by two others, and then by three 9.2in Mk Xs, each 28 tons. Bacon describes in detail how the guns were chocked up on the forecastle deck amidships, whence they could be rolled down a special timber platform on to the quayside without the need for heavy cranes, as shown in the photograph, for loading on to a gun truck for road transport.

On 24 April a net barrage was laid off the Belgian Coast, with the object of restricting the passage of U-boats to and from their bases. *Eugene* and *Wolfe* were allocated to cover the operation, which involved drifters laying nets fitted with mines, backed up by further lines of moored mines. The barrage ran for 20 miles between Nieuport and Zeebrugge, about 12 miles offshore. During the afternoon Tirpitz battery fired on *Wolfe* from 32,000yd, straddling her with four salvoes. *Wolfe* retreated at full speed but, as she could only cover about 200yd a minute, it was some time before she was out of range. Enemy aircraft then appeared on the scene, but their bombing was ineffective. Possibly *Wolfe*'s 12in fire scared them off, as it produced an impressive burst of black smoke as well as a hail of shrapnel balls. Later in the afternoon enemy torpedo boats were sighted, so the escorting British destroyers set off in pursuit. In the ensuing fight German shore batteries hit *Melpomene* but she was extricated under

the covering fire of *Wolfe* and *Eugene.*

To prevent the Germans clearing the nets and sweeping the mines, a continuous patrol of large and small monitors, destroyers and drifters was maintained all through the summer of 1916. The monitors served as rallying points for the destroyer patrols, as they were reckoned almost invulnerable to anything below a cruiser. German destroyers appeared on numerous occasions, especially during May, June and July. A strong force of 12 ships was turned back on 8 June by the combined fire of *Clive, Moore, Soult* and destroyers. The Germans soon acquired a healthy respect for 12in gunfire and usually retreated out of range on seeing the flash of the guns, while U-boats dived rapidly if spotted on the surface; the barrage and its patrols were a considerable nuisance to them. Occasionally Kaiser Wilhelm battery would open

During the summer of 1916 *General Craufurd* was used to ferry 12in Mark X guns from Chatham to Dunkirk, whence they could be moved to the front near Nieuport. This view shows the first of the guns being unloaded at Dunkirk on 5 April 1916 and being rolled on to the quayside, there being no crane heavy enough for the 58-ton lift. (HUTCHINSON GROUP)

up at the monitors, but at such long ranges the monitors were very small targets, although any hit would probably have been fatal. The most serious threat was from enemy aircraft; bombs were frequently dropped all around the monitors, but fortunately without success. On those occasions when there were no British aircraft on patrol, the monitors' AA guns could usually keep the German aeroplanes high enough to spoil their aim. Air raids on the monitors' bases at Dover and Dunkirk were commonplace, but damage was usually slight, although alarming to the civilian population.

By early July the first of the 12in guns which *Craufurd* had brought over had been erected in the Dominion battery at Adinkerke near the Franco-Belgian border. Fire was opened on the Tirpitz battery from 27,000yd on the 8th. Elaborate precautions had been taken to conceal the battery during its erection in dummy farm buildings, but it was also essential not to give away its position during firing, thus inviting retaliation. So Bacon arranged both for French 240mm (9.45in) guns ashore and *Clive* offshore to fire simultaneously to mislead the Germans as to the true source of the gunfire. *Clive* was rigged out with a dummy second funnel to make her appear as a newly arrived monitor, and she fired blanks in unison with the shells of Dominion battery. The Germans were not deceived by this ruse and retaliated at the French guns. The firings were technically successful on this and the next day but, although some forty shells landed all round the Tirpitz battery, temporarily damaging No. 2 gun, no direct hits were scored on the actual mountings. The Germans soon developed a smokescreen to hide the battery, which severely hampered spotting, and they also located and returned Dominion's fire.

During August *Craufurd* continued her role as guinea-pig ship with night bombardment trials using a gyro receiver to help train the turret to predetermined bearings. She fired thirty-eight rounds at Middelkerke in the early hours of the 16th. Shore spotting aircraft were not able to reach the area in time but, observing that the night was clear and moonlit, Altham reported that if a seaplane had been carried on board there would have been no difficulty. Four nights later he arranged with the Commodore in charge at Dunkirk to hoist aboard a Short Type 184. The seaplane was stowed on the forecastle deck abaft the funnel in the position provided for in the original design, the only difference being that the wings could not fold. Unfortunately low cloud prevented the seaplane from providing any useful reports. When Bacon heard of this trial he was furious that his express permission had not been sought first. Altham was reprimanded in writing, Bacon's open letter to the Squadron ending: 'In future, experimental work will be undertaken by ships other than

General Craufurd'. This rather childish response was typical of Bacon, a difficult commander who allowed his officers little scope for initiative, but one suspects that the main reason for his displeasure was that he had not first thought of the idea of using seaplanes at night. Although a stickler for correct uniform dress, Altham was liked by his crew and had made *Craufurd* into a happy ship.

On land, the Armies had been completely bogged down in virtually static trench warfare for nearly two years. In an attempt to break the stalemate a major British offensive was planned for the summer of 1916, the Somme campaign opening on 1 July. Later Gen Sir Douglas Haig, commanding the British forces, requested operations by the RN to simulate a landing between Middelkerke and Westende. As in the previous autumn, ships apparently associated with possible landings were exercised in the area, while the monitors softened up the enemy defences. From 8 September until Haig's offensive opened on the 15th using some of the first tanks, all the big gun monitors were in action off the Belgian Coast. Reinforcing *Soult* and the 12in stalwarts were the newly completed *Erebus* and *Terror*.

These bombardments were now being undertaken in quite a different manner from the opening rounds of twelve months earlier. The nets and spotting tripods had disappeared, but in their place considerably improved air and shore spotting techniques had been developed, as further described in Chapter 10.7. Smoke-producing motor-launches (MLs) were used to lay screens from behind which the monitors fired, invisible to the enemy spotters ashore. Although the 12in ships contributed their quota of nearly 200 out of over 300 rounds fired during this period, they also assisted the 15in monitors by acting as offshore aiming marks, especially for night firings. *Clive* notched up seventy-four rounds during the week, having taken over *Craufurd*'s experimental role, but the latter was only permitted to fire seven, Altham still being in disgrace. Generally three or four monitors would anchor offshore in the early evening and lay down a barrage for half an hour, each firing every two minutes. No great number of hits was observed, but the principal object was to tie down enemy forces and keep them occupied, especially the numerous 150mm batteries around Westende. However, Haig did write to Bacon, concluding: 'I am, however, convinced that the success of the attack carried out by the armies under my command on September 15th derived considerable assistance from your co-operation'.

After a week of intensive operations, normal duties could be resumed. On 23 September *Moore* completed her interrupted trials of the small SS Zero (submarine scout) airship, to discover whether it could be towed from ships for gunnery spotting, but the results were not very encouraging. The weather soon turned wintry, limiting any further operations during 1916. The monitors were despatched in turns to Southampton during October and November, where they could be drydocked two at a time in the large 900ft × 100ft Trafalgar Dock. As *Rupert*'s guns had been giving trouble during the recent bombardment, including three prematures at 1,000yd, and she was the slowest of the 12in monitors, she was banished to guardship duties similar to those to which the two 14in monitors were assigned. After her refit she took up a berth on 5 November at the mouth of the River Tees to protect Middlesbrough and Hartlepool, the latter having been bombarded by the Germans during the Scarborough Raid in December 1914. The patrol of the Belgian Coast barrage was abandoned for the winter, but 12in monitors maintained anti-destroyer patrols most nights during the early months of 1917 off Calais and the Downs.

3.4 Home Waters, 1917-1918

Two major schemes had been maturing in Bacon's mind for some time, one concerned with checking the activities of the U-boats using Belgian bases, the other a landing at Middelkerke to outflank the German front line. The former operation entailed putting out of action the lock gates on the Bruges Canal but, as the bombardment was planned to be made by the 15in-gun monitors, it is described on p.86. The role of the 12in ships was merely that of acting as aiming marks. The landing operation was intended to link up with an Army advance from Ypres. The 12in monitors were recognised as now being of little direct value in bombardments as their guns were completely outranged by the shore batteries. They could thus be spared for operations which, although risky, would offer worthwhile advantages if successful.

The menace of the Germans using Belgian bases

LEFT
Coaling in progress on board *Sir John Moore*, with 2cwt sacks being hoisted aboard from a collier alongside. A typical coaling rate was about 60 tons per hour, or ten sacks a minute.
(N.C. MOORE)

ABOVE
The monitors' bulges had many uses besides torpedo protection. Here a diver goes down to inspect *Sir John Moore*'s hull. The CPO is standing on one of the fenders added for the Great Landing operations.
(N.C. MOORE)

during wartime was all too apparent, but the Admiralty was equally concerned about the danger of their continuing to hold the coast after any possible armistice. If they did so they would dominate the approaches to London and much of the southern North Sea, as well as surrounding Holland from all sides on land. During the latter months of 1916 Bacon had thought out a new plan, in which troops would be put ashore between Nieuport and Ostende. They would have the opportunity of turning the German flank, destroying the coastal batteries and linking up with British forces advancing from the south. The shallow sandy coastal waters would require the use of long piers to disembark the troops, so Bacon's plan, described at length in his book, was for these to be formed by floating pontoons, which would be pushed into place by the 12in monitors.

An initial pontoon design was completed at the end of 1916: 540ft long, 30ft broad and a draft tapering from 20in forward to 9ft aft, the latter being the forward draft of the monitors. Such a pontoon displaced 2,500 tons and could carry several thousand men, as well as tanks, guns and transport equipment. One was hurriedly constructed at Chatham Dockyard, during which time other prep-

arations were made for the landings: coastal surveys, Army liaison, tank landing experiments and modifications to the monitors. The first pontoon was completed in March 1917 ready for trials. *Clive* and *Moore* had been undergoing their modifications at Southampton and arrived at the Swin off Foulness on 28 March, where they would be out of sight of any watchers ashore. The two monitors were lashed alongside each other and the pontoon was manoeuvred so that it fitted between their bows, projecting forward some 500ft, as shown in the photograph. The trials showed that using the monitors to push the pontoons was perfectly practicable.

Orders were immediately given for two more similar pontoons, and detailed planning with the Army went ahead. Haig was anxious to proceed with the operation, which, apart from clearing part of the coast and fulfilling the Admiralty's request to strike a blow at the U-boat bases, would relieve pressure on the weakened French lines further south. His objective was first the capture of the commanding Messines Ridge about five miles south of Ypres, and then an advance north-east towards the important railway junction of Roulers on the way to the Belgian Coast ports. At this point the RN would land 1

Prince Rupert (right) and *Prince Eugene* (left) linked together with one of the three 540ft pontoons for the Great Landing, from which a division of men were to have been landed in August/September 1917, had the Allied Ypres offensive progressed well. Smoke-producing gear can be seen in front of the spotting tops.
(IWM Q23387)

Division of 13,750 men at three places about one mile apart between Westende and Middelkerke. Each of the groups or columns comprised a pair of monitors, a pontoon, a brigade of men, three tanks, four 13pdr field guns, two 4.5in howitzers and transport. A large supporting fleet of cruisers, destroyers, 15in and small monitors, minesweepers, motor-launches and lighters was also required to cover the landing and the subsequent supply operations. The three 15in monitors would bombard shore batteries, *M.25* would carry the Army HQ staff and the four other small monitors would act as general escorts.

The monitors joined the three pontoons at South West Reach in the Thames in mid-July. *Clive* and *Moore* were again paired, taking the pontoon that would make the centre landing, while *Wolfe* and *Craufurd* took the eastern and *Eugene* and *Rupert* the western pontoon. *Rupert* had been recalled from the Tees to make up the numbers, and *Roberts* had been withdrawn from Yarmouth to act as reserve ship in the event of breakdown. During the last two weeks of July the monitors practised their manoeuvres, either at night or in cloudy weather to prevent observation by German aircraft. No leave was permitted and communications with the shore were strictly limited. Similarly, 1 Division was restricted in a special camp near Dunkirk, which port was to be used for final embarkation of troops and equipment on to the monitors and pontoons. Embarkation was planned to take place three days before the scheduled landing, which would be on a date that depended on the progress of the Army inland.

The Third Battle of Ypres opened with high hopes on 31 July 1917. Almost immediately, however, the weather broke and the rain and mud of Flanders, allied to strong German defences, severely hampered progress. The monitor crews and soldiers waited in vain all through August for the news that Roulers had been taken and the landing could go ahead. The September offensive was undertaken in better weather, but progress remained obstinately slow; by 20 September the British forces had advanced only two of the necessary ten miles. By this time suitable daylight hours, favourable tides and expectations of reasonable weather were all rapidly disappearing. To salvage something from all the elaborate preparations, Bacon put forward the suggestion of a modified landing operation with the limited objective of destroying enemy guns in the Nieuport-Middelkerke area. But Haig was not prepared to co-operate with such a different plan, so on 2 October the monitors and pontoons were dispersed.

Thus ended the only serious attempt to use amphibious power on the Western Front during WW1. Subsequent assessments showed that the landing, spearheaded by tanks, stood a fair chance of success, particularly if carried out while the enemy was being hard pressed by Allied forces further inland. The covering of the actual landing by smokescreens would have reduced the effectiveness of the German batteries' fire. Jacobsen later wrote that he considered the landing itself would have been successful, but that the various lines of defence inland would have halted a further advance. Although casualties would have been heavy, it seems strange that an Army leadership which could countenance the resulting slaughter of Passchendaele (which included 1 Division) was reluctant to risk one division and six relatively expendable ships in an operation which might have helped turn the enemy flank, seriously weaken his hold on the Belgian Coast and its naval bases, and open up new hope to the stalemated Allied Armies.

The six 12in monitors all arrived at Portsmouth on 4 October for drydocking in pairs. On completion *Rupert* was sent back to the Tees, where she remained for the rest

of the war, apart from a month refitting at Jarrow in April 1918. Before coming south for the Great Landing she had been relieved by *Moore* off Redcar Wharf at the end of May 1917. She was drydocked in the large Admiralty floating dock (formerly in the Medway), where Smith's Dock added teak fenders and extra mooring fittings. In mid-June *Moore* provided a similar service for *Roberts* at Yarmouth, taking the opportunity of using the shore observation stations to recalibrate her guns.

During July a barrage similar to that of 1916 was laid off the Belgian Coast. Owing to the absence of the 12in monitors preparing for the Great Landing, most of the patrols were carried out by the 15in monitors. As related

Lord Clive, paired with *Sir John Moore*, has had temporary wooden ramps erected for transferring troops from the ship to the beaching pontoon, in preparation for the Great Landing in 1917.
(AUTHOR'S COLLECTION)

in Chapter 8 they made good use of their opportunities for bombarding Ostende. The 12in monitors took up patrols again in November, firing on distant enemy destroyers and submarines as occasion offered, and in their turn being shelled by shore batteries and bombed by aircraft. These actions were inconclusive; only on rare occasions was even minor damage inflicted on either side. The barrage patrols continued throughout the winter, the monitors giving support to the smaller vessels guarding the anti-submarine minefields. Until April 1918 this burden fell mainly on *Craufurd*, *Wolfe* and *Moore*, as the other two were undergoing conversion at Portsmouth Dockyard to carry an 18in gun.[12] As described in more detail in 3.6 and 10.3, three 18in guns were available after *Furious'* conversion into an aircraft carrier. *Clive*, *Eugene* and *Wolfe* were each selected to receive one gun, to be installed at the after end of the forecastle deck. Considerable modifications were required to prepare the ships for their massive new armament. *Clive* underwent her structural modifications between 5 December 1917 and 6 April 1918, and *Eugene* between 13 December and 7 April. Owing to delays in converting the gun mountings, their new armament was not ready for shipping by April, so the two monitors returned to normal service. *Clive* got a new CO, Cdr R.J.N. Watson, who had spent the previous year in command of *Marshal Ney* at the Downs. His crew found him more easy-going than the irascible and bullying Collard. The dockyard then took the third ship, *Wolfe*, in hand on 5 April.

Meanwhile, Bacon had continued to make new plans for action against the U-boat base at Bruges. Although the 18in guns would be able to reach inland to bombard Bruges, he was anxious to mount another operation which could be put into effect rather sooner to limit the U-boat activities which had been causing increasing merchant ship losses during 1917. He planned for two 12in monitors to go alongside the outer wall of the mole at Zeebrugge under cover of a smokescreen. While troops disembarked from *Sir John Moore* to overwhelm German defences in the immediate vicinity, *General Craufurd* would fire her 12in guns directly at the lock gates of the Bruges Canal 2,000yd distant. Bacon submitted his plan to the First Sea Lord, now Admiral Jellicoe, on 4 December, but the latter, while in general agreement, suggested combining it with a blocking operation across the canal entrance. Bacon was doubtful of the efficacy of blocking; even if blockships could be accurately placed in position under heavy defensive fire, it would not be difficult for the enemy either to make a channel around them by cutting away the canal bank or to demolish their above-water structure sufficiently to allow the relatively shallow-draft submarines to pass over the obstructions

on the top of the tide. With some reluctance, however, he acceded to Jellicoe's request and included blockships in his plan.

At the same time, and unknown to Bacon, the newly appointed Director of Plans at the Admiralty, Cdre Keyes, had been preparing his own plan for blocking Zeebrugge and Ostende. As the number of U-boats passing through the Dover Straits had been seriously worrying the Admiralty for some time, Bacon was summoned to the Admiralty on 18 December in connection with the plans for patrolling the anti-submarine minefield across the Straits and for blocking Zeebrugge. At the meeting the discussion was outspoken; Keyes criticised Bacon's plan and advocated his own, while Jellicoe overruled Bacon's views on the patrols. But great changes in personnel and organisation at the Admiralty were being proposed at the same time. Neither the Prime Minister, Lloyd George, nor the First Lord, Sir Eric Geddes, had been satisfied with Jellicoe's uninspired record as First Sea Lord, so they arranged to replace him with Vice-Admiral R.E. Wemyss. Similarly, Admiralty confidence in Bacon's handling of the Dover Command had waned, particularly in regard to the continuing passage of U-boats, so Wemyss lost no time in replacing him by Keyes on 28 December.

Keyes immediately took steps to put his own plans into effect and to develop a more offensive spirit in the Dover Squadron. Extensive night patrols of the Straits minefields were instituted, the small craft being backed up by large and small monitors. Detailed planning of his own scheme for blocking Zeebrugge and Ostende went ahead rapidly. This plan required of the monitors simply that they should act as a covering force to suppress the German coastal batteries. Full details are given in Keyes' memoirs[13] as well as in *Naval Operations* Volume V, although the former does not give sufficient credit to Bacon's preparations and the latter exaggerates the importance and results of the subsequent operations.

The 12in monitors were allocated to cover only the Ostende blocking force; *Prince Eugene* and *Lord Clive's* targets being Tirpitz and Aachen batteries, *General Craufurd's* Hindenburg, while *Sir John Moore* remained in the Dover Straits, supporting the anti-submarine patrols. *Marshal Soult* was also in the force; her target was the Deutschland battery, which had been installed in 1917 three miles east of Ostende, mounting four naval 380mm (15in) guns with a normal range of 42,000yd but a maximum range of 52,000yd using special ammunition. The attempt on 11 April was called off after the blocking fleet was already at sea, the wind direction having changed, but by this time *Soult*, *Clive*, *Eugene* and *Craufurd* had fired off fifty rounds in all. After a second attempt was also abandoned due to bad weather the four

Prince Eugene after being taken in hand for conversion by Portsmouth Dockyard to carry a single 18in gun abaft the funnel. As the mounting was not yet ready she returned to service in April 1918 without the gun. The upper deck has been completely plated up at the sides and its after part strengthened for the gun. A rail has been fitted on the bulge to stop distance-controlled explosive boats hitting the main hull. (AUTHOR'S COLLECTION)

monitors set out again on the 22nd. They anchored in the West Deep and opened fire on their principal targets at 23.10 using *M.24* and *M.26* as aiming marks, later shifting to 150mm batteries on the coast. Enemy return fire was accurate, some of the monitors being spattered by shell splinters. *Soult* fired a total of eighty-seven rounds of 15in, the others about fifty rounds of 12in apiece, plus some 6in secondary. Meanwhile, *Erebus* and *Terror* covered the Zeebrugge force, as related on p.154.

When the blocking ships went in to Zeebrugge and Ostende in the early hours of the 23rd the monitors were able to draw some of the fire of the coastal batteries. Although carried out with outstanding gallantry and providing a much-needed morale booster during a particularly bad time for the Allies, neither raid was successful in its principal objective of denying the enemy the use of the bases. The blockships only partly blocked the canal entrance at Zeebrugge, so a passage round them was soon made, first for the smaller German vessels, then for the larger. The attempt to block Ostende was a complete failure as the blockships grounded some distance from the harbour entrance.

The middle of 1918 did indeed see a reduction in U-boat successes, but this owed little to the operations against Ostende and Zeebrugge. By this time the convoy system had become fully effective, while the deep mine-fields and surface patrols in the Dover Straits were making hazardous this short cut to the favourite hunting areas. In retrospect it is clear that much heavier aerial bombing would have been a more effective weapon against Bruges, but insufficient effort was devoted to such attacks.

This period also saw the fruition of developments set in train by Bacon which improved bombardment efficiency. In his memoirs Keyes claimed that the Belgian

Coast monitors had a good deal to learn from the experience of the Dardanelles bombardments, but this ignores the fact that conditions for the monitors off the Belgian Coast were totally different and vastly more difficult than at the Dardanelles. At Gallipoli there were visible targets, weak shore batteries, easy location of relative ship and target positions, better weather, deep water and lack of tides, together with Allied naval and air superiority. The improvements included more accurate charts permitting better position finding and ranging, and new longer-range projectiles. In place of the old 2cal radius of head (crh)[14] 12in projectiles, 4crh had already been introduced, but a newly designed 8crh was planned to become available during 1918, with a long pointed cap to reduce air resistance. While not sufficient to match the range of the 15in guns, the increase to 26,000yd for the 8crh was worth having, as it would enable the 12in monitors to range again on Ostende and Zeebrugge from outside the line of mine nets.

The 12in monitors were more active during 1918 than at any time since 1915. Apart from their covering the blocking operations, April saw several other bombardments, mainly from the 15in monitors, including night action against coastal batteries. Standing orders allowed for emergency bombardment of certain specified locations on receipt of a call from the Army. *Eugene* and *Moore* were on patrol on 3 May when such a call was received. Between them they dropped thirty shells near Middelkerke from behind a smokescreen. Airco D.H.4 aircraft of 202 Squadron of the newly formed Royal Air Force (RAF) spotted the fall of shot, which was being used to calibrate the firing of the new 8crh projectile. A second attempt to block Ostende was made on the night of 9/10 May. The monitors were out again to support the operation, *Craufurd* buoying the approach track while *Eugene* and *Moore* fired on the smaller coastal batteries to the west of Ostende amidst clouds of enemy star shells. Unfortunately the old cruiser *Vindictive*, which played such a gallant role at Zeebrugge, was not fully blocking the entrance channel when she was scuttled.

A new ship joined the monitor squadron in June: the ex-Norwegian coast defence ship *Gorgon*, armed with two long range 9.2in guns, as described in Chapter 6. During July *Clive* relieved *Roberts* at Yarmouth for five weeks while the latter refitted. On 16 August *Clive* arrived at Portsmouth to have her 18in gun and mounting fitted. The first gun had been allocated to *Wolfe*, the conversion of which had now been completed, and she now returned to the Dover Squadron on 15 August with a new CO, Cdr S.B. Boyd-Richardson. It was not until late September that she had an opportunity of using her 18in gun against the enemy, although not at Zeebrugge as originally intended.

The Allies' recent attacks had found a weakened enemy with little capacity for resisting a sustained offensive. The Northern Armies, comprising British, French and Belgians under the command of the Belgium's King Albert, attacked along the coast in the early hours of 28 September. They were supported by seven of the Dover monitors, i.e. all the large ships except *Clive* and *Soult*, which were in dockyard hands. Initial night bombardments were made near Ostende and Zeebrugge to mislead the enemy into thinking that a landing might be attempted. By dawn the monitors had all taken up new positions from which they could harass the German lines of communication inland. Division II, consisting of *Eugene*, *Moore* and *Craufurd*, anchored near the West

Deep, while Division III with *Wolfe* and *Gorgon* were farther out. *Erebus* and *Terror*, comprising Division I, were in the same area, but were allocated enemy howitzers for targets. A continuous fire was planned to be kept up all day, supplemented by the monitors' secondary armament. Division II also had the subsidiary role of entering Ostende harbour to land troops, if the town showed signs of being evacuated.

During the morning a regular fire was kept up, each ship firing at about 3min intervals. The weather was poor but some spotting was possible, and reported good shooting. Division II were old hands, so their effort during the day in each firing about a hundred rounds of 12in, plus their sixty rounds of 6in or 4in during the previous night, needs no further description. However, *General Wolfe*'s activity is worth describing in some detail, as it is sometimes doubted whether she ever fired her 18in in action. The gun was fitted in a semi-fixed athwartship mounting projecting over the starboard bulge, capable of only a very limited amount of training. It was therefore necessary to anchor the ship at bow and stern, broadside-on to the target. In the tidal currents off the Belgian coast this presented some difficulty, so good weather was desirable for accurate shooting. Aiming marks were set up to seaward of the monitor, where they could be seen from the second director, fitted beneath and to port of the spotting top. The director passed signals to control training and elevation as well as to the main capstans to shift the ship if larger movements were required. The recoil of firing was found to produce not only a bodily sideslip with the shallow-draft hull, but also an appreciable roll. Thus an interval of some minutes was necessary between rounds, which gave time for the heavy work of

A port broadside of *General Wolfe*, showing the rear of the open 18in mounting, the 18in ammunition derrick abaft the funnel, the cordite tanks (the shells were stowed horizontally on the upper deck beneath) and the anti-DCB rail. (IWM SP130)

reloading to be completed.

At 07.32 she opened fire from 36,000yd on the important railway bridge at Snaeskerke, 4 miles south of Ostende. In doing so she made naval history, firing the heaviest shell from the biggest gun at the longest range ever used in action to date. The enemy batteries soon returned her fire, but with little effect. Despite assistance from the tug *Lady Brassey*, *Wolfe* was soon in trouble maintaining her position broadside on to wind and tide, as her anchors started to drag. Nevertheless she managed

Not until 14 October were they able to make any further advance; the Germans began to withdraw to the east. The same targets were allocated to the monitors, but this time *Wolfe* was joined by *Lord Clive*, newly arrived with her 18in gun from Portsmouth the day before. Firing commenced at 07.10 on the 14th from 34,000yd, but *Clive* fired only a single round at this time, receiving no spot. Her gun had not been calibrated, so the actual gun range may well have been different to that estimated for the gun elevation. The other monitors were also firing, while

to keep up over two hours of 'rapid' fire, dropping in all forty-four shells near their target. The rate of fire was much better than anticipated; one round per 2min 38sec in place of 4min on trials. Later in the day she fired a further eight rounds, thus almost exhausting her outfit of sixty 18in. The monitors then all retired to Dunkirk for the night after the heaviest shore bombardment of the war; some 550 large shells. News was received that the Armies were making good progress, and that *Moore* had scored a direct hit on an ammunition dump.

The bombardment continued for the next five days, although not as heavy as on the 28th. *Wolfe* fired a further eighteen rounds on the 29th, three on 2 October and six on the 3rd. As before, the target was Snaeskerke. However, air spotting conditions were unfavourable, as the weather had worsened, limiting the accuracy and value of the bombardment. The advance of the Allied armies ashore ground to a halt once more in the Flanders mud.

one of the Great Landing pontoons was towed off the coast to give the impression of an imminent landing. Later in the day *Clive* again tried her 18in. Three rounds were got off, again all unspotted, before the order to cease fire came, to avoid hitting advancing Allied troops. As there was a shell still in her gun, the charge was reduced and the shell fired into a minefield 20,000yd to seaward. *Wolfe* fired only two 18in rounds as she received no air spots either, but the other monitors fired 174 12in.

Another sortie was made on the 17th to assist the Army but, although well within range of the shore batteries, the monitors drew no fire from the enemy. Within 48hr the whole of the Belgian Coast had been evacuated. The batteries which had menaced the monitors for so long were now silent, having been blown up before evacuation. Armistice negotiations had been under way for some weeks, and on 11 November the ceasefire came into effect. Meanwhile, *Prince Eugene* had been despatched to Portsmouth on 19 October to have her 18in gun fitted, but three days later came orders to stop all further work. So she received neither mounting nor gun and was removed from drydock, paying off on 12 December. The other 12in monitors paid off in quick succession at Sheerness: *Craufurd* on 15 November, *Wolfe* on the 19th, *Clive* on the 26th and *Moore*, first of the monitors to arrive at Dover and last to leave, on 16 January 1919. A proposal that some 12in monitors be sent to the Adriatic was not approved.

Thus ended the operations of the hard-worked Belgian Coast 12in monitors. In the days before they were severely outranged they had provided a useful bombardment capability which no other vessels could do satisfactorily. In subsequent years they were outclassed by *Erebus* and

Terror, but they continued to make a useful contribution as maids of all work. The monitors' harassment and the fear of landings forced the Germans into fortifying the Belgian Coast ever more strongly, so that by the end of 1918 it contained the strongest coastal defences anywhere in the world, with around a hundred guns between 105mm (4.1in) and 380mm (15in) calibre. Resources of men, material and heavy guns, which would have been of more value at the front, had to be diverted for this purpose. Conversely, the Allies were enabled to dispense largely with such measures on their own coastlines. Unfortunately the demolition carried out before the German evacuation made it difficult for inspection teams to distinguish the extent of damage caused by the monitors' guns. The monitors also provided a deterrent value against raids by German surface vessels in the Channel area and, in the event of an attempt by the High Seas Fleet to break through the Straits, might have helped delay them long enough for the Grand Fleet to arrive. For their crews, life was certainly more interesting than the dull routine of the big-gun ships of the Grand Fleet far away to the north.

3.5 Wartime Service in the Mediterranean

Churchill had originally planned that four of the 12in monitors should go to the Dardanelles, but this plan was cancelled after he left the Admiralty. Although the first five had been allocated to Dover, it was possible to send the sixth and seventh to be completed, *Earl of Peterborough* and *Sir Thomas Picton*, out to the Mediterranean where they could assist at Gallipoli and at the newly opened Salonika Front. *Peterborough* set off from Devonport under her own steam on 19 October 1915 and arrived at Mudros

The two 18in monitors *Lord Clive* (right) and *General Wolfe* at Dover in October 1918. *Clive* does not have the smoke producer which was fitted in *Wolfe* in front of the spotting top. *Clive*'s secondary armament comprised four modern 4in, two 3in HA and three 2pdr.
(IWM SP27)

on 13 November. She moved to a position off Suvla Bay and was soon in action, as the earlier successes of the 14in monitors and bulged cruisers had by now encouraged the Army to call on naval support with increasing frequency. She also used the Kephalo anchorage, although this was not yet fully protected by blockships. Meanwhile, *Picton* followed, arriving at Mudros on 15 December. She was briefed by *Abercrombie* and then attached to the southern squadron, which was to harass the Turkish positions on the Helles Front during the Suvla and Anzac evacuations. On 19 and 20 December she fired her first fifty rounds of 12in, while *Peterborough* undertook similar duties off Suvla. Among the transports being used to evacuate the troops were the now disarmed *Magnificent* and *Mars*; the latter's guns now being put to good use in *Picton* and *Peterborough*. The two monitors also gave close support during the Helles evacuation, as described on p.31.

By the middle of January 1916 new dispositions had been made for the monitors remaining in the Mediterranean. *Picton* moved off to Port Said, then steamed up the Suez Canal to Ismailia on 4 February to provide heavy gunfire support if the Turkish forces on the east side of the Canal should make another attempt to cross, as had been tried twelve months earlier. Her passage up the Canal was made at 6½kts; few other vessels could claim to have made a transit at their maximum speed! Following the paying-off of *Marshal Ney* (see p.84), Capt

Hugh Tweedie arrived to take command in April. Despite the availability of troops released from Gallipoli, the Turks were in no position to attempt a serious attack on the Canal so far from their bases across the wastes of Sinai. After several weeks Tweedie became impatient to adopt a more active role and, as the Turks seemed increasingly unlikely to attack the Canal again, *Picton* was allocated in May to the *Goeben* watch at Imbros, relieving *Abercrombie*. Tweedie considered his ship quite unsuited to such a role, being not only vastly inferior in armament, but quite likely to be temporarily out of action for boiler cleaning or turret repairs. He reported accordingly to the C-in-C, but with no effect; 19 months later *Raglan*'s loss proved him right.

In February 1916 *Peterborough* had been transferred to the Mitylene squadron at Port Iero, blockading the Turkish coast. Occasional bombardments were made on Turkish shore batteries protecting Smyrna, for which she sometimes carried her own spotting seaplane. Brief interludes occurred with a visit to Salonika in March, and also to Milo in June and August. The island of Milo, 80 miles south-east of Athens, was being used to harbour the Anglo-French squadron of battleships and other vessels, including *Peterborough* and *M.17*, gathered as a show of force against the Greek Government to accede to Allied requests concerning the prosecution of the war on the Salonika front against the Bulgarians. The Greek

Sir Thomas Picton leaves her builder's yard on 4 November 1915, already fitted with temporary coal bunkers for the long voyage to the Dardanelles. (IWM SP2341)

A view of *Earl of Peterborough* in 1918, probably off Venice, showing her modifications, including heat-shield over the turret, 12pdr converted to HA firing and closed-in upper deck. She was the only 12in monitor not to get a 6in secondary armament, and she retained her topmast and yards for wireless aerials.
(WORLD SHIP SOCIETY)

Navy put up no resistance at the end of August when the Allied ships, now including *Peterborough*, *M.29* and *M.33*, took over their Fleet.

The whole of 1916 saw an integration of the operations of the four remaining Mediterranean large monitors and the small monitors. One large vessel was always near Imbros on the *Goeben* watch, another at Stavros support-ing the Allies' Salonika right flank, a third with the Mitylene squadron and the fourth refitting. In August *Picton* relieved *Raglan* at Stavros, where she remained until December. These four months were more active for her, particularly after the Bulgarians occupied that part of the Greek coastline to the east. Stavros was close to the Allied right flank, which reached the sea near the mouth of the River Struma. Although the enemy was not very adventurous, the British squadron, which usually included a bulged cruiser and four or five small monitors, was able to assist feint attacks intended to tie down enemy troops, the Allied forces only having light artillery. The monitor was usually anchored bow and stern, and could readily engage in indirect fire, as by this time the calibration of the guns was accurately known. Anchoring so close to the enemy was not without its risks. On the night of 4 September an enemy mobile battery had approached unobserved and at daylight proceeded to drop shells on to *Picton*. Before she could weigh anchor she had received six hits, suffering nine casualties. Fire was exchanged but, by the time she returned after landing the wounded, the battery could not be relocated. Support was also given during the Allies' autumn attack which event-ually took Monastir (now Bitolj) in southern Serbia. During mid-September a Short 184 from the seaplane

carrier *Empress* was embarked for spotting duties. After a month at Salonika *Picton* was back at Malta in February 1917 to have her guns changed.

Meanwhile, *Peterborough* had been allocated in November 1916 to the British Adriatic Squadron at the request of the Italians, and had arrived at Venice on 4 December. The Italians had entered the war against Austria-Hungary in May 1915, the Austrians with-drawing to a strong defensive line in hilly country to the east of the River Isonzo at the head of the Gulf of Trieste. Throughout 1916 the Italians had made little progress; the battlefront remained as static as the Western Front. As the southern Austrian positions barring the way to Trieste were within range of naval guns, it was hoped to use monitors in situations where British and Italian battleships could not be risked, owing to the danger of submarines and the proximity of the Austrian Battle Fleet at Pola. The Italians were building or converting a number of monitor-type vessels. Although some mounted 15in guns they were smaller, slower and much less seaworthy than the British monitors. The Italian Army was short of heavy artillery, so, with the withdrawal of the British pre-dreadnoughts from the Adriatic in early 1917, it was thought that the monitors would prove useful, given the reduced size of the Italian battlefleet following the loss of *Leonardo da Vinci*.

Picton was sent to join *Peterborough* as soon as she was available, arriving at Venice on 22 March 1917. She was given the honour of an armoured train escort from Brindisi to Ancona. The Italians were not very keen to expose ships near the Austrian naval bases, so the first real opportunity to use *Peterborough* and *Picton* offensively

did not arise until May, when the Tenth Battle of the
Isonzo was being planned. The Italian C-in-C, Count
Cadorna, asked for a naval bombardment on Austrian
lines of communication in the Gulf of Trieste. Rear-
Admiral Mark Kerr, commanding the British Adriatic
Squadron, arrived from Taranto to take charge of the
operation but had some difficulty persuading the local
Italian Admiral that the operation was not unduly risky.

After considerable delays *Peterborough* and *Picton* sailed
from Venice on 23 May to bombard the railway line out
of Trieste and the important Austrian airfield at Prosecco.
They arrived in the firing position at 05.30 on the 24th,
intending to fire off fifty 12in shells each. The monitors
kept up a steady fire on the airfield unmolested for half
an hour, but then shore batteries opened up, although
their rounds fell short. Then eight enemy aircraft appeared
and attacked fiercely, dropping bombs all around the
monitors, splashes and splinters landing continuously on
board. One 50kg (110lb) bomb landed on *Peterborough*,
blowing a hole in the forecastle deck abaft the turret and
injuring Kerr, the only casualty. She got her revenge when
her newly modified 12pdr HA damaged an enemy aeroplane, enabling Italian fighters to finish it off. After
blasting the airfield with a good proportion of hits the
monitors turned their fire on to the Austrian headquarters
and railway station. The spotting aircraft reported good
shooting here also; the Italians were much impressed by
the monitors' cool performance so close to strong enemy
bases. The two monitors then returned safely to their
berths at Venice for another three quiet months.

The Eleventh Battle of the Isonzo also gave the
monitors a good chance to display their capabilities.
Moving up to the forward base of Grado on 19 August,
both vessels lay off the dominating Mount Hermada,
which was being attacked by the Italian Third Army.
After a few rounds of unspotted fire in poor visibility in
the morning, the arrival of spotting aircraft permitted
Peterborough and *Picton* to open rapid fire all afternoon
on enemy dugouts and ammunition dumps. Six direct
hits were obtained at about 16,000yd out of about sixty
rounds fired. Shore batteries returned a desultory fire, but
their range was too short to do any damage. A repeat
performance was undertaken on 21 August at the longer
range of 19,000yd which, with well-worn guns, necessitated heeling the monitors to gain additional elevation.
Eleven hits were obtained out of sixty-five rounds.
Spotting aircraft were able to provide a good service, as
they were covered by Italian and French fighters.

The Italian monitors *Faa' Di Bruno* and *Alfredo
Cappellini*, assisted by tugs, also added their 15in fire but,
even with their support, the troops ashore could make
little headway against the strongly defended Austrian

positions. On 23 August the British monitors switched
to bombarding lines of communication. Results were less
satisfactory as the 12in mountings were beginning to
break down under the strain of repeated firings at maximum elevation. The chances of hitting precise targets
such as railway viaducts were slight; out of fifty-four
rounds only three hits were obtained, and these only on
large targets such as villages.

During September the monitors shuttled between
Venice and Grado. In October it was the Austrians' turn
for the offensive. The blow fell on Caporetto on 24
October. The ill-prepared Italian Second Army could not
resist and fell back in rapid retreat, forcing the Third
Army on the coast to withdraw also. *Peterborough* and
Picton helped evacuate Grado on the 28th; between them
they took to Venice 1,200 people as well as guns from the
forts. The weather worsened rapidly but the British
monitors reached Venice safely; not so the two Italian
monitors, which were driven ashore despite tug assistance,
although later refloated.[15] The Austrian advance was so
rapid that the Italians were not able to make a stand before
reaching the River Piave, less than 20 miles east of Venice.
The monitors were withdrawn on 3 November to
Chioggia, but, when the Italian line had stabilised on the
Piave, they moved up again to give support.

The Austrians did their best to force crossings of the
Piave, using floating pontoon bridges. The monitors could
get within range by steaming up the shallow San Felice
channel to the north-east of Venice. *Peterborough* started
the firings on 18 November from about 19,000yd. Her
early attempts to hit such small targets were not very
successful; after twenty-eight rounds all she had to show

Exposed close off enemy-held
coastlines, nearly all the monitors
received shell hits at one time or
another, but most were minor
scratches like this one on *Sir Thomas
Picton*'s forward bulge, received off
the Salonika front in 1916.
(IWM SP3115)

Italian monitor *Faa' Di Bruno* was a much more basic concept than the British design. She mounted a twin 15in turret destined for the battleship *Cristoforo Colombo* when completed in 1917, but could only manage 3kts at best. She is seen here as floating battery *GM.194* in 1943. (A. FRACCAROLI)

for her efforts was weed-choked condensers. On the 20th she scored four hits and set fire to one of the bridges, in spite of the difficulties of spotting when enemy aircraft continually harassed the spotting aeroplanes. She was relieved by *Picton* soon afterwards; the latter continued the good shooting, obtaining hits on the narrow 10ft-wide bridges at the end of November. In December the Austrian attacks eased off, though *Picton* ventured up the channel again on the 10th to bombard Passarella, using three-quarter charges for the reduced 15,000yd range.

The two monitors remained at short notice until January 1918, when the situation appeared to have stabilised. In early February, and again in early March, they returned to the San Felice channel to bombard the Austrian positions. They both set off down the Adriatic on 18 March for the Italian west coast, where leisurely refits were undertaken: *Peterborough* at Spezia, *Picton* at Genoa. The monitors were still refitting during the Battle of the Piave in June 1918, but on completion they were sent to Valona in Albania at the western flank of the Allied Balkan Front. The Italians were preparing an offensive, so on 7 July *Peterborough* and *Picton* fired on the Austro-Bulgarian positions near the coast, earning the thanks of the Italian C-in-C.

During the next few weeks they were at Valona, Brindisi and Ancona, available for support if required. No further action occurred before the Armistice was signed, firstly with Bulgaria, finally with Austria on 3 November. Both monitors then proceeded up the now submarine-free Adriatic in easy stages, *Peterborough* going to Venice and *Picton* to Fiume as guardship at the Austrian naval base. Both ships were sent to Malta on 2 February 1919 to prepare for the voyage home, finally

arriving in Britain in mid-March to pay off and join the other monitors laid up at Immingham in May.

3.6 Modifications and Performance

The 12in monitors underwent rather more frequent modification than the 14in vessels, as conditions off the Belgian Coast were continually changing and dockyards more readily available. It was soon recognised that their weak secondary armament of two 12pdrs would not prevent a 'cutting-out' attack by destroyers from bearings and ranges which the 12in could not reach. It was also appreciated that a more powerful secondary armament would provide a supplementary medium-range bombardment capability. Accordingly either two or four 6in QF were fitted abreast the funnel on the forecastle deck of each of the Dover monitors, most of the guns being removed from the pre-dreadnought *Illustrious*. Chatham and Portsmouth dockyards carried out the installations early in 1916. *Wolfe*, *Moore* and *Craufurd* got four guns each, *Clive*, *Eugene* and *Rupert* two.

Minor changes were continually being made, especially to the HA armament. Topmasts were struck on the Dover ships, where long-range wireless aerials were not needed, and the aircraft handling derricks removed. The navigating bridge structure was extended from the original bare searchlight platform that had been the only alternative to the inconvenient conning tower under the guns. The actual arrangement of the bridge differed in each ship, providing a useful recognition feature later. The changes to the Mediterranean pair were fewer than the Dover ships; *Picton* got only a single 6in BL XII abaft the funnel, as in the 14in monitors.

Extensions were also required to the accommodation

as the numbers of the crew increased. From 194 as completed, numbers rose to 215 for ships with two 6in and to 232 for ships with four. Fortunately it was a simple matter to plate in parts of the side of the upper deck to make more cabin and mess space. This process continued until, by 1918, the whole side was plated in all ships except *Moore*, *Rupert* and *Craufurd*. During 1917 further modifications, included fitting smoke-making apparatus in front of the spotting top in the Dover ships, giving the appearance of a large rangefinder. The upperworks were often painted in a grey and white chequer pattern, although the hulls remained grey. The Adriatic monitors were painted khaki to match the colour of the water. Two-pounders and Maxims were often mounted on the turret, plus similar platforms for shooting-up the numerous mines found drifting off the Belgian Coast, as well as distance-controlled boats (DCB — see p.152). The 6in QF were gradually replaced by the more modern 6in BL VII, as the latter had a range of 13,500yd, compared with only 11,000yd for the QF which were outranged by German destroyers. These in turn were later replaced by 4in BL IX in *Moore* and *Clive*. *Wolfe* even seems to have temporarily mounted in 1917 a 6in as a high angle anti-airship gun.

The really big changes came in 1918, with the conversion of three ships to take the 18in gun. Because of the dual-purpose nature of the duties proposed after removal from *Furious*, i.e. capable of being mounted on land or on ship, a completely different design of mounting to the normal revolving turret was selected, as detailed in 10.3. The whole mounting weighed about 384 tons, including the 149-ton gun, but this figure nearly doubled when ammunition, equipment and supports were included, presenting quite a problem in mounting aboard a 6,000-ton ship. Bacon's proposals for fitting the 18in in the monitors were put forward in the summer of 1917 and included strengthening the forecastle deck abaft the funnel to take the mounting, but leaving the existing armament undisturbed. As there was insufficient space below decks, stowage for enough projectiles for a day's firing would have to be on the upper deck, with cordite in cases on the forecastle deck. A light shield over the mounting would be arranged to represent armour plating, allowing elevation to 45 degrees.

The only place to fit the mounting with its structural supports without removing the 12in turret was abaft the engine room. The large trimming moment due to this concentrated load aft would increase the draft aft to over 14ft, seriously reducing the freeboard aft to only about 4ft. The most satisfactory solution to reduce the resulting trim was to close up watertight the after inboard bulge compartments, which were normally open to the sea.

Even so, the ship's drafts as finally converted became 8ft 9in forward and 13ft 2in aft, corresponding to a displacement of 6,850 tons. The after part of the bulge was fully submerged, increasing the risk of a torpedo or DCB riding over the bulge and exploding against the main hull proper, so a heavy steel deflector was built on top of the bulge.

The actual ships to be converted to take the 18in gun were easily selected: those with the three most senior COs — *Lord Clive*, *Prince Eugene* and *General Wolfe*. The plan was to take the first two vessels in hand at Portsmouth in December 1917, fit the heavy supports in January and ship the mounting in March. After trials they would return to service in May, while the third vessel started her conversion. But delays in converting the mountings meant that work on the hulls of the first two vessels was completed long before the mountings were ready. When the first mounting finally arrived at Portsmouth, on 20

June, it was fitted into the third ship, *Wolfe*, the gun itself being lifted aboard in drydock on 9 July. After coaling and ammunitioning *Wolfe* was ready for gun trials, which were carried out successfully off the Isle of Wight on 7 August.

General Wolfe's appearance had substantially altered. The huge box-like shield over the 18in gun gave rise to the nickname 'Elephant and Castle' for the ship. The closing-in of the sides of the upper deck gave the hull a more businesslike appearance. The quarterdeck was considerably cramped by an extra boat, a proper stern anchor and windlass, and the extension aft of the forecastle deck. Apart from the two pom-poms on top of the 18in shield, the secondary armament was all concentrated forward; two 6in BL VII abreast the bridge and two 3in HA

Earl of Peterborough's 12in turret covered by sandbags to give protection against aircraft bombs while in the Adriatic. The short 35cal guns are at maximum elevation. The hatch and davit are for loading shells into the magazine. (IWM Q22881)

A starboard broadside of *General Wolfe* shortly after her 18in had been installed in August 1918. Her twin 12in turret, complete with sunshield, was retained. (IWM SP32)

abreast the 12in turret. Smaller changes included installing two 36in searchlights aft, replacing the two 24in on the mast, a slim mainmast to support the wireless aerials, bow defence gear (modified paravanes) for the bulged hulls, removal of the armoured conning tower, siting the 18 cordite stowage tanks and associated rail tracks abaft the funnel on the forecastle deck, a new ammunitioning derrick on the port side for the 18in and a more substantial bridge structure. Internally, the after half of the upper deck was given over to the 18in shell stowage and their transporters, plus the extensive structural supports for the mounting. The latter cramped the officers' accommodation, so the warrant officers were moved up to cabins on the upper deck, where crew berthing was increased for the new complement of 278. The wireless room was moved to the hold where it would be better protected, as was the new gyro compass; magazines and stores were also rearranged.

Clive returned to Portsmouth on 16 August 1918 for her missing gun, which was finally shipped on 7 September, trials being carried out on 13 October. The war was over before *Eugene* received her gun, so she retained her rather bare aft end appearance with the plated-in hull and clear forecastle deck aft.

Changes to the 12in monitors' armament were more extensive than those to any of the other classes during WW1; they are tabulated below as existing at the end of the war:

Lord Clive	1 x 18in, 2 x 12in, 4 x 4in, 2 x 3in, 3 x 2pdr
General Wolfe	1 x 18in, 2 x 12in, 2 x 6in, 2 x 3in, 2 x 2pdr
Prince Eugene	2 x 12in, 2 x 6in, 2 x 3in, 2 x 2pdr
Sir John Moore	2 x 12in, 4 x 4in, 2 x 12pdr HA, 2 x 3in, 2 x 2pdr
General Craufurd	2 x 12in, 4 x 6in, 2 x 12pdr HA, 2 x 3in, 2 x 2pdr
Prince Rupert	2 x 12in, 2 x 6in, 2 x 12pdr HA, 2 x 3in, 1 x 2pdr
Sir Thomas Picton	2 x 12in, 1 x 6in, 2 x 12pdr HA, 1 x 3in, 1 x 3pdr
Earl of Peterborough	2 x 12in, 2 x 12pdr HA, 2 x 3in, 1 x 2pdr.

During 1918 the corresponding official outfit of ammunition for each gun comprised:

　18in: 60 HE
　12in: 90 HE, 10 CPC (common, pointed capped)
　　　　(Dover); or 120 HE (Med)
　6in: 150 HE, 10 CPC, 40 shrapnel
　4in: 150 HE, 10 CP (common, pointed), 40
　　　　shrapnel
　3in: 240 HE, 60 incendiary, 32 CP
　12pdr: 150 HE, 50 CP
　2pdr: 480 CP, 320 CNF (common, nose-fuzed)

In addition, thirty rounds of star-shell were carried per ship, generally for the 3in or 4in guns.

The seagoing performance of the 12in monitors was similar to that of the 14in ships, but the extra few hundred horsepower gave the slightly higher cruising speed of about 7kts clean, except for the underpowered *Prince Rupert* at 6½. Mileage steamed at Dover was modest, *Moore* covering only 5,600 miles in her first year, requiring coaling about once a week. Coal consumption was around 50 tons a day at full speed, giving a nominal endurance of about 1,100 miles, but the official figure was about 960. This probably took account of the subsequent loss of two of the bunkers to make room for 6in magazines. *Wolfe* was the fastest of the ships in normal service and, under ideal conditions, could even better her 8kts trial speed by

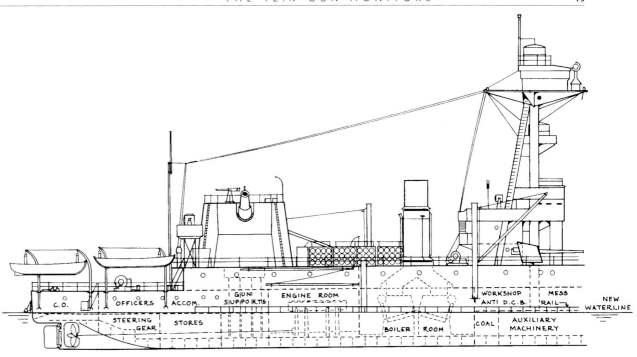

BELOW
Lord Clive's 18in at its maximum 45 degrees elevation. It had a range of up to 40,500yd, depending on type of ammunition. Some of the eighteen cordite tanks with their lifting rails can be seen, each of the twelve compartments holding two 105lb one-sixth charges. Steam heating pipes can be seen at the base to keep the water-filled tanks at an even temperature and reduce the fire risk. The fitting on the 18in muzzle was for pulling through to clean the gun bore. Also visible is part of the shield of one of the 4in BL guns.
(IWM Q19292)

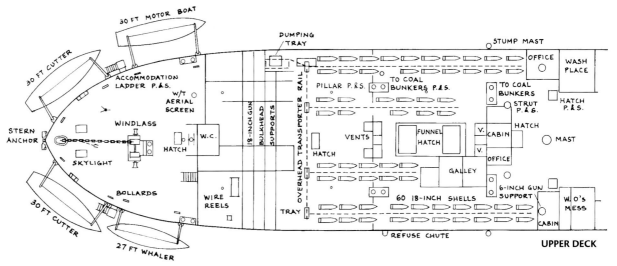

UPPER DECK

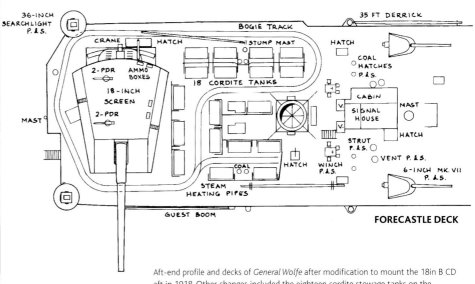

FORECASTLE DECK

Aft-end profile and decks of *General Wolfe* after modification to mount the 18in B CD aft in 1918. Other changes included the eighteen cordite stowage tanks on the forecastle deck and the bogie track, the anti-DCB rail on the bulge and the additional director for the 18in to port on the foremast below the spotting top. *Lord Clive* was generally similar, apart from her secondary armament of four 4in in place of two 6in, and three instead of two single 2pdr. See cross section on p.227.

a whisker, but needed 70 tons of coal a day to do so. After her 18in conversion, speed dropped appreciably with the extra displacement — she made only 6.7kts on trial in August 1918.

Manoeuvring was always a problem with their unsympathetic hull forms and underpowered steering gear. In the crowded conditions of Dover Harbour there were few ships which did not show some signs of a brush with one of the monitors; dents in the hull, twisted guardrails or splintered boats and fittings. Propeller-excited vibration could be serious, sometimes making writing impossible in the officers' quarters aft.

3.7 Post-war Careers

Only one ship of the class had a post-war career of any special interest, *Lord Clive*. After 19 months laid up at Immingham she was towed to Portsmouth in September 1920 to be converted to carry three 15in guns for trial purposes. The design of the projected 1921 battlecruisers included triple 16in guns, but the RN had no information on the effects of firing three-gun salvoes from a single turret. Interference and throw-off (the effect produced by firing an off-centre gun on a multiple mounting)

needed to be investigated, so it was arranged to mount three 15in guns on one of the monitors. *Clive*'s 18in and secondary armament were therefore removed, and additional strengthening fitted. The three guns were then installed on a fixed mounting by COW, covered by a canvas screen, pointing out to starboard as illustrated below. The mounting was converted from a twin 15in turntable under construction for one of the cancelled *Hood*-class battlecruisers. The new mounting weighed 520 tons complete with guns, rather heavier than the 18in. *Clive* recommissioned on 15 December 1920, but she was not ready to leave Portsmouth until 1 February. She was towed round to the Nore, for the next month firing off her test rounds up the Shoeburyness range. The trials showed that there were no serious problems with a triple mounting, so *Clive* paid off again in August 1921. She remained laid up at Portsmouth until sold on 10 October 1927 for £13,500 to P & W MacLellan of Glasgow for breaking up at their yard at Bo'ness on the Forth. She had originally been sold to Stanlee Shipbreaking of Dover in 1921, but had been withdrawn.

Three other ships saw very limited post-war service. *Prince Rupert* remained in the Tees as a temporary tender to the submarine depot ship *Vulcan*. In September 1919 she joined the other monitors laid up at Immingham. In May 1920 she went to Chatham to serve as an accommodation hulk for the dockyard police, also providing accommodation for boats' crews and serving as a lashing hulk. Two years later she took over from *Achilles* (originally an ironclad of 1863) as parent ship of the naval depot, being renamed *Pembroke*. She was sold in May 1923 to Beardmore, as the company's Dalmuir shipyard had no orders in hand, so *Rupert* was bought to provide work to help keep a nucleus of men together.

1923 to Beardmore, as the company's Dalmuir shipyard had no orders in hand, so *Rupert* was bought to provide work to help keep a nucleus of men together.

General Craufurd and *Sir John Moore* remained at the Nore after the war, and in January 1919 were recommissioned as gunnery tenders to the First Fleet firing service and to keep alive experience of bombarding techniques. Later in the year *Craufurd* was offered for sale to Rumania, but nothing transpired. Both ships were paid off again in the spring of 1920 and were put on the Sale List. The remaining four ships, *Prince Eugene*, *General Wolfe*, *Sir Thomas Picton* and *Earl of Peterborough*, were all laid up at Immingham from spring 1919 to the winter of 1920-21. They were then towed round to Portsmouth where guns and useful fittings were removed by the dockyard, after which they were moved to lie at moorings in Spithead until finally sold. *Wolfe*, *Eugene* and *Craufurd* all formed part of Ward's massive purchase in May 1921 (see p.43) but were not broken up until 1922-23. The Admiralty had reduced the price to £2 4s 0d per ton actual displacement with falling scrap market prices. The three cost Ward an average of £11,035 at 5,016 tons each, yielding an average of £24,050 each from sales of 4,897 tons of recycled materials. *Picton*, *Moore* and *Peterborough* were all sold to the Slough Trading Company on 8 November 1921 at £1 19s 0d per ton, a total of £28,085. The contract with the company allowed it to remove 32 Admiralty vessels direct to German ports, so all three were towed away and broken up in Germany in 1922. Questions were raised in Parliament about British warships being broken up in Germany while unemployment remained high in Britain. No more ships were sold in this way, which suited the Admiralty, who had been in dispute with Slough Trading about the amount of non-ferrous metals remaining on board other ships sold.

The 12in Monitors – Technical data

Displacement: 5,900 tons Navy List, 5,850 tons deep on 9ft 10½in draft, 5,170 tons light on 8ft 8½in.

Dimensions: Length 335ft 6in oa, 320ft 0in bp, breadth 87ft 2in oa, 57ft 0in main hull, depth to forecastle deck 25ft 6in

Weight distribution as designed (tons): Armament 335, ammunition 143, protection 1,824, hull 2,486, equipment 220, machinery and RFW 391, coal (nominal) 200. Designed total 5,599 tons.

Complement: 12 officers, 182 men.

Armament: 2 x 12in (twin) (60 CPC + 60 HE rpg), 2 x 12pdr (200rpg), 1 x 3in 20cwt HA (*Eugene* and *Craufurd*) (300rpg), 1 x 3pdr Vickers HA (except *Eugene*) (500rpg), 1 x 2pdr HA (except *Craufurd*) (1,000rpg), 4 x 0.303in Maxim (5,000rpg).

Protection: As 14in monitors except: sloping belt 6in C.; gunhouse 10½in front, 4in rear, 2in roof and floor (nickel steel), 5½in sides (Harveyed).

Machinery: Twin screw triple-expansion. *Wolfe:* two 4-cyl by McKie & Baxter, Glasgow (Nos. 811-12) 16in, 28in, 32in, 32in x 24in 2,500ihp at 180rpm; *Moore:* two 3-cyl by Scotts', Greenock (No. 532) 16in, 26in, 42in x 27in 2,500ihp at 190rpm; *Rupert:* two 3-cyl by McKie & Baxter, Glasgow (Nos. 807-08) 13in, 23in, 36in x 21in 1,600ihp at 180rpm; Others: two 4-cyl by Harland & Wolff, Belfast (Nos. 477-81) 15in, 25in, 30in, 30in x 24in 2,310ihp at 200rpm. Coal 356 tons.

Endurance: 1,100 miles at 6½kts on 2.1 tons per hour (H & W ships).

Speed: 10kts designed, 7 service. Trials: *Clive* 8.02, *Craufurd* 7.42, *Peterborough* 7.66, *Picton* 7.4, *Eugene* 8.2, *Rupert* 7.06, *Moore* 7.75, *Wolfe* 8.01.

Construction: Harland & Wolff, Belfast: *Lord Clive* (No. 478) laid down 9.1.15/launched 10.6.15/completed 10.7.15; *General Craufurd* (No. 479) 9.1.15/8.7.15/26.8.15; *Earl of Peterborough* (No. 480) 16.1.15/26.8.15/12.10.15; *Sir Thomas Picton* (No. 481) 16.1.15/30.9.15/8.11.15. *Prince Eugene* (No. 477G/B) H & W, Govan 1.2.15/14.7.15/2.9.15. *Prince Rupert* (No. 310) William Hamilton, Port Glasgow 15.1.15/20.5.15/12.7.15. *Sir John Moore* (No. 469) Scotts' Shipbuilding & Engineering, Greenock 13.1.15/31.5.15/22.7.15. *General Wolfe* (No. 858) Palmer's Shipbuilding & Iron, Hebburn Jan 1915/9.9.15/9.11.15.

Scrapped: *Clive* sold P & W MacLellan 10.10.27, arrived Bo'ness 17.11.27; *Rupert* sold Wm Beardmore 29.5.23, left Chatham 26.6.23 for Glasgow; All sold T.W. Ward 9.5.21: *Craufurd* arr New Holland 10.9.23; *Eugene* arr Preston 10.8.23; *Wolfe* arr Hayle c10.12.23. All sold Slough Trading Co 8.11.21 for breaking up in Germany: *Peterborough* left Portsmouth 6.5.22 for Hamburg, *Picton* left Portsmouth 21.12.22 for Bremen, *Moore* left Chatham 23.12.22 for Bremen.

Monitor stability

Ship	*Deep displacement, tons*	*Draft, ft-in*	*Tons per inch immersion*	*Height of metacentre KM ft*	*Height of centre of gravity KG*	*Metacentric height GM ft*	*Angle of maximum stability, degrees*	*Angle of vanishing stability*
14in	6,150	10-0	42.8	29.2	16.2	13.0	25	62
12in	5,850	9-10½	41.3	27.0	13.6	13.4	23	71.5
Marshals	6,900	10-5	47			13.5		63
Severn	1,520	5-7½	23.9	33.6	7.6	26.0		75
M.17	650	7-0	9.5	14.0	8.8	5.2	32	63
M.29	580	5-11	10.0	16.2	9.7	6.5	26	53
Gorgon	5,746	16-4½	32.8	26.1	18.0	7.8		62
Erebus	8,450	11-8	61.0	48.5	16.5	32.0		
Roberts WW2	9,150	13-6	54.2	36.1	17.4	18.1	31	69.5

GM is the vertical distance between the centre of gravity, G, and the metacentre, M. The metacentre can be considered as an imaginary point of suspension used to determine a ship's stability at small angles of heel. As long as G remains below M, the ship will be in stable equilibrium, i.e. will return to the upright after being heeled by wind or waves. The height of the metacentre above the keel, KM, is largely dependent on the ship's breadth at the waterline, which for some monitors (including *Erebus* and *Terror*) included the width of the bulges. The height of the centre of gravity above the keel, KG, is much influenced by top weight. Then GM = KM - KG.
GM is after free surface correction to allow for tanks not 100 per cent full of liquid, e.g, oil fuel.

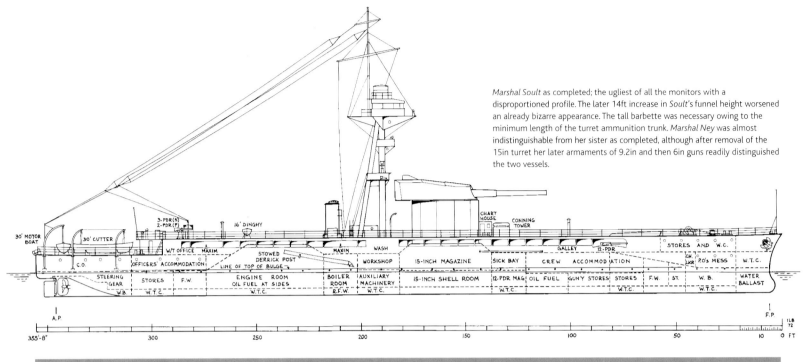

Marshal Soult as completed; the ugliest of all the monitors with a disproportioned profile. The later 14ft increase in Soult's funnel height worsened an already bizarre appearance. The tall barbette was necessary owing to the minimum length of the turret ammunition trunk. Marshal Ney was almost indistinguishable from her sister as completed, although after removal of the 15in turret her later armaments of 9.2in and then 6in guns readily distinguished the two vessels.

CHAPTER 4

The First 15in-gun Monitors

4.1 Design

Following the Battle of the Falkland Islands two eight-gun battleships of the 1914 Programme were changed into the battlecruisers *Renown* and *Repulse*, mounting only six 15in guns to enable them to achieve 32kts. With two spare 15in turrets now available, Churchill and Fisher planned to build two more monitors, whose guns could hurl a 1,920lb projectile 23,400yd. So in January, for the third time in two months, Lillicrap was called upon to design another class of monitor, provisionally identified as *M.13* and *M.14*. A twin 15in turret weighed about 760 tons, but including barbette armour and ammunition was some 300 tons heavier than a 14in installation. A hull rather larger than the two previous classes was therefore called for, but draft had to be kept at 10ft. Breadth remained fixed at 90ft from drydocking considerations, the main hull being 62ft wide, so length was the only dimension that could be increased; it went up to 340ft BP to provide the necessary displacement of 6,670 tons.

Meanwhile, DNO had been examining the detailed problems of installing the 15in Mk I mounting in a relatively shallow hull. Much to Fisher's annoyance all-round

fire could not be achieved, because the turret could not train more than 300 degrees owing to the arrangement of the hydraulic supply pipes. It was also found impossible to shorten the ammunition trunk below the length required for a battleship's aftermost turret, namely 43ft from gun axis to shell-room floor. As a result the barbette had to project 17ft above the forecastle deck, so had to be heavily armoured to protect the turntable and working chamber, being formed of 12 flat plates 8in thick in place of the usual circular shape, to speed production.

Fisher pressed the case for diesel propulsion, as Churchill had suggested for the 12in monitors. Although such relatively complex engines normally took much longer to build than steam reciprocators, there were under construction two oilers with diesel engines. The 2,400-ton deadweight oilers *Trefoil* and *Turmoil* were being built at Pembroke Dockyard; two of a number of oilers being fitted with alternative makes of diesel engine so that the performance of this new form of propulsion could be compared using non-combatant ships as testbeds. *Trefoil's* machinery had already been installed, having left Barrow on 28 November. She was about to start her trials, but it would be possible to remove her engines and transfer them into a monitor, while *Turmoil*'s engines had just completed shop trials at their maker's works and were ready for despatch to the dockyard. Here, indeed, was a fine chance to obtain two sets of diesel engines quickly, as they appeared to be the ideal prime mover for the low-powered monitors. The oilers were designed for 12kts, requiring about 1,500bhp,[1] which was to be provided by two 750bhp engines driving twin screws. This power was slightly less than installed in the earlier steam monitors, so it was expected to give a speed of about 9kts, allowing for the increased displacement.

Trefoil's 88-ton engines had been designed and built by Vickers at Barrow, being a development of its submarine engines. By contrast, *Turmoil*'s 68-ton engines had been designed by MAN of Augsburg in Germany but built under licence by J. Samuel White of Cowes in the Isle of Wight. The contracts for the complete machinery installations were worth about £40,000 for each ship,

about double that for steam reciprocators. The advantage lay in the much-reduced fuel consumption of only about 0.4 tons of oil per hour, compared with 1.3 tons of oil or 1.9 tons of coal using steam. The corresponding daily fuel costs would have been about £96 for the diesel burning shale oil at about £10.00 per ton for Admiralty supplies during WW1, £110 for oil-fired steam reciprocators (fuel oil at £3.55) and £75 for coal-fired (Welsh coal at £1.65). Although a smaller bunker capacity could be arranged, slightly longer machinery spaces were needed compared with the steam monitors. Two small oil-fired boilers were required to power the 105kW steam-driven electric generator[2], the turret hydraulic pump, the steering engines, the fresh-water evaporators, the capstans and the ballast and other pumps.

The other design features followed the pattern established by the earlier monitors, including completely ignoring AEW's advice about fining the hull lines aft, with consequences that were to be most serious. The

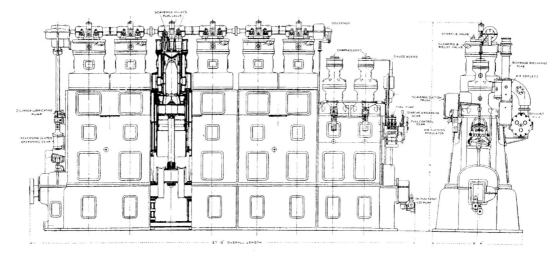

The *upper* drawing shows one of *Marshal Ney*'s two 750bhp MAN two-stroke diesel engines originally intended for *Turmoil*. The two smaller cylinders provided the compressed air for the oil fuel blast injection for the six propulsion cylinders. Despite its businesslike appearance and satisfactory test-bed performance, it never operated successfully in service.
(THE SHIPBUILDER)

The *lower* drawing shows, to the same scale, one of *Trefoil*'s 750bhp Vickers four-stroke airless injection engines, which was transferred to *Marshal Soult*. Despite the comparatively primitive appearance of the eight-cylinder engine, somewhat resembling a steam reciprocating engine, it performed well in service.
(THE ENGINEER)

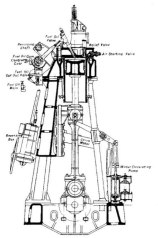
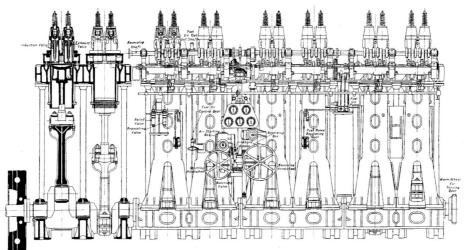
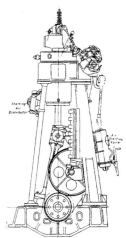

RIGHT
Marshal Soult three days before
launch at Jarrow. The brackets for
the mine-catcher wires can be
seen under the bilge. The wires
connecting the drag chains just
visible under the bilge are in place.
(AUTHOR'S COLLECTION)

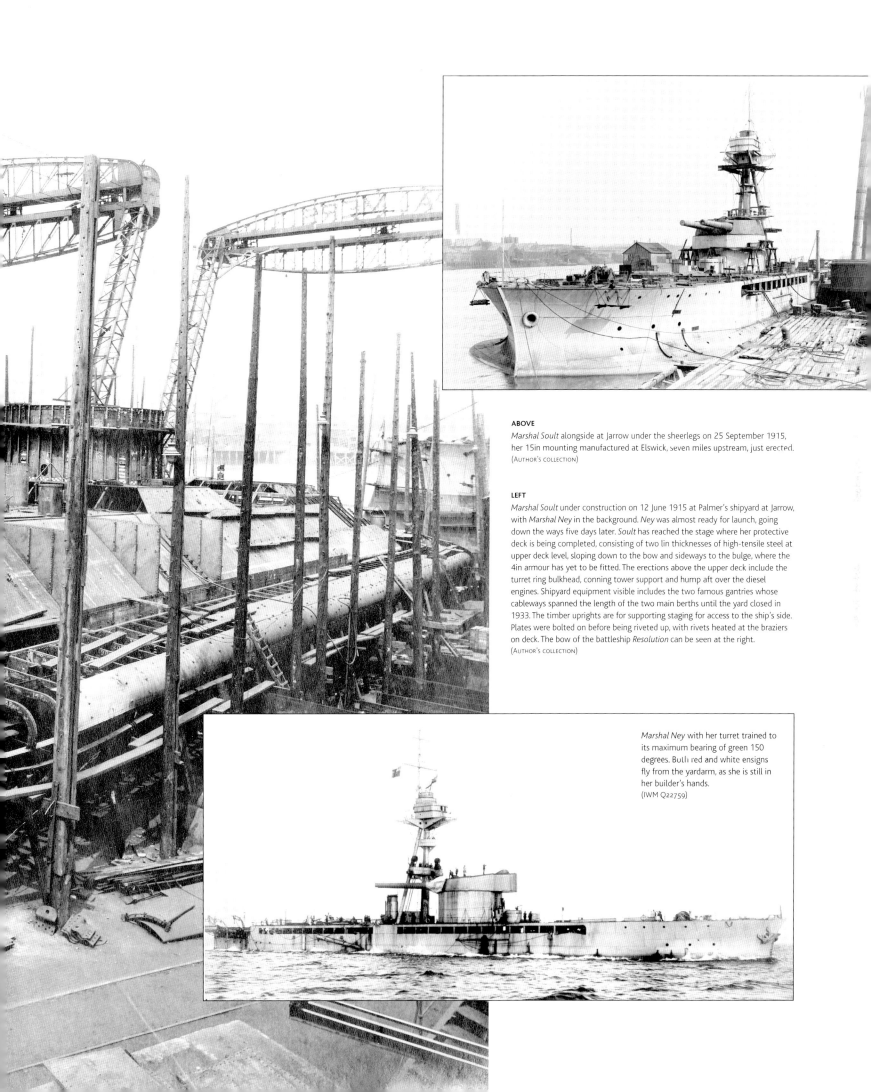

ABOVE

Marshal Soult alongside at Jarrow under the sheerlegs on 25 September 1915, her 15in mounting manufactured at Elswick, seven miles upstream, just erected. (Author's collection)

LEFT

Marshal Soult under construction on 12 June 1915 at Palmer's shipyard at Jarrow, with *Marshal Ney* in the background. *Ney* was almost ready for launch, going down the ways five days later. *Soult* has reached the stage where her protective deck is being completed, consisting of two 1in thicknesses of high-tensile steel at upper deck level, sloping down to the bow and sideways to the bulge, where the 4in armour has yet to be fitted. The erections above the upper deck include the turret ring bulkhead, conning tower support and hump aft over the diesel engines. Shipyard equipment visible includes the two famous gantries whose cableways spanned the length of the two main berths until the yard closed in 1933. The timber uprights are for supporting staging for access to the ship's side. Plates were bolted on before being riveted up, with rivets heated at the braziers on deck. The bow of the battleship *Resolution* can be seen at the right. (Author's collection)

Marshal Ney with her turret trained to its maximum bearing of green 150 degrees. Both red and white ensigns fly from the yardarm, as she is still in her builder's hands. (IWM Q22759)

decision to substitute 1,500bhp engines in place of the equivalent of about 2,000bhp in the slightly smaller 12in monitors had already meant the loss of about one knot in speed. The DNC's judgement was at fault in rejecting Froude's advice on redesigning the afterbody lines, especially as it would not have delayed construction.

4.2 Construction

The choice of a builder for *M.13* and *M.14* was not difficult. With *Repulse* transferred to Clydebank and *Resolution* launched on 14 January 1915, Palmer's two large building berths at Jarrow were now available (not being long enough for the lengthened *Repulse*), so contracts were rapidly placed. The first monitor was laid down at the end of January, while the second followed in mid-February on the adjacent berth. With completion expected in six months it was not possible to await delivery of *Renown's* and *Repulse's* fourth turrets, which were not due until 1916. As described on p.218, the deficiency was made good by transferring two of the turrets allocated to *Resolution's* sister, *Ramillies*. The cost of the turrets was not charged to the monitors, so the ships' estimated cost was only £270,000 each, compared with a probable £440,000 if built wholly from new.

Arrangements were made with Vickers and White to transfer the oilers' engines to Jarrow, where they were installed before the hulls were launched. Construction had been proceeding rapidly until the night before the launch of the first ship. In the early hours of 16 June the Zeppelin *L.10* raided the Tyne area. Attracted to Jarrow by the lights of Palmer's ironworks and workshops on night shift, it dropped twelve bombs. Severe damage and casualties were caused in the engine shops, and splinters hit the monitors. Damage to them was slight and the launch was postponed only one day. Captain H.J. Tweedie's wife launched *Marshal Ney* on 17 June, naming her after one of Napoleon's generals in tribute to Britain's WW1 ally. As well as being posted to command, Tweedie was also responsible for supervising completion and

proposing modifications. At his request a small navigating position was added halfway up the tripod mast to supplement the restricted conning tower beneath the guns. His Navigating Officer, Lt H.L. Morgan, was less successful in getting the position of her magnetic compass changed. It had been sited on a small platform on the mast just above the turret, so that whenever the latter's massive bulk trained round, the compass dutifully followed.

From Dover, Bacon repeatedly pressed for delivery as soon as possible; *Ney* was ready for trials on 26 August. Gunnery trials went off satisfactorily but her steering proved atrocious, as discussed later. Her MAN engines were found to be extremely difficult to start, exhausting a whole series of air bottles before success was achieved. Even when once started they were liable to stop whenever any change of load or speed occurred. The trials programme called for four hours' continuous steaming at full power, but this proved impossible to attain. When the news of *Ney's* dismal performance reached the Admiralty, serious consideration was given to cutting their losses with the 15in monitors by transferring their guns to other ships, as described later. Eventually, after several days' abortive trials, it was agreed to give *Ney* a chance to prove herself in service by accepting her from her builders if only one hour's continuous steaming could be obtained with both engines running. Her Engineer Officer, Lt D. Swan RNVR, who had been transferred from *Turmoil*, pulled out all the stops and got three hours' steaming out of her on the afternoon of 31 August. However, only about 6kts was obtained; like the steam monitors, about 3kts less than anticipated. The builder's men then left the ship, at 16.45 the tug *George V* took her in tow and together the pair set off for Dover at 6kts. Thus departed for action the RN's first diesel-powered surface warship. Her ungainly profile and utterly functional design, consisting only of one huge turret, tall mast and diminutive funnel projecting above the low hull, caused astonishment wherever she went.

The second ship was named *Marshal Soult* after another

The protection of the *Marshals* was basically similar to that of the 14in monitors, except for the turret and the hump necessitated by the height of the diesel engines. The sloping main deck forward, visible in the photograph on the previous spread, saved a little weight compared with a closing vertical bulkhead.

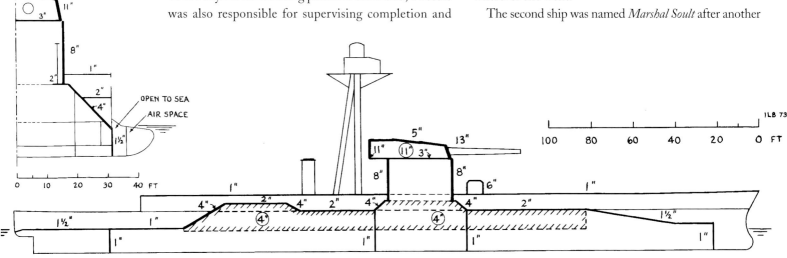

The RN's first 15in monitor, *Marshal
Ney*, leaves the Tyne for trials at the
end of August 1915. Details visible
include the 12pdr forward and the
3in HA aft.
(IWM SP122)

of Napoleon's generals. She followed about two months behind *Ney*, her engines proving much more reliable on trials. She could only make about 5kts as her engines were unable to develop full power at the designed rpm, having been fitted with wrongly pitched propellers. No official record of her displacement as completed exists, but analysis of the drafts recorded in her log show that her deep displacement was about 6,900 tons, with a draft about 5in deeper than designed. On this basis *Ney* would have been about 50 tons less, owing to her lighter engines. *Soult* left the Tyne on 3 November 1915 under Capt W.D. Paton, her future and that of her sister still under consideration.

4.3 Wartime Careers

As with the first of the 12in monitors, the original plan for sending *Marshal Ney* out to the Dardanelles had been cancelled and she had been allocated to the Dover Squadron. Her maiden voyage from the Tyne was an exciting one, as engine trouble continued to plague her. More often than not one or other of her engines was out of action. Her difficulties were accentuated by under-powered steering gear and poor response to the helm, so that, despite tug assistance, she was continually sheering off course, at times even making a complete 360-degree turn before control was regained. She eventually arrived at Sheerness on 3 September, going straight on to calibrate her guns on the Shoeburyness range, to adjust

the sights so that both guns fired to the required distance. It had been discovered by this time that the 12in monitors were outranged by the Tirpitz battery. Bacon was therefore anxious to get *Ney* into service as soon as possible to use her longer-range guns, so she was prepared for her first operation, that described on p.57. She was to steam inshore between Dunkirk and Nieuport, where it was thought that the Tirpitz guns could not bear. After waddling across to Dunkirk she joined the other monitors on 19 September in attempting to smother the fire of the coastal batteries. About midday *Ney* opened fire on Westende from 15,000yd, but she received no spotting reports as the only spotting station ashore could not obtain proper bearings from its acute angle to the line of fire. Tirpitz's guns soon showed that *Ney* was still within their arc of fire, so she was forced to withdraw out of range after only seven rounds. She returned later in the afternoon even closer off the beaches of La Panne and obtained rather better results, one hit being signalled out of sixteen rounds and the Germans being forced to evacuate temporarily the Aachen battery of four 150mm guns. Unfortunately the heavy blast from her guns blew the securing slip off the port anchor and the cable ran out while the ship was under way, bringing her to a complete halt. It proved impossible to heave the cable back in; neither could the starboard engine be started. Under power of the port engine she grounded lightly while, to add to her discomfort, Tirpitz had now found her range

Marshal Ney with her turret trained
on the broadside, probably on
gunnery trials. Blast bags are fitted
to each gun to prevent the blast
entering the turret through the gun
ports.
(IWM SP123)

and proceeded to surround her with uncomfortably close shell bursts. She soon got off the sandbank, only to find that her rudders had jammed and that the only motion possible was slow circling. Tweedie dared not stop his one remaining engine, so the destroyer *Viking* was ordered to tow her out of danger. This was successfully achieved under cover of a smokescreen, the passage back to Dunkirk being made at twice her normal speed.

She was back in action again on 25 September, supporting the big Army offensive. This time the Westende batteries were her target, receiving seventeen rounds before *Viking* again had to tow her away. A week later both engines again broke down before another bombardment. It was now abundantly clear that, if her great firepower was to be properly exploited, considerable modifications would be needed to her engines and steering gear to obtain reliable performance. So on 20 October she was drydocked at Southampton, where her rudders were modified and new steering gear was fitted. She then went across to Cowes to give her engine builders a chance to improve the starting and reversing characteristics of her diesels; of course no advice was available from the German designers.

Meanwhile, *Marshal Soult* had arrived at Dover on 6 November but had been despatched immediately to Portsmouth for a new set of propellers and to have her mine-wires removed. On her new trials she managed 6½kts without any trouble from her Vickers engines. She joined the Dover Squadron as an effective unit on 28 November and saw her first action on 23 December, when she bombarded the area around Westende Casino with six rounds. Two more similar sorties were made in late December, while on 15 and 26 January she again bombarded Westende, on the latter occasion in company with four of the 12in monitors.

Ney had arrived back at Dover on 13 December, as Bacon wanted her for supporting his planned attacks on Zeebrugge and Ostende (see p.58). But the next few weeks showed that her troubles had not really been cured. She remained as unmanageable as ever and her engines could never be relied upon, either to start or, once started, to continue running. Finally the ever-optimistic Swan had to admit defeat when a cylinder exploded, blowing parts of the engine through the deckhead. As *Soult* had shown herself a much more satisfactory performer, the Admiralty decided to cut their losses with *Ney*. By transferring her turret to one of the new fast monitors then building, they hoped to get her powerful armament back into service quickly. Accordingly *Ney* was despatched to the Tyne under tow, arriving at Elswick on 29 January

1916, where her turret was removed for transfer to *Terror*, under construction at Belfast. In April she returned to Portsmouth, where she was fitted with a reduced armament consisting of a single 9.2in and four single 6in. She was back in commission on 16 June, and new trials were undertaken with a moderate degree of success, so she returned hopefully to Dover. But her performance in service proved as bad as ever; her engines and steering prevented her from becoming an effective unit of the Squadron. She was sent back to Portsmouth, paying off for the second time on 15 August.

General patrol work occupied most of *Soult*'s time during 1916, involving occasional brushes with enemy aircraft and destroyers. It was September before she again used her 15in guns in earnest, supporting Haig's Somme offensive. Between 8 and 13 September she fired thirty-seven rounds of CPC, mostly at enemy 150mm coastal batteries. By firing from behind a smokescreen the safe firing range could be brought down to about 22,000yd. Shortly afterwards she was hit by a bomb while alongside at Dunkirk. By this time both *Erebus* and *Terror* had entered service, so *Soult* could be spared to have her gun mounting altered to give 10 degrees extra elevation up to 30 degrees, similar to the two new ships. She left for Elswick, arriving on 6 November, and returned to Dover on 12 March 1917 with her guns now capable of about 30,000yd range.

Meanwhile, further modifications had been made to *Ney* at Portsmouth. White's had another go at her engines, which performed quite well in basin trials at Portsmouth in December. But these were too late to save her from being relegated to a stationary role as a guardship. Merchant traffic along the south and east coast of England all passed through the special anchorage at the Downs off Ramsgate, where examination of vessels for blockade-running cargoes took place. Vessels also used the anchorage to lay up overnight or when enemy sorties or unswept minefields presented temporary dangers. Such a collection of ships formed a tempting target, which had to be well protected by destroyers and drifters, backed up by a 12in monitor when necessary. The need for strong protection was borne out when German destroyers raided the Downs in February and March 1917. Rather than employ one of his more active monitors, Bacon decided to convert *Ney* to a full-time guardship at the Downs, fitting her with six 6in guns. Her good underwater protection made her almost immune from U-boat attack, while her armament was still strong enough to drive off destroyers. She took up her station at the north end of the Downs on 5 April 1917, and was soon in action. On the morning of the 19th six German seaplanes appeared over the Goodwin Sands and two, which were carrying torpedoes, calmly circled *Ney* amidst a barrage of AA fire. One torpedo was dropped from low level but fortunately missed *Ney*, passed under a nearby dredger and embedded itself in the mud of Ramsgate Harbour. *Ney*'s chance came on 27 April, when she returned the fire of several destroyers shelling Ramsgate, who retired in the face of this strong opposition. Thereafter things became rather quieter as German destroyer raids virtually ceased, but she often used her HA guns against the night-time aircraft and Zeppelin raids. Not until after the Armistice did she leave her anchorage, where she had performed a dull but important service, being towed round to Sheerness on 12 December 1918.

In contrast, *Soult* saw considerable action over the next

Marshal Ney in her final WW1 appearance with six single 6in, two 3in HA and two 2pdr, plus an enlarged bridge structure. The view shows her as a motor launch base ship in the Medway early in 1919. (IWM SP154)

18 months, as Bacon was determined to make full use of his three 15in monitors. From early February 1917 he had been making detailed plans to bombard the lock gates of the Bruges Canal, which if damaged would seriously restrict the use of the important naval base at Bruges. It is worth describing the operation in some detail, as it well illustrates the difficulties the monitors faced in bombarding small targets on strongly defended coastlines. First the target: to put the lock out of action both gates needed to be hit, as otherwise passage could be made using only one gate, which could be opened for about two hours around high water. Each gate was only about 90ft × 30ft in size and invisible from the sea. Bacon calculated the chances of hitting such a target from 13 miles as one in sixty-three, but he halved the chances to allow for the difficulty of accurately laying a gun subject to all the motions of a ship. About 250 rounds would thus be required to hit both main lock gates, even before any consideration could be given to the spare gate kept nearby. Second the opportunity: to fire 250 rounds would take about 1½hr with three monitors each firing one round per minute. Such a rate was not difficult for the ships, but would be quite a strain on the spotters. But conditions had to be just right; a calm sea to prevent excessive rolling, no cloud or mist over the target so that the spotting aircraft would have a clear view, and the tide running along the coast to allow the ships to anchor broadside-on to the target. Third and most important of all, opposition: the monitors would have to fire from within the 41,000yd range of the Kaiser Wilhelm battery. This meant that an onshore wind was required so that the ML's smokescreen would continue to shield the monitors from view; that a dawn operation was desirable to achieve surprise before the enemy could retaliate seriously, jam the spotting wireless or cover the target with defensive smokescreens; that strong air patrols would be needed to prevent enemy aircraft or observation balloons spotting for their return fire, and to guard the British spotters. All in all, the chances of getting exactly the right conditions and then actually hitting the targets were slight, but Bacon judged the risks worthwhile to curb the U-boats by sealing one of their bases, despite the shortage of reliable 15in ammunition and spare guns post-Jutland. His plan was to anchor the three 15in monitors near to a predetermined position off Zeebrugge and for them to use a 12in monitor as a back aiming mark. To keep their approach within the hours of darkness, a speed of at least 9kts was required of the fleet, so each fast monitor would have to tow one of the slow ones.

All was ready by 25 March, but mist came down, forcing a postponement of the operation. A fortnight elapsed before the tides were once more suitable, but again on 8 April the weather proved too bad. On 18 April the start was delayed by *Erebus* fouling her propeller at Dunkirk and then, after the flotilla had got under way, *Soult* sheered off while being towed by *Terror*, breaking her towline. Further attempts during April were frustrated by the weather or other factors. Not until 11 May did everything again appear promising, when the 41-ship flotilla set off from Dover at about 18.00; *Terror* flying Bacon's flag and towing *Soult* at 10kts, *Erebus* towing *Sir John Moore*, followed by *M.24* and *M.26*, ten destroyers, six paddle minesweepers and nineteen MLs. They anchored in the firing position at about 04.20 on the 12th, but poor visibility forced *Moore* to anchor only 4,200yd off instead of the planned 12,000yd, thus seriously multiplying any errors of bearing. Of the three spotting aircraft, two had reported mechanical trouble and had been forced to land again, while the third had arrived as early as 03.00 and was running short of fuel by the time the monitors were in position.

Fire was opened at 04.45 from about 26,000yd, *Soult* and *Terror* taking the south gate as their target while *Erebus* took the north. The first ranging shots fell short but were soon corrected, and shooting settled down to a steady 20sec rhythm. Not all of the rounds could be spotted after their 54sec flight, as several did not burst, but the spotter reported hits with *Soult*'s twelfth round and *Erebus*'s twenty-sixth. The Germans put up smoke to screen the locks, but fortunately it was wrongly placed and did not hamper the British fire. By now Kaiser Wilhelm had begun to open fire, but the British smokescreen and strong air patrols prevented any worthwhile spotting, so after four rounds the Germans gave up. The thick white screen completely covered the ships from the shore, even hiding the red-brown cordite puffs and the occasional black smoke from their funnels. The spotting aircraft stayed as long as possible, but had to leave at 05.30, having run seriously short of fuel. Thereafter the monitors estimated their own corrections and ceased fire at 06.00, when the wind changed direction, but before a relief spotter could take over. The flotilla then retired to Dover, feeling that a good morning's work had been done: 175 rounds fired of which *Soult* had contributed fifty-one. Decorations awarded included five DSOs and ten DSMs. Subsequent reports and aerial photographs were disappointing as they showed that, although several shells had fallen very close, twenty-one of them within 50yd, no damage had been inflicted on the actual gates or pumphouses. The only results of this major effort were three enemy killed, four wounded, temporary damage to the lock pumphouse and some churned-up roads and railways, plus confirmation that the chances of hitting such small targets from long range in the face of

A close-up of *Marshal Soult*'s turret, showing the raised axis of the 15in guns permitting 30 degrees elevation. Ammunitioning is in progress at Dunkirk, with cordite cases lying on deck, each holding two 107lb quarter charges. The two 4in visible and the two 2pdr on platforms aft date the photograph as the spring of 1918. The conning tower has ceased to be used, the original searchlight platform being expanded instead. The chequer pattern was intended to confuse German rangefinders ashore and to blend into the ML's protective smokescreens.
(IWM SP926)

a host of practical difficulties were slim indeed.

The summer months of 1917 were spent on patrol, particularly from July while the 12in monitors were preparing for the Great Landing. This 'BO Patrol' consisted of one of the 15in monitors, two small monitors, a light cruiser and about nine destroyers. Arrangements were made for MLs and spotting aircraft to be on hand if conditions were favourable for bombardment. *Soult*'s first opportunity came on 4 September, when she put twenty-eight rounds into Ostende Dockyard, firing at maximum range while under way. She had another go at Ostende on 21 October, firing nineteen rounds and damaging some ships and exploding the magazine of a nearby AA battery, before the thickness of the enemy smokescreen prevented further shooting. For a short period at the end of October she was the only large monitor available for service, the other eight all being in dockyard hands. Favourable conditions for bombardment had largely disappeared with the onset of winter, so with the return of the other monitors *Soult* could be spared for a long refit at Portsmouth, which lasted from January to April 1918.

Soult's role in the forthcoming Zeebrugge raid was a relatively minor one of diversionary bombardment with three of the 12in monitors described on p.64. While waiting for the operation to take place she went out on the night of 17/18 April to fire on coastal batteries west of Ostende with *Erebus*, *Terror* and *Prince Eugene*, using *M.26* as an aiming mark. Following up the Zeebrugge raid, a bombardment was made on 9 June by *Soult* and *Terror* with *M.21* to harass enemy dredgers and salvage craft attempting to remove the blockships. The monitors opened fire from 27,000yd at 13.08 but, as the wind direction was unfavourable, no smokescreen could shield them. The enemy return fire soon became uncomfortably accurate, so after twenty-five rounds each the monitors retired to Dunkirk. *Soult*'s last bombardment of the war came on 29 July, when she and *Gorgon*, again with *M.21* as aiming mark, took on the Tirpitz battery in co-operation with Allied artillery ashore. Although the target was only 28,500yd off, her guns had fired 210efc (equivalent full charges) each and could only reach this distance by heeling the ship. Flooding the bulges increased the effective gun elevation to 33 degrees, and she was able to fire ten rounds before a combination of inadequate stern anchor, faulty firing mechanisms and about thirty retaliatory rounds from Tirpitz forced her to retire.

The next few weeks were mainly spent on the Dover Barrage patrol, guarding the deep anti-submarine mine-fields. She was back at Portsmouth for docking on 13 September, and thus missed the heaviest bombardment of the war. By the time she was back at Dunkirk the Germans had evacuated the Belgian Coast, so she was sent round to Chatham to await a decision on her future, where she arrived on 25 October 1918.

4.4 Performance and Modifications

The news of *Marshal Ney*'s trials had come as a great disappointment to the Admiralty. Here was a ship, carrying two of the most powerful guns afloat, which was not only even slower than the earlier 7kt monitors, with machinery incapable of continuous running, but which was not even able to steer a defined course. As early as

September 1915, Tudor, a gunnery specialist, had suggested removing her turret and installing it in a new monitor. Admiral H.B. Jackson, the new First Sea Lord, was in agreement about removing *Ney*'s turret, but suggested rearming both *Ney* and *Soult* with the 12in twin mountings from the pre-dreadnoughts *Caesar* or *Illustrious*. The alternative solution of re-engining *Ney* with steam reciprocating machinery was also considered. The existing engine and boiler rooms could accommodate a twin-screw installation of about 3,600ihp, but even this roughly doubled power would give at most 8kts.

However, Bacon's urgent need for ships with guns of longer range than the existing 12in overrode these plans for modifying the *Marshals*. *Ney* was temporarily reprieved, while it was appreciated that *Soult*'s different engines might turn out to be more satisfactory. In service, however, *Ney*'s performance was quite as bad as her trials had foreshadowed. She could neither steam nor steer with any degree of certainty. The steering problems arose largely from the bluff lines aft, which produced a deadness of flow around the rudders and propellers. As a result she possessed neither directional stability nor any ability to correct a swing once it had been induced by excessive use of the helm. She excelled herself on 15 October, when entering Dunkirk harbour. Her steering gear failed, her engines refused to go astern and even dropping both anchors failed to stop her. She punched a neat semi-circular hole 90ft across in the wooden pier, although she herself rebounded undamaged.

Despite their unsatisfactory performance in service, her MAN engines had run faultlessly on their 96hr test-bed trials at Cowes in December 1914. The starboard engine had developed 752bhp at 190.5rpm, burning 0.487lb of oil per horsepower per hour, with a mechanical efficiency of 62 per cent. This was a good specific fuel consumption compared with steam reciprocators, but slightly higher than some other designs of diesel, partly owing to the power absorption of the shaft-driven air compressors and the large scavenge pumps below the pistons needed to work the four-stroke cycle efficiently. In service there was found to be a fault in the design of the reversing gear, which partly accounted for the engines' erratic performance. Various modifications were tried, but the engines never proved sufficiently reliable for regular service.

Tweedie remained cheerful in the face of all these difficulties, but his crew were bitterly disappointed. They had had such high hopes of achievement and were disgusted at the failure of the ship due to no fault of their own. Their Lordships were not prepared to recognise that any of the blame was theirs in insisting on diesels and in not permitting any changes to an unsatisfactory hull form.

Thus, even though the two primarily responsible, Churchill and Fisher, were no longer in office, it was ruled that none of *Ney*'s officers or men would receive any official recognition of their time of service in her; 'a damnable injustice', as Lt Morgan later wrote.

Tweedie proved a popular commanding officer. On occasion he himself would take the helm under tricky conditions, such was his feel for the ship. Life aboard *Ney* during her brief offensive career was certainly hectic, but there was time to entertain visiting French officers while based at Dunkirk. On spotting the framed wardroom picture of Marshal Ney they would leap to their feet, don their kepis and stand to attention in front of the portrait, saluting and solemnly intoning 'Le Maréchal Ney, le brave des braves'. On the first occasion the British officers were somewhat disconcerted, but scrambled to their feet, hunted for their own caps and sheepishly mumbled 'Le brave des braves' in their best French accents. Thereafter the picture was usually removed temporarily while French officers were aboard.

The modifications that were eventually made to *Ney* in 1916 were not as extensive as originally envisaged. Although her turret was transferred to *Terror*, her diesel machinery was retained. In place of the 15in twin mounting a much lighter mounting was fitted; one of the two single 9.2in Mk VIII 40cal guns recently removed from the old first-class cruiser *Terrible*, the other being earmarked for *Soult*, although never fitted. Four single 6in QF were also transferred from *Terrible* and sited two on either side abreast the funnel. The director and topmast were removed, but a modest bridge structure was added to improve navigational facilities. She did not remain long in this state, and another extensive refit took place during 1916-17. The 9.2in was removed and mounted ashore in France, and *Ney* was given a uniform armament of six single 6in BL XI removed from the pre-dreadnought *Hibernia*. Two were sited on the centreline, one forward and one aft, while the other four were placed abreast the mast; each gun had one hundred rounds of ammunition. A fully enclosed bridge structure was provided, no doubt much appreciated by the cold and bored watchkeepers during the long months she lay at the Downs. The 12pdrs were removed and two new 3in HA fitted aft to augment her existing 2pdr. The only other noticeable change was the emergence of the bulge above the waterline, as the removal of some 1,100 tons net reduced her displacement to about 5,780 tons deep and her drafts to 7ft forward and 10ft aft.

Soult's service performance was an improvement on *Ney*'s, though hardly spectacular. A cruising speed of only 5½kts, in waters where tidal currents reached 3kts and gales were frequent, meant that sometimes the quickest progress could be made by anchoring and waiting for

Following her 1918 refit, *Soult* emerged as one of the RN's ugliest ships, with her lengthened funnel and gawky appearance. Her armament now includes eight 4in, two 12pdr HA (under the 15in guns), two 3in HA and two 2pdr. She is seen here at Devonport in 1920. (ABRAHAMS)

better conditions, as otherwise she was inclined to be driven astern, or at least sideways. The two *Marshal*s were often bracketed together when maligning diesel propulsion, but in fact *Soult*'s Vickers engines proved extremely reliable, quiet and free from vibration. Indeed, the replacements fitted in *Trefoil* in 1917 likewise gave excellent service, confirming the suitability of solid injection in four-stroke engines. The engines were usually supplied with either shale oil or Texas fuel oil, as used in submarine diesels. Endurance under ideal conditions was about 2,000 miles, but making allowance for oil for her boilers, weather, hull fouling and unusable fuel, the official figure was reduced to 1,490 miles. In practice, *Soult* never made a voyage of more than 200 miles without tug assistance, so this figure was never put to the test.

Soult's visible modifications during 1916-17 were relatively few: two 6in QF II (one from *Ney*) and a 3in HA added on the forecastle deck, and the topmast struck. A better navigational position was built on the tripod mast above the turret level, painted in distinctive grey-and-white chequers. The main modification was not readily apparent; the raising of the axis of the 15in guns about 2ft to permit them to elevate to 30 degrees. 1918 saw further modifications; first, four single 4in BL IX replaced the 6in. The 4in not only had a longer range than the 6in, but a much faster rate of fire. Then later in the year came the really startling changes which transformed her from being merely bizarre in appearance into what must surely have been the RN's ugliest ship. The most offending feature was a funnel doubled in height yet of the original diameter. Its proportions were thus those of a 30ft-long cigarette, totally disproportionate to the size of ship. Two 36in searchlights were added on tall lattice platforms abaft the funnel to replace the two 24in on the tripod mast. A control position was fitted aft and the conning tower removed. The latter was replaced by a platform carrying the two 12pdr, now converted to HA. The secondary armament was increased to eight single 4in distributed along the sides of the forecastle deck. Two single 2pdrs were retained on their platform aft, as well as two 3in HA at the break of the forecastle.

The problems of *Marshal Ney* formed one of the elements of the Churchill-Balfour controversy in the House of Commons in March 1916. Returning from France to make a speech in the Navy Estimates debate, Churchill attacked Balfour and the new Board of the Admiralty for the slowing down in the rate of construction. He compared the rapidity with which the monitor fleet had been completed with the subsequent delays in battleship construction. While he stretched a point when he claimed that the monitors had been finished in six months (the average time was eight months), there was some substance in his accusation. None of the five *Royal Sovereign*s had been completed, although contract completion dates had all been at the end of 1915. Balfour was stung to reply at length the next day, 8 March. He ridiculed Churchill for claiming credit for the speedy construction of the monitors while in the same breath criticising the delay with the battleships, pointing out that the former had only been achieved by using guns and mountings ordered for the latter. Balfour's excuse about diversions of gun mountings was a bit thin, as it only applied to two out of the fourteen big-gun monitors, the *Marshal*s, and he was quickly taken up on this point by Sir A. Markham, Liberal MP for Mansfield, who pointed out that the monitor guns had come from America. Yes, conceded Balfour, but not all of them. No mention was made of the fact that only one shipbuilder had a battleship in hand at the same time as monitors, namely Palmer. It is of course quite possible that Churchill had forgotten, or indeed had never been informed, that it had been two of *Ramillies*' turrets which had been used, rather than those from *Renown* and *Repulse*, because in *The World Crisis* he describes the turrets as coming from the 'furthest off battleships (now converted into battlecruisers)'. *Ramillies*' completion was delayed for a year, but this was partly due to the fitting of bulges.

Although his case was scarcely any stronger than Churchill's, Balfour proceeded to wade in with further criticism of the monitor fleet. Although they were doing good service, they added nothing to the strength of the Grand Fleet and, furthermore, they had design faults.

So hastily was the design of some of these vessels and so ill were they contrived to carry out their purpose that even now it has not been found possible to use some of them for the purpose for which they were originally designed. They are in process of being remodelled or remodelled so as to make them suitable for this amphibious warfare. The design was hasty, the execution was hasty and the result is therefore as might easily be expected not always satisfactory.'[3]

To speak of 'some' of the monitors having to be remodelled was quite unfair, as such a description could only be applied with any accuracy to but one vessel, *Marshal Ney*. Markham again came to Churchill's rescue, saying that although alterations had been made, they were not due in any way to the latter's 'hasty action' but rather to 'another cause', which he did not specify. Presumably he meant that it would be unfair to blame Churchill for not foreseeing the failure of *Ney*'s diesels. However, it could reasonably be argued that it was rather foolhardy of Churchill and Fisher to authorise such an untried form of prime mover for a combatant ship in wartime, especially a design with no previous operational experience. There was no overriding necessity to have taken engines already under construction, as steam reciprocators could easily have been built in the time available, as witnessed by McKie & Baxter's completion of *Prince Rupert*'s machinery in three months.

Of course, few of the MPs present could follow the significance of the allusions and vague accusations in the speeches, as the details of the construction programme of the battleships and monitors had not been made public and no ships' names were mentioned during the debate. The outcome of this particular aspect of the debate was

inconclusive, but at least 1916 did see the completion of six more capital ships.

4.5 Twilight Careers

Even before the Armistice was signed, the Admiralty realised that in *Marshal Soult* they had a very suitable ship for gunnery instruction. She carried an example of the RN's latest big-gun mounting, while her poor seagoing characteristics were no handicap for a harbour-based ship. Her upkeep costs would be modest compared with a battleship, yet she had all that was necessary for turret and director instruction. She left Chatham on 14 November 1918 to become a tender to HMS *Excellent*, the gunnery training school at Portsmouth. Four months later she was transferred to Devonport for similar duties. There she remained as Director and Fire Control Ship until March 1921, when she paid off and was put on the non-effective list. After *Glorious*, which had relieved her, had been taken in hand for conversion to an aircraft carrier, *Soult* was reinstated for gunnery instruction. She started a £35,000 refit at Portsmouth in May 1924 to bring her up to the mark, and by March 1925 she was back at Devonport as Turret Drill Ship.

Proposals for the defences of the new base to be created at Singapore were discussed in 1923 by the Admiralty and War Office. Consideration was given to stationing all three 15in monitors there (*Soult*, *Erebus* and *Terror*) but the idea was rejected in favour of shore batteries. *Soult* and *Erebus* exchanged places in April 1926, when the former berthed in No.3 Basin at Chatham, which remained her home for the next 14 years, apart from brief trips to Portsmouth for drydocking. In addition to her drill ship role, her duties also included Senior Officer Reserve Fleet, Royal Naval Reserve Training Ship and Accommodation Ship at the Nore, for which her official complement was 203. None of those duties were particularly onerous, and Cdr Spooner, who had been *Abercrombie*'s 'First and G' in the Mediterranean, remembered his period in command in 1928 as a relaxing spell of long weekends and leisurely Tuesday-to-Thursday working. In the event of mobilisation it was intended that she would pay off so that her crew could be drafted to active ships.

Marshal Ney was also put to good use after the war, although nominally on the Disposal List. In February 1919 she was base ship for MLs at Queenborough in the Medway. In September she moved back to Sheerness as an accommodation ship. She was sent round to Portsmouth in August 1920 to act as submarine school depot ship at Fort Blockhouse in place of the old cruiser *Arrogant*. For this role she was completely disarmed and her tripod mast removed. On 12 July 1922 she arrived

at Devonport to replace *Harlech* (originally the 1893 cruiser *Cambrian*) attached to the Stoker Training Establishment, and was renamed *Vivid* after the RN Barracks whose tender she officially was. She remained at Devonport for the rest of her service life, another 35 years. In her later days she became almost unrecognisable as a former monitor, her forecastle deck being buried under a mass of huts providing additional accommodation. For most of this time she remained in the dockyard, taking the parent name *Drake* in 1934. She saw out WW2, providing valuable accommodation when the barracks were bombed. She was renamed yet again in 1947, this time *Alaunia II*, as she formed part of the stoker training establishment, which included the repair ship *Alaunia*, a recently converted ex-Cunarder. She was finally disposed of in 1957, being handed over to BISCO,[4] who allocated her to T.W. Ward for scrapping at Milford Haven. Thus departed the least successful but longest-lived of all the large monitors.

Following the outbreak of WW2 the question of putting *Soult* back into active service was considered. However, a survey showed that while new engines could be installed to give 8kts, her hull was not worth refitting and it would be better to transfer her turret to a new hull. This was carried out as described in Chapter 9, so one of the turrets originally intended for *Ramillies* continued in service in a second *Roberts* for another quarter-century. *Soult* was towed to Portsmouth for the removal of her turret, as she was too beamy to enter No. 1 Basin at Chatham where the heavy-lift sheer legs were situated. She arrived on 11 March 1940, where Vickers-Armstrongs[5] refitted the turret before it was despatched to the new monitor building on the Clyde. *Soult* took up her new role as base ship for naval trawlers in December, providing administrative and maintenance facilities from her berth in the pocket of No.3 Basin. During the heavy German air attacks of 1941 she proved a popular ship, as her armoured decks made her a first-class air raid shelter. She was hit only once during these attacks, receiving a bomb forward

on the forecastle deck on 11 March, but suffered only splinter damage. She remained a trawler base ship all through the war, succouring in addition kindred vessels such as motor minesweepers and motor fishing vessels. During the Normandy landings she serviced over 200 of the various small craft taking part. She finally paid off on 31 March 1946, and four months later was towed to Troon on the Firth of Clyde for breaking up.

The Marshals – TECHNICAL DATA

Displacement: 6,670 tons Navy List, 6,900 tons deep on 10ft 5in draft, 6,050 tons light on 9ft 1½in.

Dimensions: Length 355ft 8in oa, 340ft 0in bp, breadth 90ft 3in oa, 62ft 0in main hull, depth to forecastle deck 25ft 10in.

Weight distribution as designed (tons): Armament 850, ammunition 290, protection 2,140, hull 2,600, equipment 220, machinery 450, oil fuel (nominal) 100. Total 6,650 tons.

Complement: 13 officers, 174 men.

Armament: 2 x 15in (twin) (100 CPC rpg), 2 x 12pdr (200rpg), 1 x 3in HA (*Ney*) (300rpg), 1 x 3pdr Vickers HA (*Soult*) (500rpg), 2 x 2pdr HA (1,000rpg), 4 x 0.303in Maxim (5,000rpg).

Protection: As 14in monitors except: upper deck over 15in magazine 4in NC; main deck forward 1½in HT; barbette 8in; gunhouse 13in C front, 11in C sides and rear, 5in NC roof, 3in HT floor.

Machinery: Twin-screw diesels. *Ney:* two 6-cyl MAN 14½in bore x 24in stroke by J.S. White, Cowes, 1,500bhp at 185rpm. *Soult:* two 8-cyl Vickers 17in x 27in by Vickers, Barrow, (No. 442) 1,500bhp at 150rpm. Oil fuel 226 tons.

Endurance: 1,490 miles at 5½kts on 0.6 tons oil per hour (*Soult*).

Speed: 9kts designed, 6 service. Trials: *Ney* 6.3, *Soult* 6.61kts.

Construction: Palmer, Jarrow: *Marshal Ney* (No. 859) laid down Jan 1915/launched 17.6.15/completed 31.8.15; *Marshal Soult* (No. 860) Feb 1915/24.8.15/2.11.15.

Scrapped: *Ney* Handed over to BISCO and allocated to T.W. Ward, arrived Milford Haven 6.10.57; *Soult* Handed over to BISCO 10.7.46 and allocated to West of Scotland Shipbreaking, arrived Troon 5.8.46.

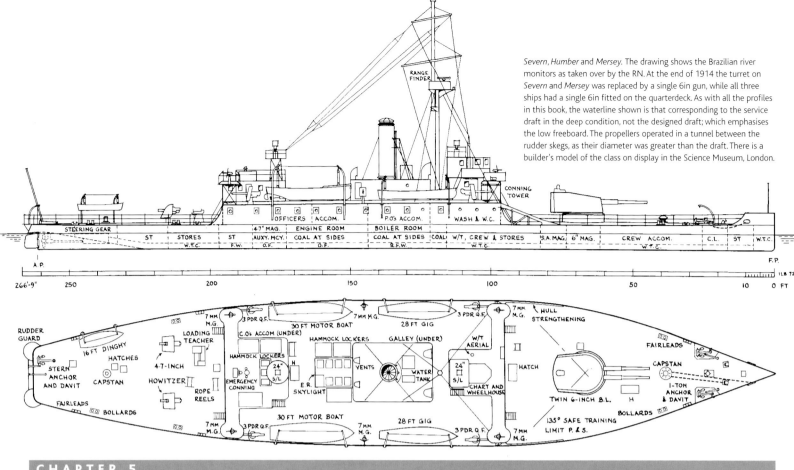

Severn, *Humber* and *Mersey*. The drawing shows the Brazilian river monitors as taken over by the RN. At the end of 1914 the turret on *Severn* and *Mersey* was replaced by a single 6in gun, while all three ships had a single 6in fitted on the quarterdeck. As with all the profiles in this book, the waterline shown is that corresponding to the service draft in the deep condition, not the designed draft; which emphasises the low freeboard. The propellers operated in a tunnel between the rudder skegs, as their diameter was greater than the draft. There is a builder's model of the class on display in the Science Museum, London.

CHAPTER 5

The Ex-Brazilian River Monitors

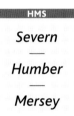

5.1 Origins

The small Brazilian river monitors taken over at the beginning of WW1 had been one of the catalysts which brought the larger monitors into existence, but both in their conception and subsequent deployment they differed considerably from their successors. The naval rivalry between South American countries and the profits from rubber exports formed the basis of a large expansion of the Brazilian Navy between 1907 and 1912. Late in 1911 negotiations were undertaken with Vickers, Son & Maxim at Barrow for vessels for the inland waters of the River Amazon; Armstrong was also approached. Three shallow-draft river monitors were required, to be well armed and well protected for their size. The Vickers design was for a vessel of about 1,200 tons carrying two 6in 50cal guns in one twin turret forward, on a draft of 4ft 6in. To obtain such a shallow draft a very beamy hull was necessary, 261ft 6in BP by 49ft. The compact twin

6in turret was an improved version of that fitted in the British *Monmouth*-class cruisers. The magazine and machinery spaces would be protected by 3in side armour, with 1in deck protection, the double bottom extending up behind the belt. Twin-screw steam reciprocating machinery to be built by Vickers with dual coal/oil-fired boilers was designed to give a trial speed of about 12kts. A powerful secondary armament was also fitted: two single 120mm (4.72in) howitzers aft, four Vickers 3pdrs and six machine guns. The main hull was only a single deck deep (8ft 6in), but with the wide superstructure there was sufficient space for accommodation well equipped for extended operations, complete with sick bay, refrigerated stores and even a prison cell.

Vickers' proposal was accepted by the Brazilians in January 1912. The three vessels were built broadside on to the water. All were named after tributaries of the Amazon: *Javary*, *Solimões* and *Madeira*. *Javary* was the first to be completed, steaming off to the Clyde in October 1913 for drydocking and trials. Although she proved capable of exceeding her contract speed of 11½kts going ahead, it was found impossible to manoeuvre her astern. As the diameter of her propellers was greater than her draft at normal load (5ft 7in *vs* 4ft 9in), they were arranged to work in a tunnel swept up into the hull. The shape was found to be such that a proper flow of water could not be obtained going astern, but the problem could be overcome by arranging a hinged flap to drop over the stern when required. Her twin rudders were increased in size, necessitating an increase of 21in in overall length to protect them. Gun trials were also undertaken at the same time. They showed up the high stress concentration at the forward end of the superstructure where it joined the main hull, necessitating strengthening of the hulls amidships by riveting a doubler plate along the edge of the boat deck and running it down to meet the upper deck abreast the turret.

The modifications were completed by December, when *Solimões* started her trials, followed by *Madeira* in February 1914. All three monitors were now complete and ready for their delivery voyage to Rio, but the Brazilians were now not in a position to be able to pay for the ships. Rubber prices had dropped dramatically in 1913 with competition from the newly established Malayan plantations, and Brazil could no longer afford

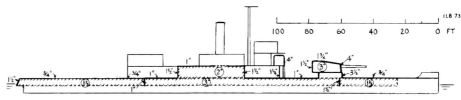

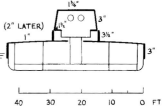

the luxury of expanding her navy. The three monitors were put up for sale at about the same time as the battleship *Rio de Janeiro*, which was sold to Turkey in December 1913. But river gunboats were not such a saleable proposition as battleships during the pre-war frenzy of capital ship construction among all the naval powers, large and small, so they remained laid up in the Devonshire Dock at Barrow. There were no takers, although the Romanians did inspect them.

Just before the outbreak of war Churchill expressed his concern about the possibility of their falling into enemy hands, minuting to the Third Sea Lord on 1 August 1914:

Simultaneously with the order to mobilise, you should notify the firms building foreign ships which are almost completed, viz the two Turkish battleships, destroyers at Messrs White and the three Brazilian monitors, of our intention in the event of war to enter into negotiations for their purchase, and warn them not to permit them to pass into foreign hands or leave the country.[1]

ABOVE
All the hull protection in *Severn*, *Humber* and *Mersey* was worked structurally except for the 3in belt. At the end of 1914 a further inch was added to the deck protection over the 6in magazine forward.

BELOW
A rare view of *Javary* passing Clydebank on her way down-river after drydocking at Glasgow in October 1913 prior to her trials. Ordered from Vickers by Brazil in January 1912, she was taken over by the RN in August 1914 and renamed *Humber*.
(JOHN BROWN)

Immediate arrangements were made to take them over for the RN on 3 August, a price of £155,000 being agreed with Vickers for each vessel, made up as follows:

Armament	£28,000
Machinery	£23,667
Hull and protection	£103,333
Total	**£155,000**

The price was high at about £120 per ton, comparable with a destroyer, reflecting the elaborate fittings and the special weight-saving construction techniques, and perhaps also a high profit margin built into the original export contract.

Although no specific use was envisaged for the monitors, they had the advantage of being complete and ready for service, while of course they would be denied to other possible belligerents. Things moved fast: declaration of war on the 4th, arrival of the COs and crews at Barrow on the 5th and commissioning on the 8th. The new names chosen were those of English rivers with initial letters as near to those of the Brazilian names as possible: *Solimões* became HMS *Severn*, *Madeira* HMS *Mersey* and *Javary* HMS *Humber*. The Senior Officer of the squadron, Cdr E.J.A. Fullerton, took *Severn* as his ship, Cdr A.L. Snagge *Humber* and Lt-Cdr R.A. Wilson *Mersey*. By 25 August the vessels had been prepared for RN service and were manoeuvred out into the Walney Channel with tug assistance. New speed trials were carried out but, instead of her previous 12kts, *Humber* could manage only 9.67, over two knots less than she had done ten months earlier. The explanation was twofold: a much deeper draft fully loaded and the fouling that had taken place during her long lay-up. Subsequent experience showed that it was almost impossible for the monitors to reach double figures even under the most favourable conditions, yet all official publications continued to show their authorised speed as an unrealistic 12kts.

The three ex-river gunboats were initially allocated to the Dover Patrol, responsible for protecting the Straits and the shipping to France and around the English coast from any German attacks. *Severn* and *Mersey* departed in company from Barrow immediately after completion of their trials, while *Humber* proceeded independently. The 3½-day voyage to Dover turned out to be a nerve-wracking introduction to navigating river craft outside sheltered waters. A strong gale blew up in the Irish Sea, causing waves to wash right over the monitors' upper decks and the hatches on their forecastles which provided the access to the crew's quarters. The messes were soon flooded and the men had to be evacuated to the wardroom at the after end of the superstructure. The monitors demonstrated quite clearly that they were unsuited to open sea operation, and that in any force of wind they were blown all over the surface of the water. They eventually reached Dover on 29 August after a most uncomfortable voyage averaging only 7½kts.

5.2 Wartime Operations

No sooner had the three monitors arrived at Dover than they were ordered to Ostende to embark Marines being evacuated to England. Early on 31 August they left Dover, undertaking gunnery trials on the way. After arriving at Ostende late in the evening they found that the Marines had already been evacuated. They were sent back to the Medway, whence they carried out patrols in the Thames Estuary for the next six weeks. The opportunity was taken for Chatham Dockyard to add an extra inch of deck protection over the 6in magazine, making 2in in all.

Meantime the 'Race to the Sea' was taking place in France as the Allied and German armies each attempted to envelop the other's flank after the initial rapid German advance had been finally halted on the River Aisne northeast of Paris. Following the fall of Antwerp on 9 October, other German forces were racing westwards towards the Channel ports, and soon virtually the whole of Belgium had been overrun right up to Ostende. The Belgian Army was attempting to hold the line of the River Yser, about ten miles east of the French border, from the sea at Nieuport inland towards Ypres, where the British Expeditionary Force was being equally hard pressed by the Germans. (see map on p.55)

On 10 October *Severn*, *Humber* and *Mersey* had left Sheerness in response to orders to provide naval cover off the Belgian Coast and to prevent any enemy landings behind the Allied lines. They anchored off Ostende the next day to assist troop withdrawal by sea before the town was finally overrun. On the way back to Dover *Severn* was attacked by *U.8*, whose torpedo, fired from only 300yd away, passed underneath her shallow hull. A squadron, which included the light cruiser *Attentive*, the three monitors and several other vessels, was then formed under Rear-Admiral Hood, hitherto Churchill's Naval Secretary, who had just arrived to take over the newly created Dover Command. Requests for assistance on their sea flank had been received from the hard-pressed Belgians, so on 16 October the squadron was ordered up in close support. But the weather was too bad for the low-freeboard monitors to proceed safely from Dover, and it was not until the 18th that they arrived off Nieuport. Their principal duties were to break up any movements of German troops, particularly along the coastal road from Ostende to Nieuport, and to prevent any enemy movements by sea. By mid-morning the Belgium Army was asking for naval gunfire to be directed at inland targets

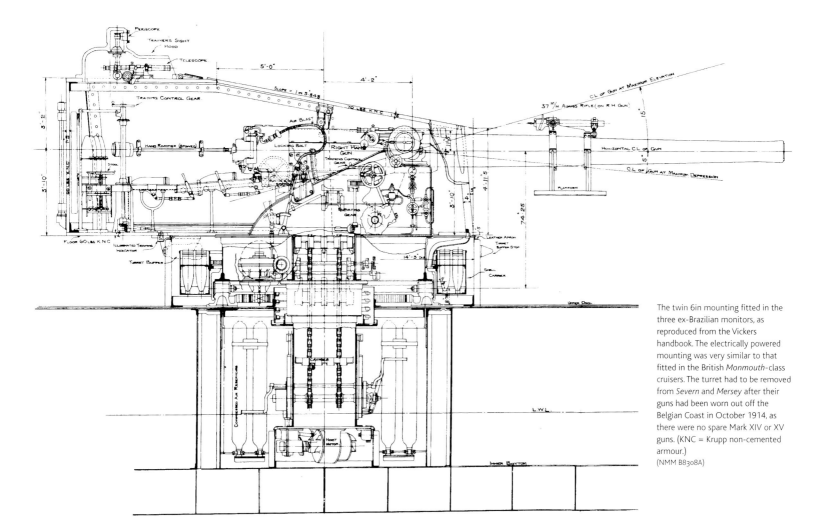

The twin 6in mounting fitted in the three ex-Brazilian monitors, as reproduced from the Vickers handbook. The electrically powered mounting was very similar to that fitted in the British *Monmouth*-class cruisers. The turret had to be removed from *Severn* and *Mersey* after their guns had been worn out off the Belgian Coast in October 1914, as there were no spare Mark XIV or XV guns. (KNC = Krupp non-cemented armour.)
(NMM B8308A)

east of Nieuport. From 2,000yd offshore the shallow-draft monitors were able to pour a heavy fire from their 6in guns and 4.7in howitzers on to enemy forces advancing on Westende, only 2 miles north-east of Nieuport. The enemy returned fire with field guns and, although none of the monitors received a direct hit, shrapnel wounded several men aboard *Humber* and *Mersey*. The monitors then lengthened the range to 10,000yd, where they were out of reach of the enemy guns. For the rest of the day continuous fire was kept up, directed by wireless messages from the Belgian headquarters, as the targets were out of sight from the sea, behind the sand dunes, and no proper spotting facilities yet existed. Firing continued the next day at various targets, including howitzers at Slype which were severely harrassing the Belgians. In the afternoon a Belgian officer arrived in *Severn* to assist co-operation, reporting that the bombardment had put fresh heart into the Belgian troops to defend the last remaining corner of their homeland.

On the 20th machine-gun parties were landed from the monitors, while the ships themselves were heavily engaged in repulsing the attack on Westende. By the afternoon all their ammunition had been shot off and the

monitors retired to Dunkirk to replenish. They were back in action on the 22nd, the squadron having been reinforced by a makeshift collection of bombarding vessels, including the old cruisers *Brilliant* and *Sirius*, the sloops *Vestal*, *Rinaldo* and *Wildfire* (CO Cdr Altham) and the ancient gunboats *Hazard*, *Excellent* and *Bustard*. For the next ten days fire was kept up whenever the opportunity arose and the weather permitted. The arrival of the pre-dreadnought *Venerable*, with her four 12in guns, helped stabilise the position later, but not before Westende had fallen. The bombardments from the sea had, however, caused the German troops great concern, considerably hampering their movement. They requested as many U-boats as possible to be sent to attack the British ships.

By now the monitors were feeling the strain of continuous action, both crews and hulls. *Mersey*'s turret had broken down on the 28th, *Severn*'s left 6in was badly scored and high rates of fire were overheating the guns, rapidly shortening their life and causing a reduction of over 2,000yd in maximum range. As the enemy entrenched themselves more firmly along the coast, heavier guns were brought up which soon inflicted damage on several of the other bombarding vessels as well as near-missing *Severn* and *Humber*. By 1 November the position ashore had fully stabilised, French reinforcements had arrived and the Nieuport sluice-gates had been opened, flooding low-lying areas to restrict further German advances. Although the German thrusts had been halted, the Allied counterattacks were unable to make any progress towards recovering Ostende, still less Antwerp. There was little more the monitors could do, so, as the U-boats were becoming more active, *Severn* and *Mersey* returned to the Medway on 3 November. *Humber* followed a week later after a final bombardment of Westende on the 7th in support of a French attack. The

not so badly worn she kept her turret, while *Severn* and *Mersey*'s four guns were sent for relining as spares for *Humber*. The 4.7in howitzers were moved from the quarterdeck to the boat deck, and a single Hotchkiss 3pdr HA was added in place of the after 24in searchlight, the latter being moved to a new platform further aft.

An invasion scare blew up during November, a possible landing being suspected in the shallow waters of the Wash. The heavily armed light-draft monitors would be ideal for resisting such an operation, so all three were hurried round to the Lincolnshire port of Boston, where they remained for three weeks until the scare receded in

A close-up of *Humber* (outboard), *Severn* and *Mersey* at Malta in April 1915. Only *Mersey* has her 3pdr HA gun actually mounted, and much equipment has yet to be replaced following the tow from England. (IWM Q46198)

Intended for operations up the Danube should the Gallipoli Expedition be successful, the three river monitors are seen here at Malta in April 1915. From left to right, *Mersey*, *Severn* and *Humber* are berthed alongside their depot ship, *Trent*. (IWM Q46200)

Germans later testified that the presence of the bombarding fleet had played a vital part in stabilising the Allied line during those critical October days, preventing a German advance to Dunkirk, Calais and Boulogne, whose loss would have been a severe handicap to British support of subsequent naval and military operations.

The next few weeks were spent in Chatham Dockyard, replacing worn-out guns. As there were no spare 6in Mks XIV and XV (as the RN designated the right- and left-hand versions of the Vickers' design), consideration was given to replacing the entire turrets with the spare mountings for the *Monmouth* class. The necessary conversion work was found to be too extensive, so the turrets were removed altogether from *Severn* and *Mersey* and replaced by two single 6in BL VII of very similar performance, one forward behind a steel breastwork and one aft. Two of the guns had been salvaged from the pre-dreadnought *Montagu*, which had been wrecked on Lundy Island in 1906, although the mountings were the new P.IIIs. Ammunition stowage was increased from 150 to 225rpg (75 CPC, 150 HE). As *Humber*'s guns were

mid-December. *Severn* and *Mersey* then returned to Dunkirk in response to French requests for naval support, while *Humber* was taken in hand at Chatham for modifications including the addition of a single 6in BL VII aft, also salvaged from *Montagu*, giving her a total of three 6in, one hardly used and two well-worn.

It was hoped that the two shallow-draft monitors would be a useful supplement to the deep-draft pre-dreadnoughts, but the severe winter weather and the limited range of their guns restricted their operations. Furthermore, Hood was only in favour of using his ships in conjunction with land offensives which would justify

This close-up shows *Severn* (nearest camera) and *Humber* after their eighteen-day tow to Malta. *Humber* retained her turret, now camouflaged, but *Severn* (and *Mersey*) has had her turret replaced by a single 6in, with another on the quarterdeck.
(IWM Q46207)

the risk of damage from shore batteries, and not for casual bombardment. The monitors therefore returned to the Medway on 11 January 1915, while Belgian Coast operations were reduced to a low key until the first large monitors arrived in August.

Early in March came orders to prepare the ships for service again, this time overseas. If the plans to force the Dardanelles were successful it would be necessary to have vessels capable of going up the River Danube for operations against Austria-Hungary. The 3,000-mile voyage out to the Mediterranean would not be possible under their own steam, so arrangements were made to tow the monitors. Their crews would be evacuated to another ship and their hulls specially strengthened and upperworks boarded over, as they would be continually washed by green seas on passage. Each monitor was taken in tow by a pair of tugs when the squadron left Sheerness on 11 March. The crews embarked in the fleet messenger *Trent*, a liner taken over from the Royal Mail Steam Packet Company, when the ten ships set off from Devonport three days later at 6½kts. Malta was safely reached on 29 March, where the monitors were readied to go on to Mudros to prepare for the forthcoming Allied landings at Gallipoli, scheduled for 25 April. Bad weather delayed their sailing for so long that insufficient time remained

Severn's forward 6in BL VII being prepared for the *Königsberg* operation in July 1915. Additional protection plates have been arranged at the rear of the shield. The 100lb shells at the rear of the gun with a band painted round the head are CPC, the others HE not yet fitted with nose fuzes. Camouflage painting in the form of palm trees can be seen on the breastwork. Sailors' washing is strung up to dry. (IWM Q46247)

to tow them the 700 miles and then complete the expected fortnight's work of putting them back into shape again, so the monitors stayed at Malta. Then, on 19 April, came new orders which were to split up the squadron for the next three years.

There had been a number of German cruisers overseas when war had broken out, most of which were quickly accounted for by the RN. The 3,400-ton cruiser *Königsberg* did, however, still remain afloat as, after operations against British shipping in August and September 1914, she had taken refuge among the shallow channels of the Rufiji River delta in German East Africa, 70 miles south of Dar es Salaam. There she was blockaded in by a superior force of British cruisers which, because of their comparatively deep draft, could not reach close enough to shell her 9 miles upstream. A stalemate had developed which could only be broken either by the *Königsberg* breaking out or the British sending well armed and protected shallow-draft vessels up one of the river entrances. The ex-Brazilian river monitors were the only suitable vessels, so Fisher ordered two of them out to East Africa. As *Humber's* armament now made her the odd one out, *Severn* and *Mersey* left Malta on 28 April under tow, together with *Trent* and a collier.

After a difficult voyage, fully described in *Severn's Saga* by E. Keble Chatterton, the convoy arrived at Mafia Island, 10 miles off the Rufiji delta, on 3 June. The island had been captured from the Germans in January 1915 and formed an advanced base for blockading vessels, which included the cruisers *Weymouth*, *Hyacinth*, *Pioneer* and *Pyramus*. It took three weeks to get the monitors operational again, removing the temporary strengthening, patching up leaks, re-storing and ammunitioning, adding further protection in the form of ½in steel plates and sandbags and filling below-deck spaces with about 9,000 empty petrol cans to provide buoyancy should the hull be damaged. The monitors were then painted green to blend better with the tropical jungle backgrounds. After the crews had rejoined, trials were needed to exercise co-operation with the RNAS spotting aeroplanes. Several of these precious machines had recently arrived from England, and they would provide the only means of directing gunfire on to the hidden cruiser.

Vice-Admiral H.G. King-Hall's plan called for them to enter the northernmost channel on the flood tide at daybreak, in order to surprise the shore defences, and then steam up to a position about 5½ miles from *Königsberg*, while one aeroplane bombed her and another spotted gunfire on to her, invisible from sea level behind the thick jungle. The two monitors entered the Kikunya mouth at 05.40 on 6 July and ran a gauntlet of fire from light guns ashore, replying with their 3pdrs. Both vessels anchored undamaged in the firing position about halfway between *Königsberg* and the river mouth, opening fire at 06.48 with their 6in guns at a range of about 11,000yd. The cruiser soon returned fire from her 105mm (4.1in), although only the five starboard guns out of her total of ten could be brought to bear. Her fire soon became uncomfortably accurate, as it was being directed by German observers hiding on the river bank near the monitors and on a hill to the northward. Her shells fell

Severn's forecastle in October 1915. On the bridge the officer of the watch can be seen in a topee, with the machine guns in the wings. On the boat deck the conning tower is visible behind the forward 6in, while two of the 3pdr can just be seen behind their shields. (IWM Q46334)

close all around the British ships but they remained unharmed until 07.30, when *Mersey* received two hits, one on her forward 6in, putting it out of action, and another aft at the waterline, which also sank her motorboat. Six men were killed; the monitor had to retire to repair the damage. At 07.51 *Severn* scored her first hit on *Königsberg*, near her foremost gun, the spotting aircraft no longer being confused by the shell bursts of both monitors. Two more hits were made before return fire also forced *Severn* to shift her berth.

Mersey was back in action by 08.10, and firing continued from both monitors on and off for several hours, whenever one of the two aircraft was available in a position to spot, during which time the cruiser's fire slackened, as she was conserving ammunition. The monitors had to withdraw at 15.30 with the falling tide but, although *Königsberg* had received three hits, she was still capable of fighting and steaming. Although 633 rounds of 6in had been fired, only seventy-eight had been spotted and others failed to burst, so it was clear that a repeat attempt would have to be made. The monitors had been severely shaken up by the repeated strain of prolonged firing and their guns were rather the worse for wear, so the next four days were spent patching them up at Mafia Island.

The river was entered again at 11.40 on 11 July. This time *Severn* anchored further up-river, to be met by several salvoes from *Königsberg* which landed uncomfortably close and showered her with splinters. Although *Mersey* opened fire at 12.15, her sister took over shortly after, quickly finding the 9,500yd range. The Henri Farman spotting aircraft reported a hit with *Severn's* eighth salvo at 12.39, and thereafter hits were registered continuously, severely damaging the German cruiser. A serious fire broke out aft, necessitating flooding of the magazines. At about 14.00 a heavy explosion was heard, followed by others, the Germans having abandoned ship and deliberately exploded two torpedo warheads amidships to disable it beyond repair. The monitors moved in closer, continuing to fire on the enemy cruiser until 14.20, making absolutely sure of her destruction. A total of 204 further rounds of 6in had been fired that day to complete the mission.

The monitors' successful action enabled the blockading force to be dispersed to other duties, although they themselves needed considerable attention. They had to be beached at Zanzibar to patch up their leaking hulls to get them back into action against other German forces in East Africa. Their shallow draft, relatively heavy guns and reasonable protection made them ideal for operations against the many small towns and harbours up and down the coast of what is now Tanzania.

continued on p.103

ABOVE
Severn, beached at Zanzibar after the *Königsberg* operation, shows her shallow draft.
(IWM Q46290)

LEFT
With no proper drydocks in East Africa, one way of getting at the monitors' underwater hull was simply to beach and wait for low tide. Shown here at Zanzibar in August 1915, after the *Königsberg* operation, *Severn* has had some leaks repaired and is getting repainted. The tunnel in which the propellers run and the hinged flap to assist astern manoeuvring can be seen. Two of the 3pdr can be seen at boat deck level, with a machine gun above the starboard one.
(IWM Q46293)

In this view, taken aboard *Severn* in 1917, the Vickers 4.7in port howitzer is sited on the boat deck, leaving the quarterdeck clear for the after 6in. The howitzer is shown at its maximum elevation of 70 degrees, with its shield removed. One of the four original 3pdr Vickers can be seen with its shield at the after end of the boat deck, with on the platform above one of the 7mm Hotchkiss machine guns and a 24in searchlight. Part of the high-angle mounting for the 3pdr Hotchkiss gun can just be seen on the platform at the top left.
(IWM Q46178)

BELOW
Humber is shown here at Mudros, still with her original turret, but with the barrel of her extra 6in just visible on the quarterdeck. A 3pdr HA is now sited on her after searchlight platform. The strengthening added after gun trials can be seen running along the boat deck and down to the forecastle.
(IWM SP912)

Severn relaxing in East Africa in 1917.
(IWM SP958)

continued from p.99

On 19 August *Severn* shot up the port of Tanga, railhead to the interior. For the next six months patrols and reconnaissances were made by both monitors until, in March 1916, *Mersey* was despatched in tow of *Trent* to Durban for a badly needed refit. The same month saw the start of serious land operations by British forces against the Germans, during which the monitors again proved their worth in company with a motley collection of other vessels. Bombardments were made, landings carried out and the Army forces supported as required, while the coast was gradually cleared from Tanga in the north to Lindi in the south. Dar es Salaam itself surrendered on 3 September 1916, although German forces remained active until after the Armistice. In December *Severn* steamed up the Rufiji to examine her former adversary. Her motor-boat parties found her hulk listed over to starboard, full of shell holes, burned out internally and stripped of useful fittings. Shortly afterwards *Severn* was towed off to Durban for refitting using some convict labour. She returned in April 1917 for a year of further patrols and minor skirmishes in company with *Mersey*. Following a decline in German activity, *Mersey* was towed back to the Mediterranean by *Trent*, leaving Zanzibar on 22 March 1918, the latter returning to tow *Severn* on 17 April. Both monitors reached Alexandria during May, where they started lengthy overhauls.

Humber had also been busy during the previous three years. She had remained at Malta during May 1915, when news came of the torpedoing of the pre-dreadnoughts *Triumph* and *Majestic* off the Dardanelles. Monitors and bulged cruisers were required as soon as possible to fill the gap caused by the withdrawal of the larger ships for fear of U-boats. She left Malta on 1 June for Mudros, arriving off Gaba Tepe on the 8th, and was in action that same day. The following day she fired on the village of Biyuk Anafarta, three miles inland, but after fifteen rounds a premature damaged her right gun. Her after 6in then took over, completing an expenditure of thirteen common and seven HE. Artillery ammunition had been running low ashore, so naval gunfire was used whenever possible. *Humber*'s usual position for the next few months was off the Anzac beaches, firing when requested on the many Turkish batteries, particularly those sited on the olive groves to the south, as these troublesome guns enfiladed the beaches used for unloading men and supplies. Her 4.7in howitzers proved a useful supplement to her 6in, while she cruised close offshore, often fired at but never seriously damaged. In December she helped to cover the withdrawal from Suvla and Anzac.

After her forward 6in turret guns were replaced at Alexandria by two relined pieces originally fitted in *Severn* and *Mersey*,[2] she was sent 150 miles west to the small harbour of Mersa Matruh. *Humber* arrived on 30 January 1916 to support British forces in the area, suppressing the Senussi sect's threat to Egypt's western frontier. Late in March she withdrew to Alexandria, leaving *M.31* to continue providing support. *Humber* then steamed through the Suez Canal to Port Tewfik at the southern end, where she formed part of the strong defences established against any possible Turkish attacks. There she remained for sixteen months, her only diversions being brief visits to Alexandria or firing at the occasional enemy aircraft. She left Port Tewfik on 4 August 1917 in tow of the cruiser *Euryalus* for Akaba at the head of that gulf, where she remained as guardship until February 1918. She then returned to Alexandria in tow of *Grafton*, which had just brought her relief *M.31*, where she was soon joined by *Severn* and *Mersey* from East Africa. In October all three monitors were sent to Mudros to assist operations against Bulgaria and Turkey, but Armistices had been signed before they could see any action.

5.3 After the War

The three monitors had come through the war far better than might have been expected for former river gunboats. Although unsuitable for operation in open waters with their already low freeboard aft reduced to only 2ft after modifications and their high GM of 26ft, they were able to deploy a comparatively powerful gun capability from a reasonably protected platform whenever called upon. Like all the monitors, their beamy shallow-draft hulls were very unmanoeuvrable. Sideways drift was always a major problem; in a Force 6 beam wind the course made good was estimated to be 45 degrees off the original heading, while above Force 6 it was wiser to stay in harbour.

Following the Armistice the three monitors were sent through the Dardanelles to Constantinople. *Humber* remained there for three months, but the other two steamed into the Black Sea and up the River Danube. They arrived at Galati on 11 December 1918, spending the winter as part of the force supervising the Armistice with Austria-Hungary. All three were ordered back to Britain in March 1919 for service with the White Sea Squadron, as operations up the River Dvina called for powerful vessels of the shallowest draft. *Humber* was the first to arrive in England, on 10 April, followed by *Mersey* on 9 May and *Severn* on 23 May. It was intended to refit them all at Devonport with triple 4in mountings, like *M.27,* but before they could be installed the decision was made to send only the first ship as quickly as possible. So *Humber* left Devonport on 20 May under tow for Murmansk, still carrying her normal armament except that her single 3pdr HA abaft the funnel had been replaced by a 3in HA. Her operations in North Russia are more conveniently described with the other small monitors in Chapter 7.5.

Severn and *Mersey* paid off into C & M and were moved to Queenstown (now Cobh) in July 1919. Both were sold to T.W. Ward in May 1921 as part of the huge block purchase described on p.43. *Humber* had returned to Chatham after her service in Russia, paying off on 24 October 1919. She was sold eleven months later to

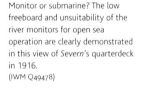

Monitor or submarine? The low freeboard and unsuitability of the river monitors for open sea operation are clearly demonstrated in this view of *Severn*'s quarterdeck in 1916.
(IWM Q49478)

Severn on the gridiron in the River Ribble at Ward's Preston shipbreaking yard in 1923. (T.W. WARD)

Dutch shipbreaking and salvage firm Frank Rijsdijk for £5,510 and converted into a crane barge for dismantling warships in the Medway. Her machinery was removed and a ring bulkhead, roller path and gunhouse floor from the German battleship *Oldenburg* (which Rijsdijk was dismantling) formed the base of her 50-ton crane, with other components salvaged from ships being broken up. She was resold in 1925 to the Upnor Shipbreaking Company and was employed on the dispersal of the wreck of the pre-dreadnought *Bulwark*, which had blown up and sunk in the Medway in November 1914. In the early 1930s she was used by Haulbowline Industries on demolition work on the 21,000-ton White Star liner *Celtic*, stranded off Queenstown in 1928. Taken over by Dover Industries, she continued work on *Bulwark* from 1935 to 1938. She was sold to French interests in 1939 for work on the French battleship *France*, wrecked on the Brittany coast in 1922, arriving at Brest on 19 May. Her ultimate fate is uncertain; probably a breaker's yard post-war.

Severn, Humber and Mersey – TECHNICAL DATA

Displacement: 1,260 tons Navy List, 1,520 tons deep on 5ft 7½in, 1,155 tons light on 4ft 4in draft.

Dimensions: Length 266ft 9in oa, 261ft 6in bp, breadth 49ft 0in oa, depth to upper deck 8ft 6in.

Weight distribution as designed (tons): Armament 116, ammunition 20, protection 308, hull 574, equipment 61, machinery and RFW 131, coal (nominal) 50. Total 1,260 tons.

Complement: 9 officers, 131 men.

Armament: 2 x 6in (twin) (50 CPC + 100 HE rpg), 2 x 120mm (4.72in) howitzers (150rpg), 4 x 3pdr Vickers (300rpg), 6 x 7mm (0.28in) Hotchkiss machine guns (5,000rpg).

Protection: Upper deck 1in nickel steel amidships, ¾in at ends; (1915) 2in over 6in magazine; side belt 3in C amidships, 1½in NC at ends; bulkheads at end of belt 1½in NC forward, 1in aft; machinery casings 1in to 2in NC; barbette 3½in C; gunhouse 4in C front, 3in N.C. sides, 1¾in NC roof, 1½in NC rear and floor; conning tower 4in sides, 2½in roof.

Machinery: Twin-screw triple-expansion by Vickers 11½in, 18in, 28½in x 17in 1,450ihp at 250rpm. Two Yarrow dual-fired boilers 250lb/sq in. Coal 187 tons, oil fuel 90 tons.

Endurance: 1,650 miles at 8kts on 0.9 tons coal per hour. 2,800 miles burning oil as well.

Speed: 12kts designed, 9½ service. Trials: *Javary* 12.18, *Solimões* 11.82, *Madeira* 12.06, *Humber* 9.67kts.

Construction: Vickers, Son & Maxim, Barrow: *Humber* (No. 433) laid down 24.8.12/launched 17.6.13/completed Nov 1913; *Severn* (No. 434) 24.8.12/19.8.13/Jan 1914; *Mersey* (No.435) 24.8.12/30.9.13/Feb 1914.

Disposal: *Humber* sold F. Rijsdijk 17.9.20, scrapped after 1945?; *Severn* sold T.W. Ward 9.5.21, arrived Preston to scrap 23.3.23; *Mersey* sold T.W. Ward 9.5.21, arr Morecambe to scrap 30.9.21.

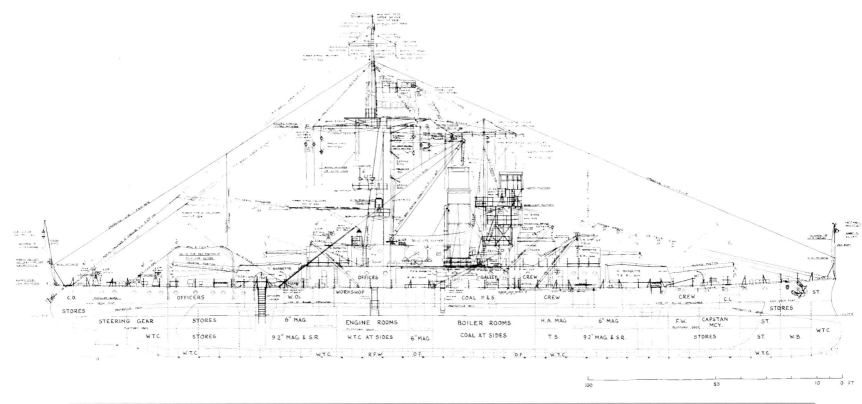

STEERING GEAR STORES 6" MAG ENGINE ROOMS BOILER ROOMS H.A. MAG 6" MAG F.W. CAPSTAN MCY. ST.

OFFICERS W.Os. OFFICES GALLEY CREW CREW C.L. STORES

STORES 9.2" MAG. & S.R. W.T.C. AT SIDES 6" MAG. COAL AT SIDES T.S. 9.2" MAG. & S.R. STORES ST. W.B.

CHAPTER 6

The Ex-Norwegian Coast-Defence Battleships

HMS

Glatton

—

Gorgon

6.1 Design and Construction

Although they were not in the mainstream of British monitor development, two coast-defence battleships intended for Norway were converted into bombardment vessels during WW1 for the RN. In 1912 the Norwegian Government envisaged a large expansion programme, which included two further vessels to add to their existing fleet of four coast-defence ships as well as destroyers and submarines. In January 1913 design and construction of the first two ships authorised in the new programme were entrusted to Armstrong, Whitworth,[1] which had built two earlier vessels, for delivery in 24 months. The hull dimensions were restricted by the only drydock at the Horten naval dockyard, near Oslo, to 290ft bp and 55ft breadth. On their designed displacement of 4,807 tons it was possible to carry two Elswick 240mm 50cal guns (9.45in) mounted in single turrets forward and aft. The secondary armament consisted of four 150mm 50cal (5.9in) also

mounted in single turrets, two superfiring over the 240mm and one on each beam amidships, plus six 100mm (3.9in). Two submerged 450mm (17.7in) torpedo tubes completed the powerful armament of these miniature battleships. In addition to the well protected citadel with a 7in belt, proof against a 9.2in projectile striking normally (i.e. at 90 degrees) at 1,500 ft/sec, there was also a 2in protective deck the full length of the hull. The armour was rolled at the company's Openshaw works.

The specified trial speed of 15kts was to be obtained from 4,000ihp twin-screw steam reciprocating machinery, ordered from Hawthorn, Leslie's Newcastle engine works. The general arrangement was well laid out on three continuous decks, although the accommodation was a trifle cramped by British standards, owing to the space taken up by the armament. The only place for the midship 150mm magazine was sandwiched between the engine and boiler rooms, an arrangement used in British

Glatton's outboard profile and deck plan is a good example of an 'as fitted' Sketch of Rig, supplied to the Admiralty by Armstrong's — after the ship had already been lost. Names of principal compartments and the scale have been added. *Gorgon* was almost identical except for a shorter funnel and different HA armament. Curiously the superfiring turret forward was named F instead of the more normal B.

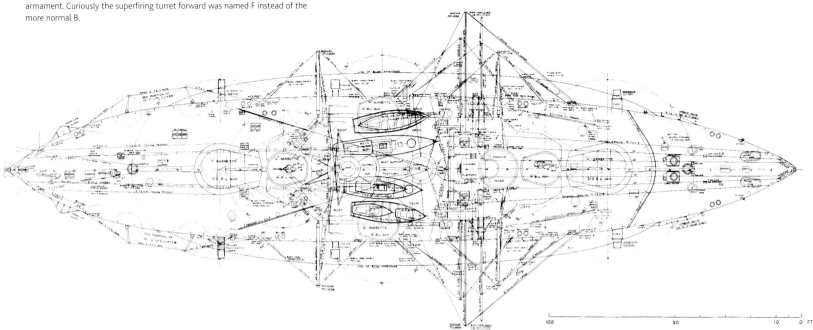

battleships, although in conjunction with insulating air spaces.

Construction proceeded to schedule at the Elswick yard, the first ship being launched on 9 June 1914. She was named *Nidaros*, the Viking name for Trondheim, while her sister was named *Björgvin*, the Viking name for Bergen. By the time of the latter's launch, on 8 August, war had broken out and work was slowed down on both ships. In November 1914 Churchill and Fisher appreciated that *Nidaros* and *Björgvin* could be readily adapted for coast bombardment. Arrangements were made with Norway to transfer the ships and for Britain to refund the instalments already paid. Two-thirds of the contract price of £370,000 each had so far been paid, the total being made up as follows:

Armament	£130,800
Armour	£60,200
Machinery	£48,400
Hull and equipment	£130,600
Total	**£370,000**

On 9 January 1915 orders went to Armstrong to complete the two ships for the RN at the earliest possible date. A number of modifications were needed, especially as neither 240mm nor 150mm guns were standard British calibres. It would not be difficult to reline the guns to 9.2in (234mm) and 6in (152mm) respectively, enabling existing service ammunition to be used. Twelve double-bottom tanks were modified to carry oil fuel to increase the endurance, and the boilers converted to dual coal/oil

firing. Names of previous heavy-gun ships were allocated on 8 April 1915, *Nidaros* becoming *Gorgon* after the turret ship of 1871, while *Björgvin* became *Glatton*, which had been the name of a sister to the previous *Gorgon* as well as a floating battery of 1855. The following month, when completion was estimated to be 10-12 months off, work was suspended by the new Board to allow faster progress to be made on *Courageous* and *Furious* at Armstrong's Naval Yard downriver.

In September 1917 orders were sent to Armstrong to complete the ships to a newly revised design. Anti-torpedo bulges were to be fitted covering about 75 per cent of the length of the hull, necessitating the removal of the torpedo tubes. The elevation of the 9.2in guns was increased to 40 degrees, enabling the remarkable range of 39,000yd to be obtained with special ammunition, as described on p.230. The eight 6in guns for the two ships were numbered in the regular Admiralty series for that calibre, Nos. 3331-3338.[2] The 100mm gun positions in the superstructure were given over to provide more accommodation, the guns themselves being modified to 4in calibre, designated Mk X and used to arm sloops. A tripod mast was fitted abaft the funnel, with a spotting top and directors for both the 9.2in and the 6in guns; other changes included a new HA armament. Over two knots' speed was lost owing to the bulges, but 12kts was still adequate for bombardment work. Deep displacement was increased to 5,705 tons (*Gorgon*) but, thanks to the bulges, the designed draft of 16ft 6in was not exceeded. The net result was the

BELOW
The original protection scheme of *Glatton* and *Gorgon* was
retained unchanged from the coast-defence battleship
design, except for the addition of bulges. The side
protection was stronger than the other large monitors,
especially in way of the wing 6in turrets, although the deck
was weaker.

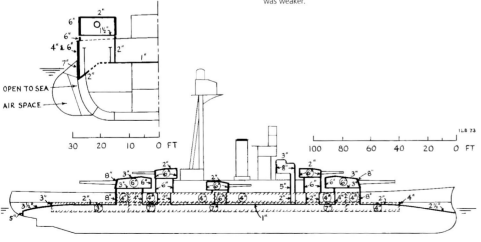

conversion of the two former coast-defence battleships
into monitors, each with two extremely powerful 9.2in
guns, which would be a useful reinforcement to the
monitor squadron off the Belgian Coast.

The modifications to the ships took some time, as there
was only one graving dock on the Tyne wide enough to
enable the bulges to be fitted; that at Palmer's Hebburn
yard. The first ship, *Gorgon*, was commissioned on 1 May
1918 under Cdr C.A. Scott. A preliminary trial was made
in the North Sea on 25 May, which included firing her
9.2in. After reasonably satisfactory trials, which showed
that her manoeuvrability had been adversely affected by
the bulges, she left for Dover on 4 June. *Glatton* commissioned at Newcastle on 31 August 1918 under Cdr
N.W. Diggle, who had earlier commanded *General Wolfe*
and *General Craufurd* for short periods. Ammunition was
taken aboard from railway wagons on 6 September and
she then proceeded for trials over the next two days. She

finally left her builders on the 9th, ready for action more than five years after her construction had started. One week later her career came to an abrupt end, as described in 6.3.

With all the changes and the ever-increasing levels of wages and material costs during the war, *Gorgon*'s final cost in Admiralty accounts amounted to £777,197 and *Glatton*'s to £513,242. There is no obvious reason for the considerable difference, unless certain costs that should have been equally divided, such as modifications to the armament, had been allocated entirely to the first ship. It is probably more representative to take the cost of each ship as about £645,000; getting on for double that of the original design, and dearer than any of the other WW1 monitors.

6.2 *Gorgon*'s Wartime Career

Gorgon's arrival at Dover on 6 June 1918 provided Keyes with a powerful addition to the monitor squadron, as he now had a vessel whose guns had a range comparable with that of the German long-range batteries. Her next few weeks were spent working-up; she took up patrols from Dunkirk at the end of the month. Her first real test came on 26 July, when she calibrated her guns on a German howitzer battery. Eight rounds were fired from 33,000yd, provoking a few retaliatory shells from the Pommern battery, which consisted of a single 380mm (15in) gun similar to Deutschland, but was sited about six miles south of Ostende. Three days later she accompanied *Marshal Soult* in a bombardment of the Tirpitz battery. August saw no firings from any of the monitors; for the next few weeks they were either out on patrol or preparing to support the big Army offensive planned for late September.

This attack started with a night bombardment by 12in and 15in monitors, as described on p.66. At daybreak on 28 September these ships were joined by the two long-range monitors, *Gorgon* and *General Wolfe*, which formed Division III. Anchored about seven miles off La Panne, *Gorgon* opened fire at 07.15 at Snaeskerke bridge, using supercharges as the range was about 36,000yd. Conditions were not too good, with a beam wind and tide. Before long her stern anchor cable had parted, swinging her round so that 'Y' turret was left to do most of the firing. No worthwhile air spots were received, so only a general spraying of the area was possible. The stationary monitors themselves provided good targets, and several air attacks were made during the morning. They remained under sporadic fire from the shore batteries all day, but few shells landed close, as the MLs' smokescreen proved reasonably effective. Although *Gorgon* fired only eleven rounds of 9.2in, a repeat performance with thirteen rounds was made the next day. One hit was reported, but later observation showed that Snaeskerke bridge itself had not been damaged.

When the Allied advance resumed on 14 October, *Gorgon* put in some concentrated shooting. Arrangements for all the monitors remained virtually identical to a fortnight earlier, except that *Lord Clive* now joined *General Wolfe* in firing at Snaeskerke, releasing *Gorgon* for action against the Middelkerke batteries. Her early-morning bombardment put forty-one rounds of the shorter-range 4crh HE into the target area from 26,000yd. In the afternoon *Gorgon* accompanied Keyes in the destroyer *Termagant* on a reconnaissance into the West Deep to ascertain whether the enemy was still holding the coast in strength, firing as she advanced. They were soon in no

Gorgon with her long-range 9.2in trained to starboard, probably taken off the Belgian Coast about September 1918.
(AUTHOR'S COLLECTION)

doubt; while *Gorgon* was off Westende the Tirpitz and Raversyde batteries opened up. At comparatively short range, they soon straddled her, landing shell splinters aboard and severely shaking the ship. She quickly turned away and worked up to 14kts to get out of range, faster than she had managed on trials, returning fire with her after guns. With her non-monitor appearance, and steaming at twice the usual speed of monitors, she must have confused the enemy spotters, as she was not hit. The next day only *Gorgon* went out, and in 20min rapid firing landed thirty shells near her bridge target. Thus to the newest monitor fell the distinction of firing the last rounds of the war at the enemy-occupied Belgian Coast, after exactly four years of almost continuous bombardments. With the German withdrawal there was nothing more for her to do, so she was sent round to Portsmouth to await a decision about her future, appropriately enough arriving on Armistice Day.

Gorgon with her guns at maximum elevation, 35 degrees for 9.2in, 20 degrees for 6in.
(ABRAHAMS)

6.3 The Loss of *Glatton*

Glatton arrived at Dover on 11 September 1918, where she prepared for the big offensive planned for later that month. Keyes and Diggle were out for a walk on the cliffs above Dover on the evening of the 16th when at 18.15 they heard a great explosion and saw a huge mushroom of smoke coming from a ship in the harbour. They saw at once that it was *Glatton* which had exploded and was now burning furiously amidships. By the time they had rushed down to the harbour the salvage tugs, including *Lady Brassey*, were already pouring their water jets on to the monitor. Lying in the next berth only 150yd away was the ammunition ship *Gransha*. Other tugs were beginning to move her, but there was still a considerable risk of her blowing up and devastating the town of Dover. Huge yellow flames from *Glatton*'s midship 6in magazine continued to shoot up through the roof of 'Q' turret (starboard midship) and reach up to the masthead among clouds of white smoke. The smoke turned to black as the fire reached the oil and coal bunkers surrounding the magazine and boiler rooms, and then began to spread aft.

Keyes and Diggle clambered aboard *Glatton*'s forecastle, to find that casualties had been heavy in messdecks and offices directly above seat of the fire. The after part of the ship was cut off by the flames, so they could not organise effective rescue operations there. Diggle was able to get the forward magazines flooded, but it was impossible to flood the after spaces owing to flames on the main deck where the magazine flooding controls were situated. Attempts to sink the ship by opening seacocks were unsuccessful, as those controlling the after compartments and the bulge buoyancy spaces could not be reached. As it was only a question of time before the after magazine exploded, Keyes reluctantly decided that his only course was to sink *Glatton* by torpedo, so he boarded the destroyer *Cossack*, which had just arrived from Hull. Her first 18in torpedo hit the bulge amidships, but embedded itself in the plating without exploding, as it had not travelled far enough to run off its safety device. At 19.40 her second and last torpedo was more successful, blowing a hole in *Glatton*'s starboard side. But 200lb of explosive were not enough to defeat her anti-torpedo bulge and she remained obstinately afloat, still burning furiously. Keyes then transferred to the destroyer *Myngs* and ordered her captain to torpedo *Glatton*. Two 21in torpedoes were fired from close range into the existing hole in *Glatton*'s side at 20.15, and under this onslaught she heeled over slowly to starboard until she came to rest at 148 degrees to the vertical, with her masts and superstructure resting on the bottom and part of her port bulge showing above the water. The fire was quickly extinguished and the danger of further explosion averted.

Glatton leaves the Tyne for trials early in September 1918. Visible further changes from the original design include the heavy tripod mast, spotting top, lengthened funnel and 3pdr on 'F' turret, as the forward superfiring 6in was named. (IWM SP2595)

Casualties had been heavy, involving over half the crew of 346; one officer and fifty-nine men were missing, and a further 124 were injured, nineteen of whom died later from their burns. A Court of Enquiry was set up immediately under Cdre A.P. Davidson to determine the cause of the original explosion. Witnesses soon confirmed the basic facts, establishing that a fire had started in the midship 6in magazine. As shown in the plan, this was sited in the hold between the boiler rooms and engine rooms, and flanked by the 6in shell rooms. The cause of the explosion was less easy to determine, and a number of theories were examined: sabotage; spontaneous ignition of the cordite; mal-operation of the oil fuel and coal bunkers; overheating of the magazine. There was no reason why the last should have occurred, as not only had insulation been provided all round the magazine, but special cooling equipment was installed. Sabotage was often suspected during wartime, but was soon ruled out, particularly as the ship had not been in contact with the shore since leaving Newcastle a week earlier. Spontaneous ignition of the cordite was also unlikely, as tests on other

charges from the same batch showed that it had not deteriorated significantly in storage. However, one alarming fact was established. The stokers were in the habit of piling red-hot ashes and clinker from the boilers against the magazine bulkhead, before periodically clearing them up the ash ejector in the starboard after corner of the boiler room. The stoker POs thought that the engine room was on the other side of the bulkhead and that there was no danger in the practice. Here was a promising line of investigation but, as most of the personnel working in that part of the ship had been killed, it would be necessary to examine her sister ship *Gorgon* closely and conduct experiments to see whether this might indeed have been the cause of the explosion.

Gorgon was carefully examined at Dover; her 6in ammunition was removed and the midship 6in magazine insulation partly stripped. The construction of the bulkhead adjoining the boiler room consisted of riveted 5⁄16in steel plates, with 5in of granulated cork covered by ¾in wood planking fitted on the magazine side. It was found that the red lead paint on the bulkhead had been blistered beneath the lagging directly behind the place where, as in her sister ship, ashes had been piled. The condition of the paint was tested at the National Physical Laboratory, which showed that temperatures of at least 400°C had been reached. Recorded air temperatures in the magazine were not particularly high, a maximum of 83°F having been noted. It was decided to undertake trials in *Gorgon* during which red-hot ashes were to be deliberately piled up against the bulkhead, while the temperatures in the magazine and in the lagging were to be recorded. The ash test results were, however, inconclusive; the average temperature in the lagging was only about 70°F, while even the hottest spot behind the ash-heaps was no more than 150°F. Such temperatures were nowhere near high enough to have ignited either the cork or the wood. It was then thought that oil might have seeped into the lagging from the double-bottom tanks beneath, but experiments with the cork soaked in oil showed that however high the fires were stoked, the cork did not ignite. Tests did show, however, that the cork could give off flammable gases in the presence of high temperatures and a supply of air under pressure. Various trials dragged on into 1919, but no really conclusive evidence appeared. Eventually, in April 1919, the Court gave its verdict, concluding that: 'The slow combustion of the cork lagging of the 6in midship magazine of the *Glatton* led to the ignition of the magazine and then to the ignition of the cordite in it and so caused the explosion.'[3]

When shown the Court's findings, both the Engineer-in-Chief, Vice-Admiral G.G. Goodwin, and the DNC, d'Eyncourt, did not accept that the cork had actually burnt. Nevertheless, the insulation in *Gorgon* was replaced by silicate cotton to be on the safe side. On stripping out the rest of her old insulation, a much more likely cause of the ignition was revealed. Behind some parts of the wood panelling was found not granulated cork, but empty spaces and folded newspapers. The latter were Newcastle journals such as the *Evening Chronicle*, bearing dates in 1916 and 1917, which must have been stuffed there by men at the Elswick shipyard. Examination of the bulkhead had already shown the existence of a number of ½in-diameter holes in the plating, where rivets had been omitted. These two discoveries point clearly to the most likely cause of the fire, although no such conclusion was ever drawn officially. The red-hot ashes could well have raised the bulkhead temperature sufficiently to have ignited any newspapers which may well have been present in *Glatton* also, with air being supplied by the forced draught pressure in the boiler room through open rivet holes. Under these conditions the cork would have given off flammable gases, charred the wood panelling and eventually ignited the cordite charges.

The monitor's wreck remained a hazard to navigation in Dover Harbour as it gradually silted up with time. Enquiries among salvage firms to undertake its removal produced either blank refusals or estimates of about £45,000. Finally Capt John Iron was asked if he could do the job. The Dover Harbourmaster had tackled many tricky jobs during the war (see p.153), but *Glatton* would be the most difficult, lying upside down at an awkward angle. He thought it might be possible to do the job for around £5,000, with the use of the salvage craft at Dover. The Harbour Board jumped at his offer, and work started in May 1925. With the aid of the salvage vessel *Dapper* and the Dover tugs, 12,000 tons of silt were cleared from under the wreck. Its mainmast and parts of the super-structure were blasted away with explosives and then sixteen 9in (i.e. 2.9in-diameter) wire ropes were passed under the hull. Four Admiralty lifting lighters were hired and connected to the wires on each side of the wreck, each capable of raising 1,000 tons when pumped dry of water. But with the silt trapped inside the wreck, 4,000 tons of lifting capacity were not sufficient to lift the 6,000-ton vessel. It was also necessary to seal all holes on the port (uppermost) side, as well as those across part of the deck and bottom. The additional buoyancy could then be obtained by making air connections to most of the watertight compartments and then pumping air into them at 70,000 cubic feet a minute.

By 2 December 1925 all was ready for the first lifting

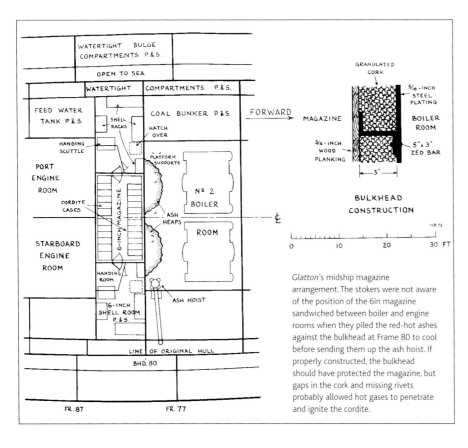

Glatton's midship magazine arrangement. The stokers were not aware of the position of the 6in magazine sandwiched between boiler and engine rooms when they piled the red-hot ashes against the bulkhead at Frame 80 to cool before sending them up the ash hoist. If properly constructed, the bulkhead should have protected the magazine, but gaps in the cork and missing rivets probably allowed hot gases to penetrate and ignite the cordite.

attempt. Just before low tide the lifting lighters were ballasted down and the wires tightened. The tide turned, the lighters were pumped out and the air compressors put on full power. The anxious watchers waited as the tide slowly rose, then suddenly the wreck began to move. Success was in sight, but the major lifting operation was deliberately held over until the following day. The wreck was again made buoyant and then moved slowly towards the shore until the ebbing tide prevented further movement. On 16 March 1926, with spring tides and better weather, she was lifted again and moved to lie in a deep gully alongside the western pier of the submarine harbour, nestling under the cliffs at the north-eastern end of the harbour. Her hulk is now buried under land reclaimed for the present car ferry terminal. Although the final cost of the operation turned out greater than Iron had anticipated, the total sum was no more than £12,000.

6.4 *Gorgon* Post-war

There was very little that the RN could do after the war with a former foreign coast-defence battleship mounting an armament of unique pattern. After the experiments to discover the cause of *Glatton*'s loss were completed, *Gorgon* moved to Devonport in April 1919 to become a temporary tender to *Vivid*, paying off on 31 August after barely a year in service. In September 1919 she joined the Devonport Reserve Fleet under the flagship *Colossus*. She was offered back to Norway, but she was no longer suitable for their requirements, especially now that she was too broad to be docked at Horten. Her name was added to the Sale List, as several South American countries had expressed interest in buying a monitor. Nothing came of Argentinian or Peruvian enquiries, but in 1920 Romania negotiated to buy *Gorgon* and six M-class destroyers. A total price of £200,000 was discussed, implying about £60,000 for *Gorgon*, but the deal fell through. The following year her armament was removed and she was sold at Devonport to Stanlee Shipbreaking & Salvage Co Ltd on 26 November 1921, but withdrawn from sale in January 1922 to become available for further trials. In June 1922 she was towed back to Portsmouth, where she was used as a guinea pig to determine the effects of heavy charges or bombs bursting underwater close to the ship, and the effects of 6in shellfire. Her relatively modern hull construction, including bulges, made her a good choice. These and other trials continued for some time and yielded useful information for future designs. She remained available for experiments until 1928, when she was sold to Ward for £10,078 and broken up at the former naval dockyard at Pembroke, after her bulges had been removed at Ward's Milford Haven yard.

Sunk after a magazine explosion on 16 September 1918, *Glatton* lay on the bottom of Dover Harbour for over seven years. The beacon on her bulge showed the angle at which she had been lying; 148 degrees to the vertical. She was raised in March 1926, this view showing her bottom between the salvage craft after her final lift.
(AUTHOR'S COLLECTION)

Glatton and *Gorgon* – TECHNICAL DATA

Displacement: (As modified) 5,700 tons Navy List, *Glatton* 5,746 tons deep on 16ft 4in draft, 4,855 tons light on 14ft 2½in.

Dimensions: Length 310ft 0in oa, 290ft 0in bp, breadth 73ft 7in oa, 55ft 0in main hull, depth to upper deck 26ft 0in

Weight distribution as completed (tons): Armament 706, ammunition 151, protection 1,082, hull 2,538, equipment 289, machinery and RFW 445, fuel 535. Total 5,746 tons.

Complement: (*Gorgon*) 22 officers, 283 men.

Armament: 2 x 9.2in single (130 HE rpg), 4 x 6in (100 CPC + 100 HE rpg), 2 x 3in HA (300rpg), 4 x 3pdr Vickers HA (*Glatton*) (300rpg), 4 (*Gorgon*)/2 (*Glatton*) x 2pdr HA (1,000rpg).

Protection: Protective deck: 2in HT on slope, 1in horizontal, 2in-2½in forward and aft; side belt: upper strake 4in C (6in abreast wing 6in turrets), lower strake 7in C amidships, 4in forward, 3in aft; bulkheads at end of belt 3in-4in; steering gear 3½in-5in; barbettes 8in C (9.2in), 6in C (6in); gunhouses 8in C front, 6in C sides and rear, 3in NC roof and floor (9.2in); 6in C front, sides and rear, 2in NC roof, 1½in floor (6in); conning tower 8in sides, 3in roof.

Machinery: Twin-screw triple-expansion by Hawthorn Leslie, Newcastle, ordered 31 March 1913 (Nos. 3020-21) 20in, 33in, 54in x 30in 4,000ihp at 150rpm. Four dual-fired Yarrow watertube boilers 250lb/sq in. Coal 364 tons, oil fuel 171.

Endurance: 2,700 miles at 11kts.

Speed: 15kts designed, 12 service. Trials: *Gorgon* 13, *Glatton* 12½kts.

Construction: Armstrong Whitworth, Elswick: *Glatton/Björgvin* (No. 861) laid down 26.5.13/launched 8.8.14/completed 8.9.18; *Gorgon/Nidaros* (No. 862) 11.6.13/9.6.14/4.6.18.

Disposal: *Glatton* blown up 16.9.18; *Gorgon* sold T.W. Ward 26.8.28 for scrap, arrived Milford Haven 29.9.28.

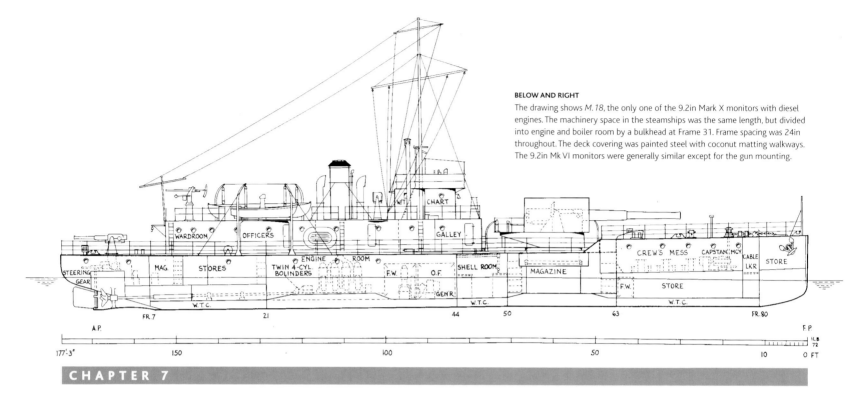

BELOW AND RIGHT

The drawing shows *M.18*, the only one of the 9.2in Mark X monitors with diesel engines. The machinery space in the steamships was the same length, but divided into engine and boiler room by a bulkhead at Frame 31. Frame spacing was 24in throughout. The deck covering was painted steel with coconut matting walkways. The 9.2in Mk VI monitors were generally similar except for the gun mounting.

CHAPTER 7

The Small Monitors

HMS

M.15 – M.33

7.1 Design of the Small 9.2in-gun Monitors

With the construction of the 15in-, 14in- and 12in-gun monitor classes well under way by early 1915, Fisher turned his attention to the possibility of obtaining further heavily armed vessels. The next-largest-calibre service gun was the 9.2in, fitted in a wide range of pre-dreadnoughts and cruisers. As it was usually installed in single mountings, the much lower weight, compared with heavy battleship twin mountings, offered the chance of arming a number of small shallow-draft monitors. A hasty search was instituted for available 9.2in mountings, as heavy mountings were always scarcer than guns. The 9.2in BL Mk X gun on a Mk V single mounting was an obvious candidate. Two single mountings had been fitted in each of five ships of the *Cressy* and *Drake* classes of armoured cruiser of 1901, but already three of the ships had been lost during the war, *Aboukir* and *Cressy* torpedoed in the North Sea in September 1914, and *Good Hope*, sunk at Coronel in November. Only two ships remained fitted with the Elswick Mk V mounting, *Drake* and *Leviathan*; all other ships of the classes had the Vickers Mk VI mounting. One spare mounting had been supplied for each ship, so four could be earmarked for new monitors and still leave one spare between the two remaining ships.

The other source of 9.2in armament was the *Edgar* class of protected cruiser of 1893. These old ships had constituted the major part of the 10th Cruiser Squadron, used for blockade work on the Northern Patrol since the outbreak of war. However, they proved quite unsuited for sustained operations in those stormy waters and were replaced by converted Armed Merchant Cruisers as soon as possible. The cruisers paid off at the end of 1914, some being converted for use at the Dardanelles. These ships were armed with two single 9.2in BL Mk VI on CP III mountings, in addition to ten 6in. It was decided to replace the 9.2in guns with 6in in all the now remaining five ships of the class, *Edgar*, *Endymion*, *Gibraltar*, *Grafton* and *Theseus*, *Hawke* having been torpedoed in October 1914. It was thus possible to arm a further ten small monitors with these old guns.

There was a considerable difference between the two types of 9.2in gun.[1] The Mk VI was a low-velocity 31cal design of hoop construction dating from 1888, with a maximum range of only 11,000yd at 15 degrees elevation using cordite Mk I. The mounting was of the old hand-worked Vavasseur type on which the gun recoiled up an inclined slide, which was visible at the rear of the open gun shield. The Mk X was a great improvement, a high-velocity steel and wire gun 46cal long, capable of ranging 15,400yd at its maximum elevation of 15 degrees using the improved cordite MD.[2] Its powered mounting and superior breech mechanism allowed it to fire about four times as fast as the Mk VI; 3½ rounds per minute. The Mk V mounting was totally enclosed in an armoured shield, with 6in front and 3in sides. As in the case of the 12in monitors, any possible increase in elevation above

ment, with a legend displacement of 540 tons. It was not practicable to fit bulges or any protection in such a small hull. The hull was only a single deck deep except forward under the raised forecastle, which housed most of the crew in very spartan conditions. The gun was sited just aft of the break of the forecastle. Abaft the gun, the superstructure housed the officers, a few ratings and the galley, with the bridge, mast, funnel and 6pdr HA gun being the only erections thereon. A single 12pdr was sited on the quarterdeck, below which was its magazine plus various store rooms. The main magazine, 9.2in gun support and machinery occupied the midship 50 per cent

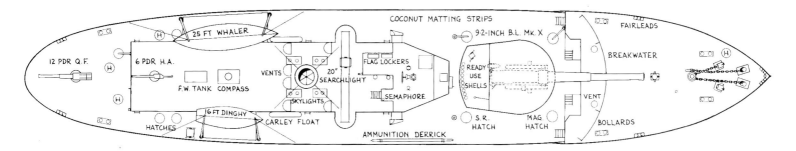

15 degrees would provide a valuable extension in range; Elswick confirmed that it would be possible to convert both types of mounting to 30 degrees elevation. The corresponding increase in range was about 45 per cent, resulting in 16,300yd for the Mk VI gun and 22,000yd for the Mk X; 25,000yd was possible with 4crh projectiles in place of the normal 2crh. The guns were intended to be operated in local control from the mounting, so no fire control equipment was provided in the monitor design.

After the armament had been selected, detailed design work could go ahead on hull and machinery. The only requirements were a draft of about 6ft, a speed of about 12kts and the simplest possible construction. The weight of the Mk VI gun and mounting was about 45 tons; the Mk X was considerably heavier at about 115 tons. Substitution of light steel plate in place of the 50-ton armoured shield would bring the latter weapon's weight down, as would the omission of the usual hydraulic machinery for working the mounting and ammunition hoists. All operations were to be by hand to keep the installation as simple as possible and save weight, so the rear of the Mk X shield had to be left open. Ammunition supply was to be by davit and whip from hatches over the magazine on to the platform at the rear of the mounting, a method calling for considerable manual effort to handle the 380lb projectiles. The weight of the 9.2in Mk X installation was thus reduced to about 70 tons, plus a further 30 tons for the 120 rounds of ammunition.

The hull was designed 170ft long with a breadth of 31ft to provide the stability needed for the heavy arma-

of the main hull. Estimating the horsepower required was nothing like as difficult as for the large bulged monitors, as the hull shape was well within existing experience. Machinery of around 700ihp would be required, which could easily be provided by steam or diesel machinery, whichever was most readily available. There was virtually no difference in the basic design for the Mk VI gun monitors as compared with the Mk X. Their overall appearance was that of a gunboat, in some respects similar to early vessels of the true monitor type, with their large gun and low-lying hull. From the start it was decided that the monitors would be identified by number only, continuing the series originally begun for the large monitors. The four Mk X monitors were thus numbered from *M.15* to *M.18* and the ten Mk VI from *M.19* to *M.28*.

Inquiries were made in mid-February 1915 among merchant shipbuilders for tenders to build the fourteen hulls. Two large companies on the north-east coast of England had not shared any of the recently allocated sloop orders, William Gray of Hartlepool and Sir Raylton Dixon of Middlesbrough. Gray was one of the biggest British shipbuilders in terms of annual tonnage built, so it certainly had the capacity to produce such relatively small vessels quickly, and was awarded contracts for four monitors, *M.15* to *M.18*. Its subsidiary company, Central Marine Engine Works, was allocated the machinery contracts. Dixon was allocated the remaining ten, *M.19* to *M.28*. As it had no associated engine works the supply of machinery had to be separately arranged.

Fisher was still keen on using internal combustion

engines wherever possible, and at this same time large orders had been placed for X-lighters (landing barges), mostly having Bolinder's engines. James Pollock & Company had been given responsibility both for the lighters' design and for the provision of their machinery, being both consulting engineers and British representative of the J. & C.G. Bolinder company of Stockholm. Here was a ready-made source of supply of diesel engines, so arrangements were made to obtain as many of these popular engines as possible to power the monitors. The most suitable standard Bolinder's engine was the four-cylinder, two-stroke M-type, developing 320bhp. Two were planned to be fitted in each monitor, 640bhp being the equivalent of about 800ihp. As there were only enough of the 22-ton engines readily available to power six monitors (*M.18, 19, 20, 23, 25* and *28*), it was arranged that four two-cylinder

units would be fitted in *M.26* and *M.27*.

The Bolinder engine was already in widespread use in small vessels for coastal and inland waterway service, as well as auxiliary propulsion for sailing vessels. It worked on the hot-bulb or semi-diesel principle, which was basically similar to a normal diesel engine except that the temperature within the cylinders was insufficient to ignite the fuel owing to the lower compression ratio. The necessary heat was provided by a hot bulb connecting with the cylinder into which the fuel was sprayed to initiate combustion. The low temperatures and pressures produced a solid durable engine with remarkable longevity. The arrangement was that the engines would be supplied by Bolinder and installed by Pollock. As the fourth Gray monitor, *M.18*, was also to have these engines, there were still three other vessels requiring

The Swedish Bolinder semi-diesel engine was popular in small vessels like coasters and fishing vessels on account of its low fuel consumption and robustness. Two of the four-cylinder 320bhp reversible engines similar to that illustrated were fitted in six of the small monitors, supplied by Pollock.
(AUTHOR'S COLLECTION)

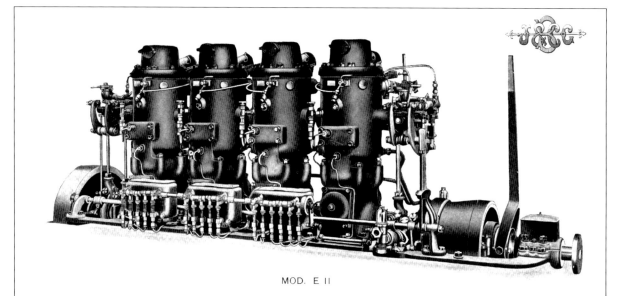

MOD. E II

DIRECT REVERSIBLE.

		Med. E II. (Four cylinder.)					
B. H. P.		**60**	**80**	**100**	**160**	**240**	**320**
Rev. pr minute		450	425	375	325	275	225
Approx. weight complete lbs.		7200	9050	11000	18500	29200	41700
Fuel consumption pr hour	Refined petroleum imp. gall.	4,52	5,8	7	10,8	15,8	21,04
	Fuel oil ...... » »	4,96	6,4	7,68	11,88	17,4	23,16
Extreme measurements of engine (only) in inches	Length	122	134	147	172	197	217
	Width	24	29	28	36	42	47
	Height	40	44	49	60	70	81
Diameter in inches of	Propeller (three blades)	37	42	45	55	67	79
	Propeller shaft (in mm.)	80	85	100	120	145	160
	Fly wheel	24	25	28	36	42	47
Shipping measurements boxed	Approx. cubic feet	219	267	339	532	810	1090
	Approx. lbs.	7500	10500	12500	21200	32700	46300
Type		R-12	R-15	R-200	R-300	R-400	R-500
Price * £							
Code		Nanna	Neptun	Niklas	Nikodemus	Nils	Nora

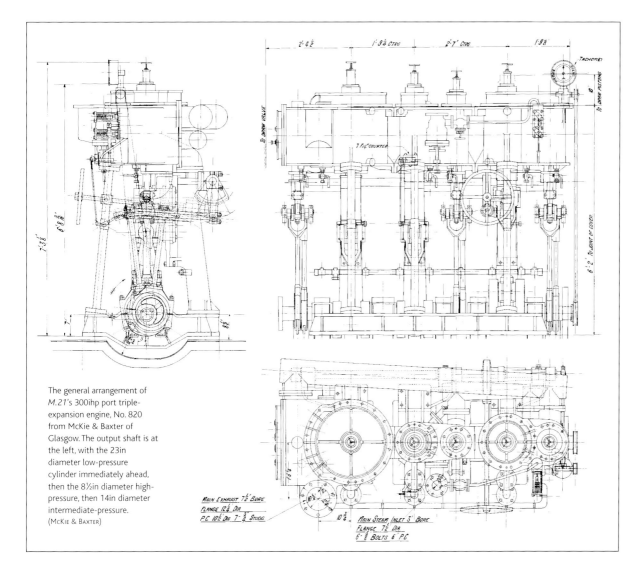

The general arrangement of *M.21*'s 300ihp port triple-expansion engine, No. 820 from McKie & Baxter of Glasgow. The output shaft is at the left, with the 23in diameter low-pressure cylinder immediately ahead, then the 8½in diameter high-pressure, then 14in diameter intermediate-pressure.
(McKie & Baxter)

One of *M.21*'s triple-expansion engines built by McKie & Baxter – original drawing at left. The output shaft is at the left, with low- and high-pressure cylinders next. The handwheel controlled the steam valve gear and engine rotation. The two small 'cylinders' were for the valve gear, which admitted steam to the HP and IP cylinders. LP valve gear at far left
(McKie & Baxter)

machinery. So *M.24* was given four paraffin engines by the Campbell Gas Company of Halifax, Yorkshire, and the remaining two, *M.21* and *M.22*, steam engines, by McKie & Baxter and Shields Engineering respectively.

The builders were instructed to adhere to normal merchant shipbuilding practice. Construction started in March 1915 and work progressed rapidly, the first vessel, *M.15*, being launched on 28 April. Fitting out took about two months, during which time the first Dixon vessel, *M.19*, overtook *M.15* and was ready for trials on 3 June, a week ahead of her near-sister and only a fortnight behind the first 14in monitor. There had been no problems installing the Mk VI guns, which had been removed from the cruisers and sent to Elswick for modification before being re-erected by EOC on the ships at Middlesbrough, ready for their gun trials. The actual allocation of the cruisers' mountings was: *Edgar*'s, two into *M.19* and *M.26*, *Theseus*'s into *M.21* and *M.27*, *Grafton*'s into *M.23* and *M.28*, *Endymion*'s into *M.24* and *M.25* and *Gibraltar*'s into *M.20* and *M.22*. The heavier Mk X was more of a problem. One of the spare

mountings allocated was at Malta, while another had been
sent out there in case it might be required for service
ashore at Gallipoli. So *M.15* and *M.16* were completed
without their main armament, which they would have to
pick up at Malta. The other two mountings were at
Portsmouth and had to be transported to Hartlepool by
road for erection by EOC, as it was considered too risky
to send them by ship owing to U-boat activity and they
exceeded the railway loading gauge.

Each group of monitors commissioned at roughly
fortnightly intervals from June to November 1915,
generally under the command of a lieutenant-commander.
Gun and speed trials were carried out as quickly as
possible, sometimes the same day. No major problems
arose, although speed fell short of the expected 12kts by
up to one knot in the lower-powered vessels. Deep
displacement was rather greater than designed, averaging
about 610 tons for the diesel Mk VI and 650 tons for the
steam Mk X increasing the mean draft by about 12 inches
and giving a trim of about 2 feet by the stern. The
probable expenditure on each vessel was around £35-
40,000, the diesel boats being the more expensive. The
true cost would have been about £50-55,000 if the
armament had not already been available. The monitors
left their builders' yards as soon as they were ready, those
destined for overseas service spending a week or two at
one of the home dockyards to be fully equipped for such
operations.

7.2 Design of the Small 6in-gun Monitors

While plans were going ahead for the fourteen 9.2in-gun
monitors, another possible source of guns presented itself.
The battleship *Queen Elizabeth* had been rushed to completion in January 1915 and was immediately sent out to
the Dardanelles. It soon became clear that the four 6in
guns of her secondary armament sited on the main deck
abreast 'Y' turret were unworkable at sea, as their casemates were only 5ft above the deep waterline. It was
therefore decided to remove the guns from this position
and resite them, but space could be found to remount
only two of them, amidships on the forecastle deck. Thus
there were two surplus guns and mountings from each of
the five ships.

So, early in March 1915, Lillicrap was called upon to
design yet another class of monitor, which was to mount
two single 6in. The guns were of a new pattern, BL Mk
XII, intended to form the secondary armament of new
capital ships and the main armament of light cruisers.
The 7-ton steel and wire gun was 45cal long and could
range 14,700yd at its maximum elevation of 17½ degrees,
although normally restricted in casemates to 14 degrees.
The mounting was transferable, i.e. merely bolted to the
deck, and as the entire installation weighed less than 18
tons, there appeared to be no difficulty in mounting two
in vessels of shallower draft than those carrying the
heavier 9.2in. The estimated total weight of armament
and ammunition came to 62 tons, compared with an

M.21 on her gun trials off the Tees in mid-July 1915, with her short 9.2in Mk VI at its increased elevation of 30 degrees. Guard rails are lowered to reduce blast damage. The painted bow wave was soon removed.
(IWM SP2033)

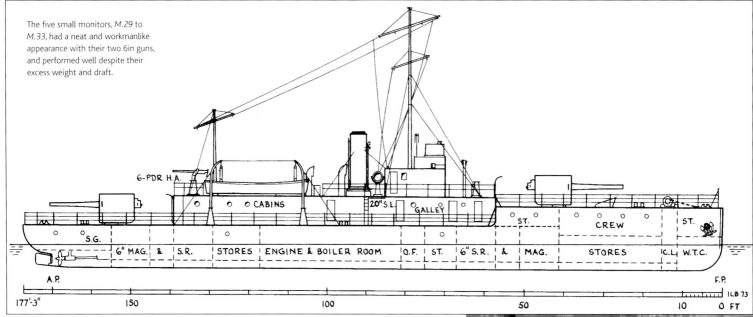

The five small monitors, *M.29* to *M.33*, had a neat and workmanlike appearance with their two 6in guns, and performed well despite their excess weight and draft.

estimated 100 tons in the 9.2in-gun vessels. As the ratio of component weights to total displacement is generally close for similar classes of ship, it was considered possible to reduce both the displacement and draft of the 6in monitors roughly in proportion to the reduced armament load. This load formed 18 per cent of the legend displacement of 540 tons in the 9.2in monitors. A similar percentage applied to the 6in monitors would give a displacement of about 340 tons and a draft of about 4ft. The design for a 10kts vessel went ahead on this basis, the legend displacement which went up to Their Lordships for approval being estimated at 355 tons.

There was, however, a fundamental error in the assumption of equal ratios. The percentages of component load are only similar for ships which are weight limited, i.e. those whose dimensions are determined by the need for buoyancy required to carry the total loads. They do not necessarily apply to ships which are space limited, i.e. those whose dimensions are determined by the need to provide a certain area of deck or a certain internal volume. In the very hurried design phase neither Lillicrap nor his superiors appreciated that, although the 9.2in monitors fell into the former category, the 6in monitors fell into the latter. The decision to mount two separate guns, one forward and one aft, meant that a deck area as large as that of the 9.2in monitors was required. The hull dimensions could not therefore be reduced, so virtually no reduction in actual hull weight was possible. As hull weight constituted about half the total displacement, the final displacement would fall not far short of that of the 9.2in monitors and the draft would be increased to nearly 6ft. By the time the error was realised the 6in monitors were committed. They continued to be listed in official

A fine view of *M.30* (nearest camera) and *M.31* on 22 June 1915, the day before the former was launched by Harland & Wolff at Belfast. Both are well advanced and ran their trials only ten days later. The keel is that of the suspended P. & O. liner *Narkunda*; *M.29* had been launched from the south side of the same Abercorn Yard berth a month earlier. The Workman Clark shipyard can be seen faintly beyond *M.31*.
(Harland & Wolff)

documents as 355-ton ships with 4ft draft, but never in their service lives would they float in such a condition.

It was not difficult to find suitable builders for the five monitors. Harland & Wolff was progressing well with the 14in monitors and would soon have some spare capacity, so orders for all five were placed with the company on 15 March 1915, as Numbers 485 to 489. When H & W came to plan out exactly how it would build the ships in the specified three months, a difficulty arose. Although the forthcoming launch of the two 14in monitors at Belfast would free a slipway on which all five could have been built, it was now needed for *Glorious*. All of its other seven berths were occupied either by monitors or suspended merchant ships. However, the keel of the 16,000-ton P & O liner *Narkunda* had only just been laid on Berth 5, so it would be possible to construct two small monitors on either side of the small amount of steel erected to date. Pirrie therefore inquired of the neighbouring shipyard of Workman, Clark & Co. if it could build one or two of the monitors. Although pre-war it had been Workman, Clark's policy not to build warships, it had in hand the conversion of *Theseus* and *Endymion*. The company therefore agreed to build two of the monitors under subcontract and was given *M.32* and *M.33*; *M.29*, *M.30* and *M.31* remained with H & W.

Construction proceeded very rapidly, the first keels being laid only eight days after the order was placed. *M.29*, *M.32* and *M.33* were all launched on the same day, 22 May, and the other two a month later with armament and machinery aboard. All five vessels commissioned in June and just about managed to scrape their designed 10kts on trials. An inclining experiment confirmed that they greatly exceeded their designed displacement and, although fortunately the extra weight did not seriously affect their stability, an undesirable trim by the head resulted. The trim caused unsatisfactory steering but was cured by six tons of permanent ballast aft. The final deep displacement came out at 580 tons as, apart from the original error over hull weight, most of the other loads were well up on the estimate. For example, oil fuel was up from 20 to 45 tons and ammunition up from 25 to 40 tons due to an increase in the number of rounds stowed.

The erroneous legend displacement of 355 tons was perpetuated in nearly every official description of the monitors. The Admiralty and naval officers showed little interest in accurate figures for the displacement of their ships, despite the vital importance of realistic figures for assessing limits of draft, stability, speed, ability to withstand flooding or the margin available for future modifications. At that period nearly every British warship's actual displacement greatly exceeded the nominal figures, which were indeed truly 'legendary'! Poor

feedback of data from completed ships into new designs, so necessary with a basically evolutionary science like naval architecture, which cannot afford to build prototypes, meant that underestimates were perpetuated. Quite possibly a few people realised the danger, but in general it was easier not to question the system, thereby avoiding inquisitions by higher authorities, political and financial, who might query why ship sizes appeared to be jumping up without a corresponding gain in military performance. The small monitors are certainly one of the worst examples in this respect and, in their case, the official 355-ton figure was so conspicuously unrealistic that it was usually assumed wrongly to be a misprint for 535 tons.

Harland & Wolff and Workman, Clark tied for the completion of the first 6in monitor. Both *M.29* and *M.32* left Belfast together on 20 June for Pembroke Dockyard, where their single 6pdr HA guns were to be mounted. The pedestals had been fitted by the builders, one forward of the bridge, one aft, but only one gun was to be supplied. The 6in vessels turned out to be the cheapest of all the monitors at about £25,000 apiece, although the cost would have been about £8,000 higher if the cost of their armament had not already been allocated. Contrary to general belief, the actual 6in used were not those removed from the battleships, but were newly constructed mountings fresh from the production line at COW, with most of the guns straight from Vickers.

7.3 Mediterranean Operations

Just before his resignation in May 1915, Churchill had arranged to send the first six 9.2in monitors out to the Dardanelles (see p.25). By the time the first vessels had been completed the newly formed Dardanelles Committee confirmed the arrangement and added all five of the new 6in monitors, as well as a further four 9.2in. The first ship, *M.19*, actually left British waters on 22 June, two days before the first of the large monitors, but, despite an occasional tow by the sloop *Aster*, *Abercrombie* overtook her at Malta. Then followed the two 6in monitors, *M.29* and *M.32*, and throughout July and August a steady procession of small monitors left Devonport: *M.33*, *M.15*, *M.16*, *M.20*, *M.30*, *M.31*, *M.17*, *M.21*, *M.22*, *M.23*, *M.28* and *M.18*. All were given some towing assistance, usually by colliers also bound for Mudros, taking three to four weeks to reach the Dardanelles. Some were held up for various reasons; *M.15* and *M.16* had to stop to pick up their 9.2in guns and mountings at Malta at the end of July. A fire in her engine room delayed *M.18*'s departure from England, the crew having to flood the magazine and shell-room before bringing the blaze under control. In September *M.23* was also delayed at Malta when a fire broke out in her funnel and spread to the bridge. Thus started a long saga of machinery-induced fires which persisted throughout the lives of the diesel monitors, causing minor damage to most of the vessels at one time or another.

As the first small monitor to arrive at Mudros, on 23 July, *M.19* was sent four days later to join *Roberts* in her berth south of Rabbit Island. From here she could help keep down the fire of the Turkish batteries on the Asiatic shore of the Dardanelles, which were harassing the British and French position at Helles on the European shore. In mid-August *M.19* was replaced by *M.17*, and thereafter two or three small monitors shared the berth with one of the large monitors for the next five months. The 9.2in Mk X proved to be a powerful and accurate weapon for this work, despite the small gun platform, usually landing its shells within 50yd of the target. Direct hits were obtained on enemy guns at ranges up to 24,000yd, although all that could reasonably have been expected of the monitors would have been the temporary silencing of enemy fire.

The Suvla landings starting on the night of 6/7 August were supported by all the available small monitors. Three of the 6in monitors were stationed off Suvla, while most of the others were supporting the 14in monitors further to the south. The fleet of bombarding vessels, monitors, cruisers and destroyers, poured an immense volume of fire on to their targets: entrenchments, field guns, supply roads and villages. Between 7 and 10 August over 8,000 rounds were fired, including about 700 from the 6in and 100 from the 9.2in monitors. Such a rate of expenditure could not be maintained for long; thereafter considerable economy of fire was enforced. A small monitor was usually stationed off Anzac, firing a dozen rounds a day at any

enemy batteries that revealed themselves, while others were off the left flank at Helles. An occasional longer-range bombardment was made several times during August; *M.15* fired at ships in the Narrows at Ak Bashi Liman, once setting a steamer on fire. Their small gun platforms proved rather lively for accurate shooting in unsheltered waters, as a broadside almost rolled the deck edge under water.

Patrols were also maintained in the Gulf of Xeros, carrying out bombardments during October and November on Turkish supply lines running down the Gallipoli peninsula. Typical targets were roads and bridges, although any likely-looking strongpoints or batteries were attacked to induce the Turks to think that a landing might be planned in the area. For this type of work the monitors with the more modern and accurate guns were preferred, usually *M.15*, *M.16* and *M.31*. Their 9.2in and 6in were used against the bigger targets, their 12pdr and 6pdr being reserved for wagons or boats. The flour mills at the town of Gallipoli on the other side of the peninsula were also a popular target, *M.16* scoring four hits out of twenty-two rounds from her long-range 9.2in during 70min on the afternoon of 8 November.

After Bulgaria had declared war a further stretch of coastline presented opportunities for bombardment. The railway between Constantinople and Salonika was a tempting target near Dedeagatch. The inland junction at Bodoma was selected, so, on the morning of 21 October, a British squadron consisting of the cruisers *Doris* and *Theseus* plus destroyers was in position close offshore, protected by drifter-laid anti-submarine nets, although their accompanying monitors, *M.16*, *M.19* and *M.29*, had been delayed by a strong headwind. Visibility was

The pre-dreadnought *Magnificent* had already surrendered her two 12in turrets to *Lord Clive* and *General Craufurd* before she was sent out to the Dardanelles as a troopship. This view, taken at Mudros about September 1915, shows *M.22* alongside with her original shorter funnel and splinter protection around the bridge.
(IWM SP69)

M.15 at Mudros in 1915, her
ammunition derrick rigged and her
12pdr aft fitted with a simple shield.
The tall narrow funnel indicates that
she is steam-engined.
(IWM SP1057)

M.30 at Mudros about October
1915. The forward 6pdr pedestal
appears to be used for a small
rangefinder.
(IWM SP570)

too bad for *Ben-my-Chree*'s seaplanes to spot fire on to the junction, so from 13.00 the bombarding ships poured a heavy fire from close range into Dedeagatch itself, the barracks, railway station, rolling stock, warehouses, fuel stocks, bridges, shipping and harbour works, joined by the monitors as soon as they arrived. By 16.00 a good bit of damage had been done, the Bulgarians being seriously alarmed that a landing by Allied troops might be heralded. A repeat operation took place five days later with *Theseus*, *M.15* and *M.28*.

The small monitors continued to support the 14in monitors off the Gallipoli peninsula, either covering them against shore batteries or firing themselves, especially during the periods when 14in ammunition was limited. On the morning of 4 December *M.19* was undertaking one such operation moored alongside *Abercrombie* off the left flank at Helles when, after her second salvo, splashes were seen all round about. At first it was thought that a shell had burst prematurely outside the gun, but after the smoke cleared it could be seen that *M.19*'s 9.2in gun (No.111) had almost disappeared. The barrel had burst 18in forward of the trunnions from a premature inside the bore, set off by a choke (see p.224). The 9.2in magazine caught fire, but *M.19*'s crew promptly flooded it, cast her off safely from *Abercrombie* and soon had the fire under control. Over two tons of fragments were found aboard *Abercrombie*, the largest weighing about 300lb. One 6lb chunk was found to have entered one of the slits of her conning tower, severing two fingers from her helmsman's hand. Two of *M.19*'s crew were killed, six badly burned and her deck buckled by fire. The destroyer *Colne* assisted her to Mudros, where the repair ship *Reliance* patched her up for the voyage to Malta, where full repairs were undertaken.

Meanwhile, some of the small monitors had been operating on the Mitylene-based patrols blockading Smyrna. *M.22* had been assigned to this squadron, which included two destroyers, from her arrival in the Aegean on 14 September, being joined three days later by *M.30* from Mudros. Long Island (Bayrakli or Chustan Island) at the mouth of the Gulf of Smyrna had just been occupied to maintain a close blockade and cover the British minefields. The monitors' duties were manifold: shooting up shore batteries and strongpoints, wagons and camel caravans, windmills and houses, soldiers and snipers, railways and bridges, searchlights and stores, shipping and boats. They also landed spies, cut telegraph wires, reconnoitred remote islands and examined suspicious steamers.

Following the evacuation from Gallipoli the squadron was strengthened to include generally one large and four small monitors, while an airfield was built on Long Island to assist reconnaissance. The enemy did not remain passive in the face of this close blockade and, under German guidance, heavy artillery was brought up and installed on the mainland to harass Long Island. By early May 1916 these heavy guns were able to shell the island and the British patrol vessels. On the night of 13/14 May *M.30* approached the island carrying stores, anchoring close inshore at about 22.00. Soon afterwards, enemy shells began to fall around her, so she moved away to try to locate the battery. No sign of its flashes could be seen, although its shells continued to land close by. Eventually a heavy shell, probably 150mm (5.9in) calibre, penetrated her machinery space, damaging one boiler and her fuel bunker and holing her bottom, killing two of her crew and wounding two others. The escaping oil caught fire, water flooded in and her engines stopped. A destroyer and motor gunboat arrived to help *M.30*, now burning fiercely amidships, but they could do little except take off most of her crew. She continued to drift inshore, her magazines having been flooded, and she grounded about 200yd offshore. Lieutenant-Commander E.L.B. Lockyer and the remaining crew took to her skiff and pulled

ashore, where they were rescued by *M.32* in the morning. Over the next few weeks an attempt was made to salvage as much useful equipment from *M.30* as possible, including her 6in guns, after which a 100lb charge of guncotton was set off to destroy her hull.[3]

While *M.22* and *M.30* had been busy off Smyrna, most of the other small monitors (*M.15*, *M.16*, *M.17*, *M.18*, *M.29*, *M.31*, *M.32* and *M.33*) had been concentrated off the Dardanelles to cover the withdrawals, first from Suvla and Anzac in mid-December, then finally from Helles in early January 1916, as described in Chapter 2.6. Generally three were at Rabbit Island, three in close support off the peninsula, and the other two fuelling or repairing at Mudros. The remaining four active monitors of the

M.30 still on fire on 14 May 1916 off Long Island in the Gulf of Smyrna after being shelled and sunk during the night. Later her guns were salvaged; and perhaps also the washing drying on the guard rails. (HUTCHINSON GROUP)

original fifteen in the Mediterranean had already been redeployed in support of operations elsewhere. *M.20* had been the first small monitor to arrive at Salonika, on 6 November, following the landing of Allied forces. She was used as a guardship, patrolling the boom, so beginning a duty which occupied one or other of the small monitors for the rest of the war. *M.28* arrived shortly afterwards, enabling one vessel to remain at Salonika and the other to move east of the Chalkis peninsula to the small port of Stavros. The remaining two, *M.21* and *M.23*, had been towed from Mudros to Port Said at the end of November to join the East Indies Squadron, so that they could be stationed in the Suez Canal to guard against any Turkish attacks from Sinai.

With the final withdrawal from Gallipoli only *M.17* and *M.29* remained with *Abercrombie* and two pre-dreadnoughts at Kephalo on the *Goeben* watch, which was occasionally enlivened by bombardment of Turkish positions on the mainland. *M.16* and *M.32* had gone to join the Mitylene patrol, while *M.18*, *M.19* and *M.33* went north to Stavros and Salonika. *M.15* and *M.31* were sent to Port Said for a quick docking, then joined *M.21* and *M.23* as Canal guardships.

The RN's role in the Eastern Mediterranean from 1916 could be summarised as:

(i)   Blockade of the Dardanelles and harassing the Turkish coastline

(ii) Supporting the Allied Salonika Army and blockading the Bulgarian Aegean coastline

(iii) Protection of the Aegean bases and retaining Greek support

(iv) Protection of the Suez Canal

(v)   Protection of Allied shipping.

Apart from the last, these duties determined the employment of the small monitors for the rest of the war. Generally, four monitors were deployed on the Mitylene patrol (4th Detached Squadron), one or two at Imbros close to the Dardanelles (2nd DS), one at Salonika (3rd DS), four at Stavros (6th DS) and four in the Suez Canal area (East Indies Squadron). One monitor was occasionally at Syra in the Central Aegean with the 5th DS, although there were none with the 1st DS based on Crete. One of the large monitors was frequently included in the main Detached Squadrons. The table summarises the usual allocation of each of the small monitors, although occasional switches occurred between the squadrons which were closest to one another, so Salonika duties are included under Stavros. Gaps of a month of two between Squadrons usually indicate refits at Malta or Mudros.

Deployment of the Small Monitors in the Mediterranean[4]

M.15 Imbros Aug 1915-Jan 1916, Egypt Jan 1916-Nov 1917 (sunk).

M.16 Imbros Aug 1915-Jan 1916, Mitylene Jan 1916-Nov 1917, Stavros Feb-Oct 1918.

M.17 Imbros Aug 1915-May 1916, Stavros May-Nov 1916, Imbros Feb 1917-Jan 1918, Stavros Jan-Oct 1918.

M.18 Imbros Oct 1915-Jan 1916, Stavros Jan 1916-Oct 1918.

M.19 Imbros Jul 1915-Feb 1916, Stavros Feb 1916-Jul 1918, Mitylene Jul-Dec 1918.

M.20 Imbros Aug-Nov 1915, Stavros Nov 1915-Apr

A 9.2in monitor, probably *M.20*, firing off Anzac during August 1915. (IWM SP3206)

1918, Syra Jun-Dec 1918.

M.21 Imbros Sept-Nov 1915, Egypt Dec 1915-Jul 1917 (Dover).

M.22 Mitylene Sep 1915-Jun 1918, Stavros Jul-Dec 1918.

M.23 Imbros Oct-Dec 1915, Egypt Dec 1915-Apr 1917 (Dover).

M.28 Imbros Sept-Nov 1915, Stavros Nov 1915-Sep 1917, Imbros Oct 1917-Jan 1918 (sunk).

M.29 Imbros Jul 1915-Jul 1916, Mitylene Jul 1916-Jan

1917, Stavros Feb-Apr 1917, Mitylene Apr-Sep 1917, Egypt Sep 1917-Mar 1918, Mitylene Mar-Dec 1918.

M.30 Imbros Aug-Sep 1915, Mitylene Sep 1915-May 1916 (sunk).

M.31 Imbros Aug 1915-Jan 1916, Egypt Jan 1916-Mar 1919.

M.32 Imbros Jul 1915-Jan 1916, Mitylene Jan-Jul 1916, Stavros Jul 1916-Sep 1917, Egypt Sep 1917-Jan 1918, Stavros Feb-Dec 1918.

The map shows the area of operations of the large and small monitors in the Aegean during WW1. The Dardanelles area is shown to a larger scale on p.35.

M.33 Imbros Jul 1915-Jan 1916, Stavros Jan-May
1916, Mitylene May 1916-Jan 1917, Syra Jan-
Apr 1917, Stavros May-Jul 1917, Mitylene Jul
1917-May 1918, Syra May-Jul 1918, Stavros
Jul-Nov 1918.

During August 1916 *M.22* and *M.33* were temporarily detached from the Mitylene patrols to assist French bombardments at Makri and Phineka on the southern coast of Turkey. Salonika guardship duties were dull, although enlivened in the early hours of 5 May 1916 when an airship was sighted overhead. Searchlights were burnt as all HA guns on ships in the harbour opened up, including those of *M.19* and *M.33*, although it was *Agamemnon* which hit the German Army Zeppelin *LZ.85* and set her on fire. The stricken Zeppelin drifted slowly eastwards before finally crashing in marshes an hour later. Several days later *M.17* found part of the wreck in the sea and towed it ashore. The Stavros squadron had a more active time, especially during the months following the Allied offensive of September 1916 and the Bulgarian occupation of Greek-held territory around Kavalla and Provista. The monitors *M.18*, *M.19*, *M.20*, *M.28* and *M.32* were usually off Chai Aghizi on the Allies' right flank, firing on Bulgarian defences and generally trying to keep the enemy troops tied down.

Some idea of the range of the daily activities of the small monitors can be obtained from the following extracts from the diary of Stoker Petty Officer C. Bass of Southsea, covering his period in *M.17* in the Aegean during 1915-16, in his original spelling (author's notes in square brackets).

10 July 1915 Commissioned at West Hartlepool. Prepared to embark ammunition.

20 July Devonport. Repairs and alterations.

26 July At sea. Hands striking down oil fuel [in drums?]. Taken in tow by HMS *Anemone*.

2 August At sea. Lost OS [Ordinary Seaman] overboard 1 p.m. Funeral service 6 p.m.

11 August In Mudros Bay. Took in shrapnel in exchange for some common shell. Took in oil and water.

20 August At Marvo [Mavro, or Rabbit Island]. Opened fire 10.30 a.m. Cease fire 11.05 a.m. at Fort 154. Opened fire 5.09 p.m. Cease fire 6.20 p.m. at Fort 160. 14 rounds. French aeroplane fell into sea near ship, both avaitors drowned.

6 October At Marvo. Went out surveying [in steam cutter] between Marvo and the entrance to the Dards. At 10.15 a.m. sighted two of the enemies Taubes [aircraft] coming from Constantinople making for Marvo and then one started droping bombs and returned then the other flew over the monitors and started dropping bombs. We returned to Marvo to see what damage was done and has [as] soon has [as] we got back they started dropping more bombs but they done no damage only killed a few fish but bombs which where [were] dropped where [were] not far from there mark. No. 21 [*M.21*] opened fire with her 9.2 and that cleared them after some good firing from the other monitors.

15 October HMS *Roberts* opened fire on Asiatic coast and

M.19, but bearing its title as MXIX, was the first of the 9.2in Mark VI monitors to be completed. (IWM SP139)

the Turks opened fire on us, one shell just missing my funnel of my boat. After the bombardment they picked up two shells and they where [were] found to be 4.7 made in New Jersey 1910.

30 October Enemy opened fire at 7.30 and done no damage. *Raglan* went around the back of Marvo and fired 21 rounds and returned in here. Seaplane went up and we had to tow her back to the ship.

31 October Went out surveying and returned at 4.30. *M.17*, *Roberts* and *M.20* all opened fire on the batteries. The enemy replied and one shell hit the *Roberts* and made a big hole in the football ground. My boat had all her bows busted open and all the after part all smashed up. Just got her hoisted in time to stop her from sinking. *Raglan* went out during the forenoon. One shell just missed the steam cutter has [as] we where [were] coming along side of the *Roberts*. Weather blowing very bad here. Already for leaving on account of the weather. *M.17* done some very good firing here today.

8 November Went away surveying. No.21 monitor arrived in forenoon with the staff Captains and left after daring French airman come over and was giving exhibitions very good.

17 November All the lighters broke away during the night. Towed two lighters off the rocks and had to let them go on account of the bad weather and had to proceed to sea. Went at the back of Marvo for shelter. HMS *Roberts* went ashore at Marvo. The collier come around to coal the *Roberts* but had to leave again on account of the gale.

25 November Watered ship already for leaving [Mudros] in the morning for Rabbit Island. Served out spuds [potatoes] first time for five months.

10 December *Roberts* played officers from monitors. [Football] Match started at 1.30 and everyone got recalled. We opened fire on 168 Fort and after firing the match was finished and the officers won 1-0.

23 December Went in the trawler to Tenedos to buy Christmas things for the mess. Come back at 4 p.m., and opened fire on 169 Fort.

28 December We opened fire on 168 Fort during forenoon and then opened on 171 Fort. After dinner we opened fire again on 168 Fort but could not reach her on account of gun being worn. Up till today we had fired 200 rounds out of our 9.2 gun.

Seen at Stavros on the Salonika front are (left to right) *M.19*, *M.32*, *M.16*, *M.20* and *M.17*. Spread awnings hide much of the deck detail, but *M.32*'s gunshield can be seen on her forecastle, probably to allow her forward 6in to be repaired. This view was probably taken early in 1918.
(IWM Q14110)

M.33 alongside the repair ship *Reliance* for work on her 6in.
(IWM SP275)

2 January 1916 7.30 a.m. went alongside the supply ship and took in stores and then left for Mudros and arrived at 3.15 p.m. and anchored off of the *Europa* and bricklayers come on here from the *Reliance* to put up the brickwork in the boilers. Served out box of chocolates gift from the Colonies. Had the gun experts on here to inspect the gun.

6 January At Mudros our parchments come on board the *Europa*. I got very good for character and exceptional for abilities. Served out winter clothing.

8 January 6 a.m. guns crews close up. Opened fire. ST Picton [*Sir Thomas Picton*] firing. *M.18* & *31* and us firing all day long. Other M [monitor] the other side of the island [Mavro] firing all day. A lot of horses and muels [mules] got smashed up on a small island here. Four Indians in charge got killed. A very nice hour sport driving them from one island to another........

26 January 10.30 a.m. went alongside SS *Trocas* [at Mudros] and filled up with oil fuel. 1.20 p.m. went alongside SS *Cairngowan*. French crane lighter come alongside of us and lifted our gun out [Mark X No.237, in *Euryalus* 1903-10] and put it on board the *Cairngowan*. 3 p.m. went alongside SS *Manchester Mariner* and French crane lighter put our new gun in [No.159 by Elswick, in *Hogue* 1901-10]. 6.35 p.m. left and anchored. Old gun fired 418 rounds [319 efc] 386 lbs each round.

27 January 4 p.m. went alongside the *Reliance* to have

our shield put on the new gun.

20 February 7 a.m. left for Gulf of Saros [Xeros] to bombard aerial station. *M.29* come out after us. 10.25 arrived 10.35 a.m. opened fire. Our aeroplanes arrived. Two destroyers scouting outside. Japanese commander on board for witnessing operations. 12.30 p.m. cease firing and rushed back to Kephalo. Whilst we were in action some snippers [snipers] where letting go but no one got hit on here. One airman who was spotting for us had to come down in Turkish territory on account of the fumes from the shells they where [were] firing at him and after 10 minutes he went up again without any damage.

8 March 8 p.m. had to go out on the gate [at Kephalo] on account of enemy submarines being reported. 1.30 p.m. went out and anchored just off Cape Hellas. *M.29 Theseus* & two destroyers come out with us and two aeroplanes. We opened fire on Cape Hellas. 5.30 p.m. ceased firing and returned to Kephalo.

14 April 9 a.m. released *M.29* on the gate [at Kephalo]. 8 p.m. aeroplanes left here for Constantinople to make an attack & Adrianople. All the ships in harbour give three cheers has [as] they flew over the Fleet. 11.40 p.m. first aeroplane arrived from Constantinople.

15 April 12.33 a.m. second aeroplane arrived back from Constantinople. 2.10 a.m. first one arrived from

M.16 steams through the busy harbour of Mudros in 1915. The breech of the 9.2in Mk X can be seen at the open rear of the shield. (P.A. VICARY)

M.32 in typical Aegean style.
(IWM SP240)

Adrianople. 5 a.m. second one just managed to land. Smashed up both pilot and observer safe. 9 a.m. went up harbour. 9 p.m. *Russell* and *Cornwallis* left here for Mudros.

2 May 7 a.m. started flooding floating dock [arrived at Mudros from Aden Nov 1915, built 1914, 1,400 tons lift capacity]. 9 a.m. went out of dock, got towed alongside oil tanker and filled up with oil fuel and fresh water. 2 p.m. went and run up and down the harbour, had a bit of a trial…….

17 May 9 a.m. towed the Zeppellin ashore that was brought down here [Salonika] on the 5 inst [see p.128]. I got a piece of angle iron. The only number reconisable was LZ [*LZ. 85*]. They have took the frame up to the French aerodrome so everyone in Salonika can go and see it.

2 June 8.30 a.m. proceeded to the nets and releaved French ships. Had some very good captures. One man and woman Salonika Jews escaping with plans of all the fortifications and of allied troops and ships here. Turned them over to the French.

20 August One of our seaplanes come down here [Kephalo]. They got lost owing to there compass giving out. 6 p.m. they left here but had to come down off of leaky bay [Aliki] and get towed in here engine troubles.

9 October 10 a.m. got releaved by the French ship [*Saint Louis*] and proceeded to Salonica following up Venizelos [Greek Prime Minister]. Passed his ship. He waved his hat three times to us. 5 p.m. Venizelos went ashore and had a great reception thousands of troops lined the streets.

22 November 1916 Dockyard men come on board [Malta]. Started pulling the ship to bits having a general refit.

In 1916 *M.29* had a surgeon aboard, F.C. Wright, to deal with the medical complaints of her crew of 74. These did not call for any great surgical skills: carbuncles, catarrh, bronchitis, haemorrhoids, influenza, injuries to scalps, elbows and wrists, and the inevitable cases of syphilis and gonorrhea.[5]

The squadron in Egyptian waters generally had a quiet time, disturbed only by an occasional enemy aircraft or sniper raid on the ships in the Suez Canal. During 1916 the British land forces were making preparations to advance through Sinai into Palestine against the Turks, laying a supply railway and water pipeline along the northern coastal road. When Turkish forces with German support attacked them in early August 1916 at El Rumana, 30 miles south-east of Port Said, *M.15* and *M.21* were able to anchor close enough inshore to land a heavy barrage on the Turkish positions around Oghratina oasis. Occasional bombardments were made of the Turkish base at El Arish, which was captured in December, the Turks being driven back to the heavily defended town of Gaza. To support the attack on Gaza on 17 April 1917, *M.21* and *M.31* were brought up to the new railhead at Deir el Belah. Together with the French coast defence ship *Requin*, they kept up a supporting fire whenever required. By the 19th the British had been heavily repulsed, although the monitors continued to fire intermittently over the next few weeks.

Driving the Turks back into Palestine had relieved the immediate threat to the Suez Canal, so the monitor forces there could be reduced. On 6 April 1917 *M.23* left Alexandria under tow for the Dover Squadron, *M.21* following three months later. Thereafter only one or two small monitors remained in Egyptian waters, but were temporarily reinforced in September 1917 by *M.29* and *M.32*. Allenby had taken command of the British land forces during the summer and, after receiving reinforcements, planned to attack the Turkish positions at Gaza again at the end of October 1917. His main thrust was to be inland at Beersheba, but he wanted naval support, not only for bombarding the defences at Gaza and the supply road and railway, but also to simulate a landing to tie down troops on the coast. By 30 October a powerful naval force had gathered at the anchorage off Deir el Belah, including *Grafton*, *Raglan*, *M.15*, *M.29*, *M.31*, *M.32*, *Requin*, the seaplane carrier *City of Oxford* and the destroyers *Comet* and *Staunch*. On the morning of the 30th *M.31* and *M.32* opened fire on Turkish defences on the coast two miles from Gaza, getting off 192 rounds from their 6in during the day. The main army attack began the next day, followed by the simulated landing on 1 November. An exceptionally heavy bombardment was kept up for several days; including the artillery ashore, it was the heaviest to date anywhere outside the Western Front. By the 7th the Army had taken Gaza, so the monitors switched their fire on to the retreating Turks. With spotting provided by *City of Oxford*'s seaplanes, *M.15* and *M.29* directed their fire against the railway line running north past Askalon, but the front line had moved out of reach of naval guns by the 9th.

The ships withdrew to Deir el Belah, anchored behind a line of anti-submarine nets about two miles offshore, as reports had been received of German U-boats in the vicinity. On the afternoon of 11 November *UC.38* managed to slip past the patrols at the ends of the nets and in two minutes had sent torpedoes into *Staunch* and *M.15*. The monitor was hit at 17.35 on the port side forward of her 9.2in gun, her magazine burning with a fierce flame but not exploding. She sank in three minutes with the loss of twenty-six men, the survivors being rescued by the other three monitors. The British defences had been caught with their pants well and truly down (*M.15*'s CO literally so, being on the WC when the torpedo struck), *UC.38* escaping unscathed. All ships were then immediately withdrawn to Port Said. After Allenby had captured Jaffa, *Grafton* moved up again with *M.29*, *M.31* and *M.32* to shell the retreating Turks north of the town on 22 December, the last occasion that the monitors were in action off Palestine. All the small monitors were withdrawn from the area early in 1918 except for *M.31*, which remained in Egyptian waters until after the Armistice.

The monitors had been keeping up their patrols off the Turkish west coast, but as heavier shore defences came to be installed they were forced to keep their distance. A particularly troublesome long-range 210mm gun (8.3in) from the disarmed cruiser *Roon* had been sited at Cape Helles, capable of shelling ships on the *Goeben* watch based at Kephalo. Early in May 1917 *M.17* and

M.18 suffered some near-misses from this well handled gun, and retaliated after its position had been located by aircraft. After *Raglan* had returned from Malta a determined effort was made to knock this gun out with a strong force of monitors. On the afternoon of 17 May *M.29*, *M.32* and *M.33* went out, covered by *Raglan* and *M.17*. The enemy did not reply on this occasion and, as none of the Helles guns had been hit, the monitors tried again early next morning. This time eleven enemy guns opened up on the 6in monitors, then only about 10,000yd off. *Raglan* and *M.17* attempted to quell this fire, managing to scatter some of the Turkish guns' crews. But even with good air spotting it was almost impossible to get the necessary direct hits on the gun mounts, so the Turks continued to harass any ships seen at Kephalo or Aliki, forcing a move to Kusu, which had recently been netted. Whenever possible *M.17* returned fire, generally firing about ten rounds over a period of half an hour from about 22,000yd. The 6in monitors then moved north to Kavalla, 40 miles east of Stavros. In the early hours of 20 May *Raglan* covered *M.19*, *M.28*, *M.29*, *M.32* and *M.33* while they opened fire on and destroyed the Custom House, which had been reported as being used to assemble submarines and motorboats. The Post Office, barracks and fort were also bombarded for 2½hr, during which time each 6in monitor got off about 100 rounds and each 9.2in monitor about fifteen, from 8,000yd.

A large and a small monitor remained based at Imbros on the *Goeben* watch, also guarding the British minefields off the entrance to the Dardanelles. On 20 January 1918 the long awaited sortie by *Goeben* and *Breslau* took place. The result was disaster for the two monitors, *Raglan* and *M.28* being annihilated as described in Chapter 2.8. By this time there were only ten of the original fifteen small monitors left in the Mediterranean, mostly at Stavros or on the Mitylene patrol, continuing their regular duties until the Armistices, first with Bulgaria, then with Turkey. *M.16*, *M.17* and *M.18* were included in the Allied Fleet which steamed triumphantly, yet three and a half years late, through the Dardanelles to anchor off Constantinople on 13 November 1918. The other monitors were sent to various Turkish ports to supervise the Armistice and dismantle the defences. Most of the monitors paid off at Mudros early in 1919, and were then laid up at Malta.

7.4 The Small Monitors at Dover

The last four small monitors to be completed were sent to join their big sisters at Dover. First to arrive was *M.25* on 6 September 1915, captained by Lt-Cdr B.H. Ramsay, who was later to command these same waters for part of WW2. She was sent into action the very next day at the bombardment of Ostende, described on p.55, but the

monitors were driven off by the Tirpitz battery before *M.25*'s short 9.2in could get within range. She was then sent round to patrol the Thames Estuary, where she soon demonstrated the lively motion of the small monitors. Bacon had serious doubts as to whether the small monitors would be effective bombarding vessels under Belgian Coast conditions. Their slow-firing guns' maximum range was 5,000yd less than those of the 12in monitors, which were already outranged by the German shore batteries. Their small gun platform meant that it was almost impossible to lay the 9.2in gun accurately in the open sea, so little more than a general strafing of large areas was possible. Gun trials had already demonstrated that the blast from firing over the bow was liable to buckle the forecastle deck, while broadside firing rolled the ship severely. Even before *M.24*, *M.26* and *M.27* had arrived, Bacon arranged to remove their 9.2in guns and mount them ashore in France, where there was a shortage of heavy artillery in the coastal sector. While *M.25*'s gun (No. 131 from *Gibraltar)* was lifted out by floating crane at Dunkirk on 1 October, the others had theirs removed at Middlesbrough before completion, for separate despatch to France.

Bacon included the small monitors as support to the large monitors in his plans for various operations described in Chapter 3.3: bombardments of Westende, anti-Zeppelin patrols and projected landings at Zeebrugge and Ostend. In the spring of 1916 all four were sent round to Portsmouth to receive a new main armament:

one 7.5in for *M.24* and *M.25* and one 6in for *M.26* and *M.27*, although *M.26*'s gun was soon replaced by a 7.5in as detailed on p.138. The guns were sited on top of a full-width deckhouse built abaft the break of the forecastle, which provided room for a sick bay. When the small monitors returned to Dover their activities were manifold, although their principal duty was patrol work, for which they were better suited with their new armament. They were able to screen the larger monitors from enemy destroyer sorties, thus relieving the burden on the more valuable British destroyers. The 7.5in gun outranged the German destroyers' guns and its 200lb projectile was capable of inflicting appreciable damage, while it could fire much more rapidly than the large monitors' 12in. The minesweepers and miscellaneous vessels supporting the barrage off the Belgian Coast in 1916 were also glad of their presence on several occasions during the summer when *M.25* and *M.26* helped drive off marauding German destroyers. Other activities included towing disabled MLs, rescuing ditched aircraft and sinking drifting mines. After 1916 they were often used as aiming marks for the large monitors. They would anchor about three miles further out to sea, out of range of the shore batteries, to provide a fixed reference point for the 12in and 15in directors. On 6 June 1917 *M.23* joined the squadron from Egypt, followed by *M.21* four months later, each having had their 9.2in replaced by a 7.5in.

After Keyes took over the Dover Command at the end of 1917, the small monitors had rather more varied

M.28 at Mudros in her final condition before her sinking on 20 January 1918. The funnel and mast have been raised in height. What appears to be a Maxim machine gun is mounted on the 9.2in gunshield. A flexible voice-pipe runs from the crows nest to the gun position. (P.A. VICARY)

activities. Patrol work continued, especially over the deep anti-submarine minefields in the Dover Straits, depth charges being added to their normal armament. The mine barrage soon took its toll of U-boats, as strong patrol forces kept them submerged. On 23 January 1918 German destroyers attacked the drifters on the old barrage patrol line off Zeebrugge. *M.26* was in support and returned fire with her 7.5in, but the enemy were difficult to locate in the smoke and were only forced to retire after two British destroyers put in an appearance. A more serious raid took place on the night of 14/15 February, this time on the Straits barrage, *M.26* again being the main defence of the patrol, as none of the regular large monitors was available on that date. The crew of *M.26* heard gunfire to the south and saw emergency signal rockets from the drifters, but a limited investigation revealed nothing and her few messages to Keyes at Dover gave no hint as the severity of the German raid. In fact, two half-flotillas had attacked the patrol line, sinking eight drifters and damaging six more, returning safely to Zeebrugge without being counterattacked by the patrolling British destroyers, which had observed them without realising they were German. When belated full reports were finally received several hours later, Keyes was furious that the Germans had got away unchallenged, unreported and unscathed. The destroyers took much of the blame, but *M.26* was criticised for not investigating fully the extensive gunfire, the signal rockets and the blazing wrecks, and for not reporting any useful information until it was too late for Keyes to redeploy his remaining forces to catch the returning German ships.

Her CO, Cdr A.A. Mellin, was replaced a month later. The organisation of the barrage patrols was tightened up but, as Bacon had pointed out before his supersession, such hit-and-run raids would always be very difficult to counter.

Three of the small monitors were in attendance at the Zeebrugge Raid, allocated to the diversionary forces bombarding Ostende. *M.21*, *M.24* and *M.26* acted as aiming marks for the large monitors. Their consorts, *M.23*, *M.25* and *M.27*, undertook similar duties at the second attempt to block Ostende on 10 May. As a small recompense for their faithful service, *M.23*, *M.26* and *M.27* were allowed to make a night bombardment of the German batteries at Westende. On the night of 14/15 May they landed fifty-one rounds near their target, supported by French artillery ashore. A repeat performance was made two nights later with a further sixty-two rounds. Two months later *M.23* and *M.25* were withdrawn from the Squadron to be prepared for service with the White Sea Squadron as described below.

The small monitors continued to accompany the large ones on their bombardments, but it was four months before they were given another chance to use their main guns, during the preliminaries to the Allies' September offensive. In the early hours of the 28th *M.26* and *M.27* opened fire with the 12in monitors on the coastal batteries around Westende. This was the last offensive operation carried out by the small monitors off the Belgian Coast, which was evacuated by the Germans shortly afterwards. The latter had left a strong minefield off the approaches to Ostende, which ensnared *M.21* on 20 October, two

M.26 entering Portsmouth, probably after her return from North Russia in October 1919. Her 7.5in was mounted in 1916, replacing her earlier 6in; she never actually mounted her 9.2in, which was sent to France. The range-finder can be seen ahead of the bridge and the tall galley funnel. Two 3in HA are now fitted aft in place of the original 12pdr and 6pdr, but the two pom-poms fitted abaft the boats have been removed. The bridge was increased one deck in height before she left for Russia. (NMM AFO 1-276)

explosions occurring at 17.35. Her whole fore end was wrecked but she could still steam, so she was brought further inshore before finally sinking in 20ft of water a mile from the West Pier. Five of her crew were missing, the remainder taking to the boats to be picked up by *Terror* and *M.27*. The three remaining monitors, *M.24*, *M.26* and *M.27*, were temporarily stationed at Ostende and Zeebrugge for the next few weeks, before returning to Dover in December. *M.27* then steamed round to Chatham, and the other two to Portsmouth, where they were refitted for service in the White Sea.

7.5 The Small Monitors in Russia

There had been a small number of British ships in North Russian waters since 1915, protecting the main supply route to the ally Russia through Archangel. After the Revolution in 1917 the main concern of the British forces was to safeguard the accumulated military stores, to stiffen resistance against any German advance from Finland and to prevent German troops being transferred to the Western Front, as well as to give help to refugees. Troops were sent to Archangel to protect the military stores and to secure the two main transport routes south; the railway to Vologda and the River Dvina to its limit of navigation at the railhead of Kotlas. For such operations shallow-draft vessels would be needed, so at the end of June 1918 *M.23* and *M.25* were ordered to prepare for service with the White Sea Squadron. They departed Chatham on 26 July after a quick docking and arrived at Murmansk on 9 August.

Archangel had already been occupied a few days earlier by a small British and French force under Capt Altham, fresh from the Belgian Coast, so *M.23* could be sent on to Kem on the south-west shore of the White Sea to assist the modest forces holding the railway south from Murmansk against possible attacks from the Bolsheviks, from whom the Murmansk region had dissociated. *M.25* was sent up the Dvina from Archangel to back up with her heavy artillery the British, American and Canadian troops, as there was a possibility of their being able to link up with the Czech Legion, formed from troops released from prisoner-of-war camps in Siberia. The Bolsheviks had withdrawn to the south-east up-river, taking several armed river steamers with them. The wide but shallow river was the only worthwhile means of communication in the area, the normally frozen ground thawing to almost impassable bog during the short summer. The Bolsheviks held the river banks down to Bereznik, at the junction with the River Vaga, some 160 miles above Archangel. Their well-armed gunboats had been able to hamper seriously any advance of the Allied forces, but the arrival of *M.25* with her 7.5in gun changed the situation

completely. She engaged the gunboats on 26 and 28 August, as well as enemy batteries on the banks near Tulgas, about 20 miles above Bereznik. Her relatively powerful armament was able to drive the gunboats off and silence the batteries, although she did suffer one hit in her captain's cabin, which caused casualties of four killed and seven wounded, mostly among the 12pdr crew on the quarterdeck. A further operation on 14 September took place to strengthen the Allied position for the approaching winter, in the course of which *M.25* sank the large gunboat *Moguchi* with two well-directed 7.5in shells. Thereafter the other Bolshevik vessels used their superior speed and shallower draft to keep well out of the range of the monitor's guns. With the imminent icing up of the river it was necessary to withdraw all ships to Archangel on 7 October, leaving the force of Allies and White Russians (anti-Bolsheviks) to hold the Tulgas-Bereznik position until the following spring, much harassed by the Bolsheviks.

By the time of the Armistice with Germany the Allied intervention had gradually developed into outright support of the White Russians against the Bolsheviks, not only in North Russia, but in the south and east as well. However, early in 1919 the Allies decided to withdraw their active forces from Russia, but in order to extricate them without loss from any Bolshevik spring offensive, reinforcements would be needed to cover the withdrawal. Churchill, now Secretary for War, organised the despatch of volunteer troops and ships, to be sent to Russia as soon as possible. Naval forces included the remaining three ex-Dover monitors, *M.24*, *M.26* and *M.27*, the last now carrying a triple 4in in place of her 6in, plus *M.31*, *M.33* and *Humber* from the Mediterranean, as well as four China gunboats. All six monitors left Britain in mid-May, ready for the break-up of the ice in the White Sea and in the Dvina.

The campaign the previous year had shown that the 7.5in monitors were really of too deep draft for satisfactory operations up the Dvina, drawing over 8ft aft. So, on arrival in North Russia, *M.24* and *M.26* were left behind at Archangel. As soon as the river ice showed signs of breaking up, *M.23* forced her way up above Bereznik, dynamiting the ice as she went, in case the Bolsheviks and their gunboats should overwhelm the scanty Allied forces before military reinforcements could arrive. She was in action the next day, 6 May, bombarding Tulgas, now held by the Bolsheviks; the four China gunboats arriving to help soon after. The flotilla was under the command of Cdr S.W.B. Green in *M.23*, as his own ship, *M.25*, was still refitting at Archangel. The latter ship joined up on 17 May, taking part in many of the minor skirmishes with the Bolshevik gunboats that took place over the next few weeks. Altham arrived in the river

From right to left, *M.27*, *M.31* and *M.33* up the River Dvina at Shestakovo in July 1919. *M.27* has a triple 4in in place of her previous 6in. (IWM Q16017)

steamer *Borodino*, now converted into a headquarters ship, to take command of the Archangel River Flotilla on 3 June. The intention had been to withdraw the Allied forces as soon as they could be safely extricated but, just at this time, one of the White Russian leaders, Admiral Kolchak, was having some success with his forces from Siberia away to the south-east. At Churchill's insistence offensive operations were continued to try to reach Kotlas and to link up with Kolchak. *Humber*, *M.27* and *M.33* arrived on 14 June, and *M.31* the following day, together with shallow-draft minesweepers to combat the troublesome drifting Bolshevik mines. These reinforcements permitted the deeper-draft *M.23* to return to Archangel on 23 June.

A major offensive was undertaken shortly afterwards to consolidate the Allied position by capturing the villages of Troitsa and Seltso, some 30 miles above Beresnik. *Humber*, *M.27* and *M.33* were all heavily engaged, not only firing on enemy batteries on the banks but also warding off any gunboats or armed barges that appeared round the bends in the river. *M.27*'s triple 4in proved a potent weapon, with a rate of fire approaching fifty rounds of HE per minute. The monitors also made good use of their lighter guns, their 3in HA generally being used for low-angle work. Owing to the relatively low maximum elevation of their main armament, the British monitors and gunboats were outranged by 2,000yd or more by the Bolshevik vessels. They did, however, have the advantage of air spotting, as kite balloons and seaplanes could operate almost unmolested and so direct fire from the anchored ships on to their targets, which were usually invisible from ground level. Altham made good use of his Belgian Coast experience by drawing up very full instructions for

controlling bombardment operations. The monitors' movements were somewhat restricted by their relatively deep draft, especially as the river depth had fallen to only about four feet by July. Their stouter hulls were better able to withstand prolonged firing than the China gunboats, while their accommodation was superior. *Humber* was a particularly valuable ship, with her three 6in, her good protection, her shallow draft and her extensive accommodation.

The Allied situation changed on 7 July, when White Russians fighting alongside the British mutinied, killing both their own and British officers. News was also received of setbacks to Kolchak, so, with the imminent withdrawal of the Allies, disaffection spread quickly among the White Russians, fearful of their fate at the hands of the Bolsheviks. The naval forces soon came under heavy Bolshevik attack, *M.33* being hit in the wardroom but without suffering casualties. She returned a heavy fire, some 200 rounds of 6in in two days, supported by *M.27*, *M.31*, *Humber*, *Cricket* and *Cicala*. By 9 July the situation had stabilised, withdrawal now being only a question of suitable opportunity. It would be several weeks before the rains would raise the river sufficiently to allow the ships to clear the sandbars, so it was necessary to obtain some freedom of manoeuvre until that time. A bombardment of Seltso on the south bank above Troitsa was made on 10 August as a preliminary to a powerful offensive by British and White Russian troops. After capture of the village with heavy enemy losses, both banks were secured with some assistance from parties of armed seamen landed from the ships.[6]

Now that the Bolshevik forces were in no position to harass the Allies, detailed preparations for the withdrawal were put in hand. Every effort was made to lighten the ships sufficiently to get them down river, transferring into barges all removable equipment and stores. *Humber* shed her 3in side armour plating as well as her after 6in, 3in HA and 3pdr guns; most of the vessels got their drafts down to about 5ft 3in, except *M.25* and *M.27*. By 30 August all the major vessels had managed to get back to Archangel with the exception of these two. Attempts were made to blast channels for them through the sandbars, but it was a losing battle as the river level had already begun to fall again. After the last troops had been withdrawn, *M.25* and *M.27* were abandoned and blown up with gun-cotton charges on 16 September.

During the summer *M.24* and *M.26* had remained at Archangel, ready to answer any calls for assistance, later being joined by *M.23* from up river. Their first action came after the mutiny of Russian troops around Onega at the southern end of the White Sea, which fell to the Bolsheviks on 22 July. On the 23rd *M.23* was sent to Onega to rescue the small British contingent and to assist 350 White Russian troops in their attempt to recapture the town, being followed by *M.26*. While *M.23* evacuated the wounded to Archangel, she was replaced by *M.24*. Heavy fighting took place on 1 August, with the two monitors firing at enemy guns on the river banks. The Bolsheviks proved to be too strong to be dislodged, so *M.24* and *M.26* returned to Archangel on the 3rd. *M.23* was sent to Kem on 27 July to cover the withdrawal of the British force that had advanced down the Murmansk railway to Lake Onega. All the remaining monitors gathered at Archangel during September to be prepared for the voyage to Britain under tow, *Humber* and *M.24* leaving first, followed by *M.26*, *M.31* and *M.33* on 27 September 1919. *M.23* was the last monitor to leave North Russia, as she had been sent to Kandalaksha at the north-west corner of the White Sea on 24 September to evacuate Allied troops, finally departing ten days later for Murmansk and arriving at Sheerness on 4 November.

Meanwhile, British naval forces had also been engaged in South Russia. They had entered the Black Sea after the armistice with Turkey and by early 1919 were supporting Gen Denikin against the Bolsheviks. With the withdrawal of German forces the Bolsheviks had taken over most of South Russia, including nearly all of the Crimea, but White Russians were still holding out in the extreme eastern corner of the peninsula in April 1919, as well as to the south-east on the mainland. Two of the small monitors were transferred from their guardship duties at Constantinople to give assistance, *M.17* arriving off Sevastopol on 24 March. She was soon in action, firing on Bolshevik-manned shore batteries at Bakal, north of Sevastopol, on 7 and 8 April. Two days later *M.18* arrived,

so both monitors were sent round into the Sea of Azov in mid-April to provide support at the ends of the White Russian lines stretching across the narrow Kertch Peninsula. While Allied battleships, cruisers and destroyers guarded the southern flank from Kaffe Bay, the monitors were anchored with two cruisers off Akhmanai in Arabat Bay on the northern flank. Their powerful 9.2in were in action right away, helping repulse Bolshevik attacks and firing on railway junctions behind the lines. On 3 May *M.29* joined the force, her two 6in being particularly useful with their solid punch and reasonable rate of fire. The 9.2in gun was much less handy than the 6in, with only about one-sixth the rate of fire, but nonetheless some 100 rounds were fired by *M.17* and *M.18* during April and May, although not without some blast damage to their hulls. The strain was felt particularly by *M.17*, which had to be towed back to Mudros, where she handed over to her replacement, *M.22*.

By the time *M.22* reached the Crimea, on 15 June, the Bolsheviks were being driven back, so she was sent to Genichesk at the north end of the Sea of Azov. In company with *M.18* she fired on Bolshevik positions and cavalry, as well as railway lines, helping the White Russians assert control of the Crimea and Lower Don area. As Denikin advanced northwards the monitors were withdrawn, *M.18* and *M.22* to Yalta, and *M.29* to Constantinople for refit. Early in August *M.18* was sent to pay off at Malta, leaving *M.22* and *M.29* to assist forthcoming operations in the north-west Black Sea, which included plans to capture Nikolaiev. To get armed barges up the Rivers Bug and Dnieper for Denikin's offensive it was necessary to reduce the forts at Ochakov and

After supporting the White Russians against the Bolsheviks, *M.27* was unable to get down the shallow River Dvina to Archangel. She was blown up on 16 September 1919 to prevent her falling into enemy hands, after her triple 4in and all useful equipment had been removed.
(IWM SP2251)

Kinburn. *M.22* had made a brief bombardment on 3 August, which was followed on the 12th and 13th by heavy fire on the 6in batteries by *M.29*, the cruiser *Caradoc* and the destroyer *Steadfast*. Nikolaiev was taken shortly afterwards, so plans were made to support the attack on Odessa, but that city fell without the British ships needing to fire. By September most of South Russia was in the hands of the White Russians, so the two remaining monitors were withdrawn. *M.22* and *M.29* left Yalta under tow on 23 September, arriving at Malta on 2 October. A number of other RN ships remained in the Black Sea into 1920, a year which was to see Denikin's defeat and total triumph for the Bolsheviks.

7.6 Armament Changes

All of the 9.2in monitors based at Dover underwent considerable armament changes. After Bacon had ordered the removal of their 9.2in guns, a makeshift armament of five 6pdr HA was provided for *M.25*, an additional three being sited in place of the 9.2in and one abaft the funnel, as well as the existing gun. The provision of a new main armament was not too easy, as most spare guns of suitable calibre, such as 6in, were required for armed merchant cruisers. However, the loss of *Triumph* in May 1915 meant that her two spare 7.5in guns became available, as she had been the only ship in the RN with the Vickers-designed 50cal Mk IV gun, because she had originally been built for Chile. The spares were dispatched from Malta to Portsmouth, where they were installed one each in *M.24* (gun No. 83) and *M.25* (No. 84) in May

1916. Both *M.26* and *M.27* were each allocated one 6in QF removed from *Redoubtable*, which were fitted at Portsmouth in March 1916. By then *Triumph*'s near-sister *Swiftsure* had left the Dardanelles and was carrying out patrols in the Atlantic. As she was unlikely to require both her spare Elswick-designed 50cal 7.5in Mk IIIs, one (No. 54) was dispatched to Portsmouth, where it replaced *M.26*'s 6in in September 1916. *M.27*'s 6in QF was also replaced, but by a longer-range 6in BL VII. When *M.21* and *M.23* arrived back in England in the summer of 1917, *Swiftsure* had been paid off at Chatham. Her fourteen-gun secondary battery could thus be raided, so both monitors got one 7.5in Mk III, while their 9.2in were sent to join the siege guns in France. Unlike the earlier 7.5in, which had been fitted with full gunshields in the monitors, only the original small semi-circular casemate shield protected these last two 7.5in. The Mediterranean vessels had no changes made to their main armament apart from the routine shifts of worn-out gun barrels.

Changes were also made to the HA armament, first of all replacing the makeshift converted 6pdr HA 1C mounting with the new HA IV mounting illustrated, which could elevate right up to 90 degrees. As 3in HA guns became more widely available they replaced the 6pdr in the Dover monitors while, later in the war, the Mediterranean monitors shipped them in place of their 12pdr. Towards the end of the war 2pdr pom-poms were being added to supplement the Dover vessels' light armament, two being mounted on platforms next to the boats, where they could be used against aircraft, DCBs

M.25's 9.2in gun was removed at Dunkirk shortly after completion for mounting as a siege gun ashore. She is seen with her temporary armament of five 6pdr HA, before getting a single 7.5in forward in 1916.
(IWM SP2969)

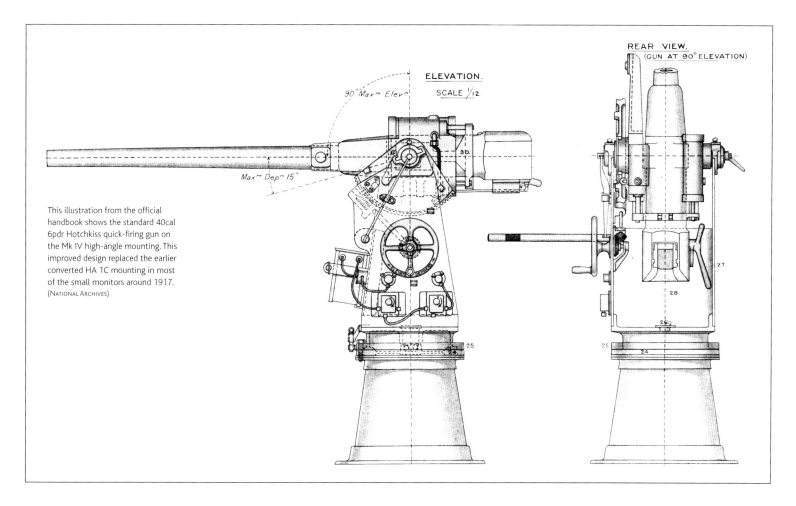

ELEVATION.

SCALE 1/12

90° Max^m Elev^n

Max^m Dep^n 15°

REAR VIEW.
(GUN AT 90° ELEVATION)

This illustration from the official handbook shows the standard 40cal 6pdr Hotchkiss quick-firing gun on the Mk IV high-angle mounting. This improved design replaced the earlier converted HA 1C mounting in most of the small monitors around 1917. (NATIONAL ARCHIVES)

or floating mines. The following table shows the armaments of the small monitors in 1918 as far as they can now be ascertained:

M.16	1 x 9.2in, 1 x 3in
M.17	1 x 9.2in, 1 x 12pdr, 1 x 6pdr
M.18, M.19, M.20, M.22	1 x 9.2in, 1 x 3in, 1 x 6pdr
M.21, M.25	1 x 7.5in, 1 x 3in, 1 x 12pdr
M.23, M.24, M.26	1 x 7.5in, 1 x 3in, 1 x 12pdr, 2 x 2pdr
M.27	1 x 6in, 1 x 3in, 1 x 12pdr, 2 x 2pdr
M.29, M.31, M.32, M.33	2 x 6in, 1 x 6pdr
M.15, M.28, M.30	All lost while still mounting original armament.

Before service in the White Sea, *M.27* had her 6in replaced by three 4in BL IX on a triple mounting, similar to the installation in *Renown* and *Repulse,* while a 3in HA replaced the 12pdr in *M.24, M.26* and *M.27,* and the 6pdr in *M.31* and *M.33.* Two 3pdr HA were fitted in *M.23* to *M.26,* their 2pdrs being removed.

7.7 Performance

The small monitors were certainly superior to the large coal-burning monitors in respect of one characteristic, namely speed. Whereas the latter were lucky to manage 7kts, the 9.2in monitors were usually good for 10½kts in

service, and the 6in for 9kts. They did, however, exhibit one feature which was not present in the large monitors: a tendency to roll excessively, due to their having been built without bilge keels, plus a relatively high GM for a small vessel of about 5.5ft. Their normal roll period was about 8sec (port to starboard and back to port again), so, without the damping of bilge keels, large amplitudes could be built up. Several cases were recorded of very large rolls, *M.25* claiming 45 degrees from the vertical when at anchor in the Thames Estuary, and *M.23* 57 degrees in the Mediterranean. Both claims are probably a little exaggerated, as a simple pendulum can overestimate angles at short periods, but the rolls were sufficient to throw ready-use ammunition out of its racks. Bilge keels were fitted at the first convenient opportunity but, although they provided some damping, the monitors' roll period remained uncomfortably short. The general handling characteristics of the shallow-draft hulls were also poor, although slightly better than those of the large vessels. The 6in monitors were worse than the 9.2in, as the 10ft² rudder area and steering gear proved inadequate, having been designed for 4ft draft. Astern steering was bad, while occasional breakdowns of the steering gear did nothing to enhance the monitors' popularity when manoeuvring in confined waters and harbours.

The machinery of the diesel ships never lived up to expectations. Designed for merchant ship conditions of steady steaming, the engines often proved unequal to the demands of naval service, with frequent speed changes, stops and starts. A recurrent problem was fires in the funnels of Bolinder-engined ships. Unburnt fuel in the exhaust could collect inside the uptakes and either produce showers of sparks or catch fire as the temperature rose after a spell at full power, or when reversing. The problem was never completely overcome, despite frequent funnel cleanings and adding 6ft extensions to their length for larger silencers. In theory, the diesel monitors had an endurance of about 2,200 miles, but in practice the unreliability of their engines resulted in their being towed on most of their longer voyages. The steamers were also towed, not because of any unreliability, but owing to their very short endurance of only about three days. Despite a specific fuel consumption nearly four times that of the diesel vessels, their bunker capacities were little larger.

The hulls proved somewhat on the light side for the relatively heavy guns mounted, and all required some stiffening, especially the decks of the 6in vessels. Various painted camouflage schemes on the hulls were tried at the whim of individual officers, *M.18* sporting green for a while, *M.19* dazzle painting, *M.21* khaki, *M.23* pale blue and *M.29* a false bow wave. Different patterns of funnel bands were painted up at various times, for example *M.17*, *M.22* and *M.30* having three, and *M.19*, *M.26* and *M.29* having none.

7.8 After the War

With the paying-off of the remaining small monitors from the White and Black Seas towards the end of 1919, thirteen were left of the original nineteen ships. There was little use for such vessels in the slimmed-down post-war RN, although a few could be converted for other duties. All of the diesel boats except *M.23* were put on the Sale List late in 1919, plus three of the steamers. With the post-war boom in merchant shipbuilding there was a brisk demand for surplus naval vessels suitable for conversion to mercantile use, thus overcoming the long delivery times being quoted by the shipyards for new construction. Early in 1920 the Anglo-Saxon Petroleum Company (now Shell) snapped up *M.16* to *M.20*, *M.24*, *M.26* and *M.32* on behalf of its Dutch associate Curaçaosche Scheepvaart Maatschappij, with the intention of converting them into small tankers. Each was sold for £7500, a good price about five times scrap value. *M.20*, *M.24* and *M.26* were converted in Britain, the latter two at Smith's Dock, North Shields, for about £19,000 each, and the others in Holland during 1920-21. Their armament was removed and four cargo oil tanks

replaced the magazines forward and aft. The average cost to Anglo-Saxon, including purchase, conversion and delivery to Curaçao, was about £40,000. As converted, the ships had a gross registered tonnage[7] of about 510 tons and could carry about 500 tons of oil cargo. With their shallow 10ft 3in draft they were mostly engaged shuttling oil from the Lake Maracaibo wells to the refineries at Curaçao. Owing to the fall in the tanker freight market in the early 1920s, most were allocated to bunkering duties in major ports. Over the next two decades many of the vessels were transferred to various Shell companies at overseas locations, as summarised in the Table.

Ship	Name	Year and port of registry
M.16	Tiga	1921 Willemstad, Curaçao; 1923 Kingston, Jamaica; 1924 Sydney
M.17	Toedjoe	1920 Willemstad; 1922 Kingston; 1922 Montreal
	Nanaimolite	1927 Nanaimo, Canada
M.18	Anam	1921 Willemstad; 1924 London for bunkering service at Hamburg
	Alcione C	1932 Genoa
M.19	Delapan	1921 Willemstad (bunkering service at Hamburg from 1925)
M.20	Lima	1920 Willemstad; 1924 Genoa; 1932 Dakar
	Marie des Fleurs	1948 Dakar, French West Africa (wine tanker)
	Maria Augusta	1954 Rio Martin, Morocco
	Alvin	1960 Panama
M.24	Satoe	1920 Willemstad
M.26	Doewa	1920 Willemstad; 1924 Gibraltar; 1924 London for service at Suez
M.32	Ampat	1920 Willemstad
	Delta	1924 Marseilles
	Colette Richard	1946 Marseilles (wine tanker)

Each first name represents a Malayan number, respectively 3, 7, 6, 8, 5, 1, 2, 4. The final fates of the vessels are shown in the Technical Data as far as they can now be ascertained. Both *M.18* and *M.32* were used by Axis forces during WW2, the latter being requisitioned by the German navy, the former by the Italians.

The five remaining small monitors were retained by the RN for further service. *M.23* was converted into a stationary drill ship for service with the RNVR. After conversion at Sheerness she was towed to Leith in August 1922, where she remained as HMS *Claverhouse* for the next 37 years. The other four were earmarked for conversion into coastal and instructional minelayers for service with Torpedo Schools. After the war large-scale mining experiments were planned, to take account of wartime experiences. The first to be converted was *M.22*, at Portsmouth early in 1920; she took part in experiments

at the Kyles of Bute and Loch Crinan from August 1920. *M.31* followed soon afterwards, completing her conversion at Portsmouth in January 1921. Their armament was stripped out and narrow-gauge mine rails added on the upper deck on either side of the superstructure, and the necessary derricks, winches and mine-handling gear were fitted. *M.31* was assigned to HMS *Defiance*, the Torpedo School at Devonport, where she remained in commission for minelaying instruction until 1937; *M.22* was based at Portsmouth for similar duties.

Both *M.29* and *M.33* had also been earmarked for conversion but, with the shortage of defence funds, the former lingered at Devonport until September 1923 when she was taken in hand by Pembroke Dockyard, while *M.33* did not arrive at Pembroke from the Nore until May 1924. The conversion work was completed in January and February 1925 respectively at a cost of about £21,000 each, these being two of the last major refits undertaken before the dockyard closed down the following year. As converted, the ex-monitors were capable of laying either fifty-two H-type moored mines (forty-four in *M.22*) or eight (later increased to sixteen) L-type loop mines, the latter laid to protect harbours and controlled by cables from observation stations on shore. Carrying

moored mines, their deep displacement was virtually unchanged at 576 tons, although with loop mines and the heavy associated cables it rose to 614 tons. The crew was reduced to twenty-six for peacetime instructional duties, but would be doubled in time of war to three officers and forty-nine men.

All four minelayers were given the distinction of names in December 1925, *M.22* being named *Medea*, *M.29 Medusa*, *M.31 Melpomene* and *M.33 Minerva*. The last was based at Portsmouth as a relief ship for *Medea*, in reserve except when the latter was refitting. *Melpomene* remained at Devonport, while *Medusa* was sent out to Malta, commissioning in May 1925 as a tender to *Egmont* to act as an instructional minelayer. For the next ten years no changes occurred in this pattern, until they were replaced by new purpose-built coastal minelayers which began to join the Fleet from 1937. *Medea* was the first to be discarded, being towed away from Portsmouth on 20 January 1939 for scrapping by Cashmore at Newport, Monmouthshire. During a heavy gale on the night of the 22/23rd she broke her tow, running on to the rocks near Trevose Head on the north Cornish coast. One of the towing crew was lost overboard, but the others were taken off safely by breeches buoy. Salvage was impossible as she

Eight of the small monitors were sold to Anglo-Saxon Petroleum (now Shell) in 1920 for conversion into coastal tankers. *M.24* was converted by Smith's Dock at North Shields into the Dutch-flagged *Satoe*, seen here on trials in October 1920. (SMITH'S DOCK MONTHLY)

TOP
M.29 was converted to a coastal minelayer in 1925 and renamed *Medusa*. She is seen here at Malta in June 1937, with a load of moored mines on the rails each side.
(A. & J. PAVIA)

ABOVE
Medea (ex-*M.22*) broke her tow on the way to the shipbreakers on 22 January 1939 and was driven on to the rocks near Trevose Head, where she was eventually broken up.
(AUTHOR'S COLLECTION)

was firmly wedged on the rocks, so she was eventually broken up *in situ*.

The other three vessels had not been sold by the time war broke out, so they were restored to naval service. *Melpomene* served the whole war at Devonport as a torpedo instruction vessel, having been fitted with a single 21in tube on her forecastle. When the small destroyer *La Melpomène* joined the Free French forces in September 1940, the ex-monitor was renamed *Menelaus* to avoid confusion. She was finally scrapped in 1948 with the great

post-war clear-out of surplus naval vessels. *Medusa* had a more varied life in the Mediterranean. She was fitted in May 1941 with the main winch from the badly damaged minesweeper *Fermoy* and used for lifting the sterns of MTBs to permit changing their propellers without the need for slipway hauling or drydocking. In September 1941 she was renamed *Talbot* and became the depot ship for the newly formed Tenth Submarine Flotilla, based in Lazaretto Creek with workshops ashore. She was damaged in the heavy Luftwaffe bombing of March 1942, which culminated in the temporary withdrawal of the Flotilla. She took up her duties again when the Flotilla returned in July, until it departed for Sardinia in December 1943. When the First Submarine Flotilla arrived, in February 1944, she adopted the name of its depot ship which had been sunk in June 1942, *Medway II*, and continued her service as a mini-depot ship. After the war she was towed back to Britain and scrapped in 1947.

7.9 The Preservation of *M.33*

Although *Minerva* was transferred to Dockyard Control for the Sale List in January 1939, she had not actually been sold before war broke out in September. Restored to naval service, she remained at Portsmouth as a floating staff office, reportedly for Wrens. Early in 1943 it was approved to convert her into a fuelling hulk to replace the coal hulk *Martin*, now numbered *C.23*, which had been

condemned. Before work could begin at Portsmouth Dockyard it was decided instead to convert her into a floating boom defence workshop. She arrived at White's Shipyard on the River Itchen at Southampton in June 1943. Her engines and boilers were removed, the whole space being given over to a workshop fitted with machine tools. Her oil fuel tank was converted to a store and her funnel and mast removed. In this form she was towed to the Clyde in the middle of 1944 to help service the anti-submarine booms protecting that important river. She was allocated *Martin*'s old number, *C.23*, although she was still generally known as *Minerva*.

She returned to Portsmouth in 1946 and was moored on the south side of the oil fuel jetty at Gosport. Here she remained as a floating workshop and office for auxiliary craft at the Royal Clarence Victualling Yard. Her designation was *C.23(M)* for some of the time, though after the Royal Maritime Auxiliary Service was set up she then became RMAS *Minerva*. She was kept in good condition with regular refits by the dockyard. When no longer required by the Ministry of Defence she was removed in 1984 to lie up harbour at Portsmouth. Efforts were made to preserve her, as one of the very few remaining First World War warships in the world. In December 1985 she was sold by the Ministry of Defence for a £8,250 to the Hartlepool Ship Preservation Trust, for possible restoration at Hartlepool,

where *Warrior* had recently been restored. She left Portsmouth together with *Foudroyant* (now restored as *Trincomalee*) on board the barge *Goliath Pacific* on 24 July 1987. Little work was possible owing to lack of funds, but in 1990 Hampshire County Council investigated the possibility of restoring her at her old base of Portsmouth. She was towed back from Hartlepool, arriving at Portsmouth on 25 August 1991. Some general hull maintenance was carried out by a small band from the RN Museum at Portsmouth. A 6in Mark XII, No. 2838, formerly at the gunnery training school *Excellent*, was fitted on the forecastle in March 1992, while she was berthed in No. 1 Basin at the dockyard. From 1994 Hampshire County Council Museums Service took over project responsibilities. On 23 April 1997 *M.33* was moved into the old No. 1 Drydock close to HMS *Victory*, clear of the water, permitting an electrolytic anti-corrosion treatment to be applied internally. A second 6in acquired from the Chilean Navy in 1994 was fitted aft. Work has continued slowly on her restoration to her 1915 appearance, including a dazzle paint scheme and interpretive panels around the drydock, but visitors are not at present (2007) allowed on board. Although the drydock entrance has been closed off by a new jetty, her future is reported as 'reasonably secure', so she should be able to participate in her own and the Gallipoli centenary in 2015.

LEFT
Minerva at Portsmouth in June 2005, showing her after 6in acquired from Chile in 1994.
(AUTHOR)

BELOW
Minerva partially restored by Hampshire County Council in No.1 drydock at Portsmouth in June 2005. Her forward gun is an original 6in Mark XII previously at Whale Island gunnery school.
(AUTHOR)

Minerva at Hartlepool in August 1988. A new funnel has been fitted by Hartlepool Ship Preservation Trust. Wooden wall *Foudroyant*, about to be restored as *Trincomalee*, lies astern.
(AUTHOR)

Minerva (ex-M.33) in August 1971 as floating workshop *C.23(M)* for auxiliary craft at Gosport. She remained in service until 1984.
(AUTHOR)

The Small Monitors — TECHNICAL DATA

M.15 — M.28

Displacement: 540 tons Navy List, (*M.15-M.18*) 650 tons deep on 7ft 0in draft, 540 tons light on 6ft 0in, (*M.19-M.28*) 610 tons deep on 6ft 7½in, 500 tons light on 5ft 7½in.

Dimensions: Length 177ft 3in oa, 170ft 0in bp, breadth 31ft 0in, depth to upper deck 12ft 3in.

Weight distribution as completed (tons) (*M.17*) Armament 75, ammunition 35, hull 340, equipment 50, machinery and RFW 118, oil fuel 32. Total 650 tons.

Complement: 5 officers, 64 men.

Armament: 1 x 9.2in single (*M.15-M.18*: Mk X; *M.19-M.28*: Mk VI) (60 CP + 60 HE rpg), 1 x 12pdr (200rpg), 1 x 6pdr Hotchkiss HA (500rpg), 2 x 0.303in Maxim (8,000rpg).

Protection: Hull nil. 9.2in gunshield (*M.19-M.28*) 4in front, 1¼in sides.

Machinery: Twin-screw triple-expansion: M.15-M.17 by Central Marine Engine Works of Hartlepool (Nos. 865, 866, 871) 11½in, 18¼in, 30in x 16in 800ihp at 210rpm; M.21 by McKie & Baxter of Glasgow (No. 820-21) 8½in, 14in, 23in x 14in 600ihp at 270rpm, two White-Forster watertube boilers 180lb/sq in; M.22 by Shields Engineering & Dry Dock of North Shields, 650ihp at 210rpm, two White-Forster watertube boilers. Twin-screw Bolinder 4-cyl semi-diesels: M.18-M.20, M.23, M.25, M.28 420mm x 480mm 640bhp at 225rpm. Quadruple-screw Bolinder 2-cyl semi-diesels: M.26 380mm x 410mm 480bhp at 275rpm, M.27 inner 160bhp each at 225rpm, outer 120bhp each at 275rpm, both 380mm x 410mm, total 560bhp. Quadruple-screw by Campbell Gas Engine, Halifax 4-cyl paraffin engines: M.24 13in x 14in 640bhp at 300rpm. Oil fuel: M.15-M.17 32 tons; M.18, M.25, M.26 25 tons; rest 28 tons.

Endurance: at 9½kts: 660 miles on 0.4 tons oil per hour (steam ships), 2,200 miles on 0.12 tons oil per hour (diesel ships).

Speed: 12kts designed, 10½ service. Trials: M.19 11.5, M.21 11.5, M.24 11.1kts.

Construction: Wm Gray, Hartlepool: M.15 (No. 865) launched 28.4.15/completed 12.6.15; M.16 (No. 866) 3.5.15/24.6.15; M.17 (No. 871) 12.5.15/14.7.15; M.18 (No. 872) 15.5.15/31.7.15. Sir R. Dixon, Middlesbrough: M.19 (No. 597) 4.5.15/11.6.15; M.20 (No. 598) 11.5.15/3.7.15; M.21 (No. 599) 27.5.15/20.7.15; M.22 (No. 600) 10.6.15/7.8.15; M.23 (No. 601) 17.6.15/28.7.15; M.24 (No. 602) 9.8.15/4.10.15; M.25 (No. 603) 24.7.15/5.9.15; M.26 (No. 604) 24.8.15/18.10.15; M.27 (No. 605) 8.9.15/3.11.15; M.28 (No. 606) 28.6.15/17.8.15.

Disposal: M.15 torpedoed 11.11.17; M.16 sold J. Stride, Sydney, 23.6.53 for scrapping; M.17 disposed Nanaimo 1939; M.18 sunk off Corsica 14.4.43; M.19 stranded near Danzig 14.4.45; M.20 scrapped Italy 1968; M.21 mined 20.10.18; M.22 wrecked 22.1.39; M.23 scrapped by Shipbreaking Industries, arrived Charlestown, Fife, 21.4.59; M.24 expended as target West Indies 29.9.36; M.25 blown up 16.9.19; M.26 sold P.C. Gallia 8.5.34 and scrapped at Suez; M.27 blown up 16.9.19; M.28 sunk 20.1.18.

M.29 — M.33

Displacement: 355 tons Navy List, 580 tons deep on 5ft 11in draft, 453 tons light on 4ft 10in.

Dimensions: Length 177ft 3in oa, 170ft 0in bp, breadth 31ft 0in, depth to upper deck 10ft 6in.

Weight distribution (tons): (As designed/as completed) Armament 35/40, ammunition 25/40, hull 180/325, equipment 25/50, machinery and RFW 70/80, oil fuel 20/45. Total 355/580 tons.

Complement: 5 officers, 67 men.

Armament: 2 x 6in single (100 CPC + 125 HE + 25 shrapnel rpg), 1 x 6pdr Hotchkiss HA (500rpg), 2 x 0.303in Maxim (8,000rpg).

Protection: Hull nil. 6in gunshield: 3in front.

Machinery: Twin-screw triple-expansion 9in, 15in, 24in x 12in 400ihp at 250rpm. M.29-M.31 by Harland & Wolff, Belfast, M.32-M.33 by Workman, Clark, Belfast. Two Yarrow watertube boilers 170lb/sq in. Oil fuel 45 tons.

Endurance: 1,440 miles at 8kts on 0.25 tons oil per hour.

Speed: 10kts designed, 9 service. Trials: M.29 10.0, M.30 9.98, M.31 10.13, M.32 9.95, M.33 9.61kts.

Construction: Harland & Wolff, Belfast: M.29 (No. 485) laid down 23.3.15/launched 22.5.15/completed 20.6.15; M.30 (No. 486) 23.3.15/23.6.15/8.7.15; M.31 (No. 487) 23.3.15/24.6.15/9.7.15. Workman, Clark, Belfast: M.32 (No. 488WC) 1.4.15/22.5.15/20.6.15; M.33 (No. 489WC) 1.4.15/22.5.15/24.6.15.

Disposal: M.29 scrapped Dover Industries, Dover, 1947; M.30 sunk 13.5.16; M.31 scrapped E.G. Rees, Llanelly, Jan 1948; M.32 scrapped France 1951; M.33 preserved at Portsmouth (2007).

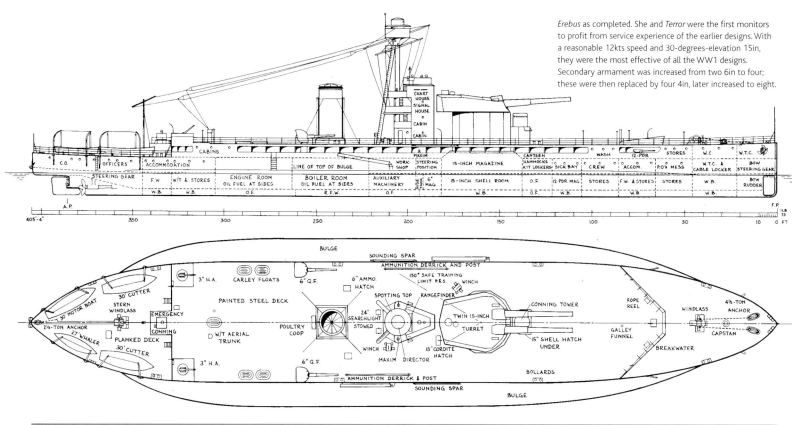

Erebus as completed. She and *Terror* were the first monitors to profit from service experience of the earlier designs. With a reasonable 12kts speed and 30-degrees-elevation 15in, they were the most effective of all the WW1 designs. Secondary armament was increased from two 6in to four; these were then replaced by four 4in, later increased to eight.

CHAPTER 8

The Second 15in-gun Monitors

8.1 The Cancelled Monitors

The protests of the Army at the decision to bring home the *Queen Elizabeth* from the Dardanelles underlined the importance of having bombardment ships carrying the heaviest guns. Although there could be no question of sending modern battleships out to the Dardanelles, *Marshal Ney* with her 15in guns was allocated on 14 May 1915, together with eight other large monitors (see p.25). On that same day the decision was taken to build four more monitors carrying 15in guns. Tudor minuted:[1]

> It has been decided to place orders for four more 15in monitors to be propelled by steam, as follows: 2 Harland & Wolff, 1 Hamilton, 1 Swan Hunter. These vessels to be completed in 6 months but not to be allowed to interfere with progress on work already in hand. The gun mountings are being ordered separately, also alternative trunks, shell-room gear

etc, in order that if so desired at a later stage, it would be possible to transfer mountings from *Royal Oak* to these four vessels. The necessary action should be taken forthwith as it is desired to place the orders for the hulls and machinery as soon as possible.

It was already known from AEW's tests that none of the large monitors would be capable of their designed 10kts, as was confirmed by *Abercrombie*'s first trial the very next day. AEW had already shown how it was possible to improve the monitors' hull form to get the designed speed, so a new set of lines was drafted out which were sent to Haslar for testing. With this new form and two more powerful minesweeper steam reciprocating engines of 3,600ihp, there would be little difficulty in attaining the required speed of 10kts. The basic ship design was similar to the earlier monitors, although the hull was slightly larger than the *Marshal*s, 350ft BP, 89ft 3in broad and

10ft draft, with a legend displacement of 6,780 tons.

Orders for the four ships, provisionally designated *M.34* to *M.37*, went to the builders on 18 May, all of whom were now finishing off their first monitors. Harland & Wolff allocated its two, *M.34* and *M.35*, the hull numbers 492G and 493G, Swan Hunter's *M.36* was No. 1009 and Hamilton's *M.37* No. 313. Although H & W quickly laid both keels at Govan, when the new Balfour/Jackson Board met on 4 June the question of continuing the new monitors' construction was reconsidered. It was appreciated that the only way of getting delivery in the specified six months would be to commandeer all of *Royal Oak*'s turrets, which would delay her completion until 1917. The new Board was not prepared to accept such a delay in the battleship programme, so on 10 June the four monitors were cancelled.

8.2 A New Design

Two months later came the disappointing news of *Marshal Ney*'s machinery trials, as described on p.82. As an ex-DNO, Tudor was well able to assess the possible ways of making better use of the *Marshal*s' valuable 15in guns. One of the possibilities considered was their transfer to two brand new monitor hulls. So once again Lillicrap was called on to work up a detailed design; he started on 6 September 1915. The new design was particularly significant as it was the only one during WW1 which incorporated from the keel up any feedback of experience from completed ships; the normal process of evolution in naval architecture. The overriding consideration was the need to achieve the specified 10kts and, if possible, to get 12kts. By 16 September Froude had sent to London the first results of the new model tests, showing that about 1,800ehp was necessary for 12kts. Lillicrap was instructed to use a propulsive coefficient no higher than 0.3, so it was estimated that about 6,000ihp would be required, over double the power of the previous vessels.

The hull was appreciably longer than those of the other monitors, at 385ft BP, but this was necessary to obtain a relatively fine entrance and run. The angle of entrance at the waterline was reduced to about 50 degrees, compared with about 120 degrees in the earlier monitors. The finer lines would give a better flow of water aft, so would improve propulsive efficiency and assist steering, although there would be insufficient space to fit twin rudders. The main hull breadth was kept at 62ft as in the *Marshal*s, but the bulge was reduced in width. Experiments with new forms of bulge construction for battleships had been carried out during 1915 using models, following up with a full-scale section of part of the side of a ship, 80ft long and 31ft 6in wide and deep, called the Chatham Float. As a result the bulge consisted of an outer and an inner

watertight compartment, the outer being empty and the inner, instead of being open to the sea, filled with steel tubes sealed at their ends. The idea was that much of the force of the explosion would be dissipated in crushing the tubes. Thus the new monitors had a bulge only 13ft wide; an air space of 9ft and a tube space of 4ft, filled with about seventy tubes of 9in diameter lying fore and aft in each bulge compartment. Inboard, 1½in of HT steel protected the hull proper. The overall breadth was thus reduced to 88ft, but there was no chance of keeping the draft as shallow as 10ft. The extra weight of the larger hull and heavier machinery meant that nearly 8,000 tons of buoyancy had to be provided, which required a draft of 11ft. The more powerful engines with four boilers in place of the usual two required a machinery space 82ft long. Using oil fuel instead of coal simplified the layout of the bunker spaces as well as reducing the number of stokers.

For the first time a proper bridge structure was provided, four decks high. Associated with a funnel large enough to keep the smoke away from the bridge, the design took on a distinctly more ship-like appearance than the earlier monitors, although the straight stem and lack of sheer forward did not enhance their looks. When it came to settling detailed design features, Bacon put forward several suggestions from Dover. His experience in *Lord Clive* on 7 September showed that maximum gun range was essential. It was therefore arranged that the 15in mountings would be modified to give 30 degrees elevation, resulting in an extra 6,000yds range. He also considered that it would be useful to be able to back off an enemy coastline while keeping the turret trained on target. Consequently a bow rudder was fitted, which necessitated a vertical stem in place of a curved profile. A further request was for a properly fitted stern anchor and windlass to make mooring head and stern easier when bombarding. The bow anchors were increased from 4 tons each in the earlier monitors to 4½ tons, with 750ft of

Erebus and *Terror* had the 'standard' WW1 monitor protection, except for the water space in the bulge being replaced by steel tubes. Splinter protection was provided for the bridge. Figures in brackets show thicknesses after 1940 rearmouring; two inches were added on the upper deck over the 15in magazine, and one inch on the main deck aft.

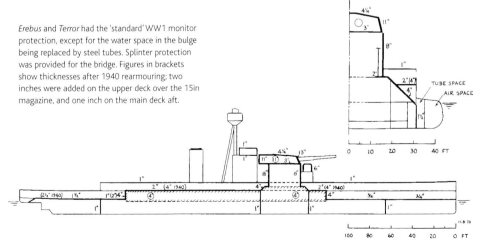

2¼in-diameter cable. It had been found on the *Marshal*s that the mass of the turret affected their magnetic compasses, so one of the newly introduced gyro compasses was fitted below the armoured deck.

The barely submerged bulge had proved a nuisance in the earlier monitors. It was neither deep enough to avoid being an underwater obstruction to boats, nor high enough to form a dry platform for access to the ship's side. The top surface was therefore raised so as to be about 18in above the waterline, thus also providing great initial stability. The spartan standards applied to outfitting in the earlier monitors were improved above the bare necessities, although not to full peacetime standards. Armour protection remained much as before: 4in on the belt slope and over the magazines, 2in on the upper deck and 1in on the forecastle deck. The turret armouring was the same as in the 15in battleships. The legend displacement put up to the Board was calculated as 7,960 tons, made up as shown in the Technical Data. A comparison with the 14in design of a year earlier shows the following differences in percentage weight distribution:

Terror on 18 May 1916, the day of her launch from No.3 slipway at Harland & Wolff's Belfast yard, the same slipway on which *Titanic* and *Lord Clive* had been built. The drag chains and bow rudder are prominent. (HARLAND & WOLFF)

	14in	15in
Armament and ammunition	13.7	13.7
Armour and protection	30.1	30.0
Machinery and fuel	12.3	17.2
Hull and equipment	43.9	39.1
Total percentage	100.0	100.0
Designed deep displacement, tons	6,157	8,460

The percentages allocated to offence and defence were identical, but the faster ship required a greater proportion devoted to propulsion and a correspondingly lesser amount to the hull.

An approximate breakdown of the estimated total cost is given below, but as the cost of the 15in turrets and one set of barbette armour had already been charged to other ships in the Admiralty accounts, there was a difference between the apparent 'as built' cost and a realistic 'if new' cost.

	'If new' cost, £	'As built' cost, £
Armament	155,000	15,000
Armour	70,000	50,000
Machinery	85,000	85,000
Hull	230,000	230,000
Total	540,000	380,000

8.3 Construction

Harland & Wolff had already laid down the keel of one of the cancelled monitors, which had remained on the slipway at Govan. The company was thus the obvious

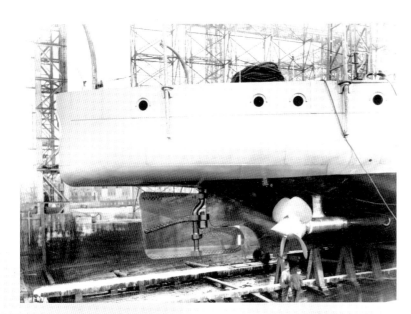

LEFT

Terror's aft end just before launch, with standing ways already greased. Her two four-bladed 9ft 3in-diameter propellers are fitted. With her finer lines than the earlier monitors, a single rudder was deemed sufficient. However, at her much deeper WW2 draft its area had to be increased to 130 sq ft to provide even barely adequate steering.
(HARLAND & WOLFF)

BELOW

Terror immediately after her launch on 18 May 1916, with Workman, Clark's North Yard in the background. The twelve-sided barbette armour and the armoured conning tower have already been fitted.
(HARLAND & WOLFF)

choice of builder for the two new monitors to take over *Marshal Ney*'s and *Marshal Soult*'s turrets, orders being placed on 29 September 1915. The previous hull numbers 492 and 493 were revived, the former for the Govan hull, the latter for the Belfast hull; machinery for both was built at Belfast. Material which had already been ordered for the cancelled ships was used, not only to speed construction but to reduce costs. Although shipbuilding steel plate only cost about £11 per ton at that time (having risen from £7 pre-war), 4in armour plate cost about £90 per ton and could not lightly be discarded. Beardmore's works at Parkhead in Glasgow supplied most of 492's armour and Cammell Laird in Sheffield most of 493's. Names were allocated on 13 October, 492 becoming *Erebus* and 493 *Terror*. Gone were the generals' names; in their place two famous names of previous bomb vessels were revived, the first *Terror* having been lost at the Siege of Gibraltar in 1704. The names had also been borne by two of the Crimean War floating batteries. Completion in six months had been specified, but with the increasing shortage of labour and the larger, more complex design, such a short period was not realistic. *Marshal Ney* only arrived at Elswick at the end of January 1916, and the work of converting her mounting to 30 degree elevation would take several months before it could be shipped to Belfast for installation in *Terror*. Furthermore, *Soult* had proved more satisfactory than *Ney*, so her turret was no longer available. It was therefore necessary to hurry on for *Erebus* one of the two turrets ordered as spares for *Furious* should her 18in prove unsatisfactory. As H & W did not have a large enough crane, *Erebus* was towed to John Brown's at Clydebank on 13 July for her turret to be erected.

No official figures of displacement as completed were recorded, although the ships' drafts suggest that it was about 8,450 tons in the deep condition, very close to the designed figure. Although the raised turret, high bridge and tall tripod mast produced a top-heavy appearance, in fact the very broad beam provided ample stability. At 32ft, the metacentric height GM² was one of the highest for any British warship; typical figures for battleships of the WW1 period being 4 to 8ft and for cruisers 2 to 4ft.

Terror was the first to be commissioned, on 22 July under Capt C.W. Bruton. Tweedie of *Marshal Ney* had originally been posted to take command but, with the longer construction period, had gone to *Sir Thomas Picton* instead. Speed trials were carried out on 1 August, and, after all the disappointments of the earlier monitors, were a great success. The 4hr full-power trial went off without a hitch, and instead of the expected 12kts she made 13.09. She left Belfast on 6 August 1916 to join the Monitor Squadron at Dover. *Erebus* followed a month later, which

gave her time to have two 6in QF guns mounted abreast the funnel on the forecastle deck to augment the meagre secondary armament of two 12pdr. Her trials went even better than *Terror*'s as she averaged 14.1kts. In place of the leisurely ten-minute cruises between the mile-posts of some of the earlier monitors, she covered the distance in just over four minutes, amidst clouds of spray thrown up off the bulges. The next day, 2 September, she was able to leave for Dover with Capt C.S. Wills in command.

8.4 Service in the First World War

The arrival of *Terror* at Dover on 8 August 1916 marked the appearance of the first monitor carrying big guns and having a reasonable turn of speed. After steaming across to Dunkirk she was soon in action on the 16th, firing at a canal bridge near Middelkerke. Her three rounds at maximum elevation were more in the nature of a gun trial than a serious attempt to hit the target. *Erebus* arrived at Dover on 5 September, just in time to join the other monitors supporting Haig's offensive described on p.60. *Erebus* and *Terror* were out on several days, but were not allowed to fire as many rounds as the 12in monitors, to avoid wearing out their guns prematurely on non-essential targets. Firing on 12, 13 and 15 September was carried out at anchor from behind a smokescreen, generally using the 12in monitors as back aiming marks in conjunction with shore spotting. About seventy rounds of HE were fired between the two ships, with no great attempt at accuracy, as only a general harassment was required. A more careful bombardment was made of Zeebrugge on 24 September by *Terror* from 27,400yd, using two seaplanes to spot. The weather proved to be too hazy for accurate observation, so firing was abandoned after twelve rounds. This turned out to be the last bombardment by any of the Dover monitors for seven months, as winter and increasingly strengthened German defences restricted operations.

At the end of January 1917 Bacon took *Erebus* and *Terror* out to bombard the German torpedo boats which usually berthed inside the mole at Zeebrugge, but the operation had to be called off at Dunkirk owing to heavy snow. The early months of 1917 had seen a number of German destroyer raids on shipping anchored in the Downs, so all 15in monitors took their turns as guardships at night. Although there were several raids in their vicinity, they never had a proper chance to fire their main guns, but such powerful defences did have a deterrent effect. Preparations had been going ahead for the bombardment of the lock gates at Zeebrugge, as related in detail on p.86. When the Zeebrugge bombardment finally took place, on 12 May, both *Erebus* and *Terror* put in some concentrated shooting, contributing sixty-three and sixty-

Terror leaves Harland & Wolff's yard on 31 July 1916 for speed and gunnery trials. The upper surface of the bulge can clearly be seen. Her 6in secondary armament was not installed until November. (HARLAND & WOLFF)

one rounds respectively.

Bacon had intended to follow up this bombardment with one of Ostende Dockyard almost immediately but, as on so many occasions, several attempts had to be abandoned before conditions were finally suitable. Although the dockyard was a much bigger target than the lock gates, great care still had to be taken in restricting the spread of shot, as the area was surrounded by civilian housing. At last all was ready on the evening of 4 June, when *Erebus* and *Terror* set out, accompanied by a fleet of twenty-two destroyers and smoke-producing MLs. The monitors anchored 13 miles north-north-west of Ostende in the early hours of the 5th. At 03.20 ranging shots were dropped deliberately short into the sea so that the splashes would check for direction; after eight rounds, fire was lifted straight into the dockyard area. Aircraft spotting corrections were obtained as dawn was not far off; good results were reported. Enemy retaliatory fire from Deutschland and Tirpitz batteries soon began and became uncomfortably hot until the spotting balloon was shot down by a Sopwith

Pup. Both sides were using smokescreens; after 15min the German one obscured the target. Firing was continued using estimated corrections until 04.00, when the monitors weighed anchor. A good morning's work had been done; twenty hits out of 115 rounds, sinking the submarine *UC 70*,[3] a dredger and two barges, and inflicting damage on other vessels and various buildings. The bombardment worried the Germans considerably, as an effective repeat performance would prohibit regular use of the dockyard.

Unfortunately neither of the two floating docks had been damaged, so Bacon was anxious to take advantage of any further favourable opportunities of bombarding the dockyard. When the BO Patrol (see p.87) was instituted, there was generally a 15in monitor available to open fire whenever conditions were favourable. Although a few rounds were fired during August, it was September before any really suitable opportunities came, first for *Soult* on the 4th, then *Terror* on the 22nd (thirty-five rounds with *M.23* as aiming mark) and again on the 25th (thirty-one rounds with *M.25*). The Germans sent up aircraft to spot on the 22nd, but Tirpitz's crashed on take-off and Deutschland's was shot down over the sea. Considerable damage was done to the dockyard installations and, in particular, one of the floating docks holding two torpedo boats was partly sunk, although both vessels were later salved. The lock gate was also hit, causing the basin to drain at low water.[4] With such continual harassments from sea and land bombardments the Germans decided to transfer most of the dockyard equipment to Bruges, and thereafter Ostende was little used.

The three 15in monitors were then sent in succession to the Tyne floating dock (later AFD 4), returning in mid-October to resume patrols. But it was not to remain so for long; both *Erebus* and *Terror* were very soon put out of action by German counterattacks, albeit temporarily. Since before the war, the Germans had been experimenting with distance-controlled explosive motorboats (DCB), but such craft only became fully operational during 1916. The 6-ton *Fernlenkboote* were 43ft long and could reach 30kts. They could be steered by means of a 30-mile trailing cable from shore in accordance with instructions signalled from an accompanying seaplane. As they were unmanned, the intention was to crash them into the side of a monitor, when it was hoped that the 700kg (1,540lb) charge would sink it. The first DCB used against the Allies in the west blew up when it hit Nieuport pier in March 1917, but later attacks on ships on patrol were more troublesome. It was thought unwise to attempt to cut the wire cable or to shoot down the guiding aeroplane, as the boat would remain highly dangerous,

circling out of control. The method adopted to combat them was great vigilance by the patrol crews, coupled with considerable skill in using the ships' lighter armaments. On 6 September *M.23* was successful in shooting up *FL.8* with her 3in at 400yd.

Another attack shortly after midday on 28 October was not so easily repelled. Amidst a hail of shells from escorting vessels ranging from 2pdr to 6in, *FL.12* was seen to approach *Erebus* as the monitor was steaming west away from the coast about 20 miles off Ostende, cross under her stern and turn 180 degrees to hit her squarely on the starboard bulge amidships. A huge explosion severely shook the ship, sending debris over a wide area, killing two and wounding fifteen of her crew. However, the monitor was not badly damaged, as the bulge took the main force of the blast. She got back safely to Dover and was then sent round to Portsmouth for repairs. In drydock it was found that about 50ft of the outer bulge had been destroyed, but that the main hull was almost unscathed apart from a minor dent in the main longitudinal protective bulkhead and a few scratches above water. She was back in service at Dunkirk on 21 November. A few more attacks were made by DCBs, but without further success. They were abandoned by the end of the year, owing to the lack of suitable targets within easy range, the small number of boats available and technical difficulties such as the breaking of the cables on the net barrages.

Terror was out of action for slightly longer. She was lying at anchor off Dunkirk at about midnight on 18/19

Erebus moored in Dover Harbour in April 1917. Apart from the chequer painting on her mast and the shield added to the 6in (just visible abaft the funnel pointing at the camera), she is as completed. Her single motor-boat is lying at the quarter-boom; it was more useful than her three pulling boats put together. (NMM GU3/29)

October when heavy explosions were felt on the port side forward. Three torpedoes from raiding German torpedo boats had struck her in quick succession, two right forward, the third about 80ft abaft the stem, at the start of the full bulge protection. The boats, *A.59*, *A.60* and *A.61*, had approached unseen and, after discharging one 450mm (17.7in) torpedo each, opened fire with their guns from close range. Although considerably damaged, with the fore part of the ship opened to the sea, *Terror* was able to beach herself with tug assistance in about 15ft of water.

Captain Iron, whom Bacon had appointed Chief Salvage Officer, was roused from bed and brought across from Dover in the tug *Lady Brassey* in the early hours of the 19th. His survey showed that the main deck, normally level with the sea, was flooded to a depth of several feet from forward of the 15in magazine. The hold below was severely damaged nearer the bows but, owing to the close subdivision, most of the compartments further aft seemed to be watertight. By now a second tug, *Lady Crundall*, had arrived, so together the two tugs brought *Terror* round to Dunkirk. With the monitor beached at low tide the damage could clearly be seen. The foremost 50ft below the main deck had been largely blown away, and damage also extended up to the forecastle deck. The hit further aft had been mostly cushioned by the bulge and the tubes, so damage was limited. As in *Erebus*'s case, the bulge had proved its worth, and these two episodes reinforced in d'Eyncourt's mind the value of including bulges in new designs where practicable.

Iron and *Terror*'s shipwright, J.S. Collacott, and their men attempted to build cement boxes over the holes, but were frustrated by the rising tide. Instead they shored up leaking bulkheads and pumped out compartments only slightly damaged, repeatedly interrupted by German air raids. By Sunday the 21st *Terror* was ready to proceed to England for full repairs. The passage to Dover was safely made going ahead at 7kts, but Iron recommended to Bruton that the longer voyage to Portsmouth should be made stern-first to reduce the strain on the damaged bulkheads and to ease steering problems resulting from the trim by the head. When *Terror* set off for Portsmouth on the evening of 23 October it was clear that the bluff-spoken Iron's advice and services were not welcomed by the prickly Bruton. Her departure was made just as the weather began to deteriorate, being towed head-first by *Lady Brassey*, assisted by *Lady Crundall*. At about midnight off Hastings the strong wind began to whip up the seas and wash them along the upper deck, being open at the sides. She became difficult to steer and, when the temporary salvage pumps broke down, water began to accumulate on the upper deck. Too late, Bruton tried to turn her 180 degrees stern-on to the sea, but she lay wallowing broadside in the trough of the seas, becoming deeper and more sluggish in the water as the waves washed over her. Although there was no sign of water below decks, Bruton gave the order to abandon ship when the head rope parted at about 03.30. *Lady Crundall was* left holding her by a single line. At about 08.00 the weather moderated, *Terror* was re-boarded and found to be sound, so *Lady Brassey* was again secured and towed her safely back to Dover.

She was readied for a second attempt to reach Portsmouth on 27 October, this time with Iron in control. The presence of a civilian officer, who had demonstrated the irritating habit of being right where ship handling and salvage matters were concerned, was not welcomed, so Iron took the precaution of having *Lady Duncannon* in attendance while two other tugs towed *Terror* stern first. All went smoothly until they were off Folkestone, when Bruton ordered that his ship be turned and proceed in the manner in which he was accustomed to command her, namely bows first. Iron's reminders of the result of her last voyage in this condition were brushed aside, so he called up *Lady Duncannon* and made to leave *Terror* and her prickly captain to their own devices. Alarmed by now at the possibility of losing his ship through pighead-edness, Bruton climbed down. Iron remained in control and *Terror* continued towards Portsmouth – stern first. In this manner Spithead was made the next morning, the Dover tugs cast off and dockyard tugs turned her bows-first for the final entry into Portsmouth.

At the Court of Inquiry into *Terror*'s abandonment, evidence centred on minor matters such as the breakdown of the salvage pumps, rather than how she was ever allowed to get into her dangerous situation in the first place. Bacon supported Bruton's decision to abandon; Iron was not called to state what recommendations he had made for the voyage. Bruton and his fellow officers could count themselves fortunate indeed in receiving a favourable verdict, as they were officially absolved of any blame.

Terror's repairs took ten weeks; she returned to Dover on 5 January 1918. *Erebus* and *Terror* continued to make the occasional bombardment of Ostende Dockyard on BO Patrols as the opportunity offered during the early months of 1918, after Keyes had taken over. German defences were continually being strengthened. Sound-ranging was developed for their coastal batteries, wireless jamming and smokescreens became more effective, and dummy shell bursts were rigged, which could be set off during a bombardment to mislead British spotting. *Terror* was hampered by unsuitable projectiles. A faulty batch of 15in had been manufactured 5in too long, so rather than scrap them they were issued to the monitors. It was hoped that

Terror early in 1918, after her
torpedo damage had been repaired.
At this stage she only had four 4in in
place of her four 6in. Her wash
always gave the impression of
greater speed; she is probably doing
about 11kts here.
(IWM Q60837)

with minor modifications to the hoists and gun-loading
cages they could be used up in shore bombardment, given
the relatively slow rate of firing. But it was found that the
clearances were too tight and the projectiles continually
jammed, disrupting serious operations. So they were
withdrawn; in any case, new longer-ranging projectiles
would soon be available. British bombardment techniques
were also steadily improving, especially the accuracy of
position-finding assisted by sound-ranging and other
features described in Chapter 10.

The big German land offensive started on 21 March
1918. That night a minor diversion was made by three
groups of German destroyers bombarding the railway
between Dunkirk and Nieuport. As usual, a force of
monitors and destroyers was anchored offshore to frustrate
such operations, the enemy vessels being spotted in the
early hours of the 21st. As the latter opened fire from
seaward, *Terror* fired star shell and followed up with her
6in. British and French destroyers from Dunkirk had
slipped and were approaching fast, so the German forces
retired to Ostende, hotly pursued. *Terror* and her patrol
consort, *M.25*, were of course too slow for such an
engagement, but when Keyes heard of the action he
ordered *Terror* to bombard the enemy ships, now holed
up in Ostende. In the afternoon she anchored offshore
and from 26,500yd put thirty-nine rounds into the
dockyard before enemy return fire and smokescreens
prevented further bombardment. Considerable damage
was done in the Gare Maritime area, although none of
the destroyers was hit. Inevitably there were also casualties

to Belgian civilians and houses.

In the plan for the blocking of Zeebrugge, *Erebus* and
Terror were assigned as part of the covering force. They
took up their position 14 miles north of the port at about
23.30 on 22 April. Having been slightly delayed en route
they were unable to bombard the locks as planned, but
opened fire directly on to the Kaiser Wilhelm battery. In
poor weather conditions there was no attempt to spot,
but a steady fire was kept up for 2hr while the main assault
took place. On the second attempt to block Ostende,
on 10 May, *Erebus* and *Terror* were both used to keep
down return fire from the Tirpitz and other heavy
batteries, firing off a total of ninety-two rounds with *M.23*
and *M.25* acting as aiming marks. Shortly afterwards a
German homing pigeon landed on *Terror* carrying a
cipher message, which revealed nothing of value.

Air raids and long-range artillery bombardments of
Dunkirk continued throughout the summer. On 7 July
Erebus was hit by two bombs on the starboard bulge; only
the second monitor to be damaged by aircraft at Dunkirk
during the whole war, despite innumerable attacks.
Damage was slight so she was soon repaired at
Portsmouth. She also received two new 15in guns in
readiness for the forthcoming Allied offensive, while at
the same time Moreton transferred from *General Wolfe*
to take command. *Terror* received her new guns two weeks
before the September offensive. Each of her old guns had
already fired about 300 rounds (including about forty
while in *Ney*), so were in no condition for a sustained
operation. *Erebus* and *Terror* carried out a 40min night

Erebus's turret and forecastle as seen after her 1918 refit, showing her twelve-sided barbette armour; quicker to make than the usual circular. Armament changes visible include the 12pdr HA under the guns, 4in on the beam and 3in HA aft (IWM SP161)

bombardment of the Zeebrugge area in the early hours of the 28th to keep enemy forces occupied in this sector. Enemy return fire was uncomfortably accurate. *Erebus* counted fifty-six rounds landing nearby from which she received many shell fragments, but fortunately nothing heavier. By 07.00 they had both taken up new positions six miles north-east of Dunkirk, whence they fired at German howitzers at Slype, about five miles south-west of Ostende. Some 120 rounds of CPC and HE were got off over a period of 8hr. Firing both types of projectile necessitated one more correction to the already large number needed to achieve accurate results; it was found that the HE ranged about 600yd further than the CPC.

Very little firing was possible over the next two weeks, but on 14 October the monitors were out again in force for another similar operation. Two hours' intensive bombardment of Slype was carried out from 05.30 at a rate of one round per ship every two minutes. In the afternoon both ships steamed up the coast to Zeebrugge, accompanied by three small monitors and 34 supporting vessels, to encourage the Germans to continue retaining troops in that sector, but in fact the Germans were busy evacuating the coast. Following the Armistice, both ships returned to Dover to await a decision as to their future. The role that *Erebus* and *Terror* had played in strengthening the Dover Patrol was fully recognised. Their modern armament, reasonable speed and generally more satisfactory design than the earlier monitors, all pointed towards their being retained in peacetime, even if only for training duties.

8.5 Between the Wars

Of all the WW1 monitors, *Erebus* and *Terror* had the most interesting post-war careers. Although *Erebus* was attached as a tender to the Chatham Gunnery School from January 1919, she remained in full commission. She was thus readily available to reinforce the British White Sea Squadron when a request came in July for a cruiser or other well armed vessel to support the forces in the Murmansk area. Orders were sent to *Erebus* on 30 July to complete to full complement, stores and ammunition. She left Sheerness three days later under Capt Moreton for the voyage to Murmansk, where she arrived on 13 August by way of the Norwegian leads. After a week at Kem she moved to Onega, 100 miles to the south-east. Onega had been taken by the Bolsheviks some weeks earlier, as mentioned on p.137; attempts to recapture it had failed. A heavy bombardment was ordered for 28 August by *Erebus* and *M.23* in collaboration with seaplanes from *Nairana*. Anchoring 18,000yd from the town, *Erebus* used her 15in and two of her 4in to fire on such varied targets as steamers, enemy headquarters, AA gun

batteries, ammunition dumps and troop concentrations. *M.23* also opened fire at noon from 10,500yd, adding twenty-eight rounds of 7.5in to *Erebus*'s twenty-eight 15in HE and twenty 4in. A similar bombardment took place next day, but without dislodging the Bolsheviks. *Erebus* moved on to Archangel on the 30th, *M.23* joining her after two more days' firing on Onega. Both monitors returned to Kem in September to cover withdrawals on the Murmansk front.

Following the final evacuation of British forces from Murmansk on 12 October, *Erebus* was on her way home when she received orders to divert to Copenhagen. A British squadron had been in the Baltic since the Armistice, helping the smaller Baltic states resist Bolshevik pressures, ensuring that German forces in the area kept to the terms of the Armistice and preventing Bolshevik naval forces from taking any offensive action. With a modest force of light cruisers, destroyers, submarines, coastal motorboats and minesweepers, Rear-Admiral Walter Cowan had been particularly successful in the last role by blockading the Gulf of Finland and attacking the naval base at Kronstadt in August 1919. Cowan had already requested the assistance of monitors for support, but had been refused on the grounds that they would be useless against forts in the area. In August he again asked for two monitors to help the Estonians deal with the Bolshevik-held forts barring the way to Petrograd (now St Petersburg). Eventually the Admiralty agreed to release *Erebus*, and on 23 October she arrived at Cowan's advanced base at Biorko, on Finland's southern shore some 50 miles west of Petrograd. She was in action early on the 27th, bombarding Krasnaya Gorka Fort in company with the cruisers *Delhi* and *Dunedin*. Some return fire from the Bolsheviks was experienced but no hits received. Damage to the fort was not great, some shells failing to explode, but the Estonians were certainly heartened by the demonstration. Bombardment continued intermittently for the next three days, but the advance of the Estonians and White Russians against Petrograd had already begun to falter and the ships could do little to help in the circumstances.

By now *Erebus* was out of ammunition, so she was sent to Libau (now Liepaja) on the Latvian coast, where the British were assisting the Letts in their fight for independence against both the Bolsheviks in the east and the Germans in the south. On 4 November the Germans had advanced right up to Libau, where British cruisers and destroyers were able to give some fire support. *Erebus* arrived on the 7th, ammunitioned from *Querida* and fuelled from *Mixol* on the 8th, and was in action on the 9th. She was able to counter German shelling of the port area over the next few days.

After receiving reinforcements the German Iron

Division attacked more strongly on the morning of the 14th, taking part of the town. A fierce Lettish counter-attack was supported by a lifting shrapnel barrage from *Erebus* and the cruisers and destroyers. The range was very short, barely over a mile, so the ships fired over open sights using half-charges. The barrage was devastating and, by early afternoon, the Germans had been driven out of range of the guns. *Erebus* had fired over one hundred rounds of 15in and over 400 4in that day between 05.50 and 13.40, expending nearly all the ammunition available. Although the Germans did not attack again, *Erebus* remained at Libau until mid-December, when the Baltic began to freeze over. She finally withdrew at the end of the year with the remaining British forces, the Baltic states having been effectively freed. The Latvians had particularly appreciated the British support, sending their 'heartfelt thanks' for the 'sublime benevolence' and 'great assistance' from the 'mighty and free British Nation and its wise Government'.[5] She returned to Chatham on 31 December 1919 to take up her interrupted duties again after having covered 7,000 miles in her five months' absence.

Meanwhile, *Terror* had relieved *Marshal Soult* as Director and Fire Control Ship at Portsmouth, where she had arrived on 3 January 1919. In addition to these duties she was also used as a firing ship in gunnery trials with ceded German warships as targets. Her first trial took place off Portsmouth in July 1919, when she fired a series of test projectiles against 100mm (3.9in) armour plates mounted on board *Swiftsure*. The plates had been removed from the German battleship *Baden*, which had been scuttled at Scapa Flow on 21 June but had been beached and subsequently salvaged. The trials were to determine the best type of projectile to use against moderately armoured vessels such as cruisers. Performance had to be assessed at the anticipated future battle range of about 16,000yd. As there was no guarantee that *Terror* could hit the target consistently from 8 miles, special reduced charges of 172lb were prepared, which would give the projectiles the same striking velocity of 1,500ft/sec from 500yd as the full 428lb charge from 16,000yd. *Terror* could hardly miss from 500yd, but the striking angle would not be correct unless the target ship was heeled 13½ degrees towards the firing ship to simulate the correct angle of descent. A whole series of 15in projectiles of the latest types was fired to compare their performance and the extent of the damage.

Several other trials were undertaken over the next two years, testing the effects of a whole range of guns from 2pdr to 15in, to determine the most suitable gun and projectile to use against different ship types. The targets were again German ships which, apart from the submarines, had been salvaged from Scapa Flow. The guns were all mounted aboard *Terror*, firing from about 300yd and simulating ranges from 7,000 to 16,000yd, the trials taking place off Portsmouth, as summarised in the table below. The guns temporarily mounted in *Terror* were:

7.5in Mk I, 6in BL XII and 4.7in BL I, the others being part of her normal armament.

Trial firings by *Terror* against German ship targets

Date	Target	Guns used	Result
30 Sept 1920	Submarine *UB.21*	4.7in, 4in, 12pdr	Target sunk
7 Oct 1920	Submarine *U.141*	4.7in, 4in, 12pdr	Severely damaged
13 & 15 Oct 1920	Destroyer *V.82*	4.7in	Damaged and beached
5 & 8 Nov 1920	Cruiser *Nürnberg*	7.5in, 6in	Damaged
8 Dec 1920	Destroyer *V.44*	6in, 4.7in, 4in, 2pdr	Damaged
2 Feb 1921	Battleship *Baden*	15in	Target sunk

The sinking of *Baden* sounds very impressive, but was not the objective of the trial. Because she had to be heeled for the trials, she flooded easily through damage holes when rolling in a moderate sea. As the vessel was in a neglected state below decks, the flooding through shell holes spread rapidly and she sank after seventeen hits. Fortunately the water was shallow and she was easily salved. Later in 1921 the trials were continued against *Baden*. This time *Erebus* was used to simulate firing from 22,000yd with the latest designs of projectile, which proved to be much more satisfactory than those used in the war, especially in terms of penetration and detonation.

Baden was badly mauled by fourteen hits from *Erebus* on 10 August off the Isle of Wight, so was towed away and scuttled in deep water off the Casquet Rocks in the Channel Islands six days later. Two important conclusions were derived from the trials: that an outfit of 100 per cent APC for battleships would prove adequate against all likely targets, and that semi-armour-piercing projectiles should be introduced for medium-calibre guns such as those carried by cruisers.

Erebus also participated at this time in trials of HA control equipment, using targets towed from kite balloons. She paid off into C & M at Chatham on 31 August 1921, but continued to be used as Turret Drill Ship there until March 1926, when she changed places with *Marshal Soult* at Devonport. After a refit she recommissioned in September 1926 as combined Turret Drill Ship, Training Ship for Special Entry Cadets and Senior Officer Devonport Reserve Fleet, with a complement of 243. Her profile remained familiar to all naval personnel because, after seven years at Devonport out in the stream, she transferred to Portsmouth in October 1933, replacing *Terror* as Turret Drill Ship and Harbour Training Ship, the cruiser *Frobisher* having taken over her cadet training duties.

It had been originally intended to dispose of *Terror*

Erebus off Whale Island at Portsmouth as Turret Drill Ship in June 1938, disfigured by the huge recreation hall and gymnasium. The bulge is serving as a useful platform for repairing the ship's boats.
(WRIGHT & LOGAN)

after her 1921 trials, but fortunately this economy measure was rescinded, so that the RN retained three monitors capable of operational use. In May 1922 she was again used for trial firings, this time against armour plates mounted on *Superb*, in connection with the design of new capital ships. *Terror* formally recommissioned at Portsmouth in May 1924 as Turret Drill Ship in place of the battlecruiser *Tiger*, with a complement of fifty-five. She remained there until 1933, when plans were made to send her out to Singapore. A huge naval base had been under construction for several years as part of the defence of British Far Eastern interests against possible Japanese expansion. A monitor would form a useful base and guardship while the dockyard and fixed defences were being completed.[6]

After a long refit at Devonport, *Terror* left on 9 October 1933 with the gate vessel *Sandgate* on the three-month voyage. Her complement of thirteen officers and 202 men was not enough for both her 15in and 4in LA armament to be manned simultaneously, but was sufficient for her general duties. Her gunnery role envisaged anti-ship operations rather than shore bombardment, so practice firings against surface targets were carried out. Her ammunition outfit now included only ten rounds of HE

to one hundred APC per gun. In April 1937 a joint shoot by *Terror* and some of the new coast-defence batteries was carried out against a high-speed target towed by the cruiser *Berwick*. *Terror* fired fifty-seven rounds of 15in at a rate of 1.8 per minute to provide information for spotting and fall-of-shot trials. She remained based at Singapore with only the occasional jaunt up the Malayan coast until the outbreak of WW2. Her war station was planned between the sandbanks south-east of the naval base, connected up with the fortress plot, and with a Supermarine Walrus amphibian aircraft attached for spotting duties.

During the 1930s the South Africans were also worried about possible Japanese threats, fearing that warships might bombard Cape Town and other major ports which were not heavily defended. The existing shore defences at Cape Town consisted of 15-degree-elevation 9.2in guns mounted around Table Bay, with a range of only about 17,000yd. It was therefore suggested by Oswald Pirow, the South African Minister of Defence, that 15in guns be mounted on Robben Island, a few miles north-west of Cape Town. The Admiralty were asked if they would provide the guns, but they considered 15in ordnance to be an over-insurance. Even if Singapore were in Japanese

Terror leaves Malta in November 1933 on her way to Singapore, with someone's motor car stowed abreast the after deckhouse. The battleship in the background is *Resolution*. (A. & J. PAVIA)

Terror shows off her lines at her annual dry docking in *AFD 9* at Singapore about 1937. Her anchors and cables are laid out on the bottom of the 50,000-ton floating dock. The bow can be seen plated over where the rudder used to be before it was blown away in October 1917.
(A.J. BRUNSDON)

hands, bombardment was judged unlikely and certainly by nothing larger than a cruiser. Instead, the Admiralty suggested additional 35-degree-elevation 9.2in and 6in guns, pointing out that the mounting of even a single 15in ashore would cost over £250,000 with all the associated works and ammunition, compared with about £40,000 for a 9.2in installation and about £15,000 for a 6in.

Pirow was not easily dissuaded from getting his 15in guns for the ports, being also Minister for Railways and Harbours, so discussions about loans of equipment dragged on during 1935-36. Eventually a compromise was reached. A 15in monitor, *Erebus*, would be loaned for the defence of Cape Town, with South Africa paying the running costs. She would be manned by a fighting crew from the South African Artillery, with deck and engine-room crews from local harbour craft, plus a nucleus of experienced RN men (219 in total). It was intended that she should operate as a self-contained unit in action, going to sea to meet any threat, relying on her own fire control equipment and whatever air spotting could be provided from shore. In 1938 steps were taken to put the plan into effect, but only as an interim measure while the fixed shore defences were being modernised, first around Cape Town, then at Durban. *Erebus* was taken in hand at Southampton for a refit in January 1939, returning to Portsmouth on 15 August. Her RN crew had been kitted out with South African Army uniforms, causing some merriment amongst their former colleagues as they paraded around Portsmouth in their riding breeches. But war broke out before she could sail and she was not destined to reach South Africa until 1942.

8.6 *Terror* in the Second World War

With the progress that had been made on Singapore's permanent shore defences, including five 15in coast-defence mountings, the question of *Terror*'s future employment was considered during 1938. A number of other British overseas bases were also awaiting the installation of up-to-date coastal defences, so it was planned to station *Terror* at one of them, either Aden or Trincomalee. The latter was considered the best place for *Terror*, which would be situated so that she could move either east or west as any threats developed. War broke out while she was undergoing a refit at Singapore, which included the fitting of six 4in HA guns and replacing her 15in guns. In November she was ordered home to prepare for service off the Channel coast. She left Singapore on 29 January 1940, but by the time she reached Suez a more urgent need arose to use her in the Mediterranean, as many of the ships there on the outbreak of war had been withdrawn to home waters when it was realised that Italy was not likely to follow Germany immediately into declaring war on Britain. On 11 March she arrived at Alexandria, which had become the main Fleet base owing to the weakness of the defences at Malta. *Terror* arrived at Malta on 4 April to supplement the island's scanty defences. She was moored behind Manoel Island and fully integrated into the fortress plot, as her main armament far outranged the island's old 9.2in. Her 4in also formed a welcome addition, as there were only thirty-four heavy A A guns on the entire island at this time.

Italy declared war on Britain on 10 June, following the

A gleaming *Erebus* newly refitted by Thornycroft at Southampton in 1939 for her South African guardship duties.
(WRIGHT & LOGAN)

Terror off Plymouth in 1933 after refitting for her Singapore guardship role. Her eight single 4in LA were replaced by six 4in HA in 1939. (MINISTRY OF DEFENCE)

collapse of France; air attacks on Malta began the very next day. A total of about 150 high-level bombers attacked in the morning and in the evening, *Terror* opening fire with all her AA guns and getting off 212 rounds of 4in in 75min. From then on, air attacks from Sicilian bases were virtually a daily occurrence. *Terror* was able to put up a good AA barrage from her berth in Lazaretto Creek; she claimed to have damaged several aircraft, without having been hit herself. She was able to start a rearmouring refit on 4 September, as new supplies of anti-aircraft guns had just arrived in Malta by sea.

The Italians invaded Greece on 28 October, which gave Britain the opportunity of using Suda Bay in Crete as an advanced Fleet base. As there seemed no likelihood of an Italian invasion of Malta, and there were no defences of any kind at Suda, *Terror* was sent as guardship on completion of her refit, escorted by the Australian destroyer *Vendetta*, air attacks on Malta having slackened off in the meantime. From 13 to 30 November she provided a useful service while shore and AA defences were being hastily improvised. She was then ordered to Alexandria, where she arrived on 2 December to prepare to give assistance to the forthcoming British offensive against the Italians, who had advanced from Libya into Egypt, thus reverting after a lapse of 22 years to her originally designed role of coastal bombardment.

The Army were to attack on the morning of 9 December, so it was arranged that *Terror*, in company with

the China gunboats *Aphis* and *Ladybird*, would bombard Italian positions at Maktila and Sidi Barrani, 200 miles west of Alexandria, to discourage reinforcements being sent further inland. Just before midnight on the 8th/9th *Terror* and *Aphis* opened fire on strongpoints and motor transport at Maktila from 10 miles offshore, meeting accurate but fruitless return fire from Italian batteries. In 73min she put down a hundred rounds of CPC, assisted by Fleet Air Arm Fairey Swordfish for spotting and flare-dropping duties. A repeat performance took place on the 11th at the small harbour of Sollum (Salum), 60 miles further west. Italian forces retreating along the exposed coastal road formed excellent targets, so firing continued during the night and day, *Terror* emptying her 15in magazine of the remaining 124 rounds. She also helped subdue the shore batteries harassing *Aphis* and *Ladybird*.

She returned to Alexandria on the afternoon of 11 December to replenish, and was back at the front on the 14th, this time to soften up the heavily defended town of Bardia, 13 miles north of Sollum. For three days she pounded the area around the town, especially the road leading west to Tobruk, being well supported by the gunboats and the Australian destroyers *Vendetta* and *Voyager*. On the 17th she engaged shore batteries while *Aphis* shot up Bardia and its harbour. The enemy's retaliation was strong, comprising coastal batteries, torpedo bombers and torpedo boats, but *Terror* emerged unscathed. During the three days she had fired 193 rounds of 15in. Wherever the range permitted, three-quarter charges were used to reduce bore wear as, although her guns had been replaced the previous year, they were half-worn pieces which had already spent 12 years in the battleship *Revenge* from 1916-28, without having been relined subsequently.[7] For the rest of the month she carried out a variety of other duties as part of the newly formed Inshore Squadron. She ferried stores and fresh water from Alexandria to Sollum, she undertook repairs on the smaller vessels, and most importantly she acted as AA guardship. Shore-based AA defences were very weak, and neither they nor *Terror* had any radar to give warning of impending attacks. All the ships which had been supporting the Army's advance had been formed into the Inshore Squadron, consisting of *Terror*, three China gunboats, four Australian destroyers, three minesweepers plus sundry small craft, so simplifying control of their operations.

The Army were preparing to capture Bardia with an attack starting on 3 January 1941. On the previous day *Terror*, *Aphis*, *Ladybird* and *Gnat* moved up in support, keeping up a heavy fire on the enemy defences in company with *Voyager* and *Dainty*, despite air attacks. The next morning the three Mediterranean Fleet battleships *Warspite*, *Valiant* and *Barham* also brought their 15in to bear, with the carrier *Illustrious* providing air cover and spotting aircraft. *Terror* bore the brunt of the ensuing Italian air attack, during which she shot down a Savoia bomber. After the huge dust clouds ashore had settled, she continued an intermittent harassing fire for the rest of the 3rd, bringing her contribution over the two days to 135 rounds. After a powerful land offensive, Bardia surrendered on 5 January.

The Army pressed on to Tobruk, where *Terror* was again called upon to soften-up the defences on the night of 20/21 January, just before the attack was to commence, supported by *Gnat*, *Stuart*, *Vampire* and *Voyager*. This time she fired off ninety-six rounds, but by now her guns were so worn that the driving bands on the projectiles were not being properly gripped in the rifling, with the result that insufficient spin stabilisation was obtained and the projectiles somersaulted their way to the targets, where they usually burst after performing a few cartwheels. Admiral Sir Andrew Cunningham, C-in-C Mediterranean, had inspected her guns himself and ordered their continued use. The effectiveness of these heavy barrages was diminished by the shortage of aircraft for spotting duties, but nevertheless they had an extremely demoralising effect on the Italians, who could not feel safe even when sheltering in deep wadis. In six weeks *Terror*'s two 15in had fired a total of 660 rounds, more than she had fired during the whole of WW1, as well as about 1,300 rounds of 4in and 4,700 of 0.5in. Including those fired whilst in *Revenge*,

each gun had fired over 600 rounds, probably a world record for a gun of such calibre at the time, with a mean wear of 0.68in corresponding to 310efc; virtually the life of the gun.

Tobruk was to be the last occasion on which her big guns were fired. After three weeks as air and sea defence guardship at that port, subjected to heavy air attacks from the end of January, on 16 February she escorted a convoy to Benghazi, which had been captured ten days earlier. Conditions in the port were very bad, especially as it was well within range of German air bases, the Luftwaffe having arrived the previous month to assist the Italians. British air cover and AA defences were almost non-existent so far to the west, particularly as forces were already being withdrawn to help in Greece. Although *Terror* was able to augment her AA armament with eight captured Italian 20mm guns, she lacked early-warning radar. She sustained damage from three near-miss bombs at dawn on 22 February, which caused flooding in some bulge compartments and started leaks into the magazines, but fortunately no casualties. That same day Cunningham ordered her return to Tobruk, as her CO, Cdr H.J. Haynes, had reported: 'I consider it only a matter of time before the ship receives a direct hit.'

On leaving Benghazi at dusk with the new corvette *Salvia* and the old minesweeper *Fareham* as anti-submarine escorts, she exploded two acoustic mines nearby, which severely shook the ship and caused further flooding. She was caught the next day by five German dive-bombers and three fighters, a few minutes after her lone Hawker Hurricane escort had departed. The bombers came in from the starboard quarter, where only the two aftermost 4in and two 20mm would bear. These guns managed to put most of the bombers off their aim, but at about 18.25 *Terror* received three very near misses amidships, two to starboard and one to port. The already weakened hull began to buckle and split between the turret and the bridge, and a list to starboard developed. An oil-fuel fire broke out in the boiler room, and was only extinguished by the rising water level, which also cut off the steam to the engines, pumps and generators. An attempt to tow by *Fareham* failed as *Terror* gradually settled by the bows. At 20.00 all the crew except those manning the AA armament were evacuated to *Salvia* and, three hours later, she began to settle more rapidly. With her sea-cocks opened and depth charges exploded to hasten her sinking, *Terror* finally succumbed, but without any casualties, at 04.20 on 24 February 1941, 20 miles north-west of Derna. She had given a fine demonstration of the value of monitor-type vessels in close support of military operations, a duty she was still able to perform efficiently after a quarter of a century of service.

8.7 *Erebus* in the Second World War

It had been planned that *Erebus* would sail for South Africa on 7 September 1939 and arrive at Cape Town eight weeks later. Her crew of 151 was already aboard when Britain declared war on 3 September. Fifty-eight of them were South Africans, while most of the rest were the RN steaming crew who would return home after she had reached the Cape. In view of the possibility of South Africa remaining neutral, her departure was immediately postponed. On the 20th Churchill, First Lord of the Admiralty again, telegraphed General Smuts:[8]

> Monitor *Erebus* is ready to sail for Cape Town. As you know, we have never considered 15in guns necessary for defence of Cape Town, but to please Pirow agreed to loan *Erebus* until those defences were modernised in view of his fear of attack by Japan. We realise the defences of Cape Town remain weak but the Germans have no battleships, and the only two battlecruisers they possess, the *Scharnhorst* and *Gneisenau*, would be very unlikely to try to reach South African waters, or if they did so to risk damage far from a friendly dockyard from even weak defences. Should they break out a major naval operation would ensue, and we shall pursue them wherever they go with our most powerful vessels until they are hunted down. Therefore it seems to me you are unlikely to have need of this ship. On the other hand, she would be most useful for various purposes in the shallows of the Belgian Coast, especially if Holland were attacked. She was indeed built by Fisher and me for this very purpose in 1914 [*sic*]. The question is therefore mainly political. Rather than do anything to embarrass you we would do without the ship. But if you can let us have her either by re-loan or re-transfer, Admiralty will be most grateful, and would of course reimburse Union. All good wishes.

Smuts readily agreed to Churchill's request, so *Erebus* remained under full RN control. However, in the weeks since the outbreak of war pro-German elements among the South African artillerymen had been causing unrest, and the detachment demanded to return to South Africa, but not in *Erebus*, which might be a target for a U-boat. Their truculent attitude was compounded by weak officers, in particular a major who had expected to be given command of *Erebus* and who became totally unco-operative when, not unreasonably, a RN officer was appointed to command her on her voyage to the Cape, Cdr I.W. Whitehorn, who had served in *Terror* in WW1. The situation was reported to Churchill, who minuted on 24 September:[9] 'Now that General Smuts has agreed to release *Erebus* for imperial uses, the sooner these sulky South African artillerymen, twenty-six in number, are sent home the better.' The South African detachment was therefore removed to the Royal Marine barracks at Eastney and sent home as soon as passages could be arranged. Meanwhile, *Erebus* remained based at Portsmouth for the next five months for gunnery instruction and occasional trial firings.

She returned to Thornycroft's at Southampton on 17 February 1940 to begin another refit, during which her AA armament and deck protection were considerably strengthened, as detailed later. She recommissioned under Capt H.F. Nalder on 10 July, by which time the Germans had overrun the Channel coast of France, Belgium and the Netherlands. Churchill, now Prime Minister, was anxious for her to repeat her WW1 performance against German-held territory; he visited her at Portsmouth on 17 July in company with Lord Beaverbrook and C-in-C Portsmouth. With an inexperienced crew, she had to do an extensive work-up before she could begin bombarding the Channel Coast, so she was sent west-about to Scapa Flow, where she arrived on 12 August. Churchill was anxious for her, as soon as possible, to bombard the heavy battery positions the Germans were constructing around Cap Gris Nez, before the guns were actually installed. But mechanical defects plagued her work-up; it was over twenty years since she had done any serious steaming. Finally, after several full-calibre bombardments around Stack Skerry, she was ready to depart for Sheerness, which was intended to be her new base for bombarding the Channel Coast. The passage without escorts was uneventful until she was off Lowestoft in the early hours of 25 September, when she was attacked by E-boats. The four torpedoes fired passed just a few yards ahead of her bows, the Germans evidently thinking that *Erebus* was doing much more than her 9kts on account of the extensive wash set up by her bulge.

Vice-Admiral Ramsay, C-in-C Dover, had planned that *Erebus* should make her first target the barges that were gathering at Calais for the projected invasion of Britain, but that if this proved impracticable the target should be the new batteries being built nearby to command the Straits of Dover. *Erebus* had set out on the afternoon of the 28th but was attacked while still in the Thames Estuary by a single German aircraft, which dropped four bombs just ahead of her. Her subsequent progress down the narrow swept channels proved very difficult owing to her lack of manoeuvrability in the prevailing weather conditions, so she had to abandon the operation.

She set out again the next day with a tug to help her. Escorted by the destroyers *Garth* and *Vesper*, she reached the firing position shortly after midnight, a specially-laid

Erebus entering Portsmouth in August 1939 after refitting as a guardship for South Africa. All the extra forecastle deck accommodation has been stripped off, the upper deck reopened at the sides and secondary armament reduced to only two 3in. The stern anchor and the platform on which the anti-DCB 2pdr were mounted can be seen.
(WRIGHT & LOGAN)

buoy eight miles east of the South Goodwin lightship. At 01.50 on 30 September fire was opened on Calais docks, but had to be stopped 15min later after seventeen rounds, owing to loading difficulties and the lack of spotting reports from the two Swordfish aircraft, so *Erebus* returned to Sheerness. Another bombardment of the Gris Nez batteries was planned for the following week, but had to be postponed until minefields off the Goodwins had been swept. The target was then switched to Dunkirk, *Erebus*'s old WW1 base, so she left the Thames again on 11 October with her WW1 consort *Lady Brassey* assisting. The operation was postponed before she could reach the firing position, owing to mechanical difficulties and the grounding of the spotting aircraft by fog. It was successfully carried out in the early hours of the 16th, when, from 25,000yd, she landed fifty rounds of CPC within the area of Dunkirk docks, although causing no serious damage as the harbour was almost empty at the time.

It was now fully apparent that she was nowhere near as effective a bombarding unit as she had been during WW1. Apart from the severe operational limitations engendered by the presence of powerful enemy air forces, *Erebus*'s general performance and mechanical condition

had deteriorated appreciably. She was sent for overhaul, firstly to Chatham, then to Tilbury for drydocking. She returned to service at Christmas, fitted with a larger rudder and sporting additional AA weapons, including rocket projectors, as described on p.173. During the early months of 1941 she was stationed off Southend as part of the AA defences against minelaying aircraft. A bombardment of Ostende took place on the night of 10/11 February. Assisted by spotting Swordfish she put fifty-four rounds into the dock area. Six hits on submarine pens were observed out of twenty-four shells which landed in the target area. She was fitted with the new Type 91 jammer to counter German coastal radar.

Erebus left Sheerness on 30 July for another working-up period at Scapa. Orders for her to sail to the Eastern Mediterranean came in mid-September, as she was urgently required to support the forthcoming British offensive against the Germans under Gen Rommel in Cyrenaica, *Terror* having served so well in this role earlier in the year. But she had yet to attain her full complement of 400, as well as her outfit of the newly available 20mm Oerlikons, so she returned to Sheerness on 22 September. Two months later she was ready for her long voyage round

Erebus in Scapa Flow on 8 August 1941, showing among her new AA armament a 3in UP launcher with its rectangular shield on the forecastle. (MINISTRY OF DEFENCE)

the Cape; sailing north-about with an escort of two destroyers to Lough Foyle, where she was joined by the new monitor *Roberts*, likewise bound for the Mediterranean. The small convoy sailed on 1 December, consisting of *Erebus*, *Roberts*, the sloop *Scarborough* and the corvette *Fritillary*. By the time she reached South Africa, Japan had entered the war and was striking a series of devastating blows at British possessions in the Far East. It was therefore decided to divert her to strengthen British defences in the Indian Ocean, so she sailed from Durban on 31 January 1942 for Ceylon (now Sri Lanka). After the longest voyage the monitor had ever made, the ship's company were disconcerted to be greeted on arrival at Colombo by the Chief of Staff remarking: '*Erebus*, *Erebus*, not the old *Erebus*? What have you come here for?' While they themselves called the ship 'Cerebos – the home for old salts', they did feel that they could contribute usefully to the protection of lightly defended Ceylon.

Erebus arrived at Trincomalee on 2 March to take up guardship duties. Early in April a powerful Japanese fleet struck at Ceylon and British ships in the surrounding waters. Trincomalee was attacked by carrier-based aircraft on the 9th at about 07.30. *Erebus* opened fire as the enemy attacked the harbour, but considerable damage was done

to shore installations, while *Erebus* suffered casualties from six near-miss bombs on the port side. Five of her crew were killed and twenty wounded, while her hull was well peppered by splinter damage. As a result of the Japanese attack on Ceylon, which caused the loss of several ships, the British Eastern Fleet was withdrawn to Kilindini (Mombasa). A proposal that *Erebus* be used to defend the entrance to the Persian Gulf was turned down, so she departed Trincomalee on the 25th, escorted by *Shoreham*. She was sent to Kilindini where she arrived on 16 May to become part of the defences at the new Fleet base. Captain H.W. D'Arcy-Evans took over command from Nalder on 3 June.

There was nothing for *Erebus* to do until early September, when she joined the force that was to land in Madagascar (now Malagasy). Diego Suarez at the north end of the island had been captured from the Vichy French in May 1942 to secure British lines of communication in the Indian Ocean, but it was later decided to occupy the whole island. A landing was therefore made at Majunga on the north-west coast on 10 September, supported by *Erebus*, but she did no shooting as there was little opposition. She remained as guardship in Madagascar for six weeks before sailing for Durban, where

she arrived on 2 November. Here she was more or less laid up, getting some new crew members from the passing troopship *Christian Huyghens*. She also acted as Turret Drill Ship, taking classes to sea for firing exercises, at three weeks' notice for operations. During a refit at Durban her ageing boilers were retubed. Such was the shortage of drydocking capacity that she shared the 1,150ft-long Prince Edward graving dock with battleship *Valiant* for a week. She finally left Durban on 9 April 1943 for the Mediterranean, to prepare for the forthcoming assault on Southern Europe from North Africa. After a stop at Kilindini, passage of the Suez Canal was attempted on 27 May without tugs, an rather unwise course of action in view of her known poor manoeuvrability. After she had touched both banks and damaged her rudder, one tug was secured ahead and another astern. On arrival at Alexandria on 1 June she had to go into the large 32,000-ton lift floating dock (AFD 5) for repairs. Such was the pressure on this dock that she had to divide her lift into three periods to allow the cruiser *Mauritius* in for more urgent repairs.

She had been allocated to the bombardment force covering the Sicilian landings, so sailed from Alexandria on 3 July. Her detailed operations in support of *Operation*

Husky are more conveniently described with *Roberts* and *Abercrombie* in the next chapter (p.196). After Sicily had been cleared of the Germans *Erebus* also supported the Allied landings on the Italian mainland near Reggio early in September. As her guns were by now worn out, she did not take part in the Salerno landing, but returned to Malta before sailing for the UK for overhaul. She departed on 18 September with the 7kts convoy MKS.25, arriving at Devonport on 6 October 1943 for a four-month refit.

Looking very businesslike with her now reduced free-board, *Erebus* left Plymouth on 10 February 1944 for the Clyde to work-up under the command of Capt J.S.P. Colquhoun. She had been allocated as one of the bombarding ships for *Operation Neptune*, the naval part of the Normandy landings, due to take place in June. Practice bombardments were made of targets on the Kintyre peninsula, using both aircraft and ground spotting, both by day and by night. As defects had begun to reappear she was sent to Glasgow for repairs in March, a tricky passage for such an unwieldy vessel. While in Glasgow, simple launchers were installed abreast the bridge for firing electronic countermeasures (ECM) rockets. More bombardment practices followed at the end of April, in company with the battleships *Rodney*,

Erebus in February 1944 with much-reduced freeboard aft. A new topmast has been shipped for the Type 79B air-warning radar aerial and the Type 272 surface-warning, while a lattice mainmast supports the Type 276 combined surface/air-warning. Compare *Erebus*'s final appearance with *Terror* as built, on p.151. (MINISTRY OF DEFENCE)

Ramillies and USS *Texas*, all of which were earmarked for *Neptune*. *Roberts* joined company on 5 May, so for three more weeks all the heavy gunfire support ships exercised in the Clyde, practising especially the newly developed technique of using fighter aircraft for spotting, described in greater detail in Chapters 9 and 10.

Erebus departed Greenock at midnight on 24 May to take her place in Bombarding Force 'A' of the Western Task Force which was to cover the two American landings on the Normandy beaches. After brief stops in Belfast Lough and Torbay she anchored off Weymouth on the 28th. She sailed at 16.30 on 5 June, taking station astern of convoy UA.1, part of the force destined for 'Utah' beach, escorted by the US

destroyer *Gherardi*. After an uneventful passage through the swept channels she dropped anchor 12 miles north-east of 'Utah' beach at 04.20 on the 6th, ready to fire on any German coastal batteries which showed signs of interfering with the landings. Allied air force bombers had already attacked the batteries, while the other ships of the bombarding fleet carried out neutralising bombardments from their positions closer inshore from 05.50 to H-hour at 06.30. *Erebus*'s first bombardment took place five minutes after H-hour with four rounds at a battery north of the beaches. Unfortunately the blast broke the port anchor cable; it was over an hour before she next opened fire with twenty-six rounds at the Pernelle battery with its three

170mm (6.7in) on the north-east corner of the Cherbourg peninsula. During the morning of D-day she remained on patrol with the US battleship *Nevada* and cruisers *Black Prince*, USS *Tuscaloosa* and USS *Quincy*, ready to open fire on any targets requested by the Shore Fire Control Parties. Ten rounds were fired at St Marcouf battery in the early afternoon, *Erebus* scoring a direct hit on No. 2 gun. By the end of the day all three of its 210mm (8.3in) Skoda guns had been knocked out by naval and air bombardment.

At about 16.40 *Erebus* received a request to fire on a radar station controlling the fire of the shore batteries. Just as her left gun was fired, the Royal Marine officer commanding the turret, Capt D.A. Farquharson-Roberts, felt a thud, followed by another. On looking out of his vision slit he saw splashes in the water ahead, and reported to the bridge that the turret had been hit. When he went into the gunhouse proper he found the guns' crews reeling about, the left gun run in at near maximum elevation and a strong smell of cordite. He then realised that the projectile in the left gun had exploded as it passed up the barrel, bursting off the jacket, splitting the gun open, and distorting the cradle and trunnion supports. The breech had held, so there were no serious casualties, but the turret was unfit for further use owing to ruptured hydraulic piping. Closer examination showed that repair of the mounting would be a major dockyard job, but the immediate fears were of the charge and projectile loaded into the right gun 'cooking off', and of the remains of the left gun breaking off and dropping through the forecastle deck. Fortunately neither happened, although *Erebus* had to remain at anchor off 'Utah' beach for two days while arrangements were made for her return passage and repair. She sailed on the 8th as Commodore of a convoy of twelve LSTs returning to Portland, having on board some 150 American glider pilots for passage. The twenty-eight British officers simply evacuated their cabins and the wardroom in the face of such numbers, and slept at their action stations. They had their reward, however: the pilots were aboard 25hr, two days by American reckoning, and the generous subsistence allowance paid to the ship covered the wardroom mess bills for quite two months.

After a few days in Stokes Bay off Gosport, *Erebus* berthed at Devonport on 14 June. All this time both guns had been at high elevation: the left gun in the position it had burst, the right gun brought up in line so that it would be less obvious that something was wrong. The next day she moved under the big 160-ton cantilever crane at No. 5 Basin. The gunhouse roof was removed, the damaged gun cut halfway along its length, and both halves

Erebus in Plymouth Sound on 4 February 1944 after her final refit, showing her camouflage. The bulge has been completely submerged. Quadruple pom-poms and Oerlikons have replaced the ineffective 0.5in machine guns and UPs.
(MINISTRY OF DEFENCE)

lifted out, followed by the cradle. The cause of the burst was traced to a faulty fuze in the American-made 15in HE projectile. As it would take some time to prepare a new cradle and gun, the turret was reassembled with only the right gun operational. She remained anchored in Plymouth Sound for the next fortnight, available for emergency use if required. On 8 July she returned to the dockyard, where a new left gun was fitted. Gun trials were satisfactorily completed on the 22nd, so she departed for the Normandy beaches again, escorted by the destroyer *Brissenden*.

By this time the Normandy front line had moved out of reach of naval gunfire everywhere except on the eastern flank, where the German batteries between the Rivers Orne and Seine continued to harass Allied shipping in Seine Bay. *Erebus* was the only big-gun bombardment ship now deployed off Normandy, though there were still a number of cruisers, destroyers and support vessels such as LCGs (Landing Craft, Gun). Her fire was therefore reserved for the longest-range targets and the well protected coast defence batteries. Between 25 July and 14 August she fired some 150 rounds at these targets, generally from an anchored position about three miles north of Courseulles, often with tug attendance to help keep her on bearing (*Dexterous*, *Schelde* or *Zwarte Zee*). Enemy retaliation was varied: coast-defence and mobile batteries, night bombing attacks, human torpedoes (Marder), pressure mines, midget submarines (Biber),

long-running torpedoes (Dackel) and explosive motor-boats (Linsen). Constant vigilance by naval and air patrols, defensive smokescreens and countermeasures such as balloons and 'Window' to spoil German fire control radar prevented *Erebus* from suffering any damage.

After the collapse of the stubborn German defence around Caen and Falaise, the whole front moved rapidly eastwards during mid-August. British I Corps was able to push along the coast towards the mouth of the Seine, so *Erebus* was called upon to help subdue the troublesome mobile batteries around Houlgate. Fire was not possible on the first day of the advance, 18 August, owing to the confused situation ashore, but on the evenings of the 19th and 20th she fired sixty-four rounds at the batteries. The latter were finally overrun shortly afterwards and, although *Erebus* replenished her ammunition from the coaster *Errol* to avoid wasting time returning to Portsmouth, no more targets remained within range for her on the Normandy coastline.

Le Havre still held out north of the Seine mouth, with a dozen batteries covering the seaward approaches, ranging from 75mm (2.95in) to 170mm (6.7in), which had been harassing Allied shipping in Seine Bay for the past three months. An even larger battery had been under construction at Octeville, north of Le Havre, planned to mount three 380mm (15in). However, construction had been seriously hampered by air bombing, and the only gun to be installed had been knocked out by a direct

A rare view of *Erebus* in Spithead early in 1945, showing her now in standard light grey camouflage with blue band.
(D.A. FARQUHARSON-ROBERTS)

hit on 9 May 1944; but the Allies could not be sure that part of the battery had not been put back into order. Following a week at Portsmouth, *Erebus* was ordered across to bombard Le Havre at the same time as I Corps closed in, the latter's artillery being insufficient to reduce the defences. She positioned herself close to a buoy 12 miles north-west of the port, opening fire at 11.32 on 5 September. After seven rounds the Germans returned fire, shell splashes being observed nearby. At 11.55 she was hit on the port bulge forward of the turret, taking a list of 3 degrees. The shell was from the enemy's 170mm battery, which had three modern guns covering the seaward sector with a range as great as *Erebus*'s guns, 32,000yd. As the enemy firing continued, *Erebus* made smoke and moved farther out of range, and then returned to Portsmouth for repairs.

She was temporarily patched up and returned to bombard Le Havre on the 8th. She opened fire at 13.00, firing ten rounds before the enemy retaliated. Despite firing 'Window', *Erebus* was hit with the second 170mm salvo in the port bulge abreast the engine room. Fortunately the hole was only about 15in x 18in, as the shell did not explode. There was only a slight list, so she carried on firing. Accurate return fire was encountered, but she was not actually hit again. On the 10th, RAF bombers attacked the Le Havre batteries, as they had been doing for several days, then *Erebus* opened an accurate fire from a position 12 miles south-west, followed by *Warspite* from further north. 'Window' and smoke-screens were put up to confuse the enemy fire control. From 10.15 onwards *Erebus* put 112 rounds into her targets, the spotting fighters reporting about thirty as hits. *Erebus* remained unmolested by the shore batteries as she was outside their principal training sector, although *Warspite* was given some attention. In the late afternoon 1 Corps launched its attack on the German defences, which had been thoroughly demoralised by the combined sea and air onslaught. Le Havre surrendered on the 12th, the British Corps Commander signalling his thanks to the bombarding ships for their support.

On returning to Portsmouth on 11 September she was taken in hand by the dockyard to complete the damage repairs and to change her guns. The unexploded 170mm shell was found in the bulge by dockyard workers, but it was a young sailor who had to remove it. *Erebus* was ordered to Dover early in October in company with *Roberts*, to support operations against the Belgian and Dutch ports and their coastal defences. The two ships formed part of the bombarding squadron for the assault on the island of Walcheren on 1 November, described in detail in the next chapter (p.207). Thereafter both monitors remained based at Portsmouth, one being at

48hr notice anchored out in Spithead on call for any further bombardments. Although several were planned, such as *Operation Deliberate* against Schouwen in the eastern Scheldt in February 1945, none took place. *Operation Nestegg*, the reoccupation of the Channel Islands planned for mid-March with *Roberts*, was deferred until after Germany's surrender.

After five years' arduous war service *Erebus* was in no condition to join her two more modern sisters allocated to the East Indies Fleet to continue the war against Japan. She was therefore sent round to the Nore, arriving on 3 July 1945, where she became Turret Drill Ship at Chatham again after a lapse of 19 years, also providing accommodation for Stoker Mechanics under training. She was approved to scrap a year later, so left Chatham under tow for Rosyth on 13 July 1946, where her gun barrels were removed. She made her final four-mile voyage to Ward's Inverkeithing yard for breaking up on 29 January 1947.

8.8 Modifications

Such was the benefit of a design that could incorporate most of the lessons learned in the earlier monitors that few modifications were made to *Erebus* and *Terror* during WW1, and those were confined mostly to secondary armament. *Terror* was quickly fitted with two 6in QF II like *Erebus*, while both ships soon got a second 3in HA and late in 1917 both got two more 6in, making a total

A 1919 view of *Erebus*'s port side looking forward, showing four 4in BL. IX low-angle guns. The ammunitioning derrick and the base of one of the 36in searchlight platforms can also be seen. A sailor is painting the bulge, which also provided useful access to the ship's side. (IWM SP163)

of four guns each. During the repairs to *Terror*'s bow at this time, her bow rudder was removed, or rather, not replaced. Her 15in magazines were fitted with the anti-flash arrangements shown to be necessary after Jutland, and were modified to take longer projectiles. Two 2pdr pom-poms were added on sponsons at the stern, while the two 12pdr were resited amidships, the original embrasures being plated up to keep the upper deck drier. Smoke apparatus was also fitted to the spotting top, giving the appearance of a large rangefinder. As in *Marshal Soult*, first four, then eight single 4in BL IX were fitted in both ships in the summer of 1918. At the same time the little-used conning tower was removed and replaced by a platform carrying the two 12pdr, now converted to HA firing. The two 3in HA remained at the after end of the forecastle deck, so that by the end of WW1 both ships carried 2 x 15in, 8 x 4in, 2 x 12pdr HA, 2 x 3in and 2 x 2pdr. A secondary control position was added abaft the funnel, while the two 24in searchlights at the base of the mast were replaced by two 36in on towers close to the funnel. A normal battleship-type 15ft rangefinder was fitted in the turret, as already existed in *Marshal Soult*.

Between the wars the ships were modified as required for their variety of duties. During 1924 three of *Terror*'s 4in were temporarily removed to provide more space on the forecastle deck. Although her major refit before going out to Singapore cost £72,000, most of the changes were not apparent, being largely internal. Improvements were made to accommodation and ventilation, while refrigerated stores were fitted for the first time in a British ship designed as a monitor. A Dreyer fire control table was installed in the lower steering position on the main deck to improve her anti-ship gunnery capability, necessary for service at Singapore. As her 12pdr and 2pdr guns were removed, changes were made to the secondary magazines, including extensions into spaces previously occupied by oil fuel tanks and kit lockers. Much of the extra space was fitted out to carry over 1,000 rounds of 8in and 6in ammunition as reserves for cruisers in the Far East. Thus, apart from a coat of white paint, *Terror*'s external appearance was little changed from 1918. Deep displacement was now 8,600 tons, so her true standard displacement[10] was about 7,830 tons. Officially her standard displacement was listed as only 7,200 tons, but this was a mistake stemming from the lack of recorded data on the ship as completed.

With the threat of war in 1939, *Terror* began a refit at Singapore in April to improve her HA armament and replace her 15in barrels. The eight low-angle 4in were replaced by six single HA/LA 4in QF V. The two 3in were removed and replaced by two quadruple 0.5in Mk III machine guns, basically similar to the gun fitted in tanks and aircraft. No changes were made to her armament at Malta in 1940, but she did get additional armour plating on the upper deck, similar to *Erebus* (see below), and her sides were fully plated up. Fresh-water capacity was trebled, this and the other changes increasing her deep displacement to a final figure before her loss of about 9,400 tons.

The modifications made to *Erebus* were considerable, especially during WW2. Her conversion to Turret Drill Ship and Cadet Training Ship in 1926 necessitated the provision of additional accommodation and classrooms. The space was obtained partly by glazing in the sides of the upper deck and partly by fitting cabins on the sides of the forecastle deck in place of six of the 4in guns, leaving only two. A tall topmast was fitted, supported by stays from a prominent 'spider' below the spotting top. Three-pounder saluting guns replaced the 2pdrs beneath the 15in muzzles. Two years later she was disfigured by the erection of a huge deckhouse on the forecastle, used as a recreation room and gymnasium by the cadets.

Her £85,000 refit in 1939 by Thornycroft for guardship duties in South Africa restored her almost to the basic simplicity of the original design. All the deckhouses were removed except for a small one abaft the funnel, while the upper deck was opened up again at the sides. New 15in guns were installed, but her secondary armament was reduced to only the two 3in HA, the 4in being considered unnecessary for her duties. In this condition *Erebus* was no longer suitable for war in European waters, so after war broke out she was soon back in shipyard hands. The original 2in upper deck was reckoned proof against 250lb SAP bombs dropped from up to 2,000ft but inadequate against the sort of attacks that were now anticipated from high-level and dive-bombers. A number of rearmouring proposals were put forward late in 1939, generally incorporating two or three inches of armour added to the existing upper and main deck plating. That finally adopted provided an extra two inches of NC armour on the upper deck over a length of 220ft amidships, making a total of 4in over the magazines and machinery spaces, and an extra inch on the main deck (see drawing on p.147). The same plans were also approved for *Terror*, and the manufacture of the necessary 366 tons of armour plate for each ship was put in hand.

The armour was fitted at *Erebus*'s 1940 refit, when the upper deck was plated-up at the sides for good. Three single 4in HA/LA were fitted in zarebas on each side of the forecastle deck as in *Terror*, with associated High Angle Calculating Positions (HACP) port and starboard. Four quadruple 0.5in guns were also fitted, two mountings forward and two aft. In addition, a brand new AA weapon favoured by Churchill was provided; the rocket launcher. Two twenty-barrel unrotated projectile (UP) mountings were fitted on a platform abaft the funnel, capable of firing a cloud of 7in parachute-and-cable projectiles into the path of an attacking dive-bomber. Each rocket released a parachute carrying a small aerial mine on a cable that was intended to catch on the aircraft's wing and explode. A normal 3in rocket motor was used, filled out to 7in diameter by the mine canister.

Other modifications included removal of the topmast, fitting of degaussing cables on the hull externally and

provision of Carley life-rafts and their launching skids, but radar was not yet fitted. All these changes considerably increased her deep displacement to 9,100 tons, with serious effects on her handling, as discussed in the next section. A substantially increased crew was required to man all the extra equipment, her authorised wartime complement being raised to 308. The usual wartime disruptive camouflage scheme was adopted, which did not include the display of the ship's pendant number. Apart from the small monitors showing their M numbers, which coincided with their pendant numbers during WW1, such numbers were never displayed on any monitor.[11] Further improvements were made to *Erebus*'s armament throughout the war, as shown in the table.

Secondary armament fitted in *Erebus*

Mounting	1938	1939	1940	1941	1942-3	1944-5
Single 4in CPI	2					
Single 4in HA III			6	6	6	6
Single 3in HA II	2	2				
Quadruple 2pdr Mk VII					3	3
Single 2pdr Mk VIII					1	1
Single 40mm Mk III				1	1	1
Twin 20mm Mk V						4
Single 20mm Mk II					7	7
Quadruple 0.5in Mk III			4	4		
20-barrel 7in UP			2	1		
Single 3in UP			3			

Normal outfits of ammunition per barrel, excluding practice rounds, were:

15in	60 CPC, 40 HE
4in	250 HETF, 150 SAP + star (50 per ship)
3in	150 + star (50 per ship)
2pdr	1,800
40mm	1,440
20mm	2,400
0.5in	2,500
7in UP	3

By the time *Erebus* left for the Indian Ocean at the end of 1941 the twenty-barrel UP mountings had been removed, as well as the three single UP mountings for 3in rockets. The latter had been mounted late in 1940, two on the forecastle and one on the quarterdeck, and differed from the 7in UP in that they carried a normal time fuze and explosive charge. This 'Harvey Projector' had been developed from a weapon originally designed for the Army; particulars are given on p.236. In practice the 7in UPs had proved ineffective at downing enemy aircraft. It was found that the wire barrage took so long to establish itself that it could easily be dodged by enemy aircraft, while the weapons were too slow to reload to allow a second salvo. They were also dangerous to the ships carrying them, because the mines tended to drift

back on to the firing ship, and there was a risk of fires
from the cordite propellant in the ammunition lockers.
The 3in was not accurate enough to score a direct hit,
and trials with an early design of proximity fuze were
unsuccessful. In place of these weapons, three quadruple
pom-poms had been installed, two sided abreast the turret
and one on the quarterdeck, plus a single 2pdr abaft the
funnel, flanked by a solitary 40mm Bofors. The multiple
pom-pom developed between the wars from the pre-
WW1 Vickers 2pdr was an impressive-looking weapon
in operation, delivering nearly 400 rounds per minute,
but its effective range was less than a mile and its accuracy
and mechanical reliability could have been better. Until
the Swiss-designed 20mm Oerlikon became available
from British production in 1941, the 2pdr was the only

British close-range weapon with any reasonable chance
of downing enemy aircraft. Late in 1941 seven single
Oerlikons were installed around the forecastle deck and
on the turret, providing a useful defence against dive-
bombers and low-flying aircraft; C-in-C Home Fleet had
commented a year earlier that he would prefer one
Oerlikon to four UPs.

The demands of war service and the increasing crew
numbers necessitated continuous extensions to accommodation, electrical generating capacity, fresh-water storage, evaporating capacity and store rooms. By the end
of *Erebus*'s 1944 refit at Devonport she carried five radar
sets: two Type 285 AA gunnery sets dating from 1941,
one for each of the HA rangefinder/directors for the 4in;
one Type 79B air warning set with aerial on the fore-
topmast in place of the previous Type 286 combined
surface/air warning; one Type 272 surface warning with
its 'lantern' just above the spotting top; and one Type 276
combined warning with aerial on the new lattice
mainmast aft, together with associated interrogators. With
all the extra equipment her bulge was now completely
submerged, as she drew 13ft 6in forward and 14ft aft,

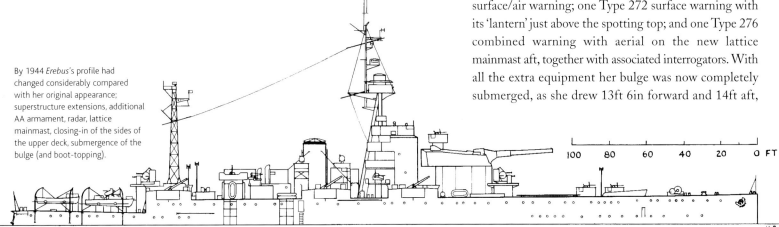

with a deep displacement of 9,800 tons, some 15 per cent above the original figure, each extra 60 tons adding one inch to her draft. The metacentric height had now been reduced from the original 32ft to about 6ft; still adequate, due to a rise of 2ft in the CG and a drop of 24ft in the height of the metacentre following the submergence of the bulge. The corresponding rolling period was increased from about five seconds to ten, making for a steadier motion when firing.

8.9 Performance

By comparison with the earlier large monitors, *Erebus* and *Terror* were relatively fast and handy vessels, although still poor when viewed against ships of normal form. In the waters around Dover they did all that was asked of them, their reliability making them the backbone of the Monitor Squadron during WW1. With clean hulls they could make a maximum of 13kts, but lost about one knot when several months out of drydock, as shown in the curves of horsepower, rpm, fuel consumption and endurance against speed.

During WW2 so many alterations were made that performance deteriorated considerably. The erections added at the aft end of *Erebus*'s forecastle deck in 1940, plus her increased draft, made her difficult to control. With wind or sea on the beam or quarter she required full rudder just to maintain course, while, if conditions worsened, even working the engines was of no avail. Her centre of pressure had been moved so far aft by the modifications that her stern was blown round, with her bows pointing upwind. In such conditions there were only two actions possible: heave to or go astern. The latter was not a popular manoeuvre as, with the reduced freeboard aft, the quarterdeck was easily swamped and the boats damaged. In pilotage waters it was not really safe to handle her without tugs, so navigation in swept channels through minefields was always risky. Only in a headwind could a course be held, but at the expense of a fair drop in speed. Often the simplest way of altering course upwind was to turn almost full circle downwind to reach the desired course.

In 1940 Nalder made urgent representations to the Admiralty about the ship's lack of control, requesting that the now plated-over bow rudder be put back into operation, as he considered that handling would be improved thereby. The DNC's Department were not keen on his suggestion, as the bow steering gear had been removed at the last refit and scrapped. Instead, a larger stern rudder was suggested, in conjunction with rigging a temporary canvas screen forward, which would balance the windage profile. A 30 per cent larger rudder of 130ft² was fitted, trials in December 1940 showing that conditions were improved without having to fit the screen forward. But the margin of improvement was modest; with beam winds of Force 6 to 7, 25 to 30 degrees of weather helm still had to be carried. On occasion *Erebus* would set a foresail, rigged from the mast or elevated 15in guns, to try to steady her course.

The weights continually being added to *Erebus* during WW2 seriously reduced her freeboard aft by about 2½ft. Parts of the quarterdeck were thus only about 5ft above the waterline so that, with the submergence of the bulge, she became a very wet ship in quite moderate sea conditions. A further consequence of these alterations was a drop in speed and endurance. Although she managed a creditable 12.53kts on the measured mile in the Clyde in February 1944, her best speed normally during WW2 was about 11½kts. This could drop well below 10kts under adverse conditions of weather and hull fouling. Indeed, when rounding the Cape in January 1942 she could make no headway against the strong current and was reputedly carried backwards at 2kts!

Fuel consumption at cruising speed was around 92 tons of oil per day at sea; in harbour about 9 tons. Her original endurance was reduced not only by her lower speed, but also by her bunker capacity being cut back by 90 tons in 1940 to provide additional space internally. By the end of the war her endurance at maximum speed was down to about 1,700 miles but, by this time, her days of long-distance voyages were over. In practice she would 'coast-hop' between frequent refuelling bases on long voyages in a manner reminiscent of the WW1 coal-burners. Less strain was put on the engines this way, and the overworked engineers given a chance to put right the endless minor breakdowns that occurred in the old ship.

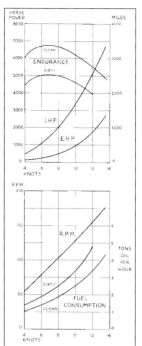

The performance curves for *Erebus* and *Terror* show the indicated horsepower developed by the engines in service, and the effective horsepower required to tow the ship, estimated from model experiments; ehp/ihp is a measure of propulsive efficiency — about 40 per cent at top speed. The endurance curves are based on 780 tons of oil fuel, and show economical speed as about seven knots. The 'dirty' condition corresponds to about six months out of dock, resulting in a loss of about 1½kts in maximum speed compared with clean out of dock (about 35 per cent more power), and a decrease of endurance of about 25 per cent.

Erebus and *Terror* – TECHNICAL DATA

Displacement: 8,000 tons Navy List, 8,450 tons deep on 11ft 8in draft, 7,100 tons light on 9ft 9½in.

Dimensions: Length 405ft 0in oa, 385ft 0in bp, breadth 88ft 2in oa, 62ft 0in main hull, depth to forecastle deck 26ft 9in.

Weight distribution as designed (tons) Armament 860, ammunition 300, protection 2,530, hull 2,970, equipment 350, machinery and RFW 700, oil fuel (nominal) 250. Total 7,960 tons.

Complement: 13 officers, 191 men.

Armament: 2 x 15in (twin) (100 HE rpg), 2 x 6in QF (200rpg), 2 x 12pdr (200rpg), 1 x 3in HA (300rpg), 4 x 0.303in Maxim (5,000rpg).

Protection: As 14in monitors except: upper deck over 15in magazine 4in NC; gunhouse 13inC front, 11inC sides and rear, 5in NC roof (4¼in *Erebus*), 3in HT floor.

Machinery: Twin-screw 4-cyl triple-expansion by Harland & Wolff, Belfast 23in, 37in, 44in, 44in x 30in 6,000ihp at 170rpm. Four Babcock & Wilcox watertube boilers 200lb/sq in. Oil fuel 784 tons.

Endurance: 2,480 miles at 12kts on 3.8 tons oil per hour.

Speed: 12kts designed and service. Trials: *Erebus* 14.1, *Terror* 13.09kts.

Construction: *Erebus* Harland & Wolff, Govan (No. 492G/B) laid down 12.10.15/launched 19.6.16/completed 2.9.16. *Terror* H & W Belfast (No. 493) 26.10.15/18.5.16/6.8.16.

Disposal: *Erebus* handed over to BISCO 10.7.46, scrapped by T.W. Ward, arrived Inverkeithing 29.1.47; *Terror* sunk 24.2.41.

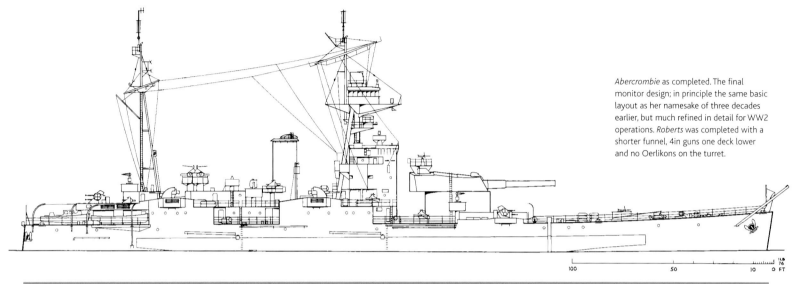

Abercrombie as completed. The final monitor design; in principle the same basic layout as her namesake of three decades earlier, but much refined in detail for WW2 operations. *Roberts* was completed with a shorter funnel, 4in guns one deck lower and no Oerlikons on the turret.

CHAPTER 9

The Last 15in-gun Monitors

HMS

Roberts
—
Abercrombie

9.1 Design

Winston Churchill returned to the Government as First Lord of the Admiralty on the day Britain declared war on Germany for the second time, 3 September 1939. He lost no time refamiliarising himself with the RN, visiting ships and naval establishments. Both at Portsmouth and Chatham he found monitors dating from WW1; *Erebus* earmarked for South Africa and *Marshal Soult* as Turret Drill Ship at the Nore. Including *Terror* at Singapore, there were but three monitors left in anything resembling their original state out of the fleet of forty that he had authorised during 1914-15. *Marshal Ney* and a few of the small monitors still existed, but converted to support roles. No new monitors had been built between the wars. Not only would they have been of limited value, but they would have been regarded as battleships under treaty tonnage quotas if they mounted guns of greater calibre than 8in.

With Germany likely to strike France again through the Low Countries, Churchill realised that coast-bombardment vessels could again play a useful role in any new conflict off the shallow waters of the southern North Sea or even in the Baltic. Anxious to make the monitors fully effective again, he minuted on 4 November:[1]

> We really must get the monitors into working order. The *Erebus* is already in good condition, but her deck must be armoured against air attack. Pray let me have at our meeting next week a definite plan for putting a strong armoured deck upon the *Erebus* and the *Marshal Soult*. How long would it take? *Soult* requires new engines. Let me have estimates in time and money for bringing her up to the mark.

A detailed survey of *Soult* showed that it would not be worth reconstructing her, but as her turret was still in reasonable condition her twin 15in guns could be transferred to a new hull with more powerful machinery.

Preliminary design work was put in hand right away. Various proposals were developed with the intention of getting a 15kts speed if possible, but the estimated power of 11,000hp was unacceptably high. Model tests at AEW were based on hull lines derived from *Erebus* which had the best of the WW1 forms. As it was estimated that

12kts could be obtained on trials with about 3,500hp, this more modest power introduced the possibility of installing diesel machinery instead of steam. Twin Atlas Polar diesels were suggested, which would be very economical in fuel consumption. However, diesels would take longer to build than steam turbines, so, as delivery was required in twelve months, it was decided to use the latter. As with the WW1 ships a bulged form was adopted which would provide good protection against torpedoes and mines for the 54ft-wide main hull. With machinery spaces about 32ft shorter than those of *Erebus*, with only two boilers but still using saturated steam, the hull length could be reduced below *Erebus*'s 385ft BP; the final figure selected was 354ft BP. In association with a moulded breadth of 88ft and a draft of 12ft, the preliminary estimate of deep displacement was about 8,380 tons; about the same as that of *Erebus* when new. Much of the design work was carried out by a young Assistant Constructor, M.C. Dunstan, under the supervision of Chief Constructor H.S. Pengelly.

The protection of the hull took particular account of the threat of air attack, but otherwise followed broadly the lines of the WW1 ships. The vertical protection was designed to resist 6in naval gun or 9in howitzer projectiles striking normally at 90 degrees to the surface of the armour. The side armour was disposed at an angle of about 35 degrees to the horizontal, corresponding to the angle of descent of long-range projectiles. The side protection system below water was designed on the pattern adopted in the new *King George V*-class battleships and Fleet carriers then under construction. A 17ft-wide sandwich layer was arranged in the bulge abreast the vitals of the ship, consisting of an outer air space, a jacket space partly filled with water and an inner air space, giving protection against torpedoes carrying a 1,000lb warhead. The theory was that detonation should take place as far as possible from the main hull proper. The outer air space served to reduce the pressure pulse set up in the sea by the explosion. The middle water space or jacket absorbed, distributed and dissipated the energy of the explosion over a wide area and reduced the momentum of splinters. The inner air space prevented the pressure waves in the water jacket from being transmitted to the protective bulkhead. The plating of this bulkhead formed the side of the hull proper in way of the bulge, consisting of a double thickness of ¾in D.1 quality steel,[2] supported by heavy stiffeners. Yet further protection was provided by watertight compartments inboard of this protective bulkhead in way of machinery spaces and main magazine to limit flooding. The side sloping armour belt, consisting of 5in NC plates abreast the magazine and 4in elsewhere, was laid on top of the two inboard bulge compartments

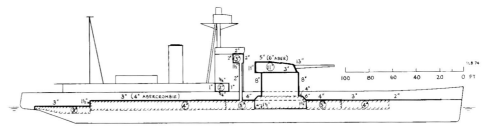

for ease of construction, unlike the WW1 ships, in which it was fitted internally. A water ballast ring main, served by four 550ton-per-hour pumps, connected all these watertight compartments. The system could be used to pump out damaged spaces, to flood magazines above the waterline, or to fill tanks to correct heel or trim.

The horizontal deck protection was intended to resist a 500lb bomb dropped from a height of 12,000ft, necessitating 3in NC plating. The protection was fitted on the main deck rather than the upper deck to reduce the height of the side armour. As the forecastle deck extended right to the stern, unlike that of the WW1 ships, this level was now described as the upper deck, the old upper deck level now becoming the main deck. The cramped circular conning tower of the WW1 designs was dropped in favour of an armoured compartment built into the bridge structure below the compass platform, as in the new battleships. Plating varied from 3in to 1½in, proof against medium projectiles and splinters.

9.2 Armament

Although the main armament was twenty-five years old, the 15in was still a very effective and accurate weapon. Apart from a general overhaul, the only important change needed was modification to load the new longer 6crh projectile, just coming into service as the standard 15in ammunition. Fire control equipment was to be installed, including a Dreyer table which would enable the corrections for firing under way to be readily calculated. As with the earlier monitors, a director was sited at the tripod masthead above the spotting top. The transmitting station with the Dreyer table was on the lower deck beneath the bridge under armour, receiving information from aloft, then calculating and transmitting bearing and elevation to the receivers in the turret. The conspicuous spotting top was much more comfortable than in the WW1 ships, as it was glassed-in and heated. A 12ft rangefinder was fitted on the compass platform, in addition to the 15ft one in the turret.

In view of the monitors' likely operations off hostile shores, the selection of anti-aircraft armament was given special attention. The original suggestion of six single 4in as in *Erebus* and *Terror* was not regarded as adequate for a new-construction monitor. Two twin 4.5in between-

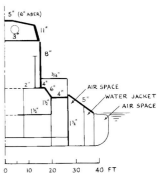

Roberts and *Abercrombie* had a well-balanced protective scheme, especially the latter with her thicker main deck, capable of resisting a wide range of air, surface and underwater attacks.

deck mountings were proposed, similar to those being fitted in the reconstructed capital ships and in the new Fleet carriers, but there were not enough available. The only remaining suitable HA equipment worthy of such a ship was the standard twin 4in HA/LA, which formed the secondary armament of cruisers and the main armament for AA sloops. The Mk XVI* gun was already proving a useful weapon, with an AA ceiling of 39,000ft and a rate of fire of 15-20 rounds per minute. In conjunction with a combined rangefinder/director, the HACP could calculate and pass to the guns the appropriate bearing, elevation and fuze-setting. The last determined the time interval between firing the shell and its detonation. Direct hits on a fast-moving aircraft were unlikely, but a near-miss burst could be lethal. Multiple 2pdr pom-poms were to be the principal close-range weapons, 0.5in machine guns being rejected, but the newly designed UP mounting for firing 7in rockets was included as a stopgap while pom-poms were in short supply. The proposal originally adopted was for two quadruple Mk VII pom-poms and three twenty-barrel UP mountings.

The siting of the 4in guns was straightforward: two twin mountings port and starboard abreast the funnel, surrounded by ¾in bulletproof screens. Each mounting was served by an endless-chain ammunition hoist, one each side from the forward 4in magazine immediately abaft the 15in shell-room to the upper deck, and another pair to the after mountings from their magazine abaft the engine room. Siting of the pom-poms was more difficult. A centreline location would give the best arc of fire, but a forecastle mounting would suffer from blast whenever the 15in guns fired on bearings within 65 degrees of the bow. If the mountings were sited on each side of the turret, one would always be usable, except when the 15in were firing within 10 degrees of the bow. The latter arrangement was the one finally adopted, plus one UP mounting on the centreline aft and one on each side of the bridge on the upper deck. The end result was an AA armament as good as a new cruiser's, and much more powerful than that of *Erebus* or *Terror*, even after their latest refits. The usual outfit of sub-calibre guns was provided: 6pdr for exercising the 15in, 2pdr for the 4in.

9.3 Construction

While design work was going ahead, preliminary arrangements for construction were being made. Building of the *Lion*-class battleships had been suspended for one year in October 1939 to speed up work on ships which could be completed more quickly. John Brown of Clydebank had been allocated the third ship of the class, *Conqueror*, so had intended to lay her keel immediately after the

launch of the battleship *Duke of York*. With *Conqueror* postponed, it was anticipated that the company could lay down and launch a monitor on its battleship berth before construction was due to be resumed. John Brown was therefore involved in discussions about design and construction from November 1939 onwards. Although the original intention had been to transfer as much equipment and auxiliary machinery as possible from *Soult*, it was found that all her electrical equipment was designed for 105 volts dc, compared with the current RN standard of 220. Deck and internal fittings were not in very good condition, so it was decided to transfer nothing other than the turret, the barbette armour and the hydraulic pumping machinery. The plan was for the turret to be refitted in the ship at Portsmouth by Vickers-Armstrongs and then shipped in pieces to Clydebank for installation in the new hull.

The preliminary design work had been carried out under the title 'Replacement *Marshal Soult*, 1939 Monitor Design' but, as the final design characteristics were not approved until 6 February 1940, the ship actually became part of the 1940 New Construction Programme. Her official identification was J.1573; her Admiralty Job Number, which system was used as a security measure for identifying new construction ships. Later she was given the name *Roberts*, the same as one of the first monitors.

As the design progressed, the estimated deep displacement crept up to 8,675 tons, with a corresponding standard displacement of 7,505 tons. Some objections had been raised to building a monitor at all, on the grounds that large quantities of armour plate would be required which could be better used in tank production. In fact, little over half of the total weight of protection was new armour-quality plate, the remainder coming from *Soult* or being D-quality material, so this objection was overruled. Although preparatory work on the new monitor had already started, the formal order for hull and machinery was not sent to John Brown until 16 March, with delivery scheduled for April 1941.

In common with most contemporary British warships, the design of the steam turbines was carried out by the Parsons Marine Steam Turbine Company of Wallsend, for building under licence at Clydebank. Parsons based the 4,800shp design on the twin-screw river gunboat *Scorpion*'s machinery of 4,500shp. The boilers, however, were similar to the Admiralty three-drum type fitted in the *Black Swan*-class sloops, although slightly modified for the lower headroom in the monitor. However, this caused problems later with serious distortion of the boiler tubes with poor circulation at full power.

Special tests were made by AEW to determine turning characteristics, as a monitor had to be as manoeuvrable as possible in view of air attacks and shore-battery fire. Twin rudders, each sited in the wake of a propeller, gave the best results; *Erebus* had only one. As *Erebus* had always been a wet ship forward, model experiments were made to check whether the spray coming over the bows and off the bulge would be a serious problem. The increased sheer and freeboard showed an improvement in this respect.

In addition to the armour and protective plating, the hull itself was strongly built. The bottom plating was generally ⅝in thick and the upper deck ¾in, both D-quality steel. The longitudinal stresses in the main hull were moderate at about 4 tons per sq in, except at the most highly stressed region in way of the barbette opening, where it rose to 5.8 tons per sq in compression at the deck. All of the main strength structure was riveted, although a number of less-important items, such as bulkhead stiffeners, were welded.

The new monitor's keel was laid on 30 April 1940 on the slipway in the East Yard at Clydebank from which *Duke of York* had been launched two months earlier. To hasten progress, the normal procedure of submitting working drawings for official approval was not followed. Instead, most decisions were made and details settled at fortnightly meetings between Admiralty and builder's representatives. Selection of fittings was based on whatever was available rather than well-established standards, while the outfit of spares, stores and equipment was based on small-ship practice, which made no allowance for a monitor being a self-supporting vessel likely to operate for long periods away from base facilities.

The work of refitting *Soult*'s turret took longer than anticipated, so in September 1940 the feasibility was examined of substituting one of the twin 13.5in turrets which had been removed from the battlecruiser *Tiger* before she was scrapped in 1932.[3] This plan was found to be practicable, although the work of conversion and overhaul would take just as long, while there would be the additional complication of ammunition supply, as the 13.5in was no longer in seagoing service. By this time sufficient AA guns were available to substitute an octuple pom-pom for the after UP mounting.

A number of discussions took place on the best way of shipping the turret. Towing *Roberts* to Portsmouth was considered too lengthy a process, while towing *Soult* to Clydebank would interfere with her base-ship role. Most of the turret components far exceeded the road or rail loading gauges, so there was no alternative left but to send the turret by sea and accept the risk of the ship being lost. There were very few vessels capable of carrying such large loads, and *Sea Fisher* was needed for transporting *Duke of York*'s 14in turrets from Barrow and the Tyne. It was therefore planned to make use of a new coaster for the

shortest possible time during February 1941. The intention was that *Roberts* would be launched on 1 February, the twelve 8in-thick barbette armour plates (despatched by rail) fitted by the 5th and the roller path and training rack completed by the 19th, ready to receive the turret. The coaster would arrive the next day and would unload the lighter components on to the dockside: the 30-ton ammunition trunk, and the 45-ton working chamber, the two 38-ton gun slides and the two 100-ton guns. The coaster would move away from the 200-ton crane, allowing *Roberts* in to receive the trunk and working chamber. The next day the 155-ton turntable would be lifted from the coaster and suspended from the crane hook while *Roberts* was manoeuvred underneath to receive it. On the

Construction at John Brown's is well under way in this view of *Roberts*, then known as No. 573, in about September 1940. Framing has reached the main deck; the armoured deck level with the top of the bulge. The double cruciform bulkheads in the magazine supporting the ring bulkhead and turret have been erected. The compartments nearest the camera are the port and starboard boiler and engine rooms.
(JOHN BROWN)

ABOVE
Roberts is seen here in March 1941 in the fitting-out basin at Clydebank awaiting her turret, which had been damaged on the voyage from Portsmouth. The twelve-sided 8in-thick barbette armour surrounds the ring bulkhead, with its forty-eight rollers covered by canvas ready to take the 760-ton turret.
(John Brown)

LEFT
Roberts is launched at 4.20 p.m. on 1 February 1941 flying John Brown's house flag, with slope armour, bulge fender and ring bulkhead in place. The guys support the slipway derrick cranes.
(John Brown)

third day the gun slides and guns would be erected, and on the fourth day the gunhouse shield and roof plates transferred from coaster to monitor. By 28 February the turret would be fully erected with the fitting of 70 tons of roof plates.

Unfortunately the whole operation turned out quite differently in practice. The newly-built 2,739-ton coaster *Goodwood* arrived at Portsmouth on 30 January to load the turret components. The intention had been to put all the readily-dismantlable parts into the forward holds, leaving the large indivisible turntable to go into the No.3 Hold. But over the previous quarter of a century the gunhouse armour plates and locking keys had become firmly welded together and could not be separated. It was therefore necessary to stow the 168-ton gunhouse in one piece in the bottom of the hold and to position the turntable above it, with its roller path sitting on the hatch coamings, all wedged up with timber shores. When *Goodwood* finally departed Portsmouth on 6 March with her precariously stowed load, the weather was fine, but during the night

Lifting *Marshal Soult*'s 15in gunhouse at Portsmouth – the cause of a three-month delay in completing *Roberts*. As it could not be disassembled into its component armour plates, it had to be shipped in one piece in the bottom of the hold of coaster *Goodwood*. The turntable thus had to be stowed above, resting precariously on the hatch coamings. When it was dislodged and damaged by heavy weather on 7 March 1941 *Goodwood* was first abandoned, but later brought into Devonport for repairs to the turntable, which was eventually delivered to the Clyde in mid-May.
(NMM N24889)

Roberts 15in finally shipped at the end of May 1941.
(JOHN BROWN)

This view, taken on 30 May 1941, shows *Roberts* with her turret now in place, together with the 4in mountings. The minor damage to equipment from the air raid earlier in the month is not apparent apart from one of the broken searchlights. The battleship in the background is *Duke of York*.
(JOHN BROWN)

a heavy gale blew up in the Channel. The violent motion of the ship dislodged the shores, allowing the turntable to drop 15ft, damaging both itself and the vessel to such an extent that the crew thought she was sinking and abandoned ship. By the morning, however, the weather had moderated and *Goodwood* was found to have survived with her precious cargo still aboard. The crew reboarded and brought her safely into Dartmouth on the 8th, where the damage was surveyed. The damaged turntable would have to be repaired at Devonport after being brought in by *Goodwood*, which arrived there on 19 March. The coaster then sailed on with the remaining undamaged parts to the Clyde.

The problem of storage then arose. There were only three cranes on the Clyde capable of lifting the gunhouse: John Brown's, Fairfield's 250-ton fitting-out crane and the Clyde Navigation Trust's (CNT) 175-ton Stobcross Quay crane. None of these three parties wished to have several hundred tons of assorted 15in turret components lying about on their dockside for several weeks, so a meeting took place at the Naval Headquarters in St Enoch's Hotel to settle the matter. At the end of the day it was the CNT that found itself the reluctant temporary

custodian of a 15in gunhouse, which was delivered by *Goodwood* on 4 April. Lighter components were unloaded at Clydebank on the 24th after she had been repaired. The turntable was not ready to leave Devonport in *Goodwood* until 9 May, being erected at Clydebank on 20 May. *Goodwood* then brought the gunhouse from Stobcross the next day, so *Roberts*'s turret was not finally erected until the end of May, three months later than planned. The two guns had already arrived by rail on 8 February, and were two of the earliest to be made by Elswick in 1915, rather than *Soult*'s pair. Completion of the ship was further delayed by the air raid of 7 May, when a landmine fell on the quay alongside *Roberts*, severely damaging boats, searchlights and HA directors.

The delay did permit a number of worthwhile modifications to be incorporated. Eight single 20mm Oerlikon guns in small pits on the upper deck and superstructure were substituted for the two remaining planned UP mountings. The Mk II gun[4] was a useful close-range weapon which the RN badly needed at that time, and was reasonably cheap at £320. Manually operated, with a rate of fire of eight rounds a second, it could open fire on and follow a target very quickly and, although it lacked

An unusual view of *Roberts* nearing completion at Clydebank on 4 September 1941, with her 15in director parked on top of her turret. Her pompoms have been shipped, but not her Oerlikons. *Duke of York* is behind.
(JOHN BROWN)

degaussing cables guarded against magnetic mines.

The modifications during construction aggravated an already serious overcrowding problem in the crew accommodation. From the original complement estimate of 308, the number crept up until *Roberts*'s official complement when she went off to war was 442, made up as follows:

	Officers	Ratings	Total
Seamen and gunners	11	237	248
Engineers	2	64	66
Royal Marines	1	40	41
Radar operators		22	22
Signallers		11	11
Shipwrights and artificers	1	16	17
Supply	2	29	31
Medical	2	4	6
Total	**19**	**423**	**442**

Few of the officers or ratings were regular RN, being mostly reservists or, like the operators of the top-secret radar equipment, specially recruited and trained young men.

9.4 *Roberts* as Completed

Although the layout of *Roberts* was basically similar to that of *Erebus*, there was no mistaking the final appearance of the two ships. The profile of the WW1 monitor as built was bare, virtually the only erections above the deck being the turret, bridge, mast and funnel, although subsequently extended during WW2. In contrast, *Roberts* had extensive superstructure, her two masts and her radar aerials, considerable AA armament, a flush upper deck and an external sloping armour belt on top of the bulge. *Roberts* had more additions during construction than normal, totalling 475 tons or over 5 per cent of her displacement, raising her deep load to 9,150 tons as built. Normally extra weight affects ship stability adversely, as most additions are high in the ship, raising the centre of gravity (G). But with the wide bulges *Roberts*'s metacentre (M) was well above G, so her metacentric height (GM) was 18ft in the deep condition, compared with 6 to 9ft in WW2 battleships and 3 to 6ft in cruisers. The main components of weight are listed in the Technical Data, showing that hull and equipment increased the most between design and completion. The percentages of the deep displacement allocated to armament and protection were remarkably similar to those of the *King George V* battleships, but in the latter a much higher percentage was taken up by machinery and fuel appropriate to a much faster ship, with a corresponding reduction in hull. Compared with the first *Roberts*, the savings from using oil-fired steam turbines as against coal-fired steam reciprocators permitted a heavier armament load to be carried:

killing power compared with the heavier 2pdr, its explosive projectile proved much more effective than the bullets of the puny 0.5in machine gun. The multiple pom-poms were originally fitted only for eye-shooting but, by mid-1941, a director with radar ranging had been developed. Although the early Type 282 was not very reliable and needed coaxing, it did provide some assistance by measuring the range of a fast-moving target, a difficult problem using optical means. Type 285 radar had also been developed for medium-range HA fire, and was fitted to the two rangefinder/directors before completion.

Moored, acoustic and magnetic mines were presenting increasingly serious threats, so *Roberts* was fitted with additional defensive equipment besides the passive bulges. Bow protection gear was installed to reduce the risk from moored mines, a modified type of paravane being streamed from a hinged A-frame lowered over the bows. Acoustic sweep gear was fitted below water forward to detonate acoustic mines at a safe distance, while internal

LEFT
Roberts's congested aft end: four boats, stern anchor, octuple pom-pom, 4in mountings, rangefinder/directors, mainmast. *Duke of York* behind.
(JOHN BROWN)

BELOW
Roberts in October 1941, with all her AA guns now shipped, including eight single 20mm, and twin rangefinder/directors with 285 radar. Compare with the same angle in 1965 on page 214.
(JOHN BROWN)

	Roberts (1915)	Roberts (1941)	K. G. V
Armament and ammunition	13.7	16.6	16.5
Armour and water protection	30.1	30.6	30.5
Machinery, fuel and RFW	12.3	9.4	16.4
Hull and equipment	43.9	43.4	36.6
Total percentage	100.0	100.0	100.0
Deep displacement, tons	6,157	9,150	41,000

Although wartime costs were not recorded in much detail, *Roberts*'s final cost was listed as follows:

	£
Hull and electrical	551,691
Machinery	168,264
Armour plating	143,000
Gun mountings and armament items	192,469
Equipment and stores	48,106
Total	1,103,530

This excluded ammunition and may not have included the gun barrels (about £70,000 total). If the 15in armament had not already existed, the total would have been about £350,000 more, at a time when the purchasing power of the pound was about 35-40 times greater than the mid-2000s.

Roberts finally commissioned six months late, on 6 October 1941, under Capt J.G.Y. Loveband. She left Clydebank three days later for the Gareloch, where she was drydocked in the floating dock AFD 4, the only dock on the Clyde wide enough to take her, which had recently

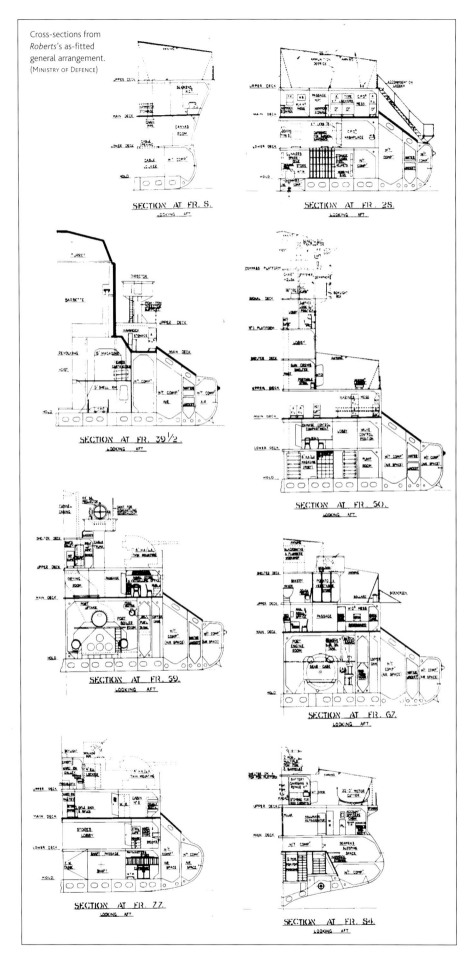

Cross-sections from *Roberts*'s as-fitted general arrangement. (MINISTRY OF DEFENCE)

been transferred from Devonport. Official trials started on 26 October with full power ahead and astern trials. As the Clyde measured miles were not available on that day, her speed had to be estimated from bearings as about 13½kts. Gunnery trials took place the following day, with the usual four rounds from each 15in at various bearings and elevations. Ten rounds from each 4in gun (newly installed mountings straight from the production line at Marshall's of Gainsborough) and about 30 from each close-range weapon rounded off a generally satisfactory trials programme. After final adjustments at the shipyard, particularly to the turret hydraulic pump, she left Clydebank on 13 November to work up and prepare for the long voyage out to the Mediterranean via the Cape to replace *Terror*, lost nine months earlier.

9.5 *Abercrombie*'s Design and Construction

Terror had given such a good account of herself off North Africa that no time was wasted ordering a replacement, *Erebus* then being the only operational monitor. The Naval Staff had recommended building a second monitor in the summer of 1940, but at that time the requirement was not sufficiently urgent and was dropped. To speed delivery the new monitor was to be a near-replica of *Roberts*, with such minor modifications as could be incorporated without too much trouble. In June 1941 *Terror*'s last CO submitted a number of suggestions for improving the design of monitors, especially those features affecting the Guard Ship and Advanced Base Ship roles which had been undertaken in the Mediterranean. Haynes's main suggestions affecting the bombardment role were:

(i) A speed of 18kts to enable the ship to move with the Fleet

(ii) Longer-range guns, about 48,000yd.

(iii) Carriage of own aircraft in view of the shortage of spotting aircraft off North Africa.

Such major changes would need a totally new design of ship, considerably bigger than *Roberts*, while no existing British naval gun could range even 40,000yd. Some of Haynes's more modest suggestions could readily be incorporated in the new ship, including larger store-room and fresh water capacity, better W/T facilities, a heavier stern anchor, more motor boats and better repair and workshop facilities. With delivery planned for September 1942, only the following differences from *Roberts* were finally permitted:

(i) 15in gun mountings brought up to latest Mk I/N standard

(ii) Deck armour over machinery spaces increased from 3 to 4in; circular and slightly shorter

Roberts leaves Clydebank for trials on 9 October 1941, sporting her camouflage. The censor has blanked out the air-warning radar aerials, but left the Type 285 on the HA rangefinder/directors. Oerlikon mountings have been fitted but not the actual guns, which were still in short supply.
(JOHN BROWN)

The nearly completed *Roberts* enters Admiralty Floating Dock 4 in the Gareloch on 13 October 1941. The dock had been towed from Devonport early in the war; it was the same one as used by the monitors drydocking in the Tyne in WW1.
(IWM AD5827)

barbette armour

(iii) More close-range weapons, and remote power control (RPC) fitted to 4in and 2pdr mountings

(iv) Shelter deck extended to full breadth of main hull to provide more accommodation and better arcs of fire for 4in guns mounted thereon

(v) Extra stowage for ammunition, stores and fresh water

(vi) Additional generating capacity necessitated by RPC and other additions, by substituting two 150kW diesel generators for the two 60kW, but retaining the two 200kW turbo-generators

(vii) Three instead of two motor boats, with only one pulling boat (a change which cramped the boat stowage even further, restricted as it was by the bulge to the extreme aft end)

(viii) Accommodation designed for up to 500 men

(ix) Various minor changes in layout and equipment, including taller funnel.

No 15in turrets had been manufactured for over 20 years, but there was still in existence at Chatham the second spare built for *Furious*. As it had been designed for a

WW1 battlecruiser, fairly extensive modifications were required to make it suitable for a WW2 monitor, as detailed on p.219.

In view of the continued suspension of construction of the battleship *Lion*, Vickers-Armstrongs' Naval Yard at Newcastle was given the contract for the new monitor's hull on 4 April 1941, the machinery contract going to Parsons. With copies of *Roberts*'s drawings sent from John Brown, construction proceeded well up to the launch on 31 March 1942. The new ship was christened *Abercrombie*, reviving a WW1 name complete with misspelling. Delays then arose, particularly with the turbines and generators, which held up completion of the structure over the engine room until September. Refitting the turret took longer than expected, so it was not ready to leave the erection pit at Elswick until January 1943. Labour troubles at the shipyard added further delays, so it was 22 April before *Abercrombie* finally left the shipyard under the command of Capt G.V.B. Faulkner. She carried out gunnery and speed trials on the way to Rosyth for drydocking but, having been lying in the Tyne for over a year, she could only manage an estimated 12kts with her fouled bottom.

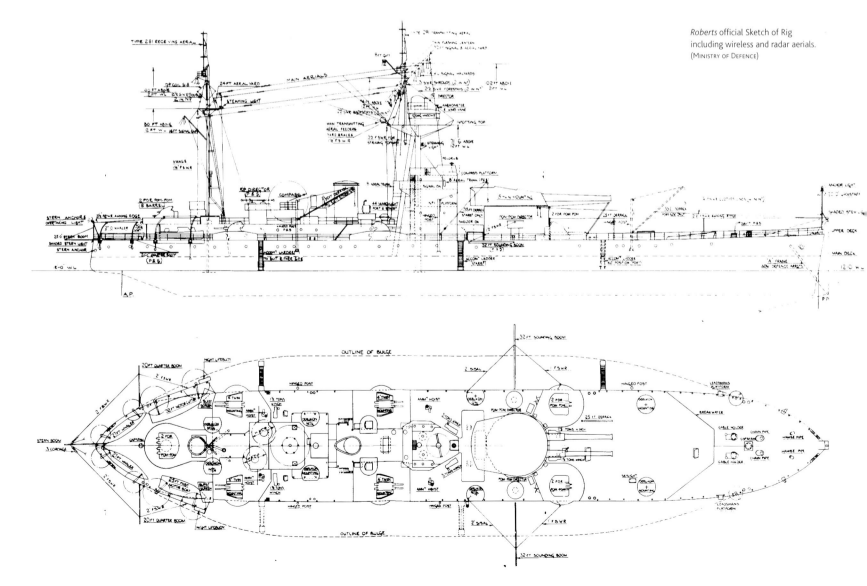

Roberts official Sketch of Rig including wireless and radar aerials.
(MINISTRY OF DEFENCE)

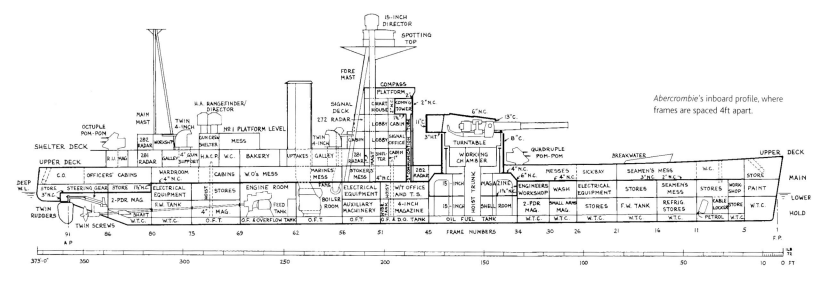

Abercrombie's inboard profile, where frames are spaced 4ft apart.

The effect of all the minor modifications was to add 567 tons to the deep displacement compared with *Roberts*, largely hull and armour. Most of the additions were aft of the turret, accentuating the trim by the stern to the extent that *Abercrombie* drew 15ft 8in aft and 12ft 1in forward, a big change from the 13ft 1in and 12ft 4in for which *Roberts* had originally been designed, negating some of the benefit of a shallow draft for inshore operations. The position of the turret was relatively further aft than *Erebus* at 41½ per cent of the length from the bow, which not only worsened the trim but severely cramped the deck, superstructure and AA gun arrangement. A shift forward of the turret of about 10ft would have been very beneficial, but *Abercrombie* had been committed before *Roberts*'s large 22in trim as completed became apparent. Standard displacement worked out at 8,536 tons, although official records continued to show the figure at its preliminary estimate of 7,850 tons, an error which was never corrected, implying that *Abercrombie* was smaller than the 7,973-ton *Roberts*. Her metacentric height (GM) was 14ft deep, 4ft less than her sister's, due to a greater submergence of the bulge as well as a higher CG. *Abercrombie* cost appreciably more than *Roberts* at £1,562,966, of which hull and machinery made up £843,177. Not only was more extensive equipment fitted, but much more work had to be done modifying the 15in turret, as well as supplying new barbette and thicker armour plating, plus the effect of wartime inflation. The price paid to the builder was based on the actual cost of labour and materials, plus a fixed profit margin of 7½ per cent.

Abercrombie's electronic and control outfit was of the most up-to-date pattern. In place of the obsolescent Dreyer table, a new cruiser-style Admiralty Fire Control Table Mark VI was fitted in the transmitting station. Her 4in armament was one of the first installations to receive RPC, whereby training and elevating of the guns were controlled directly by the HACPs with their associated rangefinder/directors and improved Type 285 radar. The octuple and two quadruple pom-poms were each controlled via RPC by their own Mk IV director and Type 282 radar. The eight twin power-operated Mk V 20mm mountings were at first fitted only for eye-shooting, later receiving gyro gunsights which considerably improved performance. The four manually-operated single Oerlikons retained their normal cartwheel-like eye-shooting sights, once described as having the appearance and durability of spiders' webs. Type 281 air warning radar at the mastheads and Type 272M surface warning in its 'lantern' below the spotting top, plus the usual interrogators, rounded off the radar outfit.

Abercrombie was completed on 5 May 1943, just in time to take part in the Sicilian landings, the newest, the best equipped and the last to be built of all Britain's big-gun monitors.

9.6 Wartime Service Overseas

When *Roberts* was allocated to the Mediterranean in October 1941 together with *Erebus*, it was hoped that she would be able to emulate *Terror* in supporting the Eighth Army's offensive against Axis forces in North Africa. Owing to enemy air superiority in the Central Mediterranean, the two monitors would have to steam to Egypt via the Cape. *Roberts* and *Erebus* left Lough Foyle on 1 December, stopping at the Azores, Freetown and Pointe Noire for fuel before arriving at Simonstown on 11 January. *Roberts* had carried out a full-calibre throw-off shoot at *Erebus* and later a sub-calibre shoot at a target towed by *St Dogmaels*. The C-in-C Mediterranean then requested *Roberts*'s presence as soon as possible, to assist forthcoming operations in Tripolitania. Delayed by boiler repairs at Durban, she did not arrive at Suez until 26

February, by which time Rommel had succeeded in pushing the Eighth Army back towards Egypt again. As the Luftwaffe had been making bombing and mining attacks on the Suez Canal, *Roberts* remained stationed at Suez as AA guardship. She was anchored about three miles south of the canal entrance, whence she could cover the approaches to the anchorages where the merchant ships supplying the Eighth Army lay. Although she closed up pom-pom crews on many nights, there were few air raids while she was there. Hot and uneventful months passed until July, when she moved down the Red Sea for a few weeks, which included some target practice at some old oil drums ashore, using up obsolete shrapnel projectiles. In August she was ordered to prepare to sail for an unspecified operation. She departed from Suez on the 17th for drydocking at Durban, as she had lost two knots' speed from hull fouling lying at anchor. Propeller shaft revolutions normally providing 8kts gave only 5kts. After leaving Durban on 20 September for Freetown, she learned that she was to support the Allied landings in North Africa, *Operation Torch*, due to take place on 8 November.

Roberts arrived at Gibraltar on 2 November, where most of the Allied covering naval and air forces were gathering. She left just after midnight on the 6th and took station with convoy KMS(A).l, which formed part of the force which was to land at Algiers. She carried the largest guns that would be available to suppress any opposition from the French forts guarding Algiers; the battleships of the main covering force were further to seaward to intercept any sortie by the Italian battle fleet. The landings were made from 01.00 on 8 November in three sectors, two to the west and one to the east of Algiers. *Roberts* stopped about seven miles offshore, ready to open fire if required. Little opposition was encountered. Fort Sidi Ferruch in *Roberts*'s sector did not resist the Allied troops, formally surrendering in the morning. Although some of the eastern forts offered some resistance, bombardment by the cruiser *Bermuda*, destroyers and naval aircraft were sufficient to suppress them. *Roberts* could therefore anchor safely on the afternoon of the 8th to act as radar guardship, warning of the approach of any German aircraft from the direction of Tunisia. The next day she anchored in Algiers Bay and opened fire with her 4in at Junkers Ju 88s attacking the Allied ships. The air attacks were sustained, necessitating a continuous standby by the crews of her AA weapons.

A further landing had been planned at Bougie (now Bejaia), 130 miles east of Algiers, to take place on the morning of the 11th. *Roberts* sailed on the evening of the

continued on p.194

This stern view of *Abercrombie* before her launch in March 1942 shows her bluff afterbody lines and the twin propellers with the rudders in their wake. The sloping armour has yet to be shipped, but some of the 1½in plating around the steering gear is visible above the propellers. The 250-ton cantilever crane in the background was used to lift the turret components from their barges after their trip from Elswick up-river, for installation in Ship No. 42. It is still in use (2007).
(VICKERS)

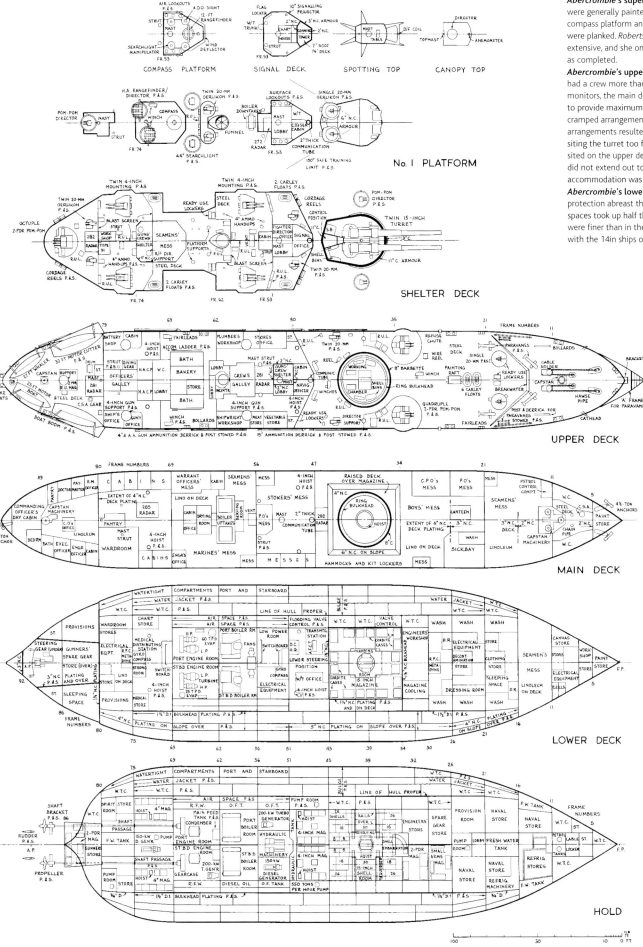

Abercrombie's superstructure decks. Decks were generally painted steel, although the compass platform and roof of the seamen's mess were planked. Roberts's deckhouses were less extensive, and she only mounted eight Oerlikons as completed.

Abercrombie's upper and main deck. As the ship had a crew more than double that of the WW1 monitors, the main deck was completely enclosed to provide maximum accommodation. The cramped arrangement of boats and after mooring arrangements resulted from the design error of siting the turret too far aft. With her 4in guns sited on the upper deck, Roberts's superstructure did not extend out to the ship's side, and her accommodation was less extensive.

Abercrombie's lower deck and hold. The side protection abreast the turret and machinery spaces took up half the breadth. The forward lines were finer than in the first monitors; compare with the 14in ships on p.15.

ABOVE

An impressive photograph of *Abercrombie* steaming down the Tyne on 20 April 1943. The circular barbette armour shows the change of camouflage pattern on the centreline.
(AUTHOR'S COLLECTION)

LEFT

Abercrombie passes South Shields on her way down the Tyne on 20 April 1943. Clearly visible are her many radar aerials, largely directed towards AA defence. Transmitting and receiving aerials for the Type 281 air-warning are at the mastheads, Type 285 on the two rangefinder/directors, and Type 282 on the pom-pom directors. The only surface-warning set is the Type 272 in its lantern under the spotting top.
(AUTHOR'S COLLECTION)

continued from p.190

10th as part of the covering force, but again no bombardment was required, the landing being unopposed by the French. The airfield at Djidjelli, 40 miles east, was also occupied, but swell prevented the troopship *Awatea* from landing petrol and air stores there. The Spitfires that were to provide air cover for the ships and troops were therefore unable to operate for two days, while the nearest airfield in Allied hands was 120 miles west of Bougie. With no carrier support, *Argus* having been withdrawn after damage, the result was that there was no fighter cover when German aircraft attacked Bougie later on the 11th, and they caused severe damage.

Roberts helped beat off the first attack by Ju 88s early in the afternoon, claiming one shot down. She continued her patrolling; at dusk another heavy attack took place. Despite concentrated AA fire from all the ships, the troopships *Cathay* and *Awatea* were bombed and sunk, while *Roberts* was attacked by three Ju 88 dive-bombers at 17.15. One came in from the bow and two from the stern in 30-degree dives, releasing their 500kg (1,102lb) bombs at about 1,000ft. One bomb was a near-miss about 30ft to port, but the other two were direct hits. Casualties were heavy, although her good protection saved her from fatal damage. One bomb hit her sloping bulge armour on the port side abreast the funnel, dishing the 4in-thick plating about ten inches and flooding two of the inner bulge compartments. A hole about 7ft × 6ft was blown in the ship's side, starting a fire on the main deck. The second hit was more serious. The bomb landed just abaft the

funnel and penetrated as far as the armoured main deck. At that instant, Engineer Lt Cdr A.W.M. Collyer was in the starboard engine room, looking up, when he saw the 3in thick deck armour deflect downwards about nine inches and then spring back, leaving a shallow depression. The explosion wrecked compartments above the main deck and started several fires. Although the damage did not appear at first to be severe, the hole in the upper deck being about 12ft × 8ft, the engine room ventilation fans had been destroyed. Despite steam being shut off, the engine room, hot at the best of times, soon became unbearable and one man died of heat exhaustion before the jammed hatches could be opened.

Considerable secondary damage was caused below decks; both turbo-generators out of action, piping and electrical systems destroyed, feed and fresh water contaminated. Above decks, the funnel was crumpled, one Oerlikon destroyed and much of the superstructure amidships damaged, although the bullet holes in the bridge were attributed to 'friendly' close-range fire. Radar sets, rangefinders and degaussing equipment were also put out of action for some time. Total casualties were seventeen killed and thirty-five wounded. Replacement crew members were obtained next day from the survivors of the AA ship *Tynwald*, sunk on the 12th, which helped *Roberts*'s close-range guns' crews maintain the constant vigilance needed to beat off surprise enemy attacks.

Roberts was effectively immobilised for two days until new engine room fans could be improvised from mess-deck fans, so she did not take part in the assault on Bone

Anchored south of the entrance to the Suez Canal, *Roberts* served as AA guardship during the summer of 1942.
(IWM E14352)

as had been intended. Air attacks continued, with *Roberts* still able to put up a formidable AA barrage. About midnight on the 12th she replenished with AA ammunition from the sloop *Pelican*, as she had fired off some 30,000 rounds in less than a week. Spitfires began patrolling from Djidjelli on the 13th, so thereafter the air attacks on the ships at Bougie became less intense. On the 16th two torpedo bombers attacked *Roberts*; fortunately both torpedoes missed, exploding harmlessly against the harbour breakwater. *Roberts* was able to repair some of the less serious damage herself, the hole in the upper deck being patched with concrete reinforced with railway sleepers and mattress frames. She was able to take up radar guardship duties on the 22nd, relieving the AA ship *Pozarica*; no shore-based radar was yet in operation. She left Bougie on 1 December for Algiers and then Gibraltar for temporary repairs. She berthed in Gladstone Dock, Liverpool, on 6 January, where Cammell Laird took her in hand for permanent repairs, lasting until the end of May 1943. The opportunity was taken to modify her magazines to handle the longer 6crh HE projectile.

Abercrombie arrived in the Clyde from Rosyth on 9 May 1943 for working up; *Roberts* arrived there on 1 June, now under the command of Capt R.E.C. Dunbar, who had been *Lord Clive*'s navigating officer at the end of WW1. The two monitors engaged in lengthy bombardment practices, exercising in particular the spotting of gunfire by shore observers. The British practice was to have a small team ashore consisting of an artillery officer called a Forward Observation Officer (FOO) to spot the fall of

shot and to estimate corrections, and a naval telegraphist to signal to the bombarding ship. On the ship, the Gunnery Officer was assisted by another artillery officer called a Bombardment Liaison Officer (BLO) in carrying out the shoot as required by the troops ashore. *Abercrombie* carried out some of her exercises with US Shore Fire Control Parties (SFCP), as she would be supporting American forces in forthcoming operations.

Both monitors had been allocated, together with *Erebus*, to provide gunfire support for the next phase of Mediterranean combined operations. With North Africa now cleared of the enemy, the next step was to land in Europe itself, first on Sicily, then on the Italian mainland. The British Eighth Army and the American Seventh Army were to make the assault early in July on the southern coast of Sicily. The three monitors would be the only heavy-gun ships in direct support, as the battleships assigned to *Operation Husky* were required to stand off to intercept any ships of the Italian fleet that might approach.

Roberts and *Abercrombie* sailed from the Clyde on 18 June as part of convoy KMS.17. On passage, *Roberts* suffered the misfortune of damage to one of her turbo-generators. The turbine blading was found to be stripped. Gibraltar dockyard could do nothing but request urgent spares from the UK, so she had to sail on her most important operation to date knowing that, if the other turbo-generator failed, she would have to withdraw, as her diesel generators had insufficient capacity. On 2 July she arrived at Algiers, where many of the invasion ships were gathering, while *Abercrombie* went on to Tunis,

Following repairs after her damage at Bougie, *Roberts* is seen here working up in the Clyde in June 1943. A number of modifications have been made, including lengthening of the funnel, new radars and additional Oerlikons. The shades of camouflage on the hull are (starting from the bow): light grey, dark grey, light grey and blue grey below the bridge (not easily distinguished in this view), dark grey (mass aft), light grey. (IWM A17511)

arriving on the 4th, after embarking the USN liaison officer and signallers who had trained with her in the Clyde. *Roberts* would join up with convoy KMS.18B coming from UK, which included the store and other ships destined for 'Bark West', the British landing beaches to the west of Cape Passero, the south-east tip of Sicily. *Abercrombie* would sail with convoy TJM.l, most of whose LSTs had been assembling at Tunis, to cover the landings on the easternmost of the American beaches, 'Cent', about 40 miles west of Cape Passero. Meanwhile, *Erebus* had been approaching from the east with convoy MWS.36, which had left Alexandria on 3 July; she would cover the northernmost British landings at 'Acid North', about 15 miles north of Cape Passero.

The two newer monitors sailed for the invasion of Sicily on 8 July, their convoys making for the rendezvous positions south of Malta. At midday on the 9th *Roberts* switched to convoy KMF.18 for the final run in, but had some difficulty keeping up with these faster ships. Bad weather was encountered that day, which slowed down the landing craft in *Abercrombie*'s convoy to a speed at which she could not be steered, so she had to pull ahead. *Abercrombie* arrived in position off Scoglitti at 02.30 on D-day, 10 July. To obtain tactical surprise, no pre-H-hour bombardments had been planned. The landing craft went in soon after she arrived; conditions were not easy although there was little opposition. Her first call for fire came at 07.15, when she was asked to fire on inland targets including Comiso Airfield. Following counterattacks by enemy tanks, *Abercrombie* was ordered up to help on the 11th. She opened fire on the town of Niscemi, eight miles inland, and managed to knock out the enemy headquarters from a range of 30,000yd. The supporting American cruisers and destroyers returned a huge volume of fire from their 6in and 5in guns on the less-distant targets. *Abercrombie* used her big guns to good effect also, but British records tend to be less comprehensive than American, and details of her targets and ammunition expenditure are not available, although she claimed a five-gun enemy battery destroyed with five rounds. The counterattack was beaten back, 'Little Dumbo', as the Americans nicknamed *Abercrombie*, scoring a direct hit on one tank that came down a hillside road in full view from the sea.

Most of the spotting had been done by the SFCPs as, although the cruisers carried observation seaplanes, the latter were vulnerable to enemy fighters during the initial period, when Allied fighter cover was poor. As the Americans pressed inland on the 13th and 14th there were fewer calls for fire as the front advanced out of range. On the 14th *Abercrombie* was called on to bombard Porto Empedocle and Agrigento on the Seventh Army's west

flank, in company with the US cruisers *Birmingham* and *Philadelphia*. Spotting conditions were not suitable until the next morning, when *Abercrombie* engaged ten separate targets including an Italian railway battery, with the help of *Philadelphia*'s spotting aircraft. Some return fire was experienced, but the shells from the shore batteries fell well short. By the evening she had expended nearly all her HE ammunition, so was sent to Malta to replenish, where she arrived on the morning of the 16th.

Meanwhile, the British and Canadian landings had also been successfully carried out. *Roberts* had opened fire at 05.10 on the 10th on the only battery to fire on the landing craft, the five 149mm (5.9in) guns near Pachino, inland from Cape Passero. The battery was silenced by fourteen rounds from *Roberts* anchored 9,000yd away, and was captured soon after. *Roberts* was then requested to bombard Pachino Airfield, but cancellation quickly followed; the airfield was taken shortly afterwards and put into service by the RAF. In the afternoon RM Commandos came under heavy mortar fire near the town of Spaccaforno. Fourteen rounds from *Roberts* induced the Italians to surrender, protesting that it was unfair to be bombarded by shells of such calibre. The next morning an enemy troop concentration near Rosolini was broken up by thirty rounds from 18,000yd, the Italian defenders quickly surrendering. No calls for fire were received by her on the 12th.

Erebus had been ready to support an airborne brigade at her bombardment position about ten miles south-east of Syracuse since 07.00 on D-day, but her first call for fire did not come until 14.15. With twelve rounds she destroyed a strongpoint east of Ponte Grande. Shortly afterwards, shipping in the 'Acid' sector was subjected to heavy air attacks by Ju 88s and Messerschmitt Bf 109s. *Erebus* suffered eight near-misses but without incurring any damage, so was able to respond to an FOO's call for fire on another strongpoint at about 20.00. Eight rounds from 19,000yd sufficed to destroy it. Owing to the speed of advance and the ineffectual coastal defences, she received no calls for fire on D+1, but spent D+2 in almost continuous bombardment. At 05.40 she began firing at a coast-defence battery on Cape San Croce, near Augusta. This and other batteries received attention during the morning in seven separate shoots to cover the advance on the important naval base of Augusta, which would permit the entry of Allied ships. The first attempt by destroyers to enter was repulsed so, after noon, *Erebus* and the cruisers *Mauritius*, *Uganda* and *Orion* switched their fire to the town of Melilli, about five miles from Augusta. *Erebus*'s total fire for the day amounted to about 130 rounds, over half her ammunition outfit.

Roberts transferred from 'Bark' to 'Acid' sector on 13 July to supplement the AA defences around the port of Syracuse, which had been captured on the 11th. *Erebus* moved north for bombardments of the strongly defended Catania area. Catania Airfield was fired on from maximum range at 11.05, and other bombardments were made in company with *Mauritius*, *Uganda*, *Orion* and *Newfoundland* of batteries harassing Allied ships offshore. Enemy air attacks continued, both monitors being shaken by near misses. Smokescreens provided some cover as continuous fighter protection was not yet available.

Roberts took over off Catania on 14 July after *Erebus* had sailed for Malta to replenish fuel and ammunition. Despite ideal firing conditions, her FOO was not in an area from which he could direct any useful fire, and nor was the exact position of the Allied troops known, so *Roberts* had to return after a fruitless day to her buoy in Augusta harbour. The next day was much more successful. In the afternoon and evening she fired some ninety rounds at Catania, its batteries, docks and the roads leading into the town. The longest-range shoots were from 25,000yd at the town of Misterbianco. During one of the shoots at a road full of German military traffic, a factory chimney was selected as the point of aim. The very first shot hit the base of the chimney, collapsing it into a heap of bricks and dust. A minor gunfire accident due to a faulty 15in projectile damaged one of her 4in and an Oerlikon, so she returned to Malta, where she joined the other two monitors on the 16th.

Abercrombie returned to Gela on 18 July, but the Americans were now advancing steadily and there was little for her to do that could not be equally well undertaken by the Army's artillery or the US cruisers and destroyers. After a period as radar guardship she therefore returned to Malta on 23 July before sailing to Bizerta to prepare for the invasion of Italy itself.

Erebus and *Roberts* arrived back at Augusta on the 18th and 19th respectively. An Inshore Squadron was formed to provide gunfire support to the Army on the east coast of Sicily, consisting of the two monitors, the Dutch gunboats *Flores* and *Soemba*, plus minesweepers and MLs. Nightly bombing and torpedo raids were frequent over Augusta, often necessitating several hundred AA rounds from each ship in the harbour, the sky being lit by scores of tracer and searchlight beams. On the night of 20 July *Erebus* was straddled by two bombs which killed six of her crew and wounded twenty-six. *Roberts* sent her shipwrights over to help patch the damage. *Erebus*'s next bombardment was on the evening of the 21st, when she put sixteen rounds into the Catania area. A shore battery returned fire, but its range was too short to reach the monitor. Thereafter virtually no calls for fire were received by either monitor for quite some time while on patrol.

Although the Germans were stubbornly defending the north-east corner of Sicily, it was clear that before long they would have to withdraw from Catania to Messina and then to the mainland. *Roberts* was therefore ordered to bombard the coastal road and railway line between those two towns at Taormina. On a cliffside, the road ran directly above a railway tunnel, so it appeared possible to block both lines of retreat. Dunbar was particularly requested by the Chief of Staff not to damage the nearby hotel, where he had spent his honeymoon. Two Army Air Co-operation Squadron Spitfires were briefed to spot for the bombardment, so initiating a technique of spotting from fighter aircraft that was to become standard method. Sailing in company with the destroyers *Brocklesby* and *Tynedale*, *Roberts* started her bombardment at 11.40 on 4 August from a range of 19,000yd. The range was found using APC spotted by the Spitfires, then *Roberts* switched to HE. After the ship had closed to 16,000yd the fall of shot could be directly observed by those on board. Fire was kept up for just under an hour, until dust blotted out the target and the aircraft had to return to base. A small battery ashore opened up towards the end of the shoot, so *Roberts* made smoke and opened the range. Most of her thirty-two shots fell in the target area, and large amounts of debris could be seen blocking the road and railway. Over the next four days destroyers continued to bombard the area to hamper repair work. Although the road had not been fully cleared when the Eighth Army took Taormina eleven days later, the Germans claimed that their withdrawal was not seriously affected by this operation.

Only two other bombardments of Sicily were carried out by the monitors: *Erebus* near Taormina on 14 August in company with *Flores*, *Ledbury* and *Wheatland*; and *Roberts* supporting a landing near Cape Scaletta on the early morning of the 16th. Forty RM Commando landed from two LSIs ten miles south of Messina to blow bridges, but found that the Germans had already almost all withdrawn. A heavy battery at Cape Pellaro on the mainland opened fire at *Roberts* at 07.00, so she increased the range and returned fire from 23,000yd when the battery began firing on the landing beaches. Neither the battery nor its gun-flashes could be seen, and low-lying mist hampered spotting, so she ceased fire after four rounds. An hour later two Spitfires arrived to spot, so another ten rounds were aimed at the battery before the ships withdrew. The following day *Erebus* fired ten rounds at another mainland battery near San Giovanni. The nights at Augusta were now much quieter following the completion of the German evacuation of Sicily on the 16th. On 21 August *Roberts* led an impressive flotilla consisting of *Erebus*, *Flores*, *Soemba*, *Ledbury*, *Wheatland*,

Aphis, *Scarab* and *Cockchafer* to Malta to rest and replenish. *Abercrombie* returned from Bizerta on the 28th, so all the monitors were together again, preparing for the assault on the Italian mainland.

Naval gunfire support was not used as extensively as it might have been at Sicily, sometimes owing to lack of a FOO in the right position. *Roberts* fired a total of 232 rounds over a six-week period, and *Abercrombie* and *Erebus* approached 200 each. No calls were made on the bombarding fleet to neutralise the coastal batteries covering the Straits of Messina, which would have allowed smaller craft to harass more effectively the vessels ferrying the Germans to the mainland.

With the Germans driven out of Sicily, the Allies planned to invade the mainland of Italy as soon as the necessary forces for a landing could be assembled. The Eighth Army was to cross the Straits of Messina and advance up the toe of Italy, while the Fifth Army was to land in the Gulf of Salerno, south of Naples. The three monitors sailed from Malta for Augusta on 30 August to support the first of these operations. *Operation Baytown* began with a heavy artillery barrage across the Straits from the hills surrounding Messina, followed by landings near Reggio on the morning of 3 September. Although the monitors expected a busy time, the landings were virtually unopposed and only *Erebus* was called upon for ten rounds in the early afternoon. The Germans were busy withdrawing northwards, while the war-weary Italians were on the point of surrender.

After anchoring for the night off Taormina, the three

monitors were back in the assault area next morning, but no calls for fire were received. In the afternoon *Roberts* and *Abercrombie* sailed for Bizerta to join the convoys preparing for the Salerno landings, leaving *Erebus* to undertake any bombardments required. Several calls for fire were received on the 6th and 7th in the Gioia area north of the Straits; most of her forty rounds were directed at enemy transport on the coastal road. The next day *Erebus* supported the landing of 231 Brigade near Pizzo, about 50 miles north-east of Reggio. The Germans were just in the process of withdrawing past this point, so gave the landing vessels a hot reception. *Erebus* fired twenty-five rounds at various targets and was met by replies from enemy artillery and Fw 190 fighters, but without being hit. With her guns now nearly worn out she was ordered to return to Malta, where she arrived on 10 September.

Meanwhile, *Roberts* and *Abercrombie* had departed Bizerta on the morning of 7 September, the former to support the British landings at the northern end of the Gulf of Salerno, and the latter the American landings at the southern end. News was received on passage of the armistice with Italy; the cheering optimists in the assault force who thought that the war was over were rudely reminded that stiff opposition was still to be expected from the Germans. Both monitors arrived in their firing positions soon after midnight, although, as no pre-H-hour bombardment had been ordered, they would not expect calls for fire for some time until their FOOs were established ashore. The Germans at Salerno were well prepared when the first troops landed at about 03.30 on the 9th. In the southern sector *Abercrombie* received her

The damage to *Abercrombie* after her mining can just be seen in this view taken on 11 September 1943. The sloped bulge armour has been pushed upwards (arrowed) and men are working on the light-coloured area, securing the armour with brackets.
(US National Archives)

first call for fire at 08.25; an enemy battery near the town of Capaccio, about five miles inland. The spotting aircraft had some difficulty identifying the target in the morning mist, so it took 50min to get off eleven rounds without any observed result. The assembled ships were under frequent air attacks; at one time *Abercrombie* was firing on He 111s on one side of the ship and Bf 109s on the other. Three more calls for fire were received during the morning, all at ranges of about 27,000yd. Tanks were engaged with nine rounds, and it is believed that she managed to destroy two of them.

In the meantime, minesweepers had been busy clearing several channels and had exploded a number of mines. At one point in the morning *Abercrombie* was warned that she was standing into danger, so she retraced her course. As the channels had not yet been properly buoyed, it was difficult to keep to safe areas; during the day *Abercrombie* drifted slowly out to sea under a light offshore breeze. By 17.00 she had drifted unknowingly into an area purposely left unswept, and three minutes later a large explosion occurred amidships on the starboard side. She had hit a moored contact mine in 450ft of water, and it had gone off under the starboard bulge abreast the foremast, throwing a great column of black water into the air. A hole was torn in the bulge about 20ft × 12ft and the ship quickly took on a heel of 10 degrees. The bulge and protective bulkhead had taken the main force of the charge, estimated to be 500lb, both being damaged over a length of about 100ft. Inboard there was little structural damage and only a few compartments were flooded, resulting from buckled or leaking bulkheads. The port

bulge was counter-flooded to bring the ship back upright, and a survey was made of the damage. The belt armour had been displaced up to 2½ft, but operationally the more serious damage was confined to fittings and equipment. The 15in director had been unseated, preventing further indirect bombardment. Although the turret could be fired, it was feared that more structural damage would result. The 281 and 272 radars had been put out of action, the latter only temporarily, together with W/T sets, while piping and lighting systems and two Oerlikon mountings were damaged. Fortunately there was only one moderately wounded casualty. The US salvage tug *Moreno* was near at hand to give assistance, so berthed alongside *Abercrombie* next morning to begin stopping leaks and securing the loose armour plating by welding. *Abercrombie* had no welding set on board, unlike *Roberts*, which had wisely privately purchased such a set in South Africa. *Abercrombie* sailed for Palermo on the 11th, her machinery being undamaged, leaving US cruisers to provide heavy gunfire support in the southern sector.

Meanwhile, *Roberts* had been busy in the northern sector, in company with four cruisers. Two shoots were made on the morning of D-day in the area of Faiano east of Salerno town, on both occasions the FOO reporting 'OK'. The next day she was ordered to bombard the road through Cava about five miles north-west of Salerno, so nineteen rounds were fired at five-minute intervals. This road to Naples was shot up twice on the 11th from ranges of eight to nine miles. The FOOs had some difficulties in observing in the hilly country, as well as in maintaining radio contact. *Roberts* also had her share of difficulties:

In the afternoon of 9 September 1943 *Abercrombie* drifted into an unswept minefield while awaiting calls for bombardment in the Gulf of Salerno. She is seen here the following day, with the US salvage tug *Moreno* assisting. No damage is apparent in this view, as the mine struck the starboard bulge amidships.
(US NATIONAL ARCHIVES)

her gyro director training gear developed a fault which prevented accurate transmission of bearing to the TS, necessitating manual control, while a round from her right gun broke up shortly after leaving the barrel, fragments landing close to the ship. The remainder of the bombardment was made using the left gun, but ordnance specialists from *Uganda* could find no fault with the gun itself. It was assumed that it was the projectiles that were faulty, some obtained at Malta having been recovered from a sunken ship. Three shoots were made on the 12th at places which were important road and rail junctions. Details of all the monitors' firings at Salerno are given in the table below. A heavy German counterattack with tanks was made down the River Sele dividing the British and American sectors on 12 September. At one time the Americans were considering withdrawing from their beach-head, but the Germans were finally halted on the 14th after three days of heavy naval bombardment by cruisers and destroyers, both British and American. Surprisingly, *Roberts*'s assistance was not requested, and indeed for the three days 14–16 September she did not fire a shot, although *Warspite*, *Valiant*, *Aurora* and *Penelope* were ordered from Malta to give gunfire support.

Monitor bombardments at Salerno, 1943

Key	Time	Target	Range, yards	Rounds	Spotting
		Abercrombie			
	9 September				
A.	08.25–09.20	Guns and troops south of Capaccio	26,600	11 HE	Air
B.	10.25–10.30	Tanks near River Sele	27,300	2 HE	Unobserved
C.	11.12–11.25	Tanks near River Sele	26,500	7 HE	Air
D.	11.35–11.41	Capaccio town	27,500	4 HE	FOO
		Roberts			
	9 September				
E.	08.45–	Area bombardment Faiano	21,500	5 HE	FOO
F.	11.00–11.05	Crossroads at Faiano	11,000	5 HE	FOO
	10 September				
G.	12.35–13.15	Road through Cava	14–15,000	19 HE	Unobserved
	11 September				
H.	13.54–	Guns and troops south of Cava	14,500	7 HE	FOO
J.	17.30–19.00	Road and bridge between Cava and Nocera	16–19,000	42 HE	FOO
	12 September				
K.	09.10–09.20	Road junction at Camerelle	20,600	7 HE	Unobserved
L.	17.45–	Tanks and troops near Battipaglia	17,000	14 HE	FOO
M.	18.24–	Enemy HQ Battipaglia	17,000	8 HE	FOO
	13 September				
N.	06.50–07.15	Transport on road to Baronissi	17,000	10 HE	Unobserved
	17 September				
P.	10.48–	Guns on road to Baronissi	18,500	10 HE	FOO
Q.	11.10–	Buildings near Baronissi	18,300	12 APC	FOO
R.	19.17–	Nocera town	25,000	2 APC	FOO
	18 September				
S.	10.18–	Guns on road between Nocera and Cava	19,200	13 APC	FOO
T.	13.20–13.40	Guns and troops near Battipaglia	13–14,000	13 HE	FOO
U.	16.21–16.46	Enemy HQ Cava	16,200	11 HE	FOO
	19 September				
V.	10.00–	Enemy HQ Cava	16,200	10 HE	FOO
W.	15.40–	Guns near Baronissi	16,700	15 HE	FOO
X.	23.59–	Enemy HQ Cava	16,200	12 HE	Unobserved

Note: Letters correspond to locations on map opposite

H.M.S. ABERCROMBIE.
MINE DAMAGE – 9th SEPT. 1944 3

PHOTOGRAPH No 1.

View looking forward of damage to starboard bulge.

PHOTOGRAPH No 2

View looking aft of damage to starboard bulge.

Close-ups of *Abercrombie*'s mine damage at Salerno on 9 September 1943, from the official damage report. Although not too severe, it took ten months to repair her at Taranto dockyard.
(MINISTRY OF DEFENCE)

During this period *Roberts* was either at anchor or steaming slowly about in the fire support channels. Air attacks were frequent. On the 11th she had the satisfaction of seeing her close-range guns down a Bf 109 off her port side. On one occasion she was able, by steaming very close inshore, to shield a group of beached LSTs with smoke floats. Enemy headquarters in Cava were engaged three times on the 18th–19th. After the second shoot *Roberts* dropped a buoy to mark her position and recorded the setting of her fire control table. She

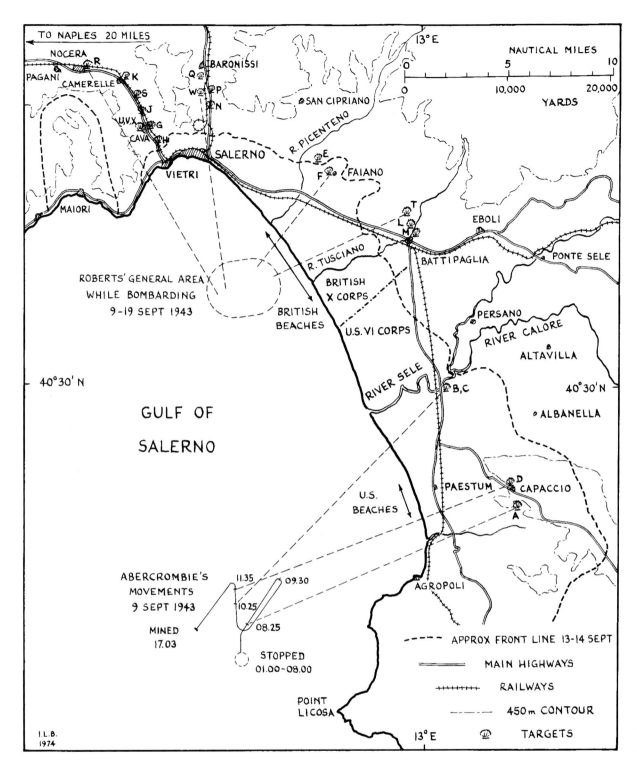

TO NAPLES 20 MILES

A map of the Salerno bombardments. Lettered targets are detailed opposite.

returned to this point at 23.59 on the 19th and thoroughly disturbed the Germans' rest with twelve rounds into her target of the previous day. The following day she left the area for Augusta and Malta, having expended 214 rounds, 175 being HE, virtually her entire outfit.

Salerno was the first combined operation in the European theatre in which naval bombardment played a crucial role. Sceptical Army officers were now convinced of the ability of the Allied navies to put down heavy and accurate fire where the Army wanted it, especially in the early stages before their own artillery was fully deployed. A detailed analysis was made of *Operation Avalanche* to point up lessons for future landings. Over a period of twelve days at Salerno the Allied warships had fired 22,800 rounds of 4in calibre and above at 322 targets, totalling about 1,000 tons. The Germans made particular reference to the important role played by naval gunfire, which severely restricted their freedom of movement anywhere within range of the sea, especially during daylight. The importance of pre-H-hour bombardment to soften up the enemy defences was emphasised and the value of spotting by fighter aircraft recognised, together with the need for special training and equipment for sustained gunfire support.

After a few days patching up at Palermo, *Abercrombie* had steamed on to Bizerta, while a decision was made about permanent repairs. After the armistice with Italy she was sent to Taranto dockyard, where she arrived on 7 October. Serious work did not start until January 1944, so she remained a total of ten months in dockyard hands. Her 15in guns were exchanged, but otherwise work was mainly confined to restoring her original condition.

Roberts also required new guns, but the nearest were at Port Said, so she was ordered to Egypt to refit, arriving on 20 October after a fortnight at Malta. Replacement turbine blades for her turbo-generator at last caught up with her, while her troublesome elderly hydraulic pump was again patched up. None of the monitors participated in the landing at Anzio in January 1944; demands for naval gunfire were relatively modest. *Roberts*'s crew thought that she might have been used in operations against German-held Aegean islands, but in fact they were able to spend nearly five relaxing months in Egypt, which included social and sporting activities, plus a bombardment practice south of Suez with 40 full-calibre rounds during February.

9.7 Wartime Service in Home Waters

The Allies recognised that the final defeat of Germany could only be accomplished by an invasion of north-west Europe, to strike directly at the heart of the Reich. Hitler had strongly reinforced the defences of all the coastlines on which landings might be made with his Atlantic Wall, so any assault would be a much more hazardous operation than those in the Mediterranean. In particular, the well-sited coast defence batteries and strongpoints would need concentrated bombardment by large numbers of warships if they were not to impede a landing. The preliminary plan for *Operation Neptune*, drawn up in December 1943, envisaged a fleet of five battleships and monitors, plus some 170 other major British warships. When later the scale of the initial assault was raised from three to five divisions, Ramsay, who had been designated Allied Naval Commander Expeditionary Force (ANCXF), encountered some difficulty in finding a sufficient number of heavy-gun ships and of landing craft. The US Navy was reluctant to release any ships which might be needed for operations in the Pacific, so RN ships had to be withdrawn from other areas, especially LSTs. The assault plans of the South-East Asia Command against Japanese-held Burma (now Myanmar) had therefore to be postponed. *Roberts*'s provisional allocation to the East Indies Fleet was rescinded

at the end of 1943. There was little likelihood that *Abercrombie* would be repaired, worked up and steamed home by the date of the invasion, planned for June 1944. As many battleships as possible were therefore required for bombardment purposes, but the Home Fleet at Scapa could not be denuded of its newer vessels, so four older ships were selected as the major units of the bombarding fleet: *Warspite*, *Rodney*, *Nelson* and *Ramillies*; in addition to the two monitors, *Roberts* and *Erebus*.

The proposed landing areas on the Normandy beaches were known to be strongly defended on their western extremity by the batteries on the Cherbourg peninsula and, to the east, by those around Le Havre and the mouth of the River Seine. With about one hundred guns emplaced either in pits or casemates and others still to be mounted, ranging from 105mm (4.1in) up to 380mm (15in), six big-gun ships were not really sufficient. The guns of the more numerous cruisers, destroyers and smaller support craft earmarked had neither the range nor the punch to take on heavily protected batteries. It was a relief to Ramsay when Admiral Ernest King, Chief of US Naval Operations, relented in April 1944 and allocated three old battleships, *Nevada*, *Texas* and *Arkansas*, together with additional cruisers and destroyers.

The strongest bombarding fleet was assigned to the easternmost of the five landing beaches, codenamed 'Sword', as not only were the coast defences strongest here, but the Germans were likely to defend nearby Caen most stubbornly as it blocked the direct route to Paris. *Roberts*, *Warspite* and *Ramillies* plus six cruisers were allocated to this sector as Bombarding Force 'D' of the Eastern Task Force, each ship being assigned one particular heavy battery as its principal target on D-day. The Mediterranean landings had shown how important it was to have a heavy bombardment to neutralise enemy defences both before and during the actual assault. While it was not expected to knock out batteries by direct hits on the guns themselves, except by a sheer fluke, the massive weight of fire would drive their crews into their shelters, disrupt control of return fire, damage communication links and generally keep the defenders' heads down. Such preliminary bombardment could only be accurately observed from the air, so the assault had to take place in daylight, after sufficient time had been allowed to pound the defences into a demoralised state. H-hour was therefore selected as 07.25 at 'Sword' beach, allowing two hours for bombardment, but ⌄ ⌄ng to the earlier tide it had to be an hour sooner tha⌄ a⌄ the two American beaches, 'Utah' and 'Omaha', so ⌄ ⌄ing only a bare 40min fire before touchdown. As described on p.168, *Erebus* had been allocated to ⌄he force covering 'Utah' beach. *Texas* and *Arkansas* were to be stationed off 'Omaha' beach, but the

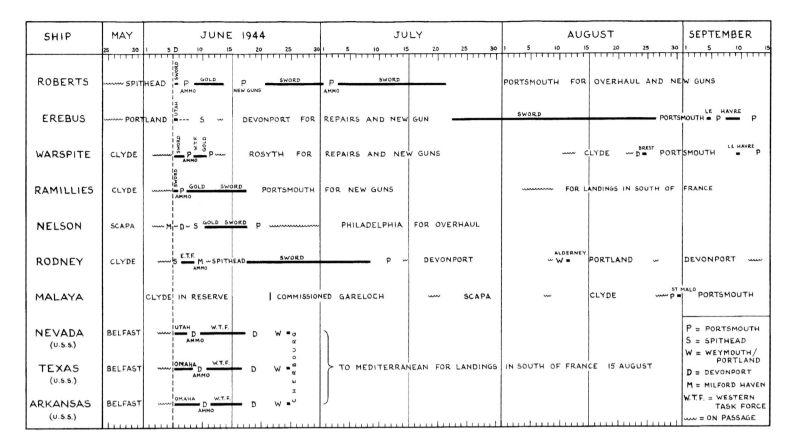

two other British beaches, 'Gold' and 'Juno', would be covered only by cruisers and destroyers. The Allies expected to have air superiority over the beaches, which would not only diminish the risk from enemy air attack but would mean that Allied spotting aircraft would be able to operate more effectively, while the enemy batteries would be denied accurate spotting. The Germans would, however, still have their gun control radar, so these stations would also be targets for air and sea bombardment.

Roberts departed Port Said on 5 March 1944 for the voyage to the UK to work up for *Neptune*. She arrived in the Clyde on 3 April to carry out practice bombardments on the Kintyre range, in company with the other ships of the five bombarding fleets. Owing to her slower speed she had to sail several days in advance of the rest of Force 'D', arriving in Spithead on 28 May to await orders for the invasion fleet to sail for France. On the evening of 5 June she set off as part of convoy S.6, joining up with the other bombarding ships and minesweepers coming from the Clyde. During the night over 1,000 British bombers attacked the German coastal batteries, followed at daybreak by US aircraft.

Roberts anchored in her fir position 11 miles west of Le Havre at 05.20 on 6 Ju nd 3min later opened fire from about 20,0 e on Houlgate battery, which had four ex-French 155mm (6.1in) guns ten miles east of 'Sword' beach. Two of the guns wer n casemates, two in concrete pits, but there were also two additional

pits from which guns had been withdrawn. As the bombarding positions were all within range of the long-range batteries around Le Havre, aircraft laid a smoke-screen along the eastern flank of the fleet. Owing to the effectiveness of this screen, electronic countermeasures and damage to the German radar, there was very little interference from these heavy batteries. The torpedo boats *Jaguar*, *Möwe* and *T.28* did, however, put out from Le Havre, penetrate the smokescreen and fire off about sixteen torpedoes into the mass of Allied shipping at 05.30. Two torpedoes were observed coming straight for *Roberts*, but one passed down one side of her and one down the other. As her 15in guns were busy engaging Houlgate she could not fire at the torpedo boats, which were out of range of her 4in, but she immediately weighed anchor and continued firing whilst under way.

A heavy fire was kept up on the enemy batteries until H-hour. *Roberts* fired twenty-seven rounds during this period, but had some difficulty spotting owing to enemy defensive smokescreens and the failure of some APC shells to explode in marshy ground. Enemy return fire from these batteries was directed mainly at the ships offshore, rather than at the more vulnerable landing craft and beaches. Periodic fire was necessary during the day to silence any batteries that showed signs of interfering with the build-up of troops, vehicles and stores on the beach-head. As the Allied Armies penetrated inland a few miles, the Forward Observers Bombardment (FOB,

This chart shows the deployment of monitors and battleships off the Channel coast of France from just before D-day to the fall of Le Havre. The thick lines show the periods when the individual heavy-gun ships were on station. After concentration of four to six ships on the firing line during the first two weeks of *Operation Neptune*, only one or two ships were required on call for fire support for the remaining three months. As well as providing direct support of Allied forces ashore on the Normandy beachheads, bombardments were made of individual fortified targets such as Brest. *Malaya* was recommissioned following the withdrawal of *Warspite* and *Nelson* in mid-June for overhaul, which included damage repairs after mining.

as the FOO was now called) deployed in positions from which they were able to report targets and call for fire, although there were some difficulties initially in communication and in spotting owing to the general fog of war over the battle area.

During the afternoon of D-day *Roberts* made a particularly successful shoot on Houlgate; after sixteen rounds the spotting fighter reported several direct hits and two large explosions. At 21.30 she had just started to fire on a troop concentration inland from 'Sword' when a crash was heard and a large chunk of metal was seen to fly up in front of the bridge. On ceasing fire it was found that the right 15in had burst its jacket, an accident similar to one on board *Erebus* during that afternoon, 35 miles to the west. The jacket had split into several pieces without the whole gun bursting, so further damage was prevented by strapping it with wire rope. The marine turret crew reckoned that they had chosen the nicknames for their guns the wrong way round: *Lousy Lou* for the left, *Sweet Sue* for the right! *Roberts* had already been ordered to Portsmouth, partly to top up with ammunition, although she had fired only seventy-five rounds so far. *Ramillies* also returned in company with her, leaving *Warspite* as the only big-gun ship off the eastern beaches until the reserve battleship *Rodney* arrived the next day. Between them the three 15in-gun ships had fired about 500 main battery rounds, mostly at the coastal defences.

Roberts's damaged gun was inspected at Portsmouth, but it was decided to defer changing it until the left gun was worn out. She sailed again for Seine Bay in the early hours of 9 June with only one of her two 15in guns operational, arriving back off 'Sword' at a time when the Germans were making heavy counterattacks. On the 10th she moved to 'Gold' beach a few miles to the west to support 7 Armoured Division's thrust towards Villers-Bocage, south-west of Caen, which was getting out of range of the cruisers' guns. For two and a half days from the early hours of the 11th *Roberts* was called upon to fire on enemy concentrations, strongpoints, road junctions, mobile batteries and motor transport in the area around Juvigny, about 11 miles west of Caen.

Shoots during daylight hours were generally spotted by fighters, given such codenames as 'Eyebrow'; those at night were usually unobserved, as they were general shoots on area targets such as troops and vehicles concentrating in woods. Each of the nineteen shoots lasted up to about half an hour, with from four to twenty rounds apiece. Although the monitor was anchored only about a mile offshore, the range was usually near the guns' maximum at about 30,000yd; on one occasion a 3-degree list was applied to get greater elevation.

Churchill paid a visit to the Normandy bridgehead on the 12th and took a trip around the bombarding fleet in the afternoon. Just as his DUKW was passing alongside *Roberts* a call for fire was received, the blast from the three rounds fired at Juvigny church somewhat disconcerting the VIPs. *Roberts* had to exercise some care to husband the 235 rounds of 15in that she was carrying, especially as one gun was approaching its nominal life of 250 rounds of HE. So devastating was the heavy-calibre naval gunfire that the Army had to be discouraged from calling for it on targets which could be tackled as readily by the smaller guns of the other bombarding vessels. *Roberts* returned to Portsmouth on 14 June with thirty-seven rounds remaining, to exchange both her guns and re-ammunition. One gun was replaced by No.102, which is now on display outside the Imperial War Museum in London. Special arrangements had been made to supply ammunition to the bombarding ships quickly, barges being preloaded with the correct outfits for the various types of ship. Most of the 2,800 15in shells stockpiled at Portsmouth and Devonport in the proportion 50:50 HE and APC were the newer 6crh, but some old 4crh were included to be used up by *Roberts* and *Ramillies.*

Roberts was again stationed on the eastern flank on her return to France on the 21st. I Corps held the ground eastwards only to the mouth of the River Orne, ten miles north-east of Caen. Further to the east the enemy held on to the coast very determinedly, using both casemated batteries and mobile field guns to harass Allied shipping off the beaches. Although the field guns were difficult to locate in woods, their fire could usually be temporarily silenced fairly quickly, as they were unprotected. Direct hits on these or emplaced guns were very unlikely; sooner or later the guns would open up again. Heavy anti-aircraft fire was often directed at the spotting aircraft. Although very few were shot down, several were attacked by 'friendly' fighters. Enemy air activity was mostly confined to night bombing and mining raids. Bombardments were usually carried out at anchor, as not only was accuracy improved but there was less danger of steaming over a mine, particularly one of the almost unsweepable pressure mines.

During the first three days following her return to the beach-head *Roberts* spread some eighty rounds between defended buildings east of Caen and the batteries east of the beaches. On 26 June she supported *Operation Epsom*, the British advance across the River Odon south-west of Caen. During the morning she was asked to fire a hundred rounds at two targets near Carpiquet village, west of Caen, but as she could not make proper contact with either her FOB or fighter spotter, the results were largely unobserved. The situation over the next few days was quiet, so she was ordered to sail for Portsmouth on

1 July to replenish ammunition and stores.

By the end of June the Americans in the west had advanced out of range of naval gunfire, so the remaining bombarding vessels were concentrated on the eastern flank; the relatively static 'hinge' around Caen about which the whole Allied advance was intended to pivot. The heavy bombardment fleet could be reduced to an average of one battleship or monitor and four cruisers, while control of fire support switched from the HQ ship *Largs* to shore headquarters at Courseulles. *Roberts* was back again on 3 July, ready to support the forthcoming attack on Caen itself. *Rodney*, *Belfast* and *Emerald* were also present to bombard the German defences, which ringed Caen at a distance of about three miles. Targets allocated to the ships were strongpoints around Carpiquet Airfield, defended villages on the roads leading north from the city, and tank concentrations. The British and Canadian attack started on 8 July, with naval gunfire backing the bombing and artillery barrage. When Canadian 3 Division asked for support when being heavily counterattacked, *Roberts* directed some forty rounds on to the road junction through which the German reinforcements were moving. The target was just outside the range of her guns, but, as it would take too long to flood the bulges to heel the ship, her Gunnery Officer, Lt Cdr H.S. Whittow, obtained the extra elevation by using an initial salvo to get the ship rolling, then timed the firing of each subsequent round to the extremity of the roll. So impressed were the Canadians by the shooting that they sent a party of eighty out in DUKWs to thank the monitor's crew personally. Caen was entered the next day, although the German defence south of the Orne remained stubborn.

Enemy batteries east of the Orne continued to fire on the shipping offshore, but the ships of the bombarding fleet received few hits, *Roberts* suffering no more than splinters through the funnel from a near miss. Although eventually four gun sites at Houlgate, two casemates and two pits, were knocked out, including one by *Roberts* on D-day, replacement guns in this battery continued their harassment, together with mobile batteries in the area. By the time Houlgate was finally overrun, on 23 August, it had taken 218 rounds of 15in and 16in from the battleships and monitors plus 928 6in from the former's secondary armament, in addition to frequent bombing raids.

The final operation in which naval gunfire could still assist active front-line engagements was *Goodwood*, the British and Canadian offensive south-east of Caen on 18 July. This time *Roberts* was supported by *Mauritius* and *Enterprise*. Most of the targets were field artillery, so both FOBs and aircraft spotting could be used. Here again the naval bombardment followed RAF bombing. In concen-

tration, accuracy and continuity of fire, the former complemented the sheer volume of explosive dropped in a short period by the latter. This was *Roberts's* last big shoot off Normandy, as she was relieved by *Erebus*, which arrived on 23 July. *Roberts* returned to Portsmouth for the next ten weeks to change her guns again, give leave and repair the wear and tear of six weeks' almost continual bombardment in which she fired a total of 692 rounds of 15in, only about sixty being APC, fired on D-day.

The lessons from the Mediterranean landings had been well learned. Fire support in *Operation Neptune* fulfilled all that was required with a lesser expenditure of ammunition than expected. German reports indicated that they found naval bombardment an extremely powerful, accurate and inhibiting weapon. Indeed, Field-Marshal von Rundstedt counted it as one of the three principal factors which determined the outcome of *Operation Overlord* (the other two were Allied air superiority and their abundance of supplies). Troop and vehicle movement and concentration during daylight rapidly brought either air attack or naval gunfire or both; the sheer weight demoralised troops whether or not direct hits were obtained.

Between them the four British battleships and two monitors fired 3,371 main battery rounds in 137 shoots. The monitors were on call for seventy ship-days, the battleships forty-five, as shown in the deployment diagram. Of the shoots, 26 per cent were against coastal batteries, 23 per cent against other artillery, 26 per cent against towns, buildings and strongpoints, and 25 per cent against tanks, vehicles, troop concentrations and miscellaneous. In all some 141,000 rounds of 4in calibre and above were expended by the Allied ships against targets at Normandy, including aircraft, the majority being 6in and below. HE projectiles were used most frequently, although they were sometimes in short supply, APC being used mainly against fortifications or buildings. The well trained fighter spotters were especially effective, so they were employed as the principal means of spotting for the big ships (52 per cent of shoots) although they had originally been intended to be used only until the FOBs got established. The FOBs spotted only 14 per cent as they were restricted by the close nature of the Normandy countryside. Ship observation (4 per cent) and Air Observation Post (2 per cent), slow and vulnerable Austers, were used a little, the remaining 28 per cent being unobserved blind shoots, often at night. Timely and accurate shooting was made possible by well-trained personnel, efficient liaison between the Army and Navy via HQs, FOBs and BLOs, and reliable spotting from air and ground, backed up by good materiel such as accurate gridded maps.

Meanwhile, *Abercrombie* had completed repairs at Taranto, arriving at Malta on 15 August 1944. She was exercising off the Delimara Light, south-east of the island, on the 21st when she had the bad luck to strike not one but two mines in 420ft of water. She hit one on her starboard side forward, which blew a hole about 16ft × 4ft, flooding part of the lower deck. The second hit was on the bottom abaft the mainmast, and did considerable damage. Although the hole was only about 10ft × 4ft, both shafts were bent and the starboard A-bracket broken, the lower deck aft flooded and radar and gyro-compasses damaged. The 4½-degree starboard heel was quickly reduced, while the ship dropped anchor to avoid hitting any more mines. The trawlers *Cava* and *Juliet* swept around her, finding four more German moored mines, then tugs towed her into

Grand Harbour. She spent the next eleven months in Malta Dockyard repairing the damage.

After the fall of Le Havre the remaining French Channel ports were either captured by the Canadian Army without the need for naval bombardment or simply surrounded until the war ended. Although Antwerp had been captured as early as 4 September, this valuable port could not be used for supplying the Allied Armies until both banks of the River Scheldt had been cleared of Germans. After a hard struggle the south bank up to the river mouth had been taken by the end of October 1944, but the Germans still held out on the strongly fortified island of Walcheren commanding the river entrance. As only a narrow and easily defended causeway connected the island with the mainland, plans were made for a

A well-known view of *Roberts* bombarding Houlgate battery on 6 June 1944. The left gun has just fired; the right is being reloaded. Extra countermeasures equipment has been fitted: the X-shaped aerial abaft the funnel is for the Type 650 missile jammer, while a 'window' rocket launcher is on top of the turret (not visible here). The cruiser in the background is *Frobisher*. (IWM A23920)

seaborne assault. A bombarding force consisting of *Warspite*, *Roberts* and *Erebus* was organised, in addition to the heavily armed converted landing craft of the Support Squadron, massed artillery on the shore opposite Flushing, and bomber aircraft. *Roberts* and *Erebus* had left Portsmouth for Dover on 5 October with US-built destroyer escort *Retalick* to prepare for the operation, which included bombardment of any batteries around Zeebrugge that might still be holding out.

The ships remained at 48hr notice throughout October, either off Ramsgate or in the Thames Estuary. After the order had been given to land a RM Commando force at Westkapelle on the western corner of the island and another force at Flushing, the bombardment force gathered at the Downs on 31 October. *Warspite*, *Roberts* and *Erebus* set sail at 23.00 at 8kts, escorted by the destroyers *Garth* and *Cottesmore*, in company with minesweepers and MLs, with the tug *Growler* in attendance in case the monitors should need help in the tricky waters. It was feared that the Germans might have spotted the ships off the Belgian coast after a de Havilland Mosquito illuminated them with flares during the night, but they sailed safely past the Knocke battery, which still remained in enemy hands.

The bombardment fleet arrived in position 11 miles west of Westkapelle at dawn on 1 November, unable to get closer owing to the minefields and sandbanks (see map on p.46). Before fire was opened, news was received that the spotting aircraft were grounded by fog at Manston Airfield; the RAF's 26 and 63 Sqns had thirty-seven Spitfires and two Hurricanes. When *Warspite* and *Roberts* opened up at 08.15, fire had, therefore, to be spotted using direct observation from the ships. *Warspite* took on the

heavy Domburg battery north-east of Westkapelle with its four 220mm (8.7in) ex-French guns. *Roberts's* first target was a radar station, the destruction of which would handicap the German gunnery. After five rounds she switched to the W.15 coastal battery at Westkapelle, which had six ex-British 3.7in and 3in guns. This battery had been allocated to *Erebus* but she was unable to open fire until 09.26, as her turret-training machinery had broken down. *Roberts* and *Erebus* then kept up a steady fire until just before the Commandos touched down at 09.45. Fire was switched to W.13 battery at Zoutelande, south-east of Westkapelle, with its six guns, four casemated naval 152mm (6in) and two 75mm (2.95in). Accurate direct observation at ranges of about 24,000yd proved very difficult for such low-lying targets, often shrouded in smoke from shell-bursts or smokescreens. Unfortunately *Roberts's* FOB and his radio operator had been killed by a mortar bomb early in the operation, so firing was stopped for three hours.

The fog over Manston lifted during the morning, so fighter spotting was available from 13.40. With the FOBs well in position, *Warspite*, *Roberts* and *Erebus* were able to pour a heavy fire on to the remaining batteries and strongpoints until darkness fell at about 17.30. Batteries W.15 and W.13 had been captured after fierce fighting, followed by Domburg at dusk. Although the bombarding ships had not been directly responsible for putting them permanently out of action, they and the fighter-bombers had contributed largely to reducing their effectiveness. The Germans had not fired on the bombarding fleet at all, reserving their ammunition for the landing craft, so there was no need for the MLs to lay their protective smokescreens. The fleet retired to lie off the Belgian Coast for the night to avoid possible E-boat attack, while *Warspite* returned to England, her guns worn out and the reporters on board anxious to file their copy.

Roberts and *Erebus* were back in position at 08.20 on the 2nd, the latter opening fire on a strongpoint almost immediately. *Roberts* turned her attention to an AA battery that had been firing at the spotting aircraft. Both monitors then switched to the troublesome W.11 battery with its four casemated naval 152mm and two 75mm guns, sited at Duinrand, between Westkapelle and Flushing. Sometimes using FOBs and sometimes fighter spotters, fire was kept up for the rest of the day on W.11. Despite continuous troubles with her working chamber frequently flooded with water to a depth of over a foot, *Erebus* put in some very good shooting at this battery. She fired ninety-nine rounds at it over four different periods of the day, twenty-seven being reported hits and a further thirty-three within 100yd. When the battery was finally captured the next day, it was found that there had been

direct hits on the casemates themselves. *Erebus* generally found the target with about the fifth round, thereafter firing for effect about twenty rounds at a rate of one a minute. Over the two days *Erebus* fired a total of 179 rounds, *Roberts* 104 and *Warspite* 353.

As there was no further need of bombardment, *Roberts* and *Erebus* departed the next morning, the latter direct to Portsmouth, the former to Sheerness for ammunition before returning to Spithead. The two monitors then took it in turns to remain on call for any further bombardments that might be required as the Allied Armies advanced into Germany, but although two operations were planned for *Roberts* in the early months of 1945, neither came off. The last operation in Europe for which she and *Erebus* were put at four hours' notice was a possible bombardment of Heligoland if its batteries should show signs of firing on the Allied minesweepers opening up the River Elbe to Hamburg following the final German collapse in early May. Much to the relief of the crews of both monitors there was no call for them to sail, so they could celebrate VE-day comfortably in harbour at Portsmouth. On 12 May ANCXF, now Vice-Admiral H.M. Burrough following Ramsay's death in January, signalled: 'On your release from "Overlord" I wish to congratulate you on the results of your operations since D-day. The recent lack of targets is a measure of your former successes.'

With the war in Europe over, the Allies turned to the final defeat of Japan, already reeling from the American Pacific island offensives. The war in the Indian Ocean was being progressed much less spectacularly owing to lack of resources, Burma being reoccupied only in May 1945. Plans to recapture Malaya included assaults on Port Dickson (*Operation Zipper*) and Singapore (*Operation Mailfist*). In view of the strong defences at Singapore, *Mailfist* required one or two monitors for bombardment purposes, so both *Roberts* and *Abercrombie* were allocated to the East Indies Fleet, under the command of Vice Admiral A.J. Power, who had been *Raglan's* gunnery officer in WW1. *Roberts* was despatched to the Mersey on 29 May for a quick overhaul by Cammell Laird, before sailing for the Indian Ocean on 27 July under command of Capt C.B. Tidd. *Abercrombie* had already left Malta on 17 July, her repairs completed. She was ordered to reach Ceylon by 1 September to allow time for her crew to become acclimatised before *Mailfist*, which was to follow about fifty days after *Zipper*, scheduled for 9 September. On the day of the Japanese surrender following the dropping of the two atomic bombs, 14 August, *Roberts* was off Port Said in company with *Loch Scavaig*, while *Abercrombie* was approaching Aden. Both vessels continued their eastwards passage until the formal Japanese surrender on 2 September. The decision to order them to return home and reduce to reserve was taken on the 11th, by which time *Roberts* had reached Kilindini and *Abercrombie* was approaching the Seychelles. *Abercrombie* reached Sheerness on 6 November 1945, and *Roberts* Plymouth on 22 November. The latter had had a busy and varied four years' operations, the other barely six months' active service owing to her misfortune with mines.

9.8 Performance

Although there was no time for lengthy trials on completion, *Roberts* took the opportunity at Suez to make some turning and stopping trials. These confirmed the model experiments, showing that she had a very small turning circle about 400yd in diameter with 35 degrees of rudder. This was accompanied, however, by a great loss of speed at full helm, so that after turning through 180 degrees in two minutes she had slowed down from 12 to 2kts. Stopping trials showed that, by going half astern at 160rpm, she could stop in 975yd, taking five minutes but ending up slewed 60 degrees to port. The small tactical diameter resulted from the use of twin rudders and the large cut-up (the rise aft of the keel from the baseline up to the stern) with corresponding lack of deadwood effect. As a consequence, course stability was not good and the response to the helm once turning had started was poor. Indeed, *Roberts* was quite capable of emulating *Marshal Ney*'s and the other WW1 monitors' trick, whereby a moderate alteration of course could not always be checked before the ship had swung in a complete 360-degree circle.

When these reports reached DNC's Department the comment was made that, as *Erebus* did not turn fast enough, special attention had been paid to this feature in *Roberts* but it appeared to have been overdone. Approval was given to fit a deadwood in the form of a vertical fin on the centreline below the cut-up, but in neither ship was this modification ever carried out. It was also found that in a strong beam wind the mass of superstructure aft of midships produced a large turning moment, which required a rudder angle of up to 25 degrees to be carried to maintain course, also resulting in considerable leeway. Experience, however, showed that the monitors' peculiar shiphandling qualities were actually quite predictable, so that they could perform quite versatile manoeuvres in capable hands.

Although the two WW2 monitors had a better hull form and higher propulsive efficiency than any of their WW1 predecessors, they still exhibited the same loss of speed at sea. The bluff form, with its large underwater area on which fouling could take place, led to losses of speed of about two knots when six months out of drydock; a serious matter when 12kts was the best cruising speed. A further 1¾kts was lost when the bow defence gear was streamed, which made station-keeping on other ships difficult. Bad weather also produced a great loss of speed; three or four knots was the best speed that could be made heading into Force 7 winds. Such losses of speed had a marked effect on the endurance. The specified endurance

Roberts leaves Malta on 8 November 1945 to pay off after returning from her intended deployment against the Japanese in Malaya. Her eight single Bofors are visible.
(A. & J. PAVIA)

of 3,600 miles at 10kts could be achieved with a clean hull, but it dropped to about 2,700 miles six months out of dock. Appreciable quantities of fuel were required to keep auxiliaries such as turbo-generators and evaporators running, so that even at the lowest speeds some 30 tons of oil a day were needed. At maximum speed, consumption rose to 66 tons per day; in harbour about 8 to 10 tons were required. The corresponding specific fuel consumption was about 1.28lb per shp per hour, which was about 50 per cent higher than that of more powerful warships using superheated steam. At higher powers there was some shaft vibration, which was serious enough to affect the operation of the Type 281 air warning radar, so rpm were generally restricted to about 225 instead of the maximum 250.

In *Roberts*'s four years of active service she steamed a total of 62,287 nautical miles, made up as shown, burning some 15,000 tons of oil fuel:

Year	Miles	Operations
1941	6,022	Two months' service
1942	25,333	Twice round the south of Africa
1943	9,967	Under repair; in Mediterranean
1944	6,579	Operations in north-west Europe
1945	14,386	Out to Indian Ocean and back.

9.9 Modifications

Because of her well-equipped start in life and her bad luck with mines, such that she spent less than twelve months in active service, *Abercrombie* experienced few of the normally extensive range of wartime modifications. During her repairs at Malta some changes were made in the internal layout, including the conversion of empty watertight compartments to carry about 180 tons of extra oil fuel. The most important modification was the installation of a full Action Information Organisation, with Operations Room, Aircraft Direction Room, Target Indicating Room and Y Office. The associated air-conditioning plant was fitted in place of one of the cabins in the shelter deck; similar plant would have been even more welcome on the mess-decks, which were very hot under the bare steel decks. Externally there was very little change, although surface warning radar was changed from Type 272M to combined surface/air warning Type 293 on the mainmasthead. The two-aerial Type 281 air warning was changed to Type 79B, with its single aerial on the foremasthead.

Roberts, however, underwent quite a number of modifications. Early experience had shown that smoke from the short funnel was troublesome on the bridge; the same problem as the WW1 coal-burners. At her first overhaul at Cammell Laird's early in 1943 following

damage off North Africa, the funnel was raised 12ft. Haynes's comments from *Terror* about lack of storage space for food and water were also borne out in service. The boilers required 12 tons of fresh water per day for make-up feed, while the ship's company used another 30 tons. Since the single evaporator could supply a theoretical maximum of 60 tons per day and there was stowage for only 100 tons, the margin for breakdown and deterioration was small. Two replacement evaporators were fitted, each with an output of 40 tons per day, while stowage capacity was increased to nearly 300 tons.

The close-range armament was increased, twin Mk V power-operated Oerlikons replacing all but the forecastle singles, making a total of fourteen 20mm (six twin, two single), while the 4in and pom-poms were converted to RPC. The radar was also augmented: Type 279 replaced the Type 281, improved versions of the Types 285 and 282 AA gunnery sets were fitted (although still not accurate enough in elevation to permit full blind-fire), and surface-warning Type 272P was added below the spotting top. The after 282 controlling the octuple pom-pom was removed. Improvements were also made to the W/T equipment, the electronic countermeasures, and the anti-ship and night-fighting capabilities, including better searchlight control. A new design of disruptive camouflage was borne by the ship when she returned to service in May 1943, with three shades of grey plus white, as illustrated on p.195.[5]

When the monitors were earmarked for the Indian Ocean in 1944-45, improvements to the accommodation were planned. It proved impossible to undertake all that was needed during *Roberts*'s two short subsequent refits, although ventilation to the 15in turret was improved for hot climates. The main outward change following her 1945 Liverpool refit was the addition of eight single Army-style hand-operated 40mm Mk III Bofors and the substitution of Type 268 for the Type 272 radar. Two of the twin Oerlikons were replaced by Bofors, as well as the two forecastle singles, while the other four were straight additions; two in place of the 44in searchlights (now completely superseded by radar and star-shell), one on top of the turret in place of the ECM rocket launcher fitted for *Operation Neptune*, and one abaft the mainmast. The Bofors had proved itself the best close-range weapon of the war, being used by both sides, with a range, rate of fire and punch that could down the larger, faster aircraft being encountered. *Roberts*'s total AA armament then comprised:

8 × 4in, 16 × 2pdr, 8 × 40mm, 8 × 20mm

The modifications that were made during the war increased her deep displacement to about 9,500 tons and *Abercrombie*'s to about 9,900 tons, mostly resulting from the additional fuel and water carried.

9.10 Post-War Careers

After the surrender of Japan *Abercrombie* arrived back at Sheerness on 6 November 1945 to be placed into reserve. Initially used as an accommodation ship, she replaced *Erebus* as Turret Drill Ship at Chatham in July 1946, lying at moorings in the Medway. Later her role was that of living ship for the Nore Reserve Fleet. In the spring of 1953 she was towed to Portsmouth and laid up in Fareham Creek until November 1954, when she was handed over to BISCO for scrapping. Allocated to Ward's Barrow yard, she arrived on Christmas Eve. Demolition work started almost immediately, but it was three weeks before there arrived from the Admiralty the list showing the items to be salvaged for return to naval stores. In addition to the usual things such as electronic equipment and spare parts, the eight 4in guns were included but, by the time Ward was notified, these had been mutilated beyond further use, in accordance with standing instructions for gunnery equipment. In preparing the 1955-56 Naval Appropriation Account, the Auditor-General drew attention to the resulting £25,000 loss and asked for a tightening-up of Admiralty procedures concerning equipment to be returned from ships to be scrapped. Breaking her up yielded about £100,000 after deduction of breaking and other costs, from 7,200 tons of recovered material, which constituted the effective sale

price under the BISCO system (see Chapter 4, note 4, p.248). It corresponded to about 6.5 per cent of the second *Abercrombie*'s original cost. The tonnage recovered was less than her 8,137 tons light displacement, owing to the removal of some equipment, steel corrosion wastage, the loss of steel from the gas-cutting process, unsaleable material such as insulation and tiling, and the inclusion of some variable items such as operating fluids in the Admiralty definition of light displacement.[6]

Roberts survived for considerably longer. She had arrived at Devonport on 22 November 1945, where she remained for the next two decades. Initially she was used as a Turret Drill Ship with a complement of about 120, and later as an accommodation ship for the Reserve Fleet base *Orion*, with a crew of about 40. Various downgradings of reserve readiness occurred, so that by 1953, in Class III Reserve, she would not have been available to the Fleet until six months after mobilisation. Although she was removed from the official 'Strength of the Fleet' in 1955, she continued to be useful at the Dockyard. She remained in the role of part living-ship, part fender-ship, berthed on the north outer wall of No. 5 Basin until 1963, when she was moved to lie at buoys in the stream. Her distinctive profile with the prominent spotting top and the raised turret made her a familiar sight to a generation of sailors at Devonport. To the older ones she was a

Abercrombie at Portsmouth in 1947 on her final commission, still very much in her as-built condition. (WRIGHT & LOGAN)

Laid up first in the Medway then at
Portsmouth, *Abercrombie* was
handed over to BISCO for scrapping
at Barrow. Here she leaves
Portsmouth under tow on 17
December 1954. Her four twin 4in
mountings were still in good
condition under their Kooncoting,
but the Admiralty letter to Ward's
asking for them to be returned to
store did not arrive until after they
had been mutilated.
(AUTHOR'S COLLECTION)

Roberts arriving at Ward's
Inverkeithing yard on 3 August 1965,
with Ministry of Defence tugs
assisting berthing.
(T.W. WARD)

Roberts is manoeuvred alongside cruiser *Mauritius* at Inverkeithing on 3 August 1965, having been purchased by Ward's for £152,600. (T.W. Ward)

reminder of the big-gun ships in which most had once served; to the younger ones, who would never see a British battleship, she gave a fleeting impression of the naval might which once had dominated the seas.

In 1965 invitations to tender for her purchase for scrap were sent out to British shipbreakers. Ward's bid of £152,600 was successful, so *Roberts* left Devonport on 19 July, under pilotage command of Cdr P.J. Cardale, who had been her navigating officer in 1943-44. The tow to Inverkeithing was made by the Royal Fleet Auxiliary tugs *Typhoon* and *Samsonia*, but she did not finally berth until 3 August, as Ward's yard was closed for the summer holiday. Ward recorded her outturn as:

Item	Long tons	Value £	£/ton
Armour quality scrap	2,228	67,175	30.1
Other ferrous scrap	4,180	65,489	15.66
Non-ferrous scrap	431	127,713	296
Reusable equipment and timber	92	3,409	37.1
Total	6,931	263,786	30.05
Demolition cost		38,670	5.58
Purchase price		152,600	22.0
Gross profit before overheads		72,516	

Roberts thus became the eleventh large monitor to be broken up by Ward out of a total of seventeen which survived the two World Wars, the last of the big-gun types whose existence had spanned exactly half a century.

Roberts and *Abercrombie* – TECHNICAL DATA

Displacement (as completed): 7,973 (*Roberts*)/ 8,536 (*Abercrombie*) tons standard, 9,150/ 9,717 tons deep on 13ft 6¼in/14ft 4¾in draft. 7,666/8,137 tons Admiralty light on 11ft 4½in/12ft 0¼in.

Dimensions: Length 373ft 4in oa, 354ft 0in bp, breadth 89ft 9in oa, 54ft 0in main hull, depth to upper deck 27ft 3in.

Weight distribution (*Roberts* as designed/as completed) Armament 970/1,012 tons, ammunition 480/504, armour and protective plating 2,130/2,200, hull 3,270/3,445, equipment 380/537, machinery 275/275. Standard displacement 7,505/7,973 tons. Water protection 580/586, reserve feed water 40/42, oil fuel 550/549. Deep displacement 8,675/9,150 tons.

Complement (*Roberts/Abercrombie*): 19/20 officers, 423/440 men.

Armament (as completed); 2 x 15in (twin) (30-60 APC + 80-50 HE + 8 practice rpg), 8 x 4in (twin) (80 SAP + 320 HETF + 12 star + 83 practice rpg), 16 x 2pdr (2 quad, 1 octuple) (1,800 HE + 114 practice rpg), 8 (*Roberts* singles)/20 (*Abercrombie* 4 singles, 8 twins) 20mm (2,400 HE + 300 practice rpg).

Protection: Main deck 4in and 6in NC over 15in magazine, 3in (*Roberts*)/4in (*Abercrombie*) machinery and aft, 2in and 3in NC forward; sloping external belt 5in NC abreast 15in magazine, 4in elsewhere; torpedo protective bulkhead 1½in D (¾in at ends); steering gear 3in NC; barbette 8in C; gunhouse 13in C front, 11in C sides and rear, 5in (*R*)/6in (*A*) NC roof, 3in HT floor; conning tower 3in NC sides, 2in front, rear and roof, 1½in floor; splinter protection l½in NC sides and floor 15in magazine, ¾in to 1in D superstructure positions.

Machinery: Twin-screw Parsons single-reduction-geared steam turbines by John Brown No. 573 (*Roberts*), Parsons Marine Steam Turbine Co, Wallsend No. 378 (*Abercrombie*). 4,800shp at 250rpm. Two Admiralty three-drum boilers, 250lb/in². Fuel oil 491 tons, diesel oil 58 tons.

Endurance: 2,680 miles at 12kts on 2.2 tons oil per hour.

Speed: 12¼kts designed and service. Trials: *Roberts* 13.5, *Abercrombie* 12.0 kts.

Construction: *Roberts* John Brown (No. 573, J.1573) laid down 30.4.40/launched 1.2.41/completed 27.10.41. *Abercrombie* Vickers-Armstrongs, Tyne (No. 42, J.4359) 26.5.41/31.3.42/5.5.43.

Scrapped: *Roberts* sold T.W. Ward 9.7.65, arrived Inverkeithing 3.8.65; *Abercrombie* handed over to BISCO 22.11.54, allocated T.W. Ward, arrived Barrow 24.12.54.

ABOVE This view from the foremasthead shows *Roberts* awaiting the shipbreaker's men on 4 August 1965. In the foreground is the roof of the spotting top. The mounting ring for a single Bofors can be seen on the turret, but the circular tubs for the two fitted on the forecastle have been removed. (Author)

ABOVE LEFT Another view from *Roberts*'s foremasthead, showing much of the preserving Kooncoting stripped. De-equipping has already taken place: the 20mm guns have been removed from the twin mountings by the funnel, the compass from the after conning position, the aerial arrays from the rangefinder/directors and the boats from the davits. (Author)

ABOVE RIGHT *Roberts* awaits the cutting torches at Inverkeithing on 4 August 1965. (Author)

LEFT Ward's men prepare to cut off *Roberts*'s 15in gun barrels. Twin Oerlikon mount in foreground. (T.W. Ward)

ABOVE FAR LEFT Ward's 50-ton crane lifts the outer section of *Roberts*'s left 15in gun barrel, with the starboard one already lying on the deck.
(T.W. WARD)

ABOVE LEFT Looking forward from *Roberts*'s mainmast, alongside cruiser *Mauritius*.
(AUTHOR)

ABOVE The last of the RN's 15in mountings in pieces at the shipbreaker's. In the foreground, a section of 11in-thick gunhouse armour, in the background a gun cradle with the recoil cylinder at left.
(T.W. WARD)

LEFT *Roberts*'s 27ft-diameter training rack and section of ring bulkhead, being prepared for shipment to Joddrell Bank radio telescope.
(T.W. WARD)

FAR LEFT *Roberts*'s ammunition hoist trunk lifted complete in October 1965. Compare with *Abercrombie*'s hoist when new on p.219.
(T.W. WARD)

MAIN PHOTOGRAPH
By late August 1965 demolition of *Roberts* at Inverkeithing is well advanced, with the masts and bridge stripped.
(AUTHOR'S COLLECTION)

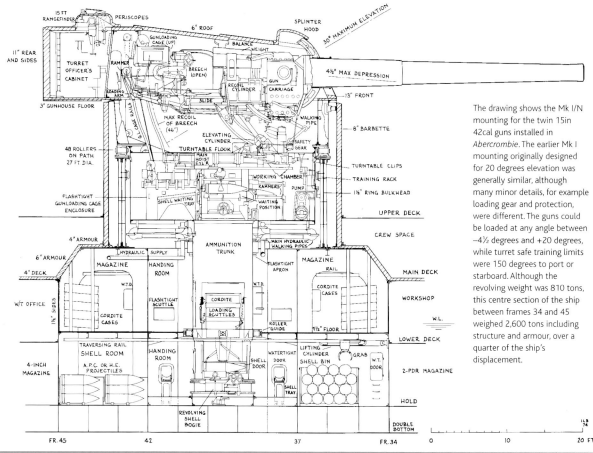

The drawing shows the Mk I/N mounting for the twin 15in 42cal guns installed in *Abercrombie*. The earlier Mk I mounting originally designed for 20 degrees elevation was generally similar, although many minor details, for example loading gear and protection, were different. The guns could be loaded at any angle between −4½ degrees and +20 degrees, while turret safe training limits were 150 degrees to port or starboard. Although the revolving weight was 810 tons, this centre section of the ship between frames 34 and 45 weighed 2,600 tons including structure and armour, over a quarter of the ship's displacement.

CHAPTER 10

Gunnery in the Monitors

10.1 The 15in Mark I Gun

When Churchill authorised the development of a 15in gun in 1912, he provided the RN with its most successful piece of heavy ordnance, which was to remain afloat for half a century. To ensure a margin of superiority over any German developments in capital ship construction, a weapon larger than the existing 13.5in was needed for the British battleships of the 1912 Programme. Although the 13.5in had only just entered service it was based on the 12in, which had developed through eleven marks. Thus when the Elswick Ordnance Company received the contract to design and build the first 15in mounting, it simply scaled up the 13.5in, while Woolwich Arsenal did likewise with the gun itself. Amidst great secrecy (the gun being called the '14in Experimental'), development was rapidly pushed ahead. The first experimental gun, Number E596 ordered on 31 January 1912, was ready for proving trials the following spring. The mounting was considerably more complex to manufacture, but the first was made ready for trial at Silloth on the Solway Firth in May 1914.

The design of the 42cal Mark I gun adopted the well-tried principles of wire-wound ordnance, used for 20 years by the RN. At this period British steel forgings could not yet be guaranteed in sufficiently large masses to make an all-steel gun built of only two or three tubes strong enough. The construction comprised the following components from the bore outwards:

i. Replaceable full-length inner A-tube in nickel steel (liner)

ii. Full-length 54ft A-tube in nickel steel

iii. 185 miles of circumferentially wound wire of 0.25 × 0.06in rectangular cross-section in high-strength steel with an ultimate tensile strength of 100 tons/sq in, tapering from seventy-nine layers at the breech to twenty at the muzzle

iv. Two-thirds-length B-tube extending 35ft from the muzzle, in nickel steel

v. Half-length jacket extending 29ft from the breech, in carbon steel

vi. Shrunk collar at breech in nickel steel

vii. Breech ring in carbon steel

viii. Renewable screwed breech bush, in nickel steel.

To complete the gun, a Welin breech mechanism with

interrupted screw thread was added, bringing the weight up to 100 tons exactly. The gun was similar in construction to that of the 18in illustrated on p.226; other characteristics are given in the Technical Data on p.222.

The twin mounting followed the now well-established British design practice using hydraulic power. The drawings on p.216 and 218 show the general arrangement as fitted in *Abercrombie* in 1943 which, although including many minor improvements, was basically similar to all the earlier 15in mountings fitted in capital ships and monitors. Each gun was mounted in a cradle, which could move in recoil on a forged steel slide. The slide was pivoted to permit elevation between trunnions which were fixed to the 3in-thick gunhouse floor, the latter also supporting the shield armour keyed to its edge. The floor also formed the top of the main rotating turntable structure, which had a diameter about two feet less than the 30ft 6in diameter of the barbette armour. Forty-eight roller bearings beneath the edge of the turntable supported the whole turret weight, which was then transferred to the hull structure by a ring bulkhead just inside the barbette armour.

Beneath the turntable was the working chamber, about 25ft in diameter. The main hoist from the magazine and shell-room below fed into the centre of this chamber via flashtight doors. After transfer to the gun loading cage, the projectile and charge were then lifted up to the breech of the gun for loading and ramming, the gun having already been brought to the normal loading angle of 5 degrees (fixed in the monitors). The chamber also contained the hoisting machinery as well as spare projectiles. The main hoist trunk was of about 8ft diameter and was made as long as required to reach the shell-room floor; only 23ft in a monitor but up to 43ft in a battleship. Each gun had two cages, one for projectile, one for cordite, which were loaded separately at shell-room and magazine handing room levels and then brought together and hoisted as one. In the shell-room the projectiles were stowed horizontally in bins each holding about twenty, from which they were lifted and traversed by hydraulically powered grabs suspended from overhead rails. In the magazine, two quarter-charges of cordite MD45[1] were stowed in each airtight cylindrical case, which were arranged nearly horizontally in layers. Ammunition was embarked by derricks on the upper deck abreast the bridge and lowered vertically to the magazine by winch and davit through hatches on the centreline.

Typical manning of a 15in installation comprised:

Gunhouse: turret officer, captain of turret, two gunlayers, trainer, four crew for each gun, four sightsetter and communication numbers	17
Working chamber	6
Magazine	12
Handing room	7
Shell-room	22
Total mounting crew	64
Control top: gunnery officer, BLO, spotting and communication numbers	8
Director: Layer, trainer, sightsetter, phone man	4
Transmitting station: officer, twelve at fire control table, four communication numbers	17
Ordnance artificers	2
Total 15in crew	95

The breakdown of the total revolving weight of the twin turret was approximately:

	Tons
Two guns	200
Two slides and cradles	80
Turntable and gunhouse floor	160
Working chamber	50
Hoist trunk	20
Gunhouse and shield plates	180
Roof plates	70
Total	**760**

A fine view of *Abercrombie*'s twin 15in turret nearing completion in No.24 Shop at Vickers-Armstrongs' Elswick Works in December 1942. The turret had been originally intended as a replacement for *Furious* should her single 18in prove unsatisfactory, but it had not been needed, so lay for 24 years in Chatham Dockyard. The ammunition trunk projected into a pit below the turret. The two 12-ton balance weights needed on the Mk I/N mounting to permit elevation to 30 degrees can be seen on top of each gun. In the foreground can be seen one of the platforms for the Oerlikons which were sited above the rangefinder hood, and what looks like a 13.5in gun, probably one of those which were to be linered down to form a hyper-velocity 8in.

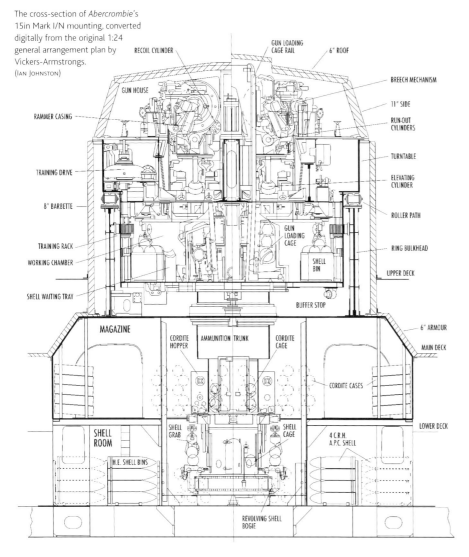

The cross-section of *Abercrombie*'s 15in Mark I/N mounting, converted digitally from the original 1:24 general arrangement plan by Vickers-Armstrongs.
(Ian Johnston)

The five battleships of the 1912 Programme, the *Queen Elizabeth* class, were designed to carry four 15in Mark I twin mountings, as were the five vessels of the *Royal Sovereign* class. The work was divided among the three main ordnance contractors: five ships by Elswick, four by Vickers and one by Coventry Ordnance Works. The contracts were of substantial value, as the armament of a battleship comprised about 25 per cent of its cost. Typical figures for the cost of one twin 15in mounting at this time were:

	£
Two slides and mountings	19,000
Turntable	13,500
Hoists	11,000
Gunhouse armour	36,500
Turning gear and shell-room machinery	11,500
Hydraulic machinery	9,000
Miscellaneous and spares	8,500
Delivery and erection	7,000
Total	**116,000**

The guns were ordered separately under a different Vote in the annual Estimates from five manufacturers. The cost of one 15in was made up approximately as follows:

	£
Steel forgings	6,900
Gun manufacture	7,500
Breech mechanism	1,600
Total	**16,000**

Mountings for only two of the four ships of the 1914 Programme had been ordered before war broke out: *Repulse*'s four from Elswick and *Renown*'s four from COW. Thus when these two ships were redesigned as six-gun battlecruisers in December 1914, it appeared that there would be two spare 15in mountings available to arm monitors. But the ships had only been ordered in May 1914, and trials of the gun mountings were not due until April 1916, whereas the monitors were to be completed in six months. The only way of obtaining the necessary turrets quickly was to take them from one of the battleships of the 1912 or 1913 Programmes. The *Queen Elizabeth* class were by now well advanced; indeed the name ship was just about to start her gunnery trials. As these 24kt ships were the most powerful battleships then under construction, it would have been a grave error to have delayed completion of one of them merely to arm two strategically much less important vessels. But the 1913 *Royal Sovereign*s were quite a different proposition. They were of an inferior design and only capable of 21kts. Although originally due to complete at the end of 1915, they had already been delayed by more urgently needed new construction. To take the turrets from one of these ships and order replacements would not have such serious repercussions on the strength of the Grand Fleet *vis-a-vis* the High Seas Fleet. The first set of mountings due to complete were the four that Vickers was building for *Ramillies*, so the two most advanced mountings, 'Y' and 'X', were taken over and transferred to Elswick for modification and erection in the two *Marshal*s building at Palmer's. Elswick used some parts from *Malaya*'s B mounting to speed the work, slightly delaying that battleship. Replacements were ordered for *Ramillies* although they would not be ready until late in 1916. As *Ramillies* would not be any further delayed by using her two remaining turrets, Fisher arranged to use them in two other battlecruiser types, each carrying four 15in and capable of 32kts. By using these two turrets and the fourth turrets from *Renown* and *Repulse*, he could get two powerfully armed ships to sea during 1916. As a result, the large light cruisers *Courageous* and *Glorious* were ordered in January 1915 and completed at the end of 1916.

Apart from having to cut the trunk of 'X' turret down to the same minimum length as 'Y' turret, the 15in mounted in the *Marshal*s were identical to the battleship mountings. At the designed elevation of 20 degrees the extreme range was 23,400yd, but experience off the Belgian Coast soon showed that this was insufficient. The subsequent conversion of the monitor mountings to 30 degrees elevation necessitated lifting the trunnions 25½in, so providing extra space for the breech end to recoil into the turntable when maximum elevation was being used. A price had to be paid for this increase: the gun could no longer be used at angles of depression. The firing angles were thus +2 degrees to +30 degrees, compared with −5 degrees to +20 degrees originally. Other changes included the fitting of a more-powerful elevating mechanism, the cutting of larger gun ports in the front armour covered by ½in-thick bonnets, and the use of fixed-angle loading at 5 degrees elevation, whereas all-angle loading was possible on the battleship mountings. This modified mounting was fitted in *Erebus*, *Terror* and *Marshal Soult*, and thus also in *Roberts* (1941) when *Soult*'s turret was transferred. *Erebus* had the slightly different shell-room loading arrangement as fitted in the battle-cruisers, as a result of her being fitted with the Elswick-

built Mark I* mounting intended as a possible replacement for *Furious*'s 18in 'Y' mounting. The Mark I* differed from the Mark I chiefly in the means by which the projectiles were transferred from the shell room to the hoist trunk. *Abercrombie*'s mounting was the second spare completed for *Furious* in 1917, converted into the Mark I/N version as fitted in the five 15in capital ships built or reconstructed from 1936 onwards. The differences between the old and the modernised mountings are best described by summarising the main points of the Admiralty order of 18 April 1941 to Vickers-Armstrongs for the reconditioning of the turret originally planned for *Furious*, then lying at Chatham Dockyard:

i. Transfer to Elswick for complete overhaul and repair, plus supply of missing parts
ii. Elevation to be increased to 30 degrees
iii. Improvement in flashtightness
iv. Modification to use both 4crh and 6crh projectiles
v. Shortening of trunk by about 7ft 6in to fit into monitor hull
vi. General modernisation of hydraulic, electrical, compressed-air and ventilation systems
vii. Improvement of ammunition supply and stowage arrangements
viii. Install mounting and hydraulic machinery in new hull.

ABOVE

Abercrombie's turntable with roller path and working chamber, a 16ft-high, 204-ton unit, leaves Elswick on 29 January 1943, loaded on to a punt for transport to Naval Yard. (VICKERS-ARMSTRONGS)

LEFT

Abercrombie's ammunition trunk is loaded at Elswick on 28 January 1943 on to the 53ft wherry *Elswick No. 2*, built for Vickers-Armstrongs in 1939 and now preserved at the Regional Museum Store at Beamish. The 22ft-long trunk weighed 16 tons, but many smaller fittings have yet to be added. The shell door is just above the toothed rack at the bottom, with the twin cordite hopper doors halfway up. (VICKERS-ARMSTRONGS)

The 30-degree elevation on the Mk I/N was achieved by moving the trunnions back 7¼in to 8ft 2¾in forward of the turret axis and raising their axis from 30½in to 39¼in above the gunhouse floor. Moving the trunnions shifted them away from the CG of the gun, so a 12-ton balance weight had to be fitted to reduce the force required to elevate the gun. Pneumatic run-out gear was fitted in place of the original hydraulic recuperator, so imposing less of a strain on the hydraulic machinery. The gun could be loaded at any elevation between 20 degrees and the maximum depression of 4½ degrees, permitting a slightly faster rate of fire than the previous monitors with their fixed-angle loading. The various changes, including the roof plates increased to 6in, increased the revolving weight to 810 tons, while the total installation weighed about 900 tons including all the associated equipment mounted on the hull proper, such as the 500hp hydraulic machinery.

The additional elevation to 30 degrees produced a useful 25 per cent increase in range, but it was still not enough to permit the WW1 monitors to keep out of range of the heavy German batteries on the Belgian Coast. A successful design of 8crh projectile weighing 1,965lb with an added ballistic cap was developed during 1918, giving an extra 3,000yd range compared with the standard 4crh. High-explosive projectiles were used the most frequently, as they had the largest bursting charge, 224lb lyddite (picric acid) or 11¾ per cent of total weight. They were made of forged steel so that their thin walls, necessitated by the large volume of the bursting charge, would withstand the shock of firing. Shrapnel were also used against targets such as troop concentrations; in form they were similar to HE except that they were filled with 13,700 1¾oz lead-alloy balls. Common pointed-capped projectiles were used against well protected targets such as coastal batteries, owing to their better penetration qualities. They were made of cast steel with a special cap to assist penetration by easing the shock of impact so allowing the point of the shell body to pierce the hard face of armour without shattering. They had a bursting charge of 129lb black powder. Armour-piercing capped were made of forged steel with a hardened head and cap to improve penetration against the most heavily armoured targets, leaving a volume for the bursting charge of only about 2½ per cent of projectile weight; they were reserved for capital ships during WW1. Based on US Navy experience in 1944, a 15in APC would be able to penetrate 18ft of reinforced concrete at 10,000yd. A typical ammunition state for the Dover monitors' magazines on 18 October 1917 showed:

Projectiles	Erebus	Terror	Marshal Soult
HE long	1	26	26
HE short	70	30	80
CPC	100	74	49
Shrapnel	34	35	44
Practice			16
Total	**205**	**165**	**215**
Full charges	188½	213½	215

The official outfit in 1918 was 90 HE and 10 CPC per gun. At the outbreak of WW1 a CPC projectile cost about £65, HE about £37 and a full charge about £40. These prices increased over the years and had nearly doubled by WW2.

The figures tabulated for range are conservative, as they are based on 2,400ft/sec muzzle velocity, corresponding to a well-worn gun. When new, a gun was capable of 2,470ft/sec, which gave about 4 per cent greater range, i.e. about 1,200yd at maximum elevation. The life of the gun firing APC was shown by service experience to be about 335 equivalent full charges. Life using HE pro-

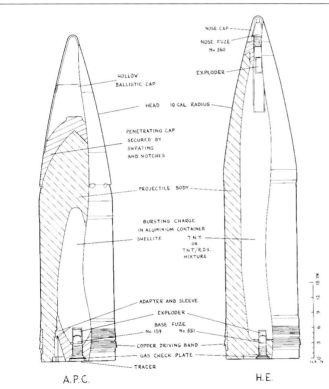

A.P.C.   H.E.

Typical 15in projectiles. The left hand part cut-away drawing shows a Mk XXIIB armour-piercing capped projectile, the right hand a Mk VIIIB high-explosive, both used during WW2. Although usually described as 6cal radius of head (crh), indicated by the B in the Mark number, the design was actually a 5/10crh, i.e. the length of the head corresponded to a 5crh shell (about 32in) but its radius was 10cal (150in). The body of the HE was longer than that of the APC to keep the same overall 1,938lb weight in spite of the larger volume of burster — respectively 130lb of TNT and 48½lb of shellite. The APC had only a base percussion fuze with a slight delay action to defer detonation until after penetration, while the HE had both nose and base percussion fuzes to reduce the chance of misfire or to allow the base fuze to function after penetrating inside a building. Sensitive tetryl exploders were used to magnify the impulse of the fuze in detonating the main charge. The gas check plate prevented gases from the cordite damaging the fuze. The conical relieved adapter was designed to allow the impact of the shell on armour plate to distort the base without dislodging the fuze. Examples of 15in projectiles are on display at the Imperial War Museum, London.

jectiles was usually restricted to about 250efc, owing to a lower limit on bore wear being set, as the longer body and greater longitudinal inertia of the HE could result in unsteady flight if the rifling was too worn to give sufficient spin stabilisation. The life of a gun was determined by the extent of erosion in the bore, caused mainly by the burning gases of the propellant charge. Erosion depended on the size of the charge. For example, a three-quarter charge caused only one-quarter the erosion of a full charge, while a proof or supercharge caused about double. Thus the wear caused by each firing could be calculated in terms of equivalent numbers of full charges. Measurements of bore wear were taken after each major firing operation, and the projected remaining life assessed. A gun was generally condemned when wear reached about 0.74in at one inch from the commencement of rifling. In practice, guns were usually replaced when their remaining life fell below the ship's normal full outfit of ammunition per gun, which ensured that the entire magazine could be safely fired in action. After removal from its mounting, a gun in good condition otherwise could be relined in about six weeks by replacing the inner A-tube at a cost of about £5,000. Guns could thus have been fitted in several ships during their overall life span; the Table shows that most of the 15in guns fitted in the monitors had either already been installed in other ships, or were so transferred later. The total numbers of rounds fired while in the monitors would be greater than those shown in the Table as having been fired in action, as trial and practice shoot figures are not included. Although these latter were often undertaken using the special sub-calibre 6pdr guns temporarily fitted in the bore, on occasion full charges would be used.

At the start of WW2 a switch was made from 4crh to the more efficient 6crh[2] projectiles in most 15in-gun ships, which increased range by about 10per cent. Only APC and HE were now being manufactured, but the monitors helped use up surplus stocks of obsolete projectiles, which included some 2,000 CPC and shrapnel left over from WW1. Nose and base-fuzed HE, now filled with TNT, were fired most frequently, being the most effective against the lighter targets such as troop concentrations and vehicles, leaving the occasional APC to cope with any heavily protected targets. The fuzes were fitted in the projectiles before embarkation in the ship but, being percussion rather than time fuzes, were unsuitable for firing at aerial targets. After WW1, experiments with improved types of cordite had been made to overcome the problems of short storage life and variation between batches. By WW2 solventless carbamite cordite (SC)[3] had become the standard, but a 432lb charge was needed to give the same performance as 428lb of cordite MD.

15in guns mounted in monitors

Date shipped	Registered number (Right or Left)	Maker	Rounds fired in action	Previous allocations	Subsequent allocations
Marshal Ney					
26.7.15	52 R	RGF	35	New	*Terror* 1916
26.7.15	75 L	VSM	35	New	*Terror* 1916
Marshal Soult					
3.9.15	27 L	COW	210	New	Dover CD 1942. *Ramillies* 1944. Scrapped 1948
3.9.15	28 R	COW	210	New	Removed Nov 1940. Scrapped 1957
Lord Clive					
10.12.20	158	COW	Trials	New	Removed Dec 1921. *Erebus* 1939. Scrapped 1950
10.12.20	159	COW	Trials	New	Gun burst Feb 1921. Scrapped 1923
10.12.20	162	RGF	Trials	New	Removed Dec 1921. *Warspite* 1937. Dover CD 1944. Scrapped 1948
11.5.21	163	RGF	Trials	New	*Warspite* 1929. *Abercrombie* 1944
Terror					
18.6.16	52	RGF	230	*Marshal Ney* 1915	*Repulse* 1935. Lost with ship Dec 1941
18.6.16	75	VSM	250	*Marshal Ney* 1915	Scrapped 1951
30.8.18	149 L	WB	70	New	*Warspite* 1942. 14in experimental 1945
30.8.18	150 R	WB	70	New	*Ramillies* 1941. Scrapped 1948
12.7.39	93	WB	330	*Revenge* 1915	Lost with ship Feb 1941
12.7.39	94	WB	330	*Revenge* 1915	Lost with ship Feb 1941
Erebus					
30.6.16	15	AW	60	Trials	*Repulse* 1935. Lost with ship Dec 1941
30.6.16	36	VSM	70	Trials	*Renown* 1941. Scrapped 1948
10.7.17	64	EOC	110	New	*Malaya* 1928. Scrapped 1948
10.7.17	65	EOC	120	New	*Vanguard* 1945. Scrapped 1960
17.6.18	143	EOC	180	New	Scrapped 1949
17.6.18	144	EOC	180	New	*Warspite* 1944. Scrapped 1948
6.1.39	72 L	VSM	170	Trials	Converted to 14in experimental 1945
6.1.39	158 R	COW	30	*Lord Clive* 1920	Removed Nov 1940. Scrapped 1950
30.11.40	60 R	EOC	160	*Royal Oak* 1916	Scrapped 1955
13.10.43	190 R	RGF	200	New	Scrapped 1948
13.10.43	76 L	VSM	20	*Royal Sovereign* 1915	Damaged Jun 1944 and scrapped
17.7.44	173 L	VSM	190	*Malaya* 1928	Scrapped 1949
15.9.44	100	RGF	90	*Repulse* 1916	Removed Jan 1947. Scrapped 1948
15.9.44	104	VSM	90	*Revenge* 1915	Removed Jan 1947. Scrapped 1948
Roberts					
May 1941	4 R	EOC	225	*Malaya* 1915	Scrapped 1955
May 1941	5 L	EOC	215	Trials	Scrapped 1949
5.11.43	33 L	VSM	230	Trials	Scrapped 1957
5.11.43	140 R	COW	40	New	Damaged Jun 1944. Scrapped 1945
19.6.44	102	VSM	215	*Resolution* 1915	I.W.M. exhibit 1968
19.6.44	10	EOC	210	*Malaya* 1915	Scrapped 1955
27.7.44	14 R	EOC	55	*Courageous* 1916 *Warspite* 1929	Scrapped with ship 1965
27.7.44	39 L	VSM	50	*Warspite* 1915 *Hood* 1936	Scrapped with ship 1965
Abercrombie					
Feb 1943	95 L	WB	110	*Royal Oak* 1916	Scrapped 1948
Feb 1943	118 R	RGF	110	*Resolution* 1916	Scrapped 1948
30.8.44	124	WB	Nil	*Resolution* 1916	Scrapped with ship 1954
30.8.44	163	RGF	Nil	*Lord Clive* 1921 *Warspite* 1929	Scrapped with ship 1954

Notes

Number of rounds fired are approximate, showing only those fired while the gun was in a monitor. Practice rounds excluded. Approximate total 4,900.

RGF = Royal Gun Factory, Woolwich
EOC = Elswick Ordnance Company, Newcastle (Sir W.G. Armstrong, Whitworth)
AW = Armstrong, Whitworth Co, Openshaw, Manchester
VSM = Vickers, Sons and Maxim, Sheffield
WB = William Beardmore, Glasgow
COW = Coventry Ordnance Works, Coventry
CD = Coast Defences (Royal Artillery)
IWM = Imperial War Museum, London

A view inside *Roberts*'s turret when she was ready for scrapping. The hydraulic cylinder and rack for opening the breech can be seen above the left gun (No. 39). The breech is open on the right gun (No. 14) although the obturator pad is missing.
(T.W. WARD)

Without any doubt, the 15in was the most successful of the monitors' various gun armaments. Indeed it was probably the most successful, tactically and strategically, of any of the world's navies' large guns. It was the mainstay of the RN's battle fleet in two world wars, and it remained in active seagoing service until 1954. Fifty-eight turrets and 186 guns, all made between 1912 and 1918, were drawn on to arm sixteen capital ships and six monitors. Although later designs were technically superior in terms of range, life or construction, the 15in remained a thoroughly reliable and effective piece of ordnance for forty years. It was a consistent weapon which could regularly drop its shells on to small targets if properly controlled. A 15in has the distinction of hitting another ship in action at nearly 15 land miles: *Warspite* firing at the Italian battleship *Giulio Cesare* from 26,200yd in the Mediterranean in July 1940.[4] While minor troubles occurred from time to time — leaky hydraulics, trouble-some air compressors, faulty firing mechanisms and even a few guns burst from imperfect projectiles — these difficulties could be overcome. Indeed, it was the intensive service in the monitors, firing some 5,000 rounds, rather than in the big ships, which was the real proving ground, not only revealing minor shortcomings and enabling them to be corrected, but also doing the most to advance the British techniques of long-range naval artillery, from

which the capital ships were able to benefit after the First World War.

15in Ordnance – TECHNICAL DATA

Mark I Gun: Length overall of gun body 650.4in; length of bore 42cal; chamber length 107.7in, volume 30,650 cu in; rifling length 516.3in, 76 grooves, twist 1 in 30cal; recoil 46in; force at 30 degrees 374 tons; weight of gun including 2.85-ton breech mechanism 100.0 tons.

Mark I / Mark I/N Twin Mounting: Revolving weight 760/810 tons; maximum elevation 30 degrees (initially 20 degrees), minimum +2 degrees/-4½ degrees; loading angle +5 degrees to +20 degrees/-4½ degrees to +20 degrees; training angle ±150 degrees; roller-path diameter 27ft; armour protection — see Ship Technical Data. Training rate 2-3 degrees/sec, gun elevating rate 4-5 degrees/sec.

Ammunition: 4crh: weight of projectile 1,920lb; length of projectile CPC/HE 63.3/63.9in; weight of bursting charge CPC/HE 129/224lb; weight of cordite MD45 428lb. 6crh: projectile 1,938lb; length APC/HE 65.0/67.0in; bursting charge APC/HE 48.5/130lb; cordite SC280 432lb. Magazine stowage — see Ship Technical Data.

Performance: Nominal muzzle velocity 2,400ft/sec; range at 30 degrees elevation 4crh MD45/6crh SC280 30,100/32,200yd. Trajectory for 4crh at 30 degrees: time of flight 64sec, angle of descent 43 degrees, striking velocity 1,400ft/sec, culminating point 17,000ft at 17,400yd. Three-quarter charge: 2025ft/sec, range at 30 degrees 4crh MD45 23,200yd. Penetration by 6crh APC 14in C at 15,000yd; maximum rate of fire 1¾ rounds per minute per gun.

10.2 The 12in Mark VIII Gun

The 12in armament of the *Majestic*-class pre-dreadnoughts of 1895 marked a major advance for the RN. Wire-wound guns were used for the first time, proving much superior to the 13.5in of the *Royal Sovereign*s of 1892 with their shrunk-on hoop construction. The 35cal 46-ton guns were designed by the Royal Gun Factory at Woolwich Arsenal, which shared the manufacture of the eighty-four ordered with the private ordnance companies. Winding high-tensile steel wire circumferentially over the inner tubes of a gun gave considerably greater radial strength, as well as greater consistency of material, thus permitting higher stresses and the use of the new more powerful 'smokeless' propellant cordite. The Elswick-designed and built mountings were also an improvement over the open barbettes of the *Royal Sovereign*s. The guns were protected by an armoured shield that also provided space for secondary loading facilities. The normal loading position required the turret to be trained fore and aft with the guns at their maximum elevation of 13½ degrees. Ammunition hoists and rammers in the pointed after end of the pear-shaped

barbette structure were then used to supply the gun in this fixed position. Hydraulic machinery was used for training, elevating, ramming and hoisting, although manual power could be used in emergency. The turret itself and the turntable immediately below were thus the only revolving parts, weighing about 264 tons altogether, as training machinery and hoists were mounted on the fixed supporting structure. As originally built, a twin B.II mounting cost about £30,000 plus a further £10,000 for each Mk VIII gun.

After twenty years' service this 12in ordnance had become distinctly obsolescent, as continuous advances had been made in naval gunnery, culminating in the new 15in. However, with two major changes the 12in could be adapted for shore-bombardment work. The first was to increase the elevation to 30 degrees to secure an additional 7,600yd range. Elswick prepared plans for recessing the fixed deck structure beneath the turret, permitting the guns to recoil through the bottom of the turntable. As with the 15in there was a penalty in that the gun could no longer attain angles of depression. The second change was to remove the primary loading posi-

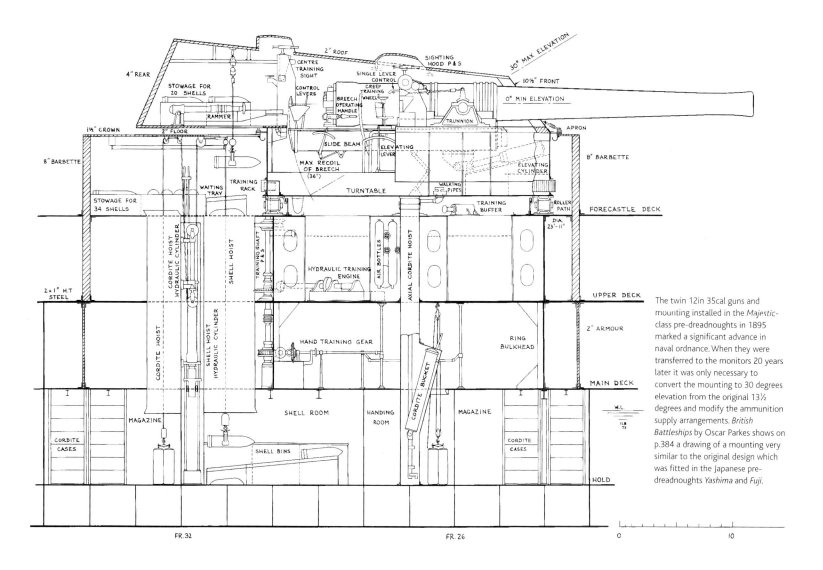

The twin 12in 35cal guns and mounting installed in the *Majestic*-class pre-dreadnoughts in 1895 marked a significant advance in naval ordnance. When they were transferred to the monitors 20 years later it was only necessary to convert the mounting to 30 degrees elevation from the original 13½ degrees and modify the ammunition supply arrangements. *British Battleships* by Oscar Parkes shows on p.384 a drawing of a mounting very similar to the original design which was fitted in the Japanese pre-dreadnoughts *Yashima* and *Fuji*.

tion in the barbette and use only that in the turret, thus permitting the guns to remain trained on target during reloading. The stowage of projectiles at the rear of the turret was increased from sixteen to twenty rounds, while the existing small centre-line trunk was used as a cordite hoist. Thus, at the normal bombardment rate of fire of one round per minute per turret, it was only necessary to replenish the turret stock every 20min. Pre-war annual gunlayers' tests had showed that a faster rate could be maintained for shorter periods: one aimed round per gun every 50sec. The original main combined projectile and cordite hoist was retained but converted to carry projectiles only, while, in place of the original inclined rammer at the back of the barbette, stowage was arranged for thirty-four projectiles. To replenish the ready-use ammunition, the turret had to be trained fore and aft and the projectiles hoisted up through hatches at the top of the barbette into the bottom of the turret at the rear. The projectiles were then stowed in bins and lifted out when required on to a bogie for loading and ramming into the gun, the four quarter-charges of cordite being transferred manually.

The eight monitor mountings were converted in early 1915 while still aboard the four pre-dreadnoughts. The conversion was carried out hurriedly; as a result the monitor mountings proved troublesome for the first few weeks in service. The twenty-year-old hydraulic systems were not fully able to meet the demands of the modified mountings. The greater elevation increased recoil and run-out forces, requiring higher hydraulic pressures to be maintained, which frequently burst the leather gaskets and inadequately brazed piping joints. Troubles also recurred throughout their life, but with careful maintenance these could be minimised. The guns were always fired singly; it is unlikely that either the mounting or the hydraulic machinery could have withstood the strain of both guns firing at once.

The guns themselves could also cause trouble. The substitution of 200lb cordite MD propellant in place of the original 174lb cordite Mk I caused problems under repeated firing, although doubling the nominal life of the

gun to 500efc. Depositions of copper in the bore from the projectile driving bands needed frequent removal, but more serious were troubles with the liners. The continual drag of the driving bands caused the liner to be gradually stretched forward. The resulting projection at the muzzle could be simply cut off, but in addition the liner began to form a ridge in the bore near the shoulders of the outer A-tube (see drawing). The ridge accumulated copper from the driving bands, which could give sufficient retardation to a projectile to start the fuze, with the result that a premature detonation could occur either within the bore or soon after leaving the muzzle. This happened on several occasions, including one when *Lord Clive* showered pieces of shell over the French destroyer *Aventurier*. While the choke could be temporarily removed by rubbing down with an emery-covered block pulled back and forth in the bore, the only permanent cure was to fit new guns with a modified design of liner, which had a different arrangement of internal shoulders and rifling.

When the 12in monitors were first completed they had no accurate information on their guns' improved performance. Range Tables for the Mk VIII only went up to 13½ degrees elevation, so approximations had to be used to estimate the figures up to 30 degrees. For some time only 2crh projectiles were available from existing stocks. The need for maximum range speeded the production of the 4crh introduced before the war, giving a 15 per cent increase in range. In 1918 a 878lb 8crh also became available, capable of reaching 26,000yd using a supercharge. The effective range of the guns in service off the Belgian Coast was considered to be about 1,000yd less than the figures quoted in the Range Tables to allow for average bore wear, cordite temperature and wind. The original nose-fuzed HE projectiles were filled with lyddite, which could be dangerous to fuze. They were replaced by TNT-filled projectiles as soon as the stocks were used up. HE projectiles were most often used, with CPC if greater penetration was required, while shrapnel with a time fuze was occasionally used as a makeshift AA projectile. A 12in HE projectile cost about £14 before the war and CPC about £25, both with a further £20 for the propellant.

The 12in Mk VIII was less accurate than the 15in but could perform adequately under good conditions, if care had been taken to equalise bore wear on the two guns and to keep the magazine temperature constant for 24hr before firing to ensure consistent performance. Off the Belgian Coast the 12in was mostly used for general bombardment, strafing back areas and keeping the enemy's heads down, while the 15in tackled the more specific targets. Taken overall, the gun and mounting performed reasonably well for their age and certainly put down some

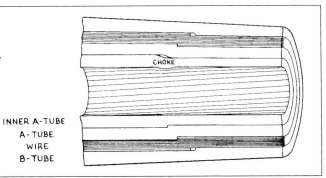

The intensive firing of the 12in Mk VIII in the monitors revealed a weakness in the liner design, whereby a choke was set up at one of the internal shoulders. Although exaggerated in the drawing, it could impart sufficient retardation to the projectile fuze to cause a premature detonation.

CHOKE

INNER A-TUBE
A-TUBE
WIRE
B-TUBE

impressive barrages, especially in 1918. The eight monitors between them fired well over 2,000 12in shells on bombardment work, while additional rounds were used to drive off enemy warships.

10.3 The 18in Mark I Gun

The 18in gun was fitted in the monitors almost by accident. Fisher's enthusiasm for the heaviest guns in the fastest ships led to an extension of the *Courageous* and *Glorious* 15in design. In March 1915 *Furious* was designed as a 'large light cruiser' of 19,100 tons mounting two 18in guns in single turrets, one forward and one aft. For security reasons the 18in gun was known as the '15in B', and indeed it was basically a scaled-up 15in. The 40cal piece was 62ft long, weighed 149 tons[5] and was constructed as shown in the drawing, similar to the 15in. The gun was also regarded as a potential coast-defence weapon, so that its official name later became '15in B CD'. Design and construction of the three guns (one spare) and the two mountings were entrusted to Elswick, with orders for completion in 1916. Like the gun, the mounting was based on the 15in design. Indeed, the barbette structure was capable of taking a twin 15in turret should the 18in prove unsuccessful. To this end two substitute 15in mountings were also ordered, both of which eventually found their way into monitors: *Erebus* and WW2 *Abercrombie*. The total revolving weight of the single mounting, including the heavily armoured gun-house, was slightly greater than the twin 15in at 826 tons.

Designed performance in *Furious* was a range of nearly 30,000yd firing a 3,320lb projectile using a 630lb charge with a muzzle velocity of 2,300ft/sec at 30 degrees elevation. This range was virtually the same as the 15in, as manufacturing difficulties prevented the use of cordite any larger than the existing MD45, which would have

given improved ballistics. The first trials of the gun were undertaken in September 1916 at Elswick's proving ground at Ridsdale, 25 miles north-west of Newcastle. Performance was not quite as good as expected, only 2,260ft/sec being obtained with the standard charge. The two mountings and their guns were shipped at Armstrong's Naval Yard at Walker-on-Tyne early in 1917, just as the Admiralty were having second thoughts about *Furious*'s design. In March 1917 the Board agreed to modify *Furious* into a seaplane carrier. Her forward turret was removed and a hangar with a flying-off deck was built over the forecastle from the bow to the bridge. Gun trials were carried out in July 1917, the remaining after gun fairly shaking the lightly-built hull. After three months' service it was decided to convert her fully into an aircraft carrier by building a flying-deck aft in place of the remaining 18in.

In the meantime some thought had been given to alternative uses for the three 18in guns. Their existence was revealed to Bacon in the summer of 1917, when he was invited to submit proposals for using two of them. In August he put up a plan to mount them inside the ruined shell of the Palace Hotel at Westende, whence they could bombard Bruges docks and Zeebrugge locks from a distance of about 18 miles. It was hoped that the

Prolonged firing of the twenty-year old 12in Mk VIII guns gave rise to rapid wear and damage to the liner. The photograph shows *Sir John Moore* exchanging her 46-ton right gun in October 1915. The work had to be done at Portsmouth rather than her home port of Chatham, as the monitors were too beamy to reach the basin at the latter yard, where the heavy-lift sheerlegs were situated.
(N.C. MOORE)

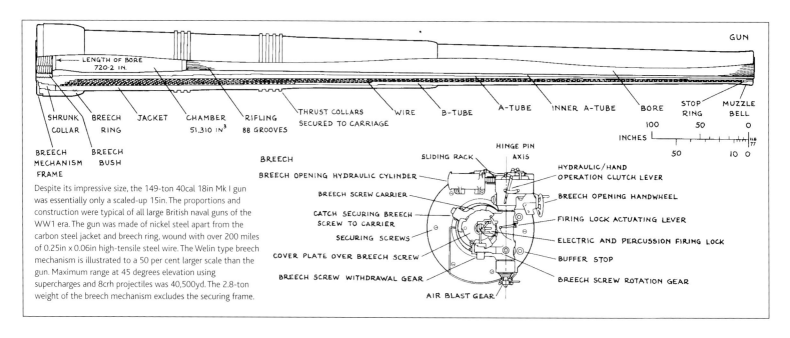

GUN

LENGTH OF BORE
720·2 IN.

SHRUNK   BREECH   JACKET   CHAMBER   RIFLING   THRUST COLLARS   WIRE   B-TUBE   A-TUBE   INNER A-TUBE   BORE   STOP   MUZZLE
COLLAR   RING   51.310 IN³   88 GROOVES   SECURED TO CARRIAGE   RING   BELL

INCHES   100   50   0

                                   50   10 0

BREECH   BREECH
MECHANISM   BUSH
FRAME

Despite its impressive size, the 149-ton 40cal 18in Mk I gun
was essentially only a scaled-up 15in. The proportions and
construction were typical of all large British naval guns of the
WW1 era. The gun was made of nickel steel apart from the
carbon steel jacket and breech ring, wound with over 200 miles
of 0.25in x 0.06in high-tensile steel wire. The Welin type breech
mechanism is illustrated to a 50 per cent larger scale than the
gun. Maximum range at 45 degrees elevation using
supercharges and 8crh projectiles was 40,500yd. The 2.8-ton
weight of the breech mechanism excludes the securing frame.

BREECH

BREECH OPENING HYDRAULIC CYLINDER

BREECH SCREW CARRIER

CATCH SECURING BREECH
SCREW TO CARRIER

SECURING SCREWS

COVER PLATE OVER BREECH SCREW

BREECH SCREW WITHDRAWAL GEAR

AIR BLAST GEAR

SLIDING RACK

HINGE PIN
AXIS

HYDRAULIC/HAND
OPERATION CLUTCH LEVER

BREECH OPENING HANDWHEEL

FIRING LOCK ACTUATING LEVER

ELECTRIC AND PERCUSSION FIRING LOCK

BUFFER STOP

BREECH SCREW ROTATION GEAR

A rare close-up of the breech of *Lord Clive*'s 18in gun. The 2.8-ton breech mechanism was hydraulically operated, although most of the work of ammunition supply was done manually. The angle-bar framework supports the transverse loading beam for taking the weight of the projectile before ramming into the gun.
(L.F. ROBINSON)

Army's Third Ypres offensive would have resulted in the capture of Westende by the time the guns became available. Bacon planned to ferry the guns and mountings across the Channel lashed on top of the bulges of a monitor; a full account is given in *The Dover Patrol*. He also conceived the alternative plan of mounting the guns on the monitors' decks to fire on Bruges from the sea, particularly when it became apparent that the Army's offensive was making little progress. A dual-purpose mounting was thus envisaged, capable of being used ashore or afloat. For use ashore the mounting required only a small arc for training but 45 degrees elevation was needed to give maximum range. Board approval to use

the guns was given on 23 September, resulting in an order to Elswick to design and construct the new mountings for delivery in five months.

The mounting consisted of two massive side girders parallel to the barrel, tied together at each end, between which the gun carriage and slide was slung. At the forward end was a strong support and a pivot about which the gun could train in a limited arc. The gun would be loaded at the fixed angle of 10 degrees, but actual firing would only be permitted between 22 degrees and 45 degrees, to distribute the firing forces fairly evenly between the forward and after supports. Ten degrees of training on either side of the centreline was achieved by a push-pull hydraulic cylinder, actually a gun elevating cylinder placed horizontally. Only the mounting itself trained, the shield being fixed to the deck. Hydraulically-operated cranes, loading tray, rammer and breech mechanism were all provided to ease the physical effort of the gun's crew. The ammunition supply parties were not so fortunate, as all movement had to be done by muscle power. The projectiles were to be stowed horizontally on the upper deck and moved by overhead transporter rail to the hatch in the forecastle deck through which they were to be lifted to the breech, while the cordite was to be transferred from the stowage tanks on to a small bogie running on rails, two one-sixth charges at a time. Total stowage was provided for some sixty projectiles and seventy-two full charges, as shown on p.75. The mounting was designed to be installed on the monitor's forecastle deck abaft the funnel, permanently trained over the starboard beam. By cutting out the armoured gunhouse and all the elaborate ammunition working arrangements associated with the revolving mounting, the weight was reduced to 384 tons, made up as follows:

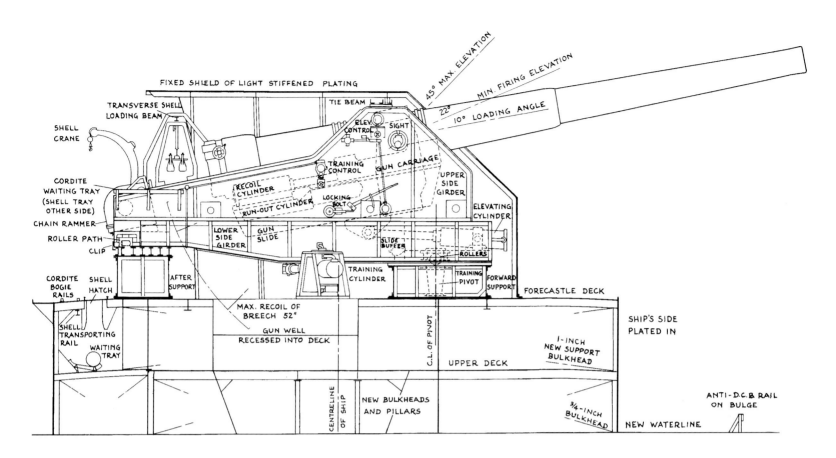

	Tons
Gun	149
Gun carriage	19
Slide	60
Elevating and training gear	7
Loading and ramming gear	14
Side girders and cross-members	68
Front and rear supports	43
Gun shield, ½in plating	24
Total	**384**

By October 1917 it was clear that there would be no chance of mounting the guns at Westende, so orders were given to proceed with the conversion of the two 12in monitors, followed by a third when *Furious*'s second reconstruction released the third gun. The work at Elswick took far longer than expected, partly due to labour troubles. Although the first two guns had been sent to Portsmouth in January, trials of the mounting at Silloth planned for January were not completed until 26 May. The mounting was then despatched in pieces to Portsmouth, where it arrived on 20 June for erection in *General Wolfe*. The actual gun shipped was Registered Number 2, which had previously been *Furious*'s 'A' gun. The gun in the second monitor, *Lord Clive*, was No. 3, *Furious*'s spare, while *Prince Eugene* would have received *Furious*'s 'Y' gun, No. 1.[6]

For bombardment purposes off the Belgian Coast it was necessary to get every possible extra yard of range. The 15 degrees increase of elevation added about 15 per cent to the original range, and a further 11 per cent was obtained by using supercharges, in which one of the six part-charges was increased to 165lb, making a total of 690lb. The combined effect increased the range to about 36,900yd using the existing 4crh projectiles. Trials of *Wolfe*'s gun showed that firing the gun produced no self-inflicted damage on the ship. As the muzzle projected some 22ft beyond the main hull, the blast was only felt right forward on the forecastle. New HE projectiles had been ordered, as the only ammunition available from *Furious* was the 500 APC of Hadfield's 'Eron' design and 500 CPC of Hadfield's 'Heclon' design. New 8crh HE projectiles with ballistic caps were also designed, adding nearly 10per cent to the range to give a maximum of about 40,500yd.

In the 18in's few weeks of service, actual rounds fired against the enemy amounted to eighty-one by *Wolfe* and four by *Clive*. Exactly which type of projectile was fired is unknown; probably 4crh APC from *Furious* modified with a ballistic cap to 8crh, since only two HE had been delivered by that time from Hadfield's.[7] The wear of *Wolfe*'s gun was measured as about 0.37in after firing 161efc (105 rounds including proof and practice, fifty-seven being supercharges). These figures indicate that the

The 18in single mounting officially known as the 15in B CD was designed by Elswick for the monitors on the lines of a land-service model of a basic type which simplified installation in *General Wolfe* and *Lord Clive*. Only 10 degrees of training was permitted from dead abeam, while fixed 10 degree angle loading was arranged. Firing could only be carried out between elevations of 22 and 45 degrees to distribute recoil forces evenly. A grid of additional bulkheads, pillars and girders was added between the forecastle deck and the inner bottom to take these forces. The drawing looking forward omits minor detail including access platforms and hydraulic piping to show the essential simplicity of the mounting. Projectiles were stowed on the upper deck, traversed by overhead rail to the hatch in the forecastle deck, then lifted by hydraulically powered winch and crane to a waiting tray on the left side of the breech. When the gun was ready to be loaded, the 1½-ton projectile was traversed across to the breech, landed on the loading tray and rammed home. The cordite charges were wheeled on a bogie along the forecastle deck, manhandled on to their waiting tray and then into the breech. See ship layout on p.75.

gun would have been good for well over 300efc, comparable with most other British heavy ordnance using cordite MD. Its range of 20 miles made it a valuable, if expensive, weapon for shore bombardment or coast-defence work. Because of the small number of spots received on the few occasions that the gun was used, it is not possible to evaluate its capability thoroughly. Being so similar to the 15in, it would probably have been an equally effective performer, especially with its much heavier projectile and bursting charge. As a ship-to-ship weapon its performance would have been much more questionable, despite an ability of the APC to penetrate about 18in of armour at 15,000yd. The chances of hitting the enemy with only two guns, as *Furious* would have

carried, would have been slight, even with the faster rate of fire of the turret mounting. While a single hit would have pulverised anything but a capital ship, it would probably have taken several hits to sink a well protected battleship, a difficult target from outside the normal range of the battleship's guns and, from inside, a dangerous task for a very lightly protected battlecruiser.

The 18in guns were removed from the two monitors in December 1920 and, together with *Eugene*'s piece, continued to be of service. Number 1 was lined down to 16in calibre by Elswick in 1921 for use in cordite-proving tests for the 45cal 16in which was to form the main armament of the four cancelled 1921 battlecruisers (see p.76), but which was actually installed in the battleships *Nelson* and *Rodney*. Number 1 remained in use for trials until 1942, being scrapped in 1947. Guns Nos 2 and 3 were installed at Shoeburyness and Yantlet ranges in the Thames Estuary, which included use for proof testing of cordite for 15in and 16in guns as new propellants were introduced. Both were sold to G. Cohen for scrap in 1933. A popular belief that they were mounted at Singapore as coast-defence guns is incorrect; five 15in Mk I were the heaviest there. One of the mountings was also used at Shoeburyness range, eventually going to Dover to mount a 14in Mk VII nicknamed *Pooh* in WW2.

18in Ordnance – TECHNICAL DATA

Mark I Gun: Length overall 744.15in; length of bore 40cal; chamber length 127.1in, volume 51,310 cu in; rifling length of rifling 585.4in, 88 grooves, twist 1 in 30 cal; recoil 52in; weight of gun including 2.8ton breech mechanism 149.0 tons.

B CD Single Mounting: Total weight including gun 384 tons; maximum elevation 45 degrees, minimum firing elevation 22 degrees.

Ammunition: Weight of projectile, 4 and 8crh 3,320lb; length of projectile, 4crh CPC 77.0in, 8crh HE 84.7in; weight of bursting charge, 4crh CPC 243lb; weight of cordite MD45 630lb, supercharge 690lb.

Performance: Nominal muzzle velocity 2,270ft/sec, supercharge 2,420; range at 30 degrees normal charge 4crh/8crh 28,900/31,400yd; at 45 degrees elevation, 4crh/8crh: normal charge 33,100/36,100yd, supercharge 36,900/40,500yd.

10.4 The 14in Mark II Gun

Until the WW2 *King George V*-class battleships the RN used no 14in guns of its own design, British requirements for this size of gun being satisfied by the 13.5in. The 14in Mk II[8] and its twin mounting installed in the first large monitors was appreciably different in many respects from the 13.5in, although it was virtually identical to the US Navy 14in 45cal. Five twin turrets manufactured by Bethlehem Steel formed the principal armament of the battleships *New York* and *Texas*, completed in 1914. Bethlehem had obtained the contract for the 14in guns for the Greek battlecruiser *Salamis* in 1912, and it was these guns which were ultimately mounted in the British monitors as described in Chapter 2. The 45cal 63-ton guns were of all-steel construction, being built up of ten shrunk-on hoops in a manner similar to British guns before wire-winding was introduced (see drawing of 9.2in Mk VI on p.232). Contrary to British practice, the rifling was made with an increasing angle of twist and a decreasing width of groove towards the muzzle. Such features had been tried in Britain but the resulting advantage of more gradual introduction of spin was not considered to outweigh the manufacturing difficulties. There were also other objections, such as copper deposited from the driving bands where the rifling increased in twist.[9] The sub-calibre gun arrangement was also different, a 3pdr being strapped on to the gun barrel, rather than inserted into the bore.

The guns were designed to use nitro-cellulose tubular (NCT) propellant, which produced considerably less erosion than the British cordite because its explosion temperature was lower. The propellant energy was correspondingly reduced, necessitating a heavier charge. The American 14in used a 350lb charge to give a 1,400lb projectile a muzzle velocity of 2,500ft/sec, while the British 13.5in Mk V required only 297lb of cordite to achieve an identical performance. Partly on account of its greater weight, an NCT charge cost about three times as much as the equivalent cordite charge.

The design of the mounting also differed considerably from normal British practice. Electric rather than hydraulic power was used, and the ammunition path to the guns and the corresponding hoists were arranged in different stages, as illustrated on p.16. The projectiles were stowed vertically in the shell-room, nose-down, and travelled in this position in both the lower and upper hoists, only swinging to the horizontal within the gun-house itself, for loading at zero elevation. The propellant was first lifted by hoists from the magazine, then delivered manually into the breech in four quarter-charges; the breech mechanism was then closed by hand. The electric power requirements were substantial, motors, hoists and fans totalling 209kW. Although there were few of the usual extensive safety features and interlocks found on British mountings, no serious accidents seemed to have occurred in RN service. The mountings proved reliable and simple to operate, especially as the bombardment rate of fire was deliberately slow; about one round per turret per 2½min, which gave time for corrections to be made.

The first stocks of ammunition were all supplied from America, the projectiles being made to British specifications. Subsequently, projectiles were manufactured in Britain; nose-fuzed 4crh HE. Propellant continued to be provided by the USA, as no British ordnance factory manufactured suitable NCT, although towards the end of the war alternative 233lb cordite charges were supplied. NCT was less stable and its performance less consistent than cordite, and the stowage containers were sometimes not airtight, so giving off a pungent odour. The silk bags were easily broken, causing NCT pellets to roll all over the turret floor. To obtain a predictable performance, care had to be taken to keep magazine temperatures constant and to select successive projectiles and charges of as nearly equal weight as possible for a particular operation. Even so, it was found that the guns never shot to their nominal muzzle velocity and range. Typically, the loss in MV was about 150ft/sec, corresponding to a drop of about 2,000yd in maximum range. The reduction was so great compared with the official Range Tables that DNO requested the provision of revised tables in 1917. Three-quarter charges were sometimes used to get a steeper angle of descent on to targets hidden behind hills. Although the gun did not fire APC in British service, its penetration would have been about 13in at 12,000yd.

The accuracy of the guns varied from ship to ship. *Abercrombie*'s always shot well, but *Raglan*'s performance often left much to be desired, with rounds sometimes dropping short. It was found that *Roberts*'s guns always shot better when they had warmed up after a few rounds. Erratic performance was partly due to variation in the ammunition and to copper deposited in the bore from the driving bands, but mainly due to the construction of the gun, as it was difficult to lock together securely all the different hoops so that the gun would behave as an homogeneous mass of steel. Gaps between the hoops soon opened up, increasing steadily until there was a space of over 0.2in between them. A droop of up to a quarter of a degree occurred in some of the guns, causing them to whip considerably when fired and lose muzzle velocity. Apart from a loss of accuracy, more in distance than in direction, the range attainable fell off rapidly and replacement guns were needed to restore performance long before the bores were fully worn. Only the eight original guns were bought from Bethlehem, the first having been proof fired at the maker's range at Redington, Pennsylvania, on 26 March 1914. As the company had no spares the US Navy supplied four guns which were basically similar, but were designated Mk IV and Mk V by the RN as they had different breech mechanisms. Two Mk IIs were made at the RGF in 1917 to a wire-wound British design, and were fitted in *Abercrombie* at Malta in May 1918, so allowing her two original guns to be closely examined by ordnance experts at Woolwich.

The British assessment was not very favourable. The potentially long life was appreciated especially as, after about 250 rounds, the bore was found to be only about one-third worn (0.17in). The slack construction, poorly locked hoops and droop were particularly criticised, as was the thin A-tube and the low designed factor of safety. The general conclusion was that there were no particular advantages to be gained by copying US practice in naval guns, mountings and propellants, but that, if large forgings of good quality could be obtained, all-steel guns constructed of only two or three tubes would be preferable to wire-wound guns. From about 1930 all-steel construction was adopted for nearly all RN guns.

14in Ordnance – TECHNICAL DATA

Mark II Gun: Length overall 642.5in; length of bore 44.5cal; rifling length 536.8in, 84 grooves, increasing twist 1 in 50cal at breech to 1 in 32cal at muzzle; recoil 46in; weight of gun including 0.8-ton breech mechanism 63.1 tons.

Twin Mounting: Revolving weight 620 tons; roller-path diameter 24ft; maximum elevation 15 degrees, minimum -1½ degrees; total crew 67 men.

Ammunition: Weight of 4crh HE projectile 1,400lb; weight of NCT propellant 350lb.

Performance: Nominal muzzle velocity 2,500ft/sec; range at 15 degrees elevation 19,900yd. Trajectory at 15 degrees: time of flight 35sec, angle of descent 22.5 degrees, striking velocity 1,345ft/sec, culminating point 4,968ft at 11,054yd. Three-quarter charge: 2,100ft/sec, range at 15 degrees 15,400yd.

Guns built: Registered Numbers, Bethlehem/Admiralty: *Havelock* 989/20, 990/21. Both sold to E.G. Rees, Llanelly, for scrap, 1922. *Roberts* left 991/22, right 994/25. Scrapped with ship 1936. *Raglan* 1013/26, 1014/27. Lost with ship 1918. *Abercrombie* right 992/23, left 993/24. Sold to T.W. Ward, Sheffield, for scrap 1919. *Abercrombie* new guns from RGF 1917 right 28, left 29. Sold to E.G. Rees, Llanelly, for scrap, 1923.

9.2in Ordnance – TECHNICAL DATA

Mark XII Gun: Length overall 485.35in; length of bore 51.4cal; chamber length 65.3in, volume 8,600 cu in; rifling length 403.0in, 46 grooves, twist 1 in 30 cal; recoil 30in; weight of gun including 0.96-ton breech mechanism 31.47 tons.

Registered Numbers: *Gorgon* A: 441, Y: 442, sold for scrap in 1923. *Glatton* A: 443, Y: 444 lost with ship 1918.

Mark IX Single Mounting: Revolving weight 194.2 tons; roller-path diameter 14ft 6in; maximum elevation 40 degrees, minimum -5 degrees.

Ammunition: Weight of projectile, 4crh/8crh HE 380/391lb; length of projectile, 4crh HE 33.3in; weight of bursting charge 4crh HE 40lb; weight of cordite MD37, normal/supercharge 128½/152lb.

Performance: Nominal muzzle velocity, normal/supercharge 2,900/3,060ft/sec; range at 40 degrees elevation, 4crh normal/8crh supercharge 30,000/39,000yd; maximum rate of fire two rounds per minute.

10.5 The 9.2in Mark XII Gun

The 240mm (9.45in) guns intended for *Nidaros* and *Björgvin* (see Chapter 6) were typical of Elswick designs of their period, consisting of inner and outer A-tubes, wire winding, B-tube over the muzzle portion and jacket over the rear portion. The single-turret mountings were hydraulically operated, with the centreline ammunition hoist cranked through the working chamber to deliver to the left side of the gun. The projectile was then moved on to a tray which swung round to the breech, in line with the hydraulic rammer. The original specification called for a gun capable of penetrating 8.75in of Krupp cemented armour at 7,000m (7,650yd), using a 419lb projectile, with 144lb of propellant giving a muzzle velocity of 2,900ft/sec. As designed, each gun cost about £6,000, a single turret £26,000, a CPC projectile about £15 and a charge £11.

When the two Norwegian ships were taken over by Britain in 1915 the guns were modified to 9.2in calibre so that standard Service ammunition could be used, and designated Mk XII. A new thicker inner A-tube was fitted, making a slightly stronger gun. It was thus possible to reduce the volume of the chamber, resulting in a greater gas pressure and increased MV. Using the existing 9.2in Mk XI 128½lb charge gave an extra 65ft/sec. The corresponding range at maximum elevation of 35 degrees would have been about 28,500yd, but the guns had not been installed or tested by the time work was suspended in May 1915. In 1917 plans were discussed to complete the ships for use off the Belgian Coast, where it was clearly desirable to obtain the greatest possible range. At a meeting in August between the Admiralty and Elswick, the possibility of increasing the elevation to 40 degrees was discussed. Elswick was asked to provide this elevation and to include arrangements to handle a new long 8crh projectile; a 4crh with an added ballistic cap. To get the maximum possible range, 152lb supercharges were also made available. The combined effect of increased MV, increased elevation and 8crh shells was to give the 9.2in Mk XII the prodigious range of 39,000yd, only surpassed in the RN by the modified 18in.

During *Gorgon*'s brief active service she fired about 200 rounds but, as many of these were supercharges, the guns were already half-worn by October 1918. After *Glatton*'s loss, *Gorgon*'s two guns were the only ones of that design in service and so of little practical value post-war. They were removed from the ship in 1921, although surprisingly two spare guns had been completed in 1921.

10.6 Other Monitor Weapons

Under the press of wartime necessity the monitors had to be fitted out with whatever guns could be obtained most readily. As a consequence they mounted a miscellany

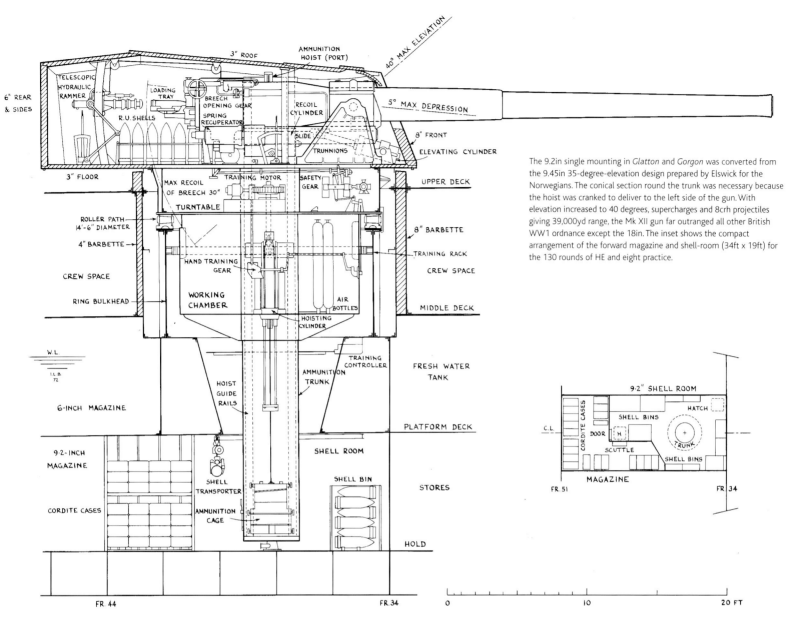

The 9.2in single mounting in *Glatton* and *Gorgon* was converted from the 9.45in 35-degree-elevation design prepared by Elswick for the Norwegians. The conical section round the trunk was necessary because the hoist was cranked to deliver to the left side of the gun. With elevation increased to 40 degrees, supercharges and 8crh projectiles giving 39,000yd range, the Mk XII gun far outranged all other British WW1 ordnance except the 18in. The inset shows the compact arrangement of the forward magazine and shell-room (34ft x 19ft) for the 130 rounds of HE and eight practice.

of pieces, whose origins and other uses are too numerous to spell out in detail individually. Reference is made in the ship chapters to ordnance of particular interest, while the following Tables summarise the principal characteristics of the main armaments of the small monitors, the various secondary armaments and the anti-aircraft weapons. Wherever possible, data relate to the period in which the weapon was fitted in the monitors and the ammunition which they generally used; in other ships and at other times, different mountings, projectiles or propellants may have been used, giving a different performance. For example, the 9.2in Mark VI would have had an increased range and life if cordite MD and 4crh projectiles had been used all the time in place of the more usual cordite Mark I and 2crh; the 4in QF V used different ammunition for low-angle firing.

Range data is quoted for the nominal muzzle velocity corresponding to a part-worn gun for which the Range Table was drawn up; the maximum MV of a new gun was usually slightly greater than the nominal value, giving a small increase in range. For the close-range weapons maximum range was not a significant factor, even though four to six times longer than the effective range. Only the initial part of the trajectory was of use against aircraft targets, where it corresponded quite closely with the line of sight and short flight time of the projectile. Life of gun was a more important factor for older or larger guns as replacement of worn guns was usually a dockyard job. In newer guns of moderate calibre, replacement barrels or loose liners were designed, which could usually be replaced by ship's own staff. Nearly all of the smaller calibres were standard weapons used in a wide range of other British ships. A few remained in service to the end of the 20th century in various navies, such as the 4in QF XVI*, 40mm Bofors and 20mm Oerlikon.

continued on p.236

The monitors provided examples of three main stages of British naval ordnance development. The top illustration of the 9.2in Mk VI fitted in *M.19* to *M.28* shows a design of the late 1880s, when heavy guns had to be built up of a large number of tubes and hoops. This basic type of construction was also used in the 14in monitors' Bethlehem guns. The stumpy profile with many shoulders gave rise to its nickname of the 'soda-water bottle' gun. The construction of the 6in Mk XII used wire wound circumferentially to provide radial strength, and was typical of modern RN designs of the WW1 era. The gun was installed in *M.29* to *M.33* and as secondary armament in three of the large monitors. The lowest illustration shows how an all-steel design was built up of fewer pieces, made possible by improvements in steel forgings and manufacturing techniques. The 4in Mk XVI* used as an HA/LA gun in *Roberts* and *Abercrombie* was typical of medium-calibre designs of the WW2 era. Breech blocks and other fittings are not shown.

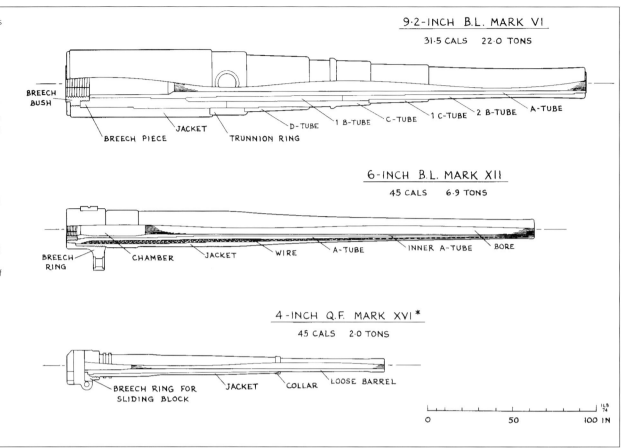

All the early large monitors received one 3pdr semi-automatic and one 2pdr pom-pom as high-angle armament. The photo shows *Sir John Moore*'s 50cal 3pdr fitted with HA range dials. Elevation up to 80 degrees was possible on this Vickers design, compared with only about 15-20 degrees on the contemporary low-angle mountings.
(N.C. Moore)

Towards the end of WW1 the 6in secondary armament on the large Dover monitors was replaced by 4in BL Mk IX. The photograph shows the crew of one of *Sir John Moore*'s four guns at drill. The gun used separate ammunition: one man is holding the 31lb projectile, and two others are holding leather cartridge cases with cordite. The shaded light on top of the shield was for night action. (N.C. MOORE)

All the large Dover monitors received a 6in secondary armament in 1916. *Sir John Moore* was originally fitted with four 6in QF on the forecastle deck abreast the funnel, two of which were replaced by 6in BL Mk VII. One of the latter is illustrated, having been allocated pre-war to the Royal Marine Artillery. (N.C. MOORE)

Main armament of the small monitors

Gun

Calibre	9.2in	9.2in	7.5in	6in	6in	6in
Mark	BL X	BL VI	BL III	BL XIV & XV	BL XII	BL VII
Length of bore, calibres	46.7	31.5	50	50	45	44.9
Length overall, in	442.5	310.0	388.2	309.7	279.7	279.2
Length of rifling, in	353.8	243.4	325.2	265.2	230.6	233.6
Construction	S. & W.	Steel hoop	S. & W.	S. & W.	S. & W.	S. & W.
Weight including breech mechanism, tons	28.3	22.0	15.75	8.10	6.90	7.51
Life with normal propellant, efc	450	350	500	ca l,000	700	1,200

Mounting

Type	Turret	Vavasseur	Transferable	Vickers	Transferable	Transferable
Mark	V	CP.III	P.III	Special Twin Turret	P.IX	P. III
Weight including gun and shield, tons	70 (R)	45 (T)	32 (T)	100 (R)	17.9 (T)	16.3 (T)
Maximum elevation, degrees	30	30	15	15	17½	15
Minimum elevation, degrees	0	-5	-5	-5	-7	-7

Ammunition

Typical projectile	4crh HE	2crh CP	4crh HE	4crh HE	4crh CPC	4crh HE
Weight, lb	380	380	200	100	100	100
Length, in	32.1	35.4	29.7	22.0	23.5	22.9
Weight of bursting charge, lb	33.0	30.0	23	ca 11	7.5	13.3
Weight of propellant, lb	120 MD37	53.5 C30	54.25 MD26	28.62 MD26	27.12 MD19	28.62 MD26

Performance

Nominal muzzle velocity, ft/sec	2,700	2,065	2,700	2,800	2,750	2,725
Range at max elevation, yards	25,000	16,300	15,000	14,000	14,700	13,500
Armour penetration by CPC	5in at 10,000yd	5in at 6,000yd	4in at 10,000yd	3½in at 7,500yd	3½in at 7,500yd	3½in at 7,500yd
Maximum rounds per minute	1	½	4	6	6	6

Fitted in

	M.15-M.18 (1915)	M.19-M.28 (1915)	M.26 (1916) M.21, M.23 (1917) Mk IV in M.24, M.25 (1916) See Note 2	Severn, Humber, Mersey (1914)	M.29-M.33 (1915)	Severn, Humber, Mersey (1915), M.27 (1917), Clive, Craufurd, Eugene, Moore, Rupert, Wolfe (1916-17) See Note 3

Notes

1　S. & W. = steel and wire; C = cordite Mk I; MD = cordite MD; R = revolving weight; T = transferable weight; P = pedestal (mounting); CP = centre pivot (mounting); CP = common, pointed (projectile). All mountings single except as indicated.

2　7.5in Mk IV on Mk IV mounting generally similar to Mk III. Mk I gun in M.26 from 1917.

3　Some 6in Mk VII had 20 degrees elevation.

Secondary armament in the monitors

Gun

						4in BL IX		
Calibre	9.2in	6in	6in	6in	120mm (4.72in)	4in		3in
Mark	BL VIII	BL XVIII	BL XI	QF II	Howitzer	BL IX		12pdr 18cwt QF l
Length of bore, calibres	40	48.9	50	40	18	44.4		50
Length overall, in	384.0	303.9	309.7	249.3	89.9	184.6		154.7
Weight including breech mechanism, tons	25.0	8.65	8.70	7.00	0.57	2.12		0.90
Life, efc	250	1,200	1,000	1,200		2,350		1,200

Mounting

Mark	CP. IV	IV	P. V	P. II	Vickers	CP. I	Triple I	P. IV
Weight including gun and shield, tons	79 (R)	65.7 (R)	16.2 (T)	15 (T)	4.65 (T)	5.4 (T)	18.5 (T)	1.71 (T)
Maximum elevation, degrees	13½	20	13	19	70	30	30	20
Minimum elevation, degrees	-5	-5	-7	-7	-5	-10	-10	-10

Ammunition

Typical projectile	2crh. CP	4crh CPC	4crh HE	2crh CP	2crh HE	3crh HE	2crh HE
Weight, lb	380	100	100	100	45	31	12.5
Weight of propellant, lb	66 C	28.62 MD	32.09 MD	13.25 C	1.78 MD	7.69 MD	2.75 MD

Performance

Nominal muzzle velocity, ft/sec	2,329	2,800	2,900	2,154	1,200	2,600	2,600
Range at max elevation, yards	12,000	16,000	13,600	11,000	ca 9,000 at 45 degrees	13,700	9,300
Maximum rounds per minute	1	3	6	6	ca 10	10	15

Fitted in

Ney (1916)	Glatton, Gorgon (1918)	Ney (1917)	Erebus, Terror, Wolfe, Moore, Craufurd, Soult, Ney, (all Mk II 1916) Roberts, Clive, M.26, M.27 (all Mk I 1916) See Note 2	Severn, Humber, Mersey (1914)	Erebus, Terror, Soult, Clive, Moore (1918) M.27 triple (1919) See Note 3	All 14in, 12in and 15in (1915-16) M.15-M.28 (1915) See Note 4

Notes

1　All guns hand-worked except 6in Mk XVIII. All mountings single except 4in triple.

2　6in QF I on CP I generally similar to QF II on P. II. Roberts's gun on special HA mounting.

3　4in Mk IX was BL version of 4in QF Mk V.

4　12pdr 18cwt mountings later converted for HA firing.

High-angle guns in the monitors

Gun

	4in	4in	3in	57mm (2.24in)		47mm (1.85in)	47mm (1.85in)
Calibre							
Designation and Mark	QF XVI*	QF V	20cwt QF I	Hotchkiss 6pdr QF I		Hotchkiss 3pdr QF I	Vickers 3pdr QF I
Length of bore, calibres	45	45	45	40		40	50
Length overall, in	190.5	187.8	140.0	97.6		80.6	98.9
Weight including breech mechanism, tons	2.00	2.15	1.02	0.36		0.23	0.29
Life, rounds	600	1,600	1,250	6,000		6,000	ca 5,000

Mounting

Type	Twin HA/LA	Single	Single	Single	Single	Single	Single
Mark	XIX	HA III & IV	HA II	HA 1C	HA IV	HA IC	HA III
Weight including gun and shield, tons	15.2	6.8	2.83	0.84	0.93	0.58	0.70
Maximum elevation, degrees	80	80	90	60	90	60	80
Minimum elevation, degrees	-10	-5	-5	-8	-15	-8	-5

Ammunition

Weight of HE projectile, lb	35.87	31.43	16	6	3.31	3.31
Weight of propellant, lb	9.0	5.87	2.12	0.54	0.45	0.83
Total weight of round including cartridge case, lb	63.5	54	27	9.7	5.7	6.6

Performance

Nominal muzzle velocity, ft/sec	2,600	2,350	2,000	1,765	1,873	2,575
Range at 45 degrees elevation, yards	19,600	16,300	11,200	8,700	7,900	5,600 at 12 degrees
Maximum AA. ceiling, feet	39,000	29,000	23,000	ca 10,000	ca 10,000	ca 15,000
Maximum rounds per minute per gun	16	10	20	20	20	25

Fitted in

- **4in QF XVI***: Roberts (1941), Abercrombie (1943)
- **4in QF V**: Terror (1939), Erebus (1940)
- **3in 20cwt QF I**: Abercrombie, Havelock, Roberts (1917), Ney (1915), Soult (1916), All 12in (1915-17), Glatton, Gorgon (1918), Erebus, Terror (1916), Humber (1919), M.16, M.18-M.27 (1917), M.31, M.33 (1919) See Note 1
- **57mm Hotchkiss 6pdr QF I**: M.15-M.33 (1915) See Note 2
- **47mm Hotchkiss 3pdr QF I**: Severn, Humber, Mersey (1915) See Note 2
- **47mm Vickers 3pdr QF I**: All 14in (1915), Soult (1915), All 12in except Eugene (1915), Glatton (1918), Severn, Humber, Mersey (1914), M.23-M.26 (1919) See Notes 2 & 3

Notes

1 3in 20cwt originally fired a 12½ lb projectile at 2,500ft/sec.
2 Effective AA range of Hotchkiss 3pdr and 6pdr about 1,200yd, Vickers 3pdr about 2,000yd.
3 Four Vickers 3pdr in *Severn* class were Mk II on low-angle mountings.

Close-range automatic weapons in the monitors

Gun

	40mm (1.575in)	40mm (1.575in)		40mm (1.575in)	20mm (0.787in)		0.5in	0.303in
Calibre								
Designation	2pdr Vickers	2pdr Vickers HV		Bofors	Oerlikon		Vickers machine gun	Maxim MG
Mark	QF I & II	VIII		N.1	II		III	I
Length of bore, calibres	39.4	39.4		56.25	70		62	94
Length overall, in	96.0	115.6 over guard		130	87		52	42.4
Weight, lb	572	850		423	141		56	60
Life, rounds	5,000	7,200		11,000	30,000			

Mounting

Type	Single	Quadruple	Octuple	Single	Single	Twin	Quadruple	Single
Mark	HA I & II	'M' VII*	'M' VIA*	III*	IIA	V	'M' III	Pedestal
Weight including guns, tons	0.70	9.15	15.68	1.18	0.56	1.01	1.31	0.072
Maximum elevation, degrees	80	80	80	90	85	70	80	20
Minimum elevation, degrees	-10	-10	-10	-5	-5	-10	-10	-47

Ammunition

Weight of HE projectile, lb	2.15	1.81	2.00	0.272	0.083	0.031
Weight of propellant, lb	0.21	0.26	0.56	0.061	ca 0.015	0.0045
Total weight of round including cartridge case, lb	2.95	2.87	4.80	0.53	0.18	0.060

Performance

Nominal muzzle velocity, ft/sec	1,900	2,300	2,800	2,725	2,520	2,060
Effective AA range, yards	ca 1,200	1,700	2,500	1,000	800	500
Rounds per minute per barrel	200	115	120	480	700	450

Fitted in

- **40mm 2pdr Vickers QF I & II**: All 14in (1915), All 12in (1915), Ney, Soult (1915), Erebus, Terror (1918), Glatton, Gorgon (1918), M.23, M.24, M.26, M.27 (1918)
- **40mm 2pdr Vickers HV VIII**: Erebus (1941), Roberts (1941), Abercrombie (1943) See Note 2
- **40mm Bofors N.1**: Erebus (1941), Roberts (1945)
- **20mm Oerlikon II**: Erebus (1941), Roberts (1941), Abercrombie (1943)
- **0.5in Vickers machine gun III**: Terror (1939), Erebus (1940) See Note 3
- **0.303in Maxim MG I**: All 14in, All 12in, All WW1 15in, M.15-M.33 (1915-16) See Note 3

Notes

1 Maximum range four to six times effective range.
2 *Erebus* also had one 2pdr Mk VIII on single Mk VIII mounting, 1941. Weight 1.15 tons. HV = High-velocity.
3 Fired solid projectiles, no burster.

continued from p.231

Anti-aircraft rocket weapons

Designation	3in UP Mark I	7in UP Mark I
Type	Harvey Projector	Naval Wire Barrage
Projectile diameter, in	3	7
Weight of round, lb	56	35
Length of round, in	76	32
Type of projector	Single	20-barrel
Length of launcher, in	144	ca 90
Weight of mounting, tons	0.5	4
Effective range, yd	1,500	1,000
Fitted in	*Erebus* (1941)	*Erebus* (1940)

10.7 Bombardment Techniques

Before 1914, gunnery techniques in the RN concentrated on the problem of hitting an enemy ship; a directly visible target. The problem of indirect fire, where the target could not be seen, was considered to be the prerogative of the Royal Artillery. To hit an enemy ship it was necessary to know the relative positions of the two vessels, predict their relative motion and, knowing the ballistic performance of the gun, translate this information into the appropriate angles for training and elevating the guns. Fire-control instruments, the director system, the training of personnel, the gunnery exercises, the principal types of ammunition: all were devised to this end. On the rare occasions before WW1 when shore bombardment was undertaken, the target, such as a fort, was usually visible from the ship and the fire was controlled by direct observation as if at a stationary ship. The corresponding problem where the target was not visible was much more difficult to solve, so nearly four years of WW1 elapsed before the RN developed a reliable system that could be used even under the most demanding conditions.

Successful shore bombardment requires that all of the following operations be accurately carried out:
  (i) Identification of the target and its location on a suitable map
  (ii) Selection of a suitable firing position for the ship and accurate fixing of this position relative to the target
  (iii) Selection of a suitable point of aim for laying and training the gun, which might not be in direct line with the target
  (iv) Calculation of the exact range and height of the target, calculation of all the necessary ballistic corrections to allow for the current performance of the gun, and translation into gun elevation and training angle
  (v) Laying, training and firing the gun in the required direction
  (vi) Observation of the fall of shot
  (vii) Communication of the results of the observation back to the ship
  (viii) Application of the necessary corrections to bring the gun right on to the target.

This complex sequence often had to be carried out in the face of strong enemy opposition, while the key to success was accurate observation and communication. Given the inevitable slight inaccuracies of making and firing ordnance, it was virtually impossible to land the first round exactly on target, however carefully steps (i) to (v) had been carried out. In a general bombardment of a neutralising and harassing type, extreme accuracy was not so vital, but destructive fire to hit a precise target such as a shore battery or a lock gate from a dozen miles called for the highest standards of performance in every aspect. The individual techniques used for each step underwent progressive refinement as experience grew, from the makeshift arrangements off the Belgian Coast in October 1914, through the improvisations of the Dardanelles Campaign in 1915, to the sophistication off the Belgian Coast during 1918.

It is worth taking each of the eight steps in turn and tracing the changes that developed, particularly during WW1. Location of targets right on the coastline such as harbour installations presented no difficulty, as the normal navigational charts were sufficiently accurate in most cases. Targets inland were much more difficult to relate to the ship's position on a chart, which showed little detail of land features. Conversely, land maps included few offshore features, while their grid system did not correspond with the chart's grid of latitude and longitude. The existing maps of Gallipoli were insufficiently accurate to permit target location by map reference until the peninsula had been photographed, surveyed and remapped after the landings. Aircraft soon proved their worth in locating the position of hidden targets such as mobile batteries on the reverse slopes of hills, so, by the end of 1915, almost any target at the Dardanelles could easily be referenced in relation to prominent landmarks. While the targets at the Belgian Coast were more clearly identifiable (dockyards, locks, batteries etc), resurveying was eventually necessary, to provide larger-scale maps of the coast as well as to re-chart those shallow areas of shifting sandbanks which had last been fully surveyed in the 1840s. During 1918 the precise latitude and longitude of every likely target had been established so that ships could calculate directly from tables and diagrams the true range and bearing from any firing position offshore.

The second step also presented many problems: selecting and fixing accurately the ship's firing position. The position had to be chosen to give a good line to the target, to avoid if possible the fire of enemy shore batteries, and to permit safe navigation, allowing for wind and tide. The ship's position then had to be fixed relative to the target location by sighting on prominent landmarks ashore, a difficult task off the low-lying, relatively featureless Belgian Coast, where German shore batteries drove the monitors almost out of sight of land. New methods were developed, such as that in which a drifter would lay a buoy in advance at the firing position and then a destroyer would drop two depth charges, one on each side of the buoy. Direction finding stations on the Kent coast would pick up the sound of the explosions on hydrophones, cross-plot the exact position to within a few yards and signal it to the monitors. Such a method was not without its hazards, as the Germans also had sound-ranging equipment and could then range their shore batteries on to any ships near the buoy. However, they could be confused by dropping a number of depth charges whether or not a bombardment was about to take place.

With the exact position of ship and target determined, the next step was to give the gun-sight a point to aim at. In the large monitors the newly developed director system was used to aim the guns from aloft, the necessary elevation and training angles being transmitted electrically from the layer and trainer in the director to their counterparts in the turret, who had to match pointers to bring the turret on to the target. In the small monitors, layer and trainer used the normal telescope sights on the gun itself to sight the point of aim. There was little difficulty at the Dardanelles in finding a suitable aiming mark such as a prominent rock or tree more or less in line with the target. The angle between the mark and the target was then calculated and set on the horizontal deflection scale of the gun-sight so that, although the sights were pointing at the mark, the barrel was pointing at the target. Similarly, after the necessary angle of elevation for the range had been calculated, the elevation to the mark was measured by sextant and subtracted from this angle to give the setting on the sights.

Conditions were much more difficult off the Belgian Coast, especially after the monitors were driven out to firing positions ten miles or more offshore. The introduction of smokescreens to protect the ships finally ruled out any further use of shore marks. Bacon therefore used another ship as an aiming mark, generally one of the smaller monitors. Anchored out of range of the shore batteries, the ship burned a searchlight about four to six miles to seaward of the firing monitor. As the angle between the mark and the target now approached 180 degrees, it was necessary to fit a special dial sight in the director so that it could be aimed off, yet still transmit the correct training angle to the turret. During 1916

Altham had rigged up in the 12in turret a repeater from the gyro compass which had been newly installed in *General Craufurd*, so that the turret could be trained on any true bearing to an accuracy of less than half a degree. The widespread installation during the summer of similar equipment in the monitors' directors called Gyro Director Training Gear enabled the Dover monitors to keep their guns on targets whilst under way, an operation which could otherwise only be undertaken by very special arrangements of buoys and subsidiary marks.

Calculation of the fourth step, the actual range to set on the sights, was complicated owing to the great number of sources of potential error. For naval guns with high velocities and flat trajectories, inherent inaccuracies in bearing (or deflection) were relatively small, especially if both monitor and target were stationary, as was usually the case. The most important sources of deflection error for long-range firing were:

(a) Wind across the line of fire
(b) Drift, i.e. the tendency of a spinning projectile to wander to one side
(c) Correction for parallax between the lines of sight from the director and from the turret
(d) Heel of the ship, unless firing over the beam
(e) Rotation of the Earth, especially at long range. Possible sources of error in range and elevation were more serious, particularly anything that affected muzzle velocity, including:
(f) Bore wear, with MV dropping appreciably as the gun became worn
(g) Type and quality of propellant and projectile
(h) Temperature of the propellant
(i) Wind along the line of fire
(j) Air pressure and temperature
(k) Height of the target above sea level
(l) Curvature of the Earth
(m) Tilt and installation errors in guns and mountings
(n) Errors in the sights and equipment generally.

A number of these factors could be incorporated in the Range Table issued for the gun, but, for the others, estimated corrections had to be applied at the time of firing. Range Tables gave the necessary angle of elevation for a particular gun and specific ammunition to achieve a certain range under standard conditions, which had been calculated from full-scale trial firings before the gun entered service. Each tabulated data for range steps of 100yd, including time of flight, striking velocity of projectile, angle of descent and culminating point. Separate corrections were given for: bore wear, propellant temperature, muzzle velocity, drift and atmospheric conditions. A standard calculation form was used to convert the actual map range into the equivalent Range Table range, so that the elevation for the gun could be read off. Especially in a well-worn gun, the two range figures could easily differ by several thousand yards. Even after making all these corrections there still remained a number of other sources of error which all contributed to an overall 'error of the gun', including:

    (i) increase in temperature of the gun during firing
    (ii) droop of the gun as its tubes slackened with use
    (iii) deflection of the mounting and throw-off from recoil forces
    (iv) inaccuracies of installation of mountings and sights, plus deflections of the hull at sea
    (v) extent of ramming of projectile into the rifling
    (vi) unsteady flight of the projectile resulting from manufacturing errors or mishandling.

The fifth step of laying and training the gun to the required angles was relatively simple in calm weather. In any sort of a sea, however, the gunlayer and trainer had a much harder job, as it was necessary to try to fire the gun at the instant that the motion of the ship brought the telescope crosswires exactly into line with the aiming mark. While it was sometimes possible to lay on the horizon, sophisticated types of spirit levels with telescopes, such as clinometers, proved more satisfactory. The task was simplified after the introduction of the Henderson gyro firing gear in 1918, which automatically fired the gun at the instant that the director sight was elevated for the correct range.

The existence of all these actual and potential sources of error meant that it was almost impossible to land the first round exactly on target. The first few rounds had therefore to be fired on what was in effect a trial and error basis, which placed great importance on the accurate observation and rapid reporting of the fall of shot, so permitting the necessary correction to be applied. During the 'Race to the Sea' in 1914 only very crude ground-level spotting was possible in support of the Belgian troops, rough corrections being laboriously telephoned to Nieuport for signalling by acetylene lamp out to the bombarding ships. Such a method could not possibly suffice for accurate sustained fire, so experiments were started using aircraft spotting and wireless communication. The preliminary bombardments of the Dardanelles forts early in 1915 had nearly all been made using only observation from the firing ships, but after the landings at Gallipoli arrangements could be made for more effective methods. Early attempts were made at spotting from a kite balloon tethered to a balloon ship. Although the balloon was not directly over the target, its height was sufficient to give a marked improvement over ground-level observation. Communication was simple, using a telephone with the wire running down the mooring cable, but the balloon was vulnerable to enemy aircraft. Early experiments with aircraft were not very successful. The first seaplanes were unreliable and had insufficient power to reach a good altitude, while their wireless sets were weak, temperamental and only capable of transmitting, not receiving. The observers were not sufficiently trained, while standard spotting codes had yet to be developed.

Gradually the difficulties were overcome. More-powerful aircraft arrived, the observers became more experienced and the wireless sets were improved. By late 1915 the RNAS spotting service had developed into a reliable means of observing and controlling fire at Gallipoli. If the target was close to the front line, shore observation was normally used, spots being telephoned back to the main Naval Observation Station and then relayed out to the monitors, e.g. by acetylene signalling lamp or telephone to the moored Rabbit Island ships. The small monitors' 9.2in Mark X earned the reputation of being able to place its shells regularly within fifty yards of its target at a range of 24,000yd; an ability retained during its coast defence deployment until after WW2.

When the first large monitor arrived at Dover, Bacon's plans had been prepared on the basis of ground-level observation. When firing near to the front line, fire could be observed from vantage points in two or more high buildings, telephoned to a shore plotting station which drew out the bearings and then signalled the results to the ship. This was a slow procedure and not very accurate unless the observers were widely spaced, with good lines of sight. As time went on, enemy artillery demolished more and more of the suitable vantage points. Bombardment of targets well behind enemy lines, such as at Zeebrugge in August 1915, had to be observed by ships of the bombarding fleet, at first using the spotting tripods which were dropped into the sea offshore, as described on p.54. The observers on the vulnerable tripods had a poor view of the shell bursts from their position only a few feet above sea level, while their lamp signalling apparatus was feeble and slow, so the method had to be abandoned. Bacon tried adapting submarines *A.11* and *A.13* as floating observation platforms, but these were found of little practical use.

Despite some earlier failures with aircraft spotting, the experiments were continued. Those organised by Altham in November 1915 yielded a basic method which was refined into a very successful system by 1917-18. The system devised enabled one observer to spot for several ships all firing at the same target. Up to six ships would each fire a round at about 20sec intervals. Each ship would wireless a buzz to the aircraft at the moment of firing, so that the observer would know from the estimated time of flight when the projectile would be expected to burst. On spotting the burst he would wireless back another buzz, followed by the fall-of-shot details, so that each ship could tell whose round was being spotted from the timing. By this time the Army clock spotting method was adopted, which was similar to rifle shooting in that several circles at standard distances from the target were imagined, in conjunction with bearings measured in 'hours' from the 12 o'clock position, which represented due north. The observers studied aerial photographs of the targets beforehand, so that the circles and 12 o'clock could be related to features on the ground. A special Artillery Clock and Deflection Indicator was developed so that spots could be translated directly into changes of gun range and deflection.

It was usually necessary for the first ranging shots to be brought on to the target as quickly as possible, especially if the enemy was using defensive smokescreens to hide the target or was jamming W/T transmissions. Once the guns got on target, 'firing for effect' could take place more or less blind. Spotting services for the Dover monitors were generally provided by No. 1 Wing RNAS, based at Dunkirk. Aeroplanes such as the Nieuport 12 soon replaced seaplanes owing to their better performance and endurance. After the corrections were received in the W/T office in the monitors, they were sent by telephone or voice-pipe to the Gunnery Officer and his team in the draughty spotting top, where the necessary alterations to gun elevation and deflection could be applied. After an operation, aircraft observation and photographs proved invaluable in assessing the results.

During WW2 the techniques established during WW1 and formalised in successive post-war editions of bombardment manuals were further refined, although more concerned with operational control and improved spotting methods than with changes in material. Radar was of little use for bombardment, apart from assisting navigation and permitting the removal of rangefinders from bridge or spotting top; although the 15ft rangefinder in each 15in turret was retained. Apart from improved projectiles, the 15in as used in WW2 differed very little from that of WW1. One technical improvement that did prove useful was the installation of a proper transmitting station with a fire control table, which simplified the problem of firing with the ship under way, or stopped but drifting with tide or current. Other refinements included the introduction of gyro-stabilised director sights and, from 1943 onwards, the use of direct voice radio communication between observer and ship.

The greatest changes occurred in observation and communication techniques, with most bombardments being in direct support of military operations rather than

aimed at predetermined coastal targets. In the earlier Mediterranean operations naval aircraft such as Swordfish and Albacores were used for spotting, as well as for dropping flares during night bombardments. For the later combined operations new systems were devised to enable close support of the Army to be maintained during a landing. Forward Observer Bombardment teams of artillery officers and naval telegraphists signalled their spotting reports to the bombarding vessel, usually via an HQ ship, and these were interpreted by the Bombardment Liaison Officer and the ship's Gunnery Officer to give the necessary corrections. Both FOBs and BLOs had undergone special training in naval gunnery and its capabilities; the former were also parachute trained. With large numbers of ships allocated to bombardment duties and as many as thirty FOBs, it was necessary to channel

all requests for fire support through a Bombardment Control Organisation on board the HQ ship for a particular sector. The HQ ship was usually a specially converted merchant ship with a wide range of communications equipment plus accommodation for personnel from the three services. *Largs* served Force 'S' at Normandy; others who served the monitors during 1943–44 included *Hilary*, uss *Ancon* and uss *Bayfield*. In response to requests from Army HQ ashore, the senior BLO and Staff Gunnery Officer aboard the HQ ship allocated targets, FOBs and spotting aircraft to a particular bombarding vessel, using special radio channels. The HQ ship had the latest tactical information on the front-line situation and air activity, and was an indispensable part of any combined operations fleet.

During the early stages of a landing operation, spotting was mainly by aircraft but, as the Armies pushed inland,

This sketch by John Worsley shows *Roberts*'s turret during the Salerno bombardment on 10 September 1943. The breech-worker in the left foreground, like the others, is not wearing flashproof gear, probably owing to the heat and lack of serious enemy retaliation. (IWM LD3377)

the FOB was used in preference wherever enemy targets were close to the front line. When the FOB made a call for fire, giving the map reference and other details, the first round was on its way within about five minutes, usually landing within about 300yd of the target in a position where it could be observed by the FOB, yet not alarming own forces. After two or three more rounds the shells would be falling within 50yd or so of the target; firing for effect required typically a further ten to twenty rounds. Nearly all of the monitor firings during the

This drawing by Stephen Bone shows *Roberts*'s spotting top during the Walcheren operation, 1-2 November 1944. The Bombardment Liaison Officer, Capt S.W.T. Musto RA, is standing at the plot; on his left is a map of Walcheren, and through the window is the island itself. Seated are the communication numbers, with the Gunnery Officer, Lt-Cdr H.S. Whittow RNVR, in the duffle coat. (IWM LD4670)

Sicilian and Italian landings were made under the control of FOBs, although there were sometimes difficulties owing to their being in the wrong position or from radio communication problems. Until forward airfields had been secured during the Mediterranean operations, air cover and spotting facilities tended to be limited.

Careful analysis of experiences in the Mediterranean during 1943 emphasised the importance of good communications and extensive training. The use of fighter-reconnaissance aircraft for spotting, first used in Sicily, had been so successful that it soon became the principal means of observation thereafter, especially at Normandy. In addition to spotting fall of shot, the aircraft were invaluable in detecting tactical targets worthy of bombardment. Spotting by such fast aircraft was only effective if the pilot could devote his full attention, so it was necessary for him to be accompanied by another fighter as escort. The spotter would circle at about 5,000ft over the target, with his 'weaver' guarding his tail and ready to stand in should the former be brought down by AA fire. Owing to the distance from British airfields, the fighters could only spend about 45min over the target

in Normandy, so at any given time there were two on station, two returning to base and two more approaching to relieve. Large numbers of aircraft with specially trained pilots were needed to sustain such an operation. Nine squadrons totalling about 170 aircraft participated on *Neptune* D-day: Fleet Air Arm Seafires of Nos. 808, 845, 886 and 897 Sqns, RAF Spitfires of Nos. 26 and 63 Sqns, RAF Mustangs of Nos. 2, 268 and 414 Sqns, and US Navy Spitfires of Sqn VC S-7. On D-day alone 435 sorties were flown, spotting for 135 shoots. After D-day the Mustangs were withdrawn and the naval pilots based at Lee-on-Solent carried out most of the remaining 1,700 sorties made during June 1944, covering some 400 shoots.

This substantial effort was well worthwhile, as aircraft had the clearest view of enemy movements in the close Normandy countryside, even though it was sometimes difficult to distinguish the exact front line. With Allied air superiority over France the number of fighters required was not a problem, while losses were relatively few, only four spotters being lost. Best results were obtained when one aircraft spotted for one ship.

The American Shore Fire Control Parties (SFCP) operated slightly differently to the British FOB system, which was basically an Army link between observer and ship. The SFCP itself interpreted the military requirements into naval terms and passed the corresponding orders to the ship, which put a great responsibility on to a team which might be under pressure in the field. The British considered that their system, in which there was a greater degree of centralised control, was more suitable for the conditions under which they operated. The experiences that the Americans learned in Europe were applied in the Pacific operations during 1945, when Grumman Wildcat fighters from escort carriers spotted many of the devastating bombardments of Iwo Jima and Okinawa.

CHAPTER 11

In Retrospect

The RN was the only navy to build ships exclusively for coast-offence purposes in significant numbers. Was its policy justified? The answer must certainly be yes. One has only to ask what other vessels it would have had to use in the absence of special-purpose vessels, and whether the resources required could have been more usefully deployed elsewhere. In answering the latter question it is pertinent to consider some figures, which have been estimated from the published accounts of Britain's war expenditure. The WW1 fleet of 40 monitors, large and small, cost about £8 million to build. Each large monitor cost about £100,000 a year to run — payments for its crew, fuel, ammunition, stores, repairs etc — while a small monitor cost about £30,000 a year. The total cost of Britain having a monitor fleet during WW1 thus amounted to about £17 million, after making some allowance for 'overhead' costs of the naval establishment ashore. The total cost of the naval votes for 1914/15 to 1918/19 inclusive was £1,080 million, so that the monitors accounted for only 1.6 per cent of the total. The proportion of seagoing personnel serving in the monitors was also under 2 per cent. As the monitors were nearly

all built by merchant shipbuilders, there was no question of sacrificing construction of warships, although there was an appreciable effort required by the three main ordnance companies.

The WW2 fleet of two old and two new monitors absorbed fewer resources, even without allowing for the value of sterling having approximately halved between WW1 and WW2. The total cost of building and running the monitor fleet, with its average strength of only two ships available most of the time, amounted to about £11 million, out of a total for the RN of £3,130 million for 1939/40 to 1945/46 inclusive, or only 0.35 per cent. Building *Roberts* and *Abercrombie* in warship specialist yards did, however, mean the sacrifice of the equivalent of five destroyers, but this was not a large price to pay for two vessels which made a major contribution to important amphibious operations.

The essential features of a monitor which no other vessel shared were the combination of hitting power and riskability. Compared with heavy land artillery, their principal attribute was mobility, and with aircraft bombing, accuracy and sustained fire. These potentialities were only realised to the full in later WW2 operations in which, after the fiasco of Dieppe, no major British assault on any enemy European shore except Anzio took place without monitors in support. In most cases it was necessary to supplement their limited number by battleships and cruisers, but the monitors were more cost-effective than such vessels. Compared with a battleship they needed only about one-third the men and resources to provide a similar capability, as the battleship's greater number of guns was but a small advantage at the slow bombardment rate of firing. Their shallow draft and riskability enabled them to get closer to their target, so increasing their effective range inland, while their training for a single purpose ensured maximum efficiency in shore bombardment compared with ships for which this was only a subsidiary role. Cruisers certainly made a major contribution in terms of rounds fired, but lacked the range and hitting power of the big-gun ships; their high speed and long endurance were of no particular value in this role.

With its vast resources during WW2, the US Navy had less need than the RN to operate the most cost-effective vessels. Battleships and cruisers were used to lay down immense barrages as the American troops assaulted the succession of islands in the Pacific in 1943-45. The Japanese fleet having largely ceased to exist as a fighting force towards the end of WW2, the newest US battleships as well as the oldest could be devoted primarily to bombardment duties, while their anti-aircraft batteries provided valuable close-range cover. The statistics of US heavy-calibre naval bombardments are staggering: 23,210 rounds of 12in and above plus 261,000 5in to 8in on Okinawa alone between March and June 1945, excluding heavy AA fire. This barrage was essentially for destruction which, in the absence of large numbers of heavy bombers within range, called for a much greater weight of fire than in the neutralisation role, which was that more commonly required in the European theatre. By comparison, bombardment expenditure at Normandy was 58,600 British rounds out of 141,000 Allied of 4in and above.

The monitors' role during WW1 was less clear-cut. The plans of Churchill and Fisher for a North Sea offensive supported by monitors were never put into effect, so the ships were used instead off the Dardanelles and Belgian Coast. In the Mediterranean they relieved the Army of the necessity of deploying the heaviest artillery ashore, especially during the early stages of operations, and an equally important role was the substitution for more valuable vessels such as battleships. After the evacuation of Gallipoli the large and small monitors were useful as patrol vessels off enemy coasts, again relieving other more versatile ships like cruisers and destroyers for duties elsewhere. In terms of positive damage to the enemy, the Mediterranean monitors could point to no great successes, but their presence did certainly inhibit enemy freedom of manoeuvre on coastal front lines such as Salonika, Palestine and the northern Adriatic. They and the other patrol vessels spared the Allies the need to devote resources to the defence of their own seaward flanks; in this role the bulged monitor with its relative invulnerability to submarine attack proved most valuable. This latter attribute was demonstrated even better off the Belgian Coast, where British and French coastal defences were minimal compared with the heavily fortified German sector. The monitors patrolled with immunity only a few miles offshore, in effect constituting a mini-battle squadron with a considerable deterrent value on German surface-ship operations in the area. It must be conceded, however, that their primary role of shore bombardment was less successful off the Belgian Coast. The exceptionally strong German coastal batteries and their accurate shooting made it difficult to destroy specific targets. It was never realistic to expect to put the inland U-boat base at Bruges out of action by gunfire alone, although it was possible to render the forward base at Ostende of little use to the Germans by the last year of the war.

Towards the end of WW1 the improvements in bombardment techniques enabled the monitors to make a more effective contribution, but only the newer, faster vessels with longer-range guns. The earlier vessels were of relatively little value by this time and could be deployed on guardship duties with no reduction in front-line offensive capability. The monitors' operations were always excellent morale boosters for the troops ashore. Even when their gunfire was not able to achieve much on the ground, their mere presence offshore, remaining on station in spite of all the enemy's attacks, was always welcome. Accounts and pictures of the monitors' bombardments were also good for civilian morale.

Of the forty WW1 monitors, there is no doubt which vessels were the most valuable: *Erebus* and *Terror*. The 12in and 14in monitors were handicapped by their slow speed and comparatively short-range guns. There was little that could have been done about the latter shortcoming; the early monitors were only built because the 12in and 14in guns were readily available, it was a question of those or nothing. The handicap of their slow speed is less excusable. The model experiments at AEW clearly showed as early as December 1914 that the first monitors would never achieve their designed ten knots. While understandably Fisher would brook no delay in the construction of the four 14in ships, he was either pig-headed or badly advised by his DNC when refusing to allow a modified hull form and more powerful machinery for the eight 12in and two 15in *Marshal*s. There was time enough to draw new lines and order machinery of about double the power which would easily have given the required 10kts without delaying completion.

The decision to use diesels in the *Marshal*s was also an error of judgement by Churchill and Fisher. Such new and untried machinery should never have been risked in vessels carrying the most powerful guns the navy could provide. There is no time and little necessity in war to innovate in matters that are not vital to operational performance and for which adequate solutions already exist. Although *Soult*'s engines were not unsuccessful, the fiascos with *Ney*'s engines contributed to the bad name that diesels generally obtained in the eyes of the RN. Diesels had to be tolerated in vessels like submarines and in auxiliaries, which did not really count, but in surface combatant ships the anti-diesel lobby remained strong up to WW2. In the case of the *Marshal*s it was not appreciated that their slow speed was due not so much to their type of machinery but to their bluff lines, poor design of propellers and low installed horsepower.

As is so often the case, the most successful ship designs were those in which the principal features were well balanced: armament, speed, protection, seaworthiness. Insufficient performance in any one respect could jeopardise a design, but so too could 'excess' performance. The heaviest-armed of the small monitors were by no means the most successful. The 9.2in gun was really too heavy for 600-ton vessels and the 6in monitors proved a better-balanced design, despite the increased weight and reduced speed of *M.29* to *M.33* as completed. The use of a single turret in most of the monitors might be considered something of a risk, as one mishap could cripple the ship operationally, as was shown by *Erebus* on D-day. The alternative of two turrets was, however, not realistic, as the guns were always in short supply, so it was preferable to distribute those few available over as many hulls as possible.

In all the bulged designs, removal of the bulges would have added about two knots speed, but the loss in protection would not have been worth this increase, particularly after the bulged forms were properly designed. A slight relaxation of the specified shallow draft would also have improved speed by enabling finer lines to have been drawn. An increase of one or two feet would not have been a serious handicap even off the shallow Belgian Coast as, apart from *Marshal Ney*, there are no records of any of the monitors grounding. The long period between the wars when no monitors were built meant that the WW2 designs did not benefit much from the natural evolution that occurred in other ship types. Problems with steering were never properly overcome owing to lack of prolonged Service experience. Design shortcomings like

siting the turret too far aft in *Roberts* and *Abercrombie* would have been less likely to occur, as would the generally inadequate standard of outfit and equipment.

One great service the monitors performed during WW1 was to consolidate the increasing degree of professionalism in naval gunnery. Percy Scott had laid the groundwork before the war, but it was the monitors' firing of large numbers of shells to maximum ranges that ensured that gunnery techniques and problems were fully appreciated, evaluated and developed. The operational conditions enabled proper care to be taken to estimate all the necessary corrections on as exact a basis as possible and to control the fire using the most accurate means; aircraft spotting and wireless reporting. Unlike ship targets, the monitors' targets could easily be photographed before and afterwards and a careful analysis made of every firing. The ability to fire at long range was recognised as an essential feature of a naval gun. Before the WW1 monitors no British large-calibre gun had an elevation of more than 20 degrees; after them, none had an elevation less than 40 degrees.

Virtually every calibre of gun in the RN was used by the monitors and, with the large number of rounds fired compared with Fleet vessels, plenty of experience was obtained, especially of such factors as bore wear and corresponding loss of performance. Normally gun life was not a particularly important operational factor in most ships, but in the monitors it sometimes had an influence, e.g. *Erebus* unable to participate at Salerno. All the guns mounted in the monitors were existing naval designs, i.e. high-velocity low-trajectory guns. Howitzers were never seriously considered after Churchill's suggestion in December 1914 (see p.44), although a design for a self-propelled Army-manned floating howitzer platform was proposed during WW2.

There must have been little anticipation of much monitor or even shore bombardment activity pre-WW2, as stocks of suitable shells were small in 1939; 84 per cent of the 23,210 15in held were APC. By the end of the war considerably more heavy shells, mostly HE, had been fired at shore targets than ships. Aircraft bombing was certainly more effective in many roles, but its value was more restricted once the troops were ashore and requiring close support. It was reckoned that bombing accuracy was only about one-tenth that of naval gunfire and, while it was extremely rare for naval gunfire to fall on Allied troops, the same could not be said of aircraft bombing in close support. For saturation or general neutralisation fire, one 15in round was considered equivalent to about four 6in, whereas the ratio of shell weight was about 17 to 1. For destruction, especially of protected or distant targets, the 15in was the principal weapon as it could range about four miles further than a cruiser's guns.

Nearly every navy had coast-defence vessels of one description or another, but the only one apart from the RN that made any attempt to build coast *offence* vessels was the Italian. A considerable fleet of hastily-built and -converted craft was pressed into service in 1916-18 for use on the Adriatic front (see p.71). The nation that had pioneered the original monitors had given up their construction after the completion of USS *Florida* in 1903; these low-freeboard designs were in any case only suitable for coast-defence or river use. During the Vietnam War, however, the US Navy revived the monitor concept for riverine craft; specially-built or -converted vessels for inshore offensive operations. For example, some 60 LCMs were converted to carry one 105mm (4.1in) howitzer and several smaller guns on a well protected 80-ton hull. For work off the coast of Vietnam the US Navy repeated its WW2 tactic by deploying cruisers and destroyers, supplemented during 1968-69 by the reactivated battleship *New Jersey*. Supplied with special ammunition for her nine 16in guns, she was capable of delivering a great weight of fire at ranges in excess of those possible with the same ordnance in WW2. Such was the nature of the war in Vietnam, and the general lack of concentrated targets, that the overall effect was not great, merely curtailing the enemy's use of the coastal strip. However, she was recommissioned in 1982, and used her guns to effect off the Lebanon against the Syrians in 1983-4. Her sisters *Iowa*, *Missouri* and *Wisconsin* were recommissioned in 1984-88 largely for the land attack role, having also been fitted with thirty-two Tomahawk cruise missiles and sixteen Harpoon anti-ship missiles. The latter two battleships were deployed in the first Gulf War, using both guns and missiles against Iraqi positions early in 1991. But the resources required to man and maintain such elderly large vessels were disproportionate. All four ships had been decommissioned by 1992, and are now preserved as memorials to the big-gun warship.

The RN applied the term 'monitor' to one other design during the twentieth century, but not in the context of its previous use. The three modified K-class submarines of 1918, *M.1* to *M.3*, were described as 'monitor submarines', as they mounted one 40cal 12in Mk IX. This weapon was not, however, intended for coast-offence purposes, but as a supplement to the normal torpedo armament in cases where the latter would not be effective. The concept was not a success. A design of shallow-draft monitor was proposed in 1935 under Lillicrap's supervision, a diesel propelled 14kt 1,400-ton vessel carrying six twin 4.7in mountings, but as the estimated cost exceeded that of a sloop, it was not taken any further.

In planning for the invasion of Sicily, the idea of

building a new fleet of small monitors was put forward. Various designs were proposed in 1942-3, including a 14kt 800-ton design with two 6in guns, but it was found that the number required, a first batch of ten, followed by a further forty, could only be built at the expense of escort vessels or landing craft. Other means of providing fire support were therefore examined, including the conversion of tank landing craft to carry 4.7in destroyer guns. Twenty LCT(3) were therefore taken straight from their building yards to ship repair yards from early 1943 for conversion to Landing Craft, Gun, Large; monitors in all but name. They carried two single 4.7in QF IX or BL I on a displacement of about 500 tons, as *LCG(L)3 1-20*. The tank deck was filled in with magazines, gun supports and accommodation. In addition to providing gunfire support on amphibious operations, they also proved useful for other roles, such as patrol work off the Normandy beaches, where their low 9kts speed was not a handicap. A further thirteen LCT(3) and (4) (some ex-Landing Craft, Flak) were converted in 1944, followed by nine more in 1945, although few of the latter were completed; all were disposed of rapidly after the war. A class of purpose-built medium LCG was completed from 1944 onwards, mounting two 17pdr or 25pdr anti-tank guns for close support of the Army. Some 200 LCG(M) were ordered, although many were cancelled in 1945.

Despite their impressive firepower, it was always recognised that the monitors were not of themselves able to disprove the old dictum about ships versus forts:[1]

Nothing has occurred to invalidate the maxim based on the experience of centuries that ships cannot engage properly armed and well designed shore defences with any hope of success unless the strength and equipment of the fort is greatly inferior to the armament carried by the ships.

The introduction of aircraft spotting did a little to even-up the odds against the ship due to its relative degree of vulnerability; a single hit could sink a ship, but near-direct hits on each main gun position were necessary to destroy a fort's fighting ability permanently. Second World War experience emphasised that the morale and experience of those manning the forts were perhaps the most important factors. There was no difficulty in inducing demoralised Italian coast defenders to surrender in 1943, but, at the same period, even relatively modest Japanese defences could only be overcome by total annihilation. When time and resources permit, purpose-built designs always prove superior to adaptations. The ex-Brazilian river monitors and ex-Norwegian coast-defence battleships were welcome 'windfalls' and were able to contribute usefully to

Erebus's officers relax more informally in WW2 style on the quarterdeck. Smoke canisters can be seen on the twin Oerlikon platform. (D.A. FARQUHARSON-ROBERTS)

particular operations, but were discarded as soon as WW1 was over, while *Erebus* and *Terror* were retained. Only the largest navies can afford to build ships for limited roles; the others must make do with general-purpose designs. When those special-purpose vessels have few peacetime uses it becomes more attractive to add the specialist role to some existing design. Indeed, the gunfire-support role is one of the main reasons for retaining guns of 4in to 5in calibre in modern destroyers and frigates, so that a bombardment capability is available from more or less any significant vessel taking part in an operation, as was seen in the Falklands in 1982. The role of the long-range heavy-calibre gun against ship or shore targets has now been taken over by the air-, surface- or submarine-launched precision-guided missile.

The British monitors were not normally thought of as regular navy ships. Their crews were largely reservists and many of their officers were either older men passed over for further promotion, or relatively junior. Apart from Ramsay and Tweedie, no ex-monitor CO rose to flag rank in the RN, but this did not mean that the monitors were not well run and efficiently handled. The monitors and those who manned them have never been given the credit they deserve, especially the small monitors with their additional handicap of numbers instead of easily remembered names. It is hoped that this account of the origins, activities and ultimate fates of the forty-two British monitors, which had a life span of half a century from 1914 to 1965 and played an important role in both world wars, will help put the record straight. The Royal Navy will never build their like again.

Bibliography and Sources

Published Sources

There are not many published works that give monitors more than a passing mention. Among those that I have found helpful are:

E. Altham, 'Monitors in Modern Naval Warfare', *Journal of the Royal United Service Institution* (*JRUSI*),Vol. LXIX, 1924

E. Altham, 'The Dwina Campaign', *JRUSI*, Vol. LXVIII, 1923

R.H. Bacon, *The Dover Patrol 1915-1917*, 2 vols. (Hutchinson, 1919)

R.H. Bacon, *From 1900 Onward* (Hutchinson, 1940)

The Belgian Shiplover, 'British Monitors, Class "M"', No. 127, Jan/Feb 1969

F.C. Bowen, 'Ships of the Monitor Type', *Shipbuilding and Shipping Record*. 30 Aug 1945

Brassey's Naval Annual. Various years, e.g. 1921

I.L. Buxton, *His Majesty's Monitor M33 1915-2001*, Hampshire County Council 2001

E.K. Chatterton, *'Severn's' Saga* (Hurst & Blackett, 1938)

E.K. Chatterton, *Seas of Adventure* (Hurst & Blackett, 1936)

W.S. Churchill, *The World Crisis: 1911-14; 1915* (Thornton Butterworth, 1923)

J.S. Corbett and H. Newbolt, *Naval Operations*, 5 vols. (Longmans, 1920-31)

R.H. Davis, *Deep Diving* (St Catherine Press, n.d.)

K.G.B. Dewar, *The Navy from Within* (Gollancz, 1939)

K. Edwards, *Operation Neptune* (Collins, 1946)

The Engineer, 'The British Monitors', 14 Feb 1919

—'Some Notes on the Vickers Diesel Engine', 22 Aug 1919

M. Gilbert, *Winston S. Churchill*, Volume III and Companion Volume III (Heinemann, 1971)

J.G.Hamilton, 'Naval Bombardment', *JRUSI*, Vol. XC, 1945

J. Iron, *Keeper of the Gate* (Sampson, Low, n.d.)

A.D. Jacobsen, *Trutzig und Treu* (Behrs Verlag, Berlin, 1935)

Jane's Fighting Ships. Various years, e.g. 1919

H.A. Jones and W. Raleigh, *The War in the Air*, 6 vols. (Oxford, 1922-37)

P. Kemp, *British Monitors* (ISO Publications, 1988)

R. Keyes, *The Naval Memoirs of Admiral of the Fleet Sir Roger Keyes. Scapa Flow to the Dover Straits 1916-1918* (Thornton Butterworth, 1935)

Der Krieg zur See: Die Mittelmeer Division. H. Lorey (Mittler, Berlin, 1928);

Der Krieg in der Nordsee, 7 vols. D. Groos; W. Gladisch (Mittler, Berlin, 1920-37; Frankfurt 1965);

Die Kampfe der Kaiserliche Marine in den Deutschen Kolonien. K. Assman (Mittler, Berlin, 1935)

The Marine Engineer and Naval Architect, 'The New Navy', January, February 1919, July 1920

S.E. Morison, *History of US Naval Operations in World War II*, Vol. 9: *Sicily-Salerno-Anzio*, Vol. 11: *The Invasion of France and Germany*, (Little, Brown, 1954 & 1957)

S.W. Roskill, *The War at Sea*, 3 vols. (HMSO, 1954-61)

The Shipbuilder, 'The White Diesel Marine Oil Engine', January 1920

G. Smith, *Britain's Clandestine Submarines* (Yale University Press, 1965)

B. Stjernfelt, *Alarm i Atlantvallen* (Horsta Forlag, Stockholm, 1953)

R.H. Thompson, 'The Rise and Fall of the Monitor 1862-1973', *Mariner's Mirror*, August 1974

H. Tweedie, *The Story of a Naval Life* (Rich & Cowan, 1939)

Unpublished Sources

The bulk of the sources I have used comprise official records held primarily by the following institutions:

The National Archives (formerly Public Record Office)

Among many hundreds of records consulted, the following contained the most useful information:

Histories and Reports of Proceedings (WW1) ADM 137/177, 398, 496, 507, 630, 774, 782-3, 1565-6, 1668, 1684, 1700, 1734, 1741-3, 2095, 2112-3, 2168, 2170, 2215, 2236, 2268, 2272, 3329, 3791

Cases and Reports of Proceedings (WW2) ADM 199/360, 426, 904, 946-7, 949, 1386, 1598, 1645, 1655, 1661

Naval Historical Monographs (WW1) ADM 186/606, 611, 613

Ship's Logs ADM 53 series

Ship's Books ADM 136/23 (*Terror*)

Cases (miscellaneous reports, e.g. losses) ADM 116/1348-9, 1433, 1625, 2461, 3584, 5053

Secretary's Papers (miscellaneous reports, e.g. *Erebus* transfer) ADM 1/8513-4, 8547, 8557, 9832, 9876, 10543, 11292

Pink Lists (ships' movements) ADM 187 series

Navy Lists ADM 177 series

Armament Lists ADM 186 series, e.g. 170

Quarterly Appropriation of Gun Mountings ADM 186 series, e.g. 197

Range Tables ADM 186 series, e.g. 181

Gunnery Handbooks ADM 186 series, e.g. (71, 315, 329

National Maritime Museum, London

Ships' Covers (DNC design files) ADM 138/433 (*Severn, Humber & Mersey*); 436 (*Erebus & Terror*); 502 (Oilers); 600 (*Glatton & Gorgon*); 647 (Small monitors)

Admiralty Drawings (all WW1 monitors)

Gunnery Handbooks

Vickers and Armstrongs' ordnance drawings

D'Eyncourt Papers

Diary of CPO Bass

Naval Library, Portsmouth

Includes many naval historical references, some also in TNA, NMM and IWM

Records of Warship Construction During the War (WW1)

Technical History of the War (WW1) especially Nos. 28, 33,34

Naval Historical Monographs (WW1) e.g. Dover Command

Battle Summaries (WW2) B.R. 1736 series

Pink Lists

Navy Lists

Steamships of England (WW1)

War Vessels and Aircraft

Gunnery Handbooks (OU and BR series)

Range Tables

Ships' Log Summary Cards (WW1)

Details of Estimates (WW1 costs)

Admiralty Fleet Orders

Ministry of Defence, London

War Diary (WW2 chronology, Naval Historical Branch)

Damage Reports (e.g. *Abercrombie*)

Lillicrap Workbooks 188/1-3 (Bath, now at NMM)

Gun Registers (Priddy's Hard, now at Hampshire Record Office)

Ship's Cover, Ship's Book and Drawings (*Roberts* and *Abercrombie*) now at NMM

Range Tables (Ordnance Board)

Model Test Records (Admiralty Experiment Works, some now at TNA)

Imperial War Museum, London

Gunnery Handbooks Books of Reference (BR)

General and historical works

Miscellaneous

M.33 A Diary Douglas C. Whitfield (Jnr), privately published 1990

Just a Number: The History of the 6" Gun Monitor HMS *M.30 1915-16*. Michael Hanna, privately published 2000

Acknowledgements

Since so little has been previously published about monitors, I have particularly appreciated the help and information provided by a very large number of individuals and organisations. With a correspondence file extending to well over a thousand letters, it is not possible to acknowledge everyone by name, but nevertheless I am grateful to all who helped, most of whom are no longer alive. I am particularly grateful to those who served in monitors: Cdr L.G. Addington, Capt Sir J.M. Alleyne, Mr A.J. Brunsdon, Capt N.D. Campbell, Cdr P.J. Cardale, Cdr A.W.M. Collyer, Capt R.E.C. Dunbar, Capt R.H. Errington, Rev D.A. Farquharson-Roberts, Cdr C.J. Gordon, Capt G. Lydekker, Capt N.C. Moore, Cdr H.L. Morgan, Capt H.F. Nalder, Cdr L.F. Robinson, Major C.R.J. Scott, Capt L.A.W. Spooner, Cdr P.H.B. Taylor, Mr G. Watson, Capt K.U. White, Lt Cdr H.S. Whittow, Capt M.F. Wilson.

Those whose knowledge of naval matters filled many gaps: Mr A.D. Baker III, Mr J.G. Bedford, Mr D.K. Brown, Dr N.J.M. Campbell, Mr D.B. Cochrane, Mr R.J. Coleman, Col R.A. Colenso, Mr. J.J. Colledge, Mr J. David, Mr J. Dixon, Lt Cdr R.O. Dulin, Mr M.C. Dunstan, Mr R.H. Gibson, Mr J.W. Goss, Mr W.G. Hall, Mr P.H. Judd, Mr D.J. Lyon, Mr P.S. Millington, Mr G.A. Osbon, Mr A.W. H. Pearsall, Mr A.M. Preston, Mr G. Ransome, Mr H.C. Rayner, Mr V.C. Richards, Lt Cdr D. Trimingham.

The staff of the following companies, who were most helpful in providing information or access to records and photographs (the company names are those appropriate at the time consulted, although many have since changed, or ceased operation):

Bolinder Company, John Brown (Clydebank), Dunford-Hadfield, Eisen und Metall, Harland & Wolff, Hawthorn Leslie (Engineers), McKie & Baxter, Lithgows, Palmer Hebburn, Scott's Shipbuilding & Engineering, Shell International Marine, Swan Hunter Shipbuilders, Vickers Shipbuilding Group (Barrow), Vickers Engineering Group (Elswick), T.W.

Ward, J.S. White, and not forgetting the staff of the North Tyneside and South Tyneside Public Libraries.

But no adequate history of British warships can be written which does not make full use of the resources and records of those institutions whose staff made such efforts to see that the monitor history was given every assistance:

The National Archives (Public Record Office)

National Maritime Museum

The Naval Library/Naval Historical Branch

Imperial War Museum and the Ministry of Defence, including the Admiralty Experiment Works; HM Dockyard, Chatham; HM Dockyard, Portsmouth; HMS *Excellent*; Naval Home Division; the Ordnance Board; Royal Armament Research and Development Establishment; Royal Naval Armament Depot, Priddy's Hard.

I owe a particular debt to the University of Newcastle upon Tyne, which provided financial assistance for the first edition, and to the World Ship Society, both of whom recognised the importance of publishing a history of monitors. The latter's knowledgeable members pointed to many sources of information, not least their own and the Society's records. I am especially grateful to my wife and my mother, who have given support and assistance during the long years of research.

For this second edition I reiterate the above and add Hampshire County Council, owner of *M.33*, plus the many correspondents who have written over the intervening years with helpful comments.

Finally, I would point out to those who have previously copied large amounts of material and illustrations from the first edition, without permission or acknowledgement, that the publishers of this edition will take action against any infringement of their rights.

Illustrations
Compared with more numerous and more publicised warship types, there are not many photographs of monitors, as their active careers were short and surrounded by security restrictions at the time. I am therefore especially grateful to the organisations credited on each illustration. Their names are those when they first gave permission; some have since changed their names or gone out of business. The line drawings are nearly all my own.

Notes

Chapter 1

[1] *The Life of John Ericsson* by W. C. Church, p.254

[2] D'Eyncourt papers, National Maritime Museum

Chapter 2

[1] All tons in this book are the tons used at the time, i.e. long tons of 2,240lb (1016kg)

[2] Block coefficient is the ratio between the underwater volume of a ship's hull and the rectangular circumscribing block having the same length, breadth and draft

[3] Cemented armour (C) had a specially hardened face to resist initial impact but a tough back. Non-cemented armour (NC) was more ductile and intended to deflect projectiles attacking obliquely, e.g. for deck protection. Armour plating was ordered by weight in pounds per square foot. The weight of one square foot one inch thick was nominally 40lb, but was actually 40.8lb. Thus '4in' armour ordered as '160lb' was actually 2 per cent thinner, 3.92in. Nominal thicknesses are used in the book

[4] Horsepower to be delivered to the propellers is determined by dividing ehp by propulsive efficiency

[5] The ship was never completed, but her hulk was usually referred to as *Salamis* until it was scrapped in 1932. Reconstruction was considered in the mid 1920s, but by then her design was outdated and her main armament would have had to be built anew. Her proposed secondary armament of twelve 6in guns had also been sold by Bethlehem to Britain, being used to strengthen the shore defences at Scapa Flow

[6] Breech-loading guns have their propellant charge in a silk case, the gas-tight seal being formed by an elastic obturator pad on the breech block itself

[7] In quick-firing guns, the propellant is contained in a brass cartridge case which forms the gas-tight seal at the breech

[8] H & W applied a suffix to their yard numbers to indicate the yard of construction other than Belfast, e.g. G = Govan, with G/B indicating hull at Govan, engines at Belfast

[9] The measure of power used for steam reciprocating engines, so called because the power was calculated from 'indicator' diagrams showing the pressure in each cylinder throughout the length of the piston stroke. The power delivered to the propeller was usually about 85 per cent of the ihp, most of the losses being due to friction

[10] COW had been formed in 1902 but was purchased by steel company Cammell in 1903, which merged with shipbuilder Laird Brothers that year. The company enabled a group of shipbuilders to compete with Vickers and Armstrongs, particularly on foreign warship contracts by supplying armaments as well as hull, armour and machinery. By 1905 ownership was shared by John Brown (50 per cent), Cammell Laird (25 per cent) and Fairfield (25 per cent). Naval gun mountings were built at a new factory at Scotstoun, Glasgow, guns at Coventry. The Scotstoun works were sold to Harland & Wolff in 1920 for diesel engine building, but reverted to gun mounting manufacture in 1936

[11] *The World Crisis 1915*, by W.S. Churchill, p.161

[12] *The World Crisis 1915*, p.347

[13] *The World Crisis 1915*, p.355

[14] The National Archives (formerly the Public Record Office) TNA file ADM 137/177

[15] *Winston S. Churchill*, Volume III, by M. Gilbert, p.542

[16] Quoted by Capt E. Altham in 'Monitors in Modern Naval Warfare', *Journal of the Royal United Services Institution*, November 1923

[17] *Naval Operations*, Volume IV, by J.S. Corbett and H. Newbolt, p.128

[18] *Breslau* now carried eight 150mm in place of her original twelve 105mm (4.1in)

[19] *Goeben* carried ten 280mm (11in) and ten 150mm

[20] ADM 116/1348

[21] ADM 116/1348

[22] BL XII = Breech-loading gun, Mk XII

Chapter 3

[1] *Winston S. Churchill*, Companion Volume III, p.305

[2] At that time the Admiralty normally held heavy-ordnance reserves of one mounting per eight in ships and two gun barrels per five in ships

[3] For example, *M.9* was first to have been *Wolfe*, then *Sir James Wolfe*, finally *General Wolfe*

[4] The names were often abbreviated in everyday use by dropping the titles

[5] Unlike the 14in monitors, the turrets were powered by hydraulic fluid supplied by steam powered pumps. As a result smaller electric generators were sufficient, two at 74kW each

[6] See Monitor Stability Table on p.77

[7] See map on p.55. All distances in this book are given in nautical miles (1.15 statute miles, 2,025 yd or 1.852km)

[8] Renamed *Redoubtable* in August 1915 after the new battleship *Revenge* was launched

[9] Two volumes published in 1919; concise revised volume in 1932

[10] *Trutzig und Treu*, p.49 (see Bibliography)

[11] *Der Krieg zur See, Nordsee*, Vol. IV, p.328

[12] *Wolfe* had exchanged her lyddite-filled HE for TNT in May 1917

[13] *The Naval Memoirs of Admiral of the Fleet Sir Roger Keyes. Scapa Flow to the Dover Straits 1916-1918*

[14] The crh figure denoted the radius of the ogive forming the head of the projectile, e.g. 2-calibre or 24in radius indicated a relatively short blunt projectile

[15] *Alfredo Cappellini* was wrecked off Ancona on 16 Nov 1917

Chapter 4

[1] Brake horsepower. The ratio of bhp. to ihp was a measure of the mechanical efficiency, typically about 75 per cent at that time

[2] There were also two 74kW diesel-driven generators

[3] *Hansard*, 8 March 1916, p.1,567

[4] After WW2 British warships were not sold for breaking up but were handed over to the British Iron and Steel Corporation (Salvage) Ltd (BISCO), which then allocated them to an appropriate shipbreaker and returned to the Exchequer the net proceeds of the sale of recovered material after deducting demolition costs

[5] Vickers and Armstrongs merged in 1927, retaining the joint title until 1965, when the company reverted simply to Vickers

Chapter 5

[1] ADM 137/880

[2] Vickers No.1421A or RN No.3102 replaced 1420A which had fired 1,068efc, and Vickers No.1425A or RN No.3105 replaced 1423A

Chapter 6

[1] Armstrong's of Elswick, Newcastle, and Whitworth's of Openshaw, Manchester, had merged in 1897

[2] The Admiralty numbered all BL guns of the same calibre in one sequence irrespective of Mark; with

QF in a separate sequence. Mountings, however, had a separate number series for each Mark.

[3] ADM 138/600

Chapter 7

[1] Further details of the guns are given in the Table on p.234

[2] See Chapter 10, note 1 for types of cordite

[3] Two photographs of her wreck are included in *Seas of Adventure* by E. Keble Chatterton. The salvaged 6in were put to good use subsequently: No. 2590: *Raglan* (1916-17), *Cairo* (1918-32), *Valiant* (1934-37), *Revenge* (1939-46), scrap 1948. No. 2628: *M.33* (1916-19), *Enterprise* (1925-40), *Ranpura* (1941-44), scrap 1947

[4] For a more detailed account of some operations, especially by *M.33*, see 'His Majesty's Monitor *M33* 1915-2001'

[5] ADM 101/575

[6] For a more detailed account of some operations, especially by *M.33*, see 'His Majesty's Monitor *M33* 1915-2001'

[7] Gross registered tonnage was a measure of volume, not weight. 1grt represented 100 cu ft of enclosed space. The vessels' deadweight was about 550 tons including cargo, fuel, stores, water and crew

Chapter 8

[1] Lillicrap Workbook 188/1

[2] See Monitor Stability Table on p.77

[3] Later raised, repaired and returned to service, but sunk again in the North Sea August 1918

[4] *The Dover Patrol* includes two aerial photographs showing the dockyard after these bombardments

[5] ADM 137/1668

[6] A proposal in 1924 to station the three 15in monitors at Singapore in lieu of fixed defences was rejected

[7] There is no explanation as to why her 15in, which had fired about 140efc, were replaced in 1939 by un-relined guns from *Revenge* which had already fired about 160efc, so having a projected remaining life of only about 100 HE using full charges

[8] ADM 1/9876

[9] ADM 1/10543

[10] Standard displacement was introduced by the Washington Treaty of 1922, defined as: 'The standard displacement of a ship is the displacement of the ship complete, fully manned, engined and equipped ready for sea, including all armament and ammunition, equipment, outfit, provisions and fresh water for crew, miscellaneous stores and implements of every description that are intended to be carried in war, but without fuel and reserve feed water on board'. Ships built before the Treaty had new figures of more or less doubtful accuracy established to bring them into line

[11] WW2 numbers were *Marshal Soult* F.01, *Erebus* F.02, *Terror* F.03, *Roberts* F.40, *Abercrombie* F.109

Chapter 9

[1] *Roberts* Ship's Cover, NMM

[2] D and D.1 quality steels were improved high-tensile steels introduced by the Admiralty in the 1920s

[3] Three of her other turrets had been sold to Turkey in 1939, but owing to the war were never delivered

[4] Mk I was the Swiss-made version

[5] A coloured drawing of this pattern is given in *Royal Navy Warship Camouflage* by P. Hodges

[6] The Admiralty included variable items such as crew, and some stores in their light displacement, unlike merchant ships, where it is effectively an empty ship weight

Chapter 10

[1] The 'modified' cordite introduced before WW1 to give increased gun life was designated MD, the number being the nominal diameter of the sticks in hundredths of an inch, i.e. 0.45in. Increasing the proportion of nitrocellulose from 37 per cent in cordite Mk I (with 58 per cent nitro-glycerine and 5 per cent mineral jelly) to 65 per cent (with 30 per cent nitro-glycerine) approximately doubled gun life

[2] The 6crh was actually a 5/10crh, i.e. the length of the head was equivalent to a true 5crh but the ogive was formed with a 10cal-radius curve, non-tangential at the shoulder. The 4crh was actually a 3/4crh. See figure on p.220

[3] The manufacturing process was 'solventless', the carbamite acting as a stabiliser to improve storage quality, constituting 9 per cent by weight, with 41 per cent nitro-glycerine and 50 per cent soluble nitrocellulose. SC was designated by its stick diameter in thousandths of an inch; that used for the 15in was SC280, i.e. 0.28in

[4] A 15in mounted ashore at Wanstone near Dover hit the German blockade runner *Munsterland* at about 30,000yd in January 1944, but she had run ashore near Cap Gris Nez and so was an easy target

[5] While some sources quote 152.3 tons, this figure is based on Ordnance Board minutes

[6] More detail on the installation is given in *Warship No.12* (Conway Maritime Press, 1979)

[7] There is an 18in projectile at the 'Explosion' Museum, Gosport

[8] The 14in Armstrong guns in the Chilean battleship *Almirante Latorre* were designated Mark I when she was taken over as the RN's *Canada* in 1914

[9] A.J. Power, when a lieutenant commander, reported that after a full day's firing (in *Raglan*), the copper filled two ½lb tobacco tins (SUPP 6/291)

Chapter 11

[1] *The Gunnery Manual*, Vol. 1, 1922. ADM 186/171

Index

The index is arranged to include the most important subjects, but excludes passing references to people, places and ships, e.g. names of vessels escorting monitors. Illustrations are indicated by italic type.